AI Powered Healthcare in the Metaverse

Virtual Ecosystems

Editors

Balasubramaniam S

Assistant Professor, School of Computer Science and Engineering
Kerala University of Digital Sciences, Innovation and Technology
Digital University Kerala, Thiruvananthapuram, Kerala, India

Seifedine Kadry

Professor, Department of Computer Science and Mathematics
Lebanese American University, Beirut, Lebanon

CRC Press
Taylor & Francis Group
Boca Raton London New York

CRC Press is an imprint of the
Taylor & Francis Group, an **informa** business
A SCIENCE PUBLISHERS BOOK

First edition published 2027
by CRC Press
2385 NW Executive Center Drive, Suite 320, Boca Raton FL 33431

and by CRC Press
4 Park Square, Milton Park, Abingdon, Oxon, OX14 4RN

CRC Press is an imprint of Taylor & Francis Group, LLC

Library of Congress Cataloging-in-Publication Data (applied for)

ISBN: 978-1-041-10585-5 (hbk)
ISBN: 978-1-041-15426-6 (pbk)
ISBN: 978-1-003-67937-0 (ebk)

DOI: 10.1201/9781003679370

Typeset in Times New Roman
by Prime Publishing Services

Preface

The convergence of Artificial Intelligence (AI) and the Metaverse is poised to revolutionize various industries, with healthcare emerging as one of the most promising areas. Over the past decade, healthcare has undergone a rapid transformation through the adoption of AI technologies, ranging from machine learning for diagnostics to AI-driven drug discovery and personalized treatments. Simultaneously, the development of immersive virtual environments, including the metaverse, has opened new frontiers in virtual interaction, training, and simulation.

At the same time, the pandemic has accelerated the shift toward remote healthcare services such as telemedicine, highlighting the potential for virtual care ecosystems that transcend physical limitations. As AI becomes more sophisticated, it is now capable of creating virtual hospitals, digital twins, and AI-driven monitoring tools that offer unprecedented levels of patient care. The metaverse, often associated with gaming and entertainment, is evolving into a platform where healthcare services can be delivered in immersive, interactive, and real-time virtual environments. This combination of AI-powered healthcare in the metaverse promises a future where patients can receive personalized, continuous care regardless of location.

This book explores the emerging field of AI-powered healthcare in virtual environments and helps readers understand how this technology will reshape the future of medicine care. By combining the potential of AI with the immersive capabilities of the metaverse, the book aims to offer a roadmap for the future of healthcare, emphasizing how virtual health ecosystems can improve diagnostics, treatment, and patient engagement.

Balasubramaniam S
Seifedine Kadry

Contents

CHAPTER

1

The Convergence of AI and Metaverse: A New Era in Healthcare

C. Arun[1*], B. Hariharan[1], Gopirajan P V[1], Anupama C G[1] and Po-Ming Lee[2]

[1] Department of Computational Intelligence, School of Computing, SRM Institute of Science and Technology, Kattankulathur, Chennai, Tamilnadu, India

[2] Department of Electronics and Engineering, Southern Taiwan University of Science and Technology, Taiwan

The convergence of Metaverse and AI makes a paradigm shift in the healthcare industry and transforms healthcare service delivery. This chapter explores synergistic integration of AI technologies, such as Machine Learning, natural language processing, and predictive analytics, with an immersive metaverse environment to enhance various aspects of the healthcare industry. Begins with an overview of AI's role in diagnostics and decision-making alongside the emerging metaverse as a virtual healthcare space. Virtual clinics are transforming remote healthcare by integrating AI-driven chatbots with real-time health monitoring, thereby enhancing the speed, intelligence, and responsiveness of patient interactions. These digital environments frequently employ avatars and patient "digital twins" to provide care that is not only individualized but also predictive, anticipating health complications before they arise. In medical education, immersive simulations and AI-assisted surgical training facilitate the acquisition of practical skills in realistic virtual settings, enabling collaboration across distances. This digital transition raises major concerns about data privacy, algorithmic fairness, and the need for clear regulations to guarantee the responsible use of these technologies. Future advancements, such as blockchain, may be essential in safeguarding patient data and facilitating the smooth integration of AI and metaverse systems. This integration of AI and the Metaverse facilitates

*Corresponding author: arunc@srmist.edu.in

DOI: 10.1201/9781003679370-1

a more interconnected, individualized, and immersive healthcare experience for providers and patients.

1. Introduction to AI and Metaverse in Healthcare

Disruptive technologies, including Artificial Intelligence, Blockchain, Virtual Reality, Augmented Reality, Web 3.0, and Mixed Reality, have created countless prospects for immersive experiences in areas such as conference rooms, gaming, virtual test drives, and virtual classrooms. Artificial Intelligence has revolutionized healthcare and disrupted traditional methodologies by enhancing disease identification from X-rays and CT scans with Convolutional Neural Networks (CNN). AI, renowned for its computer vision, natural language processing, and machine learning, has been extensively implemented in predictive analytics, disease diagnosis, and treatment optimization [1–2].

Disease prediction ability can be enhanced by encompassing AI-driven systems that analyze healthcare data more precisely and accurately. Similarly, the robotic surgery assisted by an AI-system facilitates minimally invasive procedures with increased accuracy and shortened recovery periods. The ever-changing landscape of healthcare advocates the need for integration of advanced technology to enhance patient care, medical research, and education. The change in living conditions has prompted new and essential demands that need to be addressed in healthcare.

The current healthcare system faces substantial challenges, including extensive shortages and a lack of proficient medical professionals, which restricts coverage of chronic disease management. Also, the uneven distribution of medical expertise and technology across geographical regions leads to disparities in care and considerable pressure on cost control, particularly on the medical insurance funds. These hurdles force the contemporary technical platform to enhance efficiency, improve the quality and accessibility of healthcare, and reduce resource waste. The healthcare industry faces numerous challenges, including a lack of doctor-patient communication, which hinders their understanding of their disease and treatment, leading to increased anxiety and diminishing their compliance with treatment. Improvements in surgical precision and safety are crucial, especially for elderly patients who require tailored approaches that currently involve risky, irreversible procedures. Conventional rehabilitation environments lack immersion, seclusion, and stimulating equipment, resulting in monotonous experiences that hinder patient motivation and recovery.

The advancement of disruptive technologies such as AI, AR, VR, and Metaverse can create realistic simulations of healthcare scenarios, analyze patient data, and provide personalized recommendations based on individual health needs. Metaverse converging with other technologies transforms healthcare in numerous ways, such as connecting experts across the globe through a virtual world to examine patient records and do collaborative surgery in real-time, enabling patients to get virtual consultations, and offer health advice, track medication adherence, and alert human doctors, when necessary, which was depicted in Fig. 1. The metaverse enables virtual replicas of patients, known as digital twins, which help clinicians make informed decisions and simulate treatment outcomes before actual intervention.

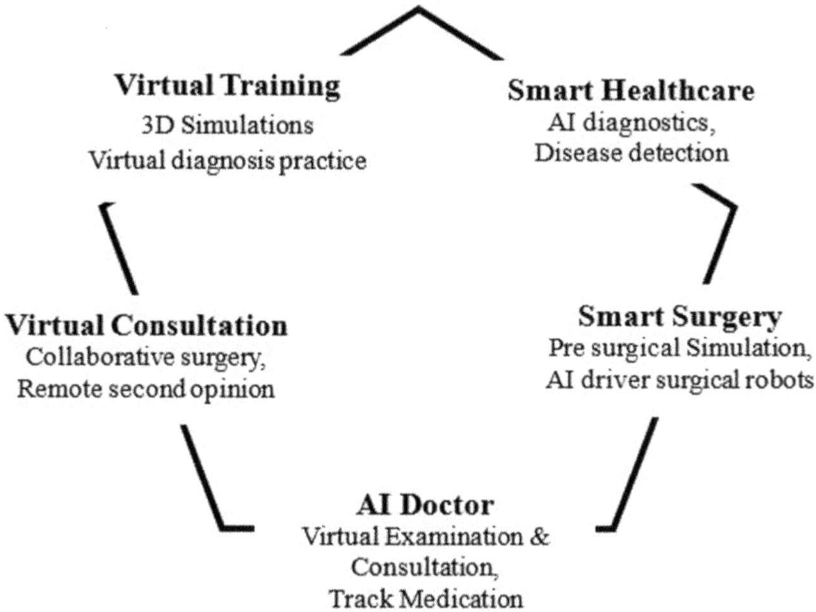

Figure 1: Metaverse enabled smart healthcare applications.

2. Metaverse Potential Applications in Healthcare

2.1 Virtual Consultation through Metaverse

Virtual consultation is made possible through the metaverse, eliminating the geographic barriers for patients from remote or mobility-impaired users. Patients can interact with healthcare professionals through virtual engagements, which offer personalized engagement to patients and improve comfort and trust. Conventional telemedicine offers one-on-one interaction, whereas the metaverse-enabled virtual consultation offers multi-user collaboration, which allows patients to receive consultation from experts around the globe. It also improves spatial presence, which increases empathy and understanding among people.

Telemedicine laid the foundation for remote patient care, while the metaverse enhances it by providing an interactive, immersive, and collaborative experience through virtual clinics, which enhance clinical decision-making, patient satisfaction, and accessibility. Convergence has many benefits, but it also has difficulties, such as data privacy concerns, problems with interoperability, regulatory monitoring, and biases in AI algorithms. Using disruptive technologies in medical records requires strong cybersecurity measures and an ethical governance framework [3]. Despite these problems, healthcare is changing to be more patient-centered, fair, and digital.

2.2 Metaverse in Medical Education and Training

A metaverse-based platform provides a realistic simulation for the education and training of medical professionals, enabling improved learning compared to conventional methods. Clinical instruction for medical students primarily relies on instructor demonstrations, theoretical frameworks, and observational learning. Limitations, such as working hours and ethical standards, hinder the integration of theory and practice. Metaverse-based learning environments significantly enhance teaching effectiveness, decrease training duration, and boost learner interest, confidence, and engagement across various disciplines, including surgery, anatomy, and dentistry. Medical education utilizes metaverse tools for an immersive study of three-dimensional anatomy, virtual surgical practice, and collaborative clinical simulations in a secure and repeatable environment. High-fidelity anatomical models enable detailed visualization of organs and vessels in a layer-by-layer manner, allowing for virtual dissection without the need for cadavers. Enhance user involvement in surgical procedures by utilizing haptic input and real-time assessment, while encouraging participation in collaborative scenarios to improve decision-making and communication abilities. Studies show these technologies improve learning outcomes, surgical precision, and confidence, providing scalable and adaptable training options beyond conventional classroom and laboratory settings.

A simulation framework called MAGES 4.0 enables medical training applications to function together. It uses virtual reality (VR), augmented reality (AR), and mixed reality (MR) [4]. This is a low-code or no-code platform that teaches medical professionals how to deal with trauma events in real time, such as accidents, war injuries, minimally invasive surgeries, and the use of real-time anesthetic procedures. The first step in the MAGES operating protocol is storyboarding, when a user uses a visual script editor to make a step-by-step plan for a complicated situation. After that, virtual assets like surgical tools and 3D human body models are created. Next, write down the steps that need to be taken to do the surgery by using action scripts that follow the rules of prototype design. The assembled technique will also be built and put into use so that it may be used on a variety of devices. MAGES did a great job of showing fourth simulation surgeries, including complete knee arthroplasty, liver dissection, and an interactive heart model, to name a few.

Similarly, students from the University of Newcastle have been provided with a distinctive opportunity to explore the intricate complexities associated with pregnancy, thereby enhancing their comprehension of the challenges that may arise during this period using virtual simulations [5]. Through virtual reality, a highly realistic three-dimensional representation of pregnancy has been developed, allowing users to navigate seamlessly through various stages, spanning from the first week to the forty-fourth week.

In addition, the MOOG Simodont Dentistry Trainer is a Virtual Reality (VR) haptic simulator that teaches dentistry students and professionals about hand dexterity and tactile feedback during dental treatments [6]. It uses haptic technologies, 3D visualization, and realistic simulations to provide an interesting, safe, and repeatable educational experience. It gives a high-definition imagery of dental equipment and teeth with 3D projection and a handpiece to execute a dental procedure with precision and accuracy. The Academic Centre for Dentistry Amsterdam included this into their curriculum to instruct students on numerous dental treatments, including cavity preparation, crown shape, and endodontic access.

Metaverse, an immersive technology that blends physical reality with virtual experience through AR and VR, and facilitates virtual hospitals and a health care ecosystem where patients and providers can interact in a virtual world, seems to be in a real world. The implementation of virtual worlds in healthcare is becoming a demanding one post-pandemic due to growing limitations of traditional healthcare models and increased demand for remote, scalable, and immersive solutions. Ullah et al. [7] proposed a four-phase holistic process of Medical Metaverse development, which was depicted in Fig. 2.

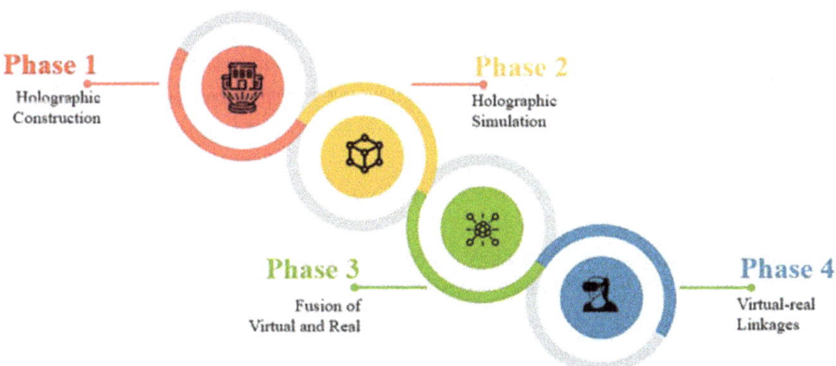

Figure 2: Framework for the implementation of the metaverse in medical applications.

The process begins with the creation of geometric representations of the environment, encompassing medical instruments, facilities, and spatial elements where medical professionals interact, such as surgical rooms, and capturing dynamic exchanges between individuals and the environment. Holographic reconstruction and technology like sensors and diagnostic equipment provide us with a lot of information about how the body works, which makes it possible to make digital twins, or virtual copies of real patients. These connect the real and virtual world, making clinical decision-making more effective and simulations more accurate.

The second phase is holographic simulation, which generates realistic and spatially precise representations of objects, including medical tools, human anatomy, and settings. This leads to the development of immersive, interactive medical environments in which healthcare workers can visualize, modify, and interact with virtual patients or organs as if they were physically there. In the third stage, real-world and virtual realms are combined, with virtual components interacting with patients and gathering real-world inputs such as physiological movements, sensor data, and medical imaging. Capture information is presented via augmented reality, resulting in a new relationship with the current natural environment.

The next step is the integration of real and virtual linkage, which refers to the dynamic connection between physical healthcare facilities and their digital counterparts, for continuous data flow, synchronization, and interaction between these two domains. This link supports metaverse-driven medical systems, allowing real-time diagnosis, simulation, intervention, and learning.

2.3 Surgical Training and Education through Metaverse

Traditional surgical training and teaching face numerous challenges, including restricted patient availability, a wide range of case types, time limits, and the expensive expenditures involved with cadaver laboratories. Immersive technologies, such as AR, VR, and MR, enhance surgical training by providing a virtual environment, complete with tools and 3D anatomical models. This allows trainees to practice repeatedly on the complex surgical procedure and pre-operative plans, improving their precision and decision-making skills. Platforms like Osso VR, FundamentalVR, and Medicalholodeck simulate entire operating rooms, integrating haptic feedback and real-time performance analytics to enhance precision and decision-making.

These simulations facilitate team-based training, enabling multidisciplinary groups to collaboratively rehearse emergency scenarios or complex surgeries, enhancing communication, coordination, and procedural fluency. The metaverse facilitates personalized learning paths, competency assessments, and skill refinement by integrating AI-driven feedback and performance tracking, independent of patient involvement [8]. Studies indicate that surgical residents trained using virtual reality demonstrate superior performance in speed, accuracy, and confidence relative to those trained through traditional methods.

2.4 Rehabilitation and Therapy through Metaverse

In rural or resource-restricted settings, fragmented manual procedures, extended recovery times, and limited access to specialized care might make traditional rehabilitation and therapy less effective. Patients frequently experience issues such as a lack of motivation, a lack of involvement, and treatment regimens that are overly generic and fail to consider their unique needs. Also, the lack of educated specialists and real-time feedback or objective progress tracking makes rehabilitation even harder. These problems make therapy less effective, make people less likely to stick with it, and slow down recovery. This shows how important it is to find new, immersive, and individualized solutions like those offered by the metaverse.

Neurorehabilitation, cognitive treatment, psychological therapy, and rehabilitation for children and the elderly are some of the most significant domains where the metaverse plays an integral part. The metaverse enhances engagement, repetition, sensory input, and personalization—all of which are essential to many forms of therapy. A metaverse-enabled gamified platform presents an optimal environment for treating patients with conditions such as stroke, spinal cord injuries, and Parkinson's disease through guided physical activity. It will enhance motor coordination, balance, and muscle strength through repetitive, engaging activities. XRHealth provides VR-based stroke rehab programs with real-time feedback.

An identical environment can be established to train patients experiencing cognitive decline, memory impairment, and executive function disorders. Virtual tasks and simulations enhance memory, attention, and problem-solving skills. Individuals diagnosed with Alzheimer's engage in immersive cognitive training programs to mitigate the progression of degeneration. Virtual reality environments that are safe and controlled are utilized for exposure therapy in the treatment of anxiety, post-traumatic stress disorder, and phobias. Metaverse environments replicate real-life stressors, facilitating gradual desensitization in a controlled clinical setting. Likewise, involving children and elderly people in interactive, age-appropriate therapy enhances adherence and motivation.

3. Challenges and Considerations

The primary obstacle was the substantial expenses associated with Metaverse hardware, and the requirements for infrastructure and interoperability complications with existing health systems. High-end VR/AR headsets, haptic feedback apparatus, and motion-tracking technologies are costly and need regular enhancements. The hospital required substantial investment in developing networks, data storage, and servers that facilitate real-time immersive environments. The existing health record systems and IT infrastructure in hospitals are not readily compatible with these immersive solutions. Furthermore, there is an absence of standardized data formats, APIs, and integration protocols to facilitate the seamless exchange of virtual simulation data with patient records. The virtual environment presents vulnerabilities to patient-sensitive data by bringing cybersecurity and compliance problems.

4. Virtual Clinics and AI-driven Patient Interactions

Healthcare has never experienced a paradigm shift like this, with virtual clinics and AI-run patient interactions coming to the fore. In the remodelling of the way of life through technology, its integration into healthcare is one avenue worthy of delving into. The traditional spatial barriers of delivering and receiving healthcare are being redefined as the clinical visit metamorphoses into a digital interface offering convenience, accessibility, and personalized care. The emerging advent of virtual care and AI-enabled interventions has propelled a vast wave of opportunities for action, particularly after the COVID-19 pandemic, which urged the call for scalable remote health solutions [9].

Rather than the convention of face-to-face consultations, virtual clinics realize doctor-patient communication from afar via digital platforms. These clinics break down all barriers of time and distance by allowing patients to access real-time care, even in the remotest and most underserved locations. In conjunction with this shift is the emergence of AI as a forceful ally providing automation, intelligent, and situationally aware responses to patient needs through chatbots, virtual assistants, and real-time monitoring systems. Together, these technologies are engendering a paradigm shift in healthcare—proactive, preventive, and deeply patient-centric.

4.1 Virtual Clinics: The Building Blocks of Remote Care

Virtual clinics are the building blocks of digital care today. It can be defined as websites or telecommunication that facilitate medical consultations meant to occur remotely. The advancement of virtual clinics has greatly facilitated the delivery of healthcare for patients who would not have been able to access timely medical advice. Virtual clinics often employ video conferencing, mobile applications, and secure portals to achieve doctor-patient interactions while minimizing the need for a physical visit to the hospital except for appropriate cases [10].

An additional strength of a virtual clinic is that it can reach patients in geographically remote areas. In regions with extensive rural populations without healthcare infrastructure, a virtual clinic may represent an invaluable service for those patients. Virtual clinics can also alleviate patients in action-packed urban centres, freeing healthcare systems to focus on more relevant issues without being overwhelmed.

Typically, virtual clinics include several important resources. There are typically digital interfaces for scheduling appointments, tools for video consultations, electronic medical records (EMR), digital prescriptions, follow-up reminders, and even AI-based pre-screening tools in some cases. The digitization of the virtual clinic ensures care continuity from consultation to diagnosis, and follow-up is efficiently followed, monitored, and accessible.

Virtual clinics also increase patient empowerment. Patients can access their medical records and become engaged and involved in their health management. Patients can connect with specialists who may be several cities or countries away, reducing delays in diagnosis for timely intervention and improved outcomes. Nevertheless, virtual clinics must address challenges, including maintaining patient confidentiality, ensuring regulatory compliance, and bridging a digital literacy gap for patients of all ages.

4.2 AI Chatbots and Virtual Assistants in Patient Care

Artificial Intelligence (AI) has created new levels of automation, personalization, and efficiency in how healthcare is delivered. One of the more obvious and more widely adopted use cases for AI is chatbots and virtual assistants. These systems leverage Natural Language Processing (NLP), machine learning, and data analytics to engage with patients, replicate human conversation, and provide intelligent responses.

AI chatbots often appear on healthcare websites and mobile apps and typically respond to basic patient inquiries, triage symptoms, offer preliminary diagnoses, and assist in making appointments. For instance, a chatbot can ask a patient a series of structured questions regarding symptoms and refer them to emergency care, schedule a virtual consultation, or if there wasn't an emergency; recommend alternative treatments. This benefits healthcare providers by saving time and providing patients with immediate assistance, something felt most often in non-emergency care encountered, such as when someone doesn't feel well but is uncertain whether to visit a healthcare provider. The potential services that are enhanced with the integration of a chatbot are depicted in Fig. 3.

Virtual assistants expand on this capability. AI-powered assistants, now available through smartphones, smart speakers, or wearable health monitors and devices, can continuously monitor a patient's health metrics, remind them to take medications, track fitness goals, or provide lifestyle recommendations. Additionally, they may access electronic health systems to obtain patient data, update records, or deliver alerts to caregivers.

These AI technologies have considerable promise to improve chronic disease management. People with chronic conditions like diabetes, hypertension, or asthma can use AI technologies to help manage their conditions daily and receive alerts when there are variations in their health. AI chatbots can harness user input to provide a basic level of cognitive-behavioral therapy (CBT), emotional support, or crisis intervention. While these chatbot skills are useful, the limitations of chatbot technology must also be acknowledged. For example, these chatbots are limited in their ability to comprehend nuanced language, cultural differences, and sometimes the complexity of patients' medical conditions. While the potential and applications of AI in healthcare are continually evolving, AI cannot yet replace our natural human responses, such as empathy, nor our professional clinical judgment. It is well-established within the clinical sphere of human interactions that AI has potential utility to augment our understanding of disease management; however, we must move forward with caution and not replace what clinicians can personally offer their patients with AI technologies.

24/7 Patient Support	• Provide round-the-clock responses to common health queries.
Appointment Scheduling	• Automate booking, reminders, and rescheduling of appointments.
Symptom Checker & Triage	• Analyze patient-reported symptoms using NLP.
Medication Reminders	• Send personalized alerts to patients for timely medication intake.
Mental Health Support	• Provide anonymous, real-time emotional support and check-ins. • Used widely in depression and anxiety monitoring tools.
Health Education	• Deliver tailored health tips, lifestyle advice, and preventive care info.
Pre-Consultation Data Collection	• Gather medical history, current symptoms, and vitals before a doctor's visit.
Post-Treatment Follow-up	• Automate follow-up messages to monitor recovery progress.
Language and Accessibility Support	• Communicate in multiple languages, including voice-to-text and text-to-speech.

Figure 3: Applications of AI chatbots in health care.

5. The Integration of Avatars with Real-Time Monitoring Systems

An intriguing new frontier for digital health is the inclusion of animated avatars with real-time physiological monitoring systems. Ideally, automated avatars and real-time physiological monitoring systems will work together to enhance the virtual-patient experience, allowing consumers/patients to receive more engaging, personalized, and continuous care or treatment.

Avatars in health care are humanoid, computer-generated figures that interface with patients while in a digital space. They can be customized to present as a physician, physician assistant, nurse, or "health care guide," and they offer health information and data in a friendly, non-threatening manner. For example, avatars can simulate doctor's visits to explain medical procedures in a gentle approach for paediatric care. Avatars can be used in mental health therapy to simulate interactive counselling sessions while giving patients and clients a safe venue to discuss their feelings without fear of judgment.

For elderly care, avatars can simulate visiting friends and, combined with speech synthesis and facial recognition, create virtual companions. These avatars can check on seniors' well-being through a phone or other device, remind them to take their medications, and even engage them in cognitive activities that combat feelings of social isolation and cognitive decline. The psychological effects of these avatars are beginning to be realized, particularly when used with patients who have anxiety or dementia.

Real-time tracking and monitoring systems are closely associated with the Internet of Things (IoT). Wearable smart devices such as smartwatches, fitness bands, and biosensors can routinely collect physiological data, including heart rate, blood oxygenation, glucose level, quality of sleep, and body temperature; the collected data can be analysed on the device and via cloud using an AI algorithm to identify anomalies, predict medical events, and generate alerts. Due to the essence of this and emerging technology, real-time tracking and monitoring will be especially applicable for patients with acute conditions and/or chronic disease states. For example, a known heart patient could wear a device that alerts their physician to any abnormal ECG; similarly, diabetic patients would use a continuous glucose monitor (CGM) that provides continuous regulatory feedback regarding blood sugar ebbs and flows, informing their food intake choices and decisions about the consumption of insulin.

While the potential is significant, easy access and incredible utility among consumers raise serious questions of privacy, security, and data ownership. The realities of real-time tracking and monitoring mean the presence of consent and protocols around secure data transmissions to mitigate unauthorized access and the inappropriate use of sensitive health data.

6. Transforming Healthcare

Virtual clinics and AI-based patient connectivity are not just improvements—they signify a disruption to how we think about and deliver healthcare. By adding convenience with intelligence, these new technologies are helping to develop a healthcare system that can be more responsive, more inclusive, and more efficient. Whether through avatars that transform digital consultations to feel more human, chatbots that are always there for patients, or real-time monitors that continually check in on health, the confluence of virtual platforms and AI is redefining the patient pathway.

Like any implications of a changing technology, an intentional process is required. Ethical design principles, human-centered principles, and regulatory frameworks are all very important, as is training healthcare workers and educating patients to feel confident about engaging with digital capabilities. In the end, it is not to take away from traditional care, but to improve on it. Arriving at the right equilibrium could lead to virtual clinics and AI-based patient engagements to provide customized, proactive, and easy-to-access care for all.

7. Issues and Challenges

7.1 Digital Healthcare Challenges and Opportunities

While virtual clinics and AI-enhanced patient interactions have enormous potential, significant barriers to adoption remain. One of those challenges is the digital divide—not every patient has access to a fast internet connection, a mobile phone, or is comfortable leveraging a digital interface (in these cases, primarily in low-income populations and elderly patients). Without inclusive design and education approaches, these innovations could unintentionally exclude the very patients who could benefit the most [11].

Another challenge to contend with is interoperability. Providers use different systems that do not promote smooth and effective exchanges of patient data across care systems. A lack of digital health infrastructure hamstrings the coordination of care teams and ultimately dilutes the impact of virtual clinics and AI-enabled tools.

7.2 Data Safety and Cybersecurity also Create Considerable Threats

Due to the digitalization of medical records and the use of connected devices, data breaches will pose a serious challenge. It is critical to have healthcare providers who have to navigate through the regulatory framework of the Health Insurance Portability and Accountability Act (HIPAA) or the General Data Protection Regulation (GDPR).

In contrast, the opportunities are plentiful. AI will become better, and predictive analytics will allow for levels of concern for patients who appear healthy for now, but we can identify likely conditions. Virtual clinics combined with remote labs and diagnostic imaging centers can support full spectrum digital care.

The incidence of these technologies is mostly effective when a public health emergency exists or during a natural disaster, when access to healthcare on site is not an option, or in conflict zones, when physical care is under duress or not an option. These technologies allow for continuity of care to occur, can be supported with contactless consultations, and reduce the load on healthcare service structures.

7.3 Ethical, Privacy, and Regulatory Considerations

Integrating multiple technologies and global data access capability leads to problems in following the regulatory considerations. Each country focuses on individual aspects with respect to data privacy and concerns. As per the data given by “UN Trade and Development”, the developed countries provide 98% of legislative data privacy, whereas the least developed countries and landlocked least development countries have around 50% of legislative data privacy [12]. Various challenges of data privacy and digital identity are given in Fig. 4.

Figure 4: Challenges of data privacy and digital identity in healthcare.

7.4 Challenges of Data Privacy and Digital Identity

- **Sensitive Health Data in Virtual Environments:** Applications developed with AI and Metaverse get health-related datasets from individual patients. Accessing their data without getting their consent leads to a greater threat to their privacy. Private data generated from patients' cush as blood group, biometric information, and disease details, creates a high risk of data exposure or leakage [13].
- **Digital Identity in the Metaverse:** Even though there is a possibility to create avatar-like patients, a few of the patient's identity is required to show the model in the real-world environment. This creates a challenge to replicate the patients without disclosing their personal data as an avatar [14].
- **Data Ownership and Consent:** Data generated from virtual consultations with metaverse applications has a challenge of authenticity. There is a potential for users to claim the data as it is available online. Strong methodology is required to claim one's dataset generated through the metaverse.

- **Cybersecurity Risks:** Metaverse platforms that store healthcare data are vulnerable to hacking by hackers. Also, ransomware attacks could encrypt the data generated. Other cyber security risks, such as malware, distributed denial of service to our data, man-in-the-middle attacks, and fraudulent interpretations, must also be focussed on to avoid data theft [15].
- **Cross Border Data Jurisdiction Issue:** Metaverse-based models face the cross-border data jurisdiction issue since they follow the globally virtual data. Determining which part of the country is following which type of legal framework is a challenging task.

7.5 AI Bias and Transparency Issues

Data generated through AI or with the help of AI may have a biased or inconsistent information present. Figure 5 shows a few of the possible AI bias and transparency issues.

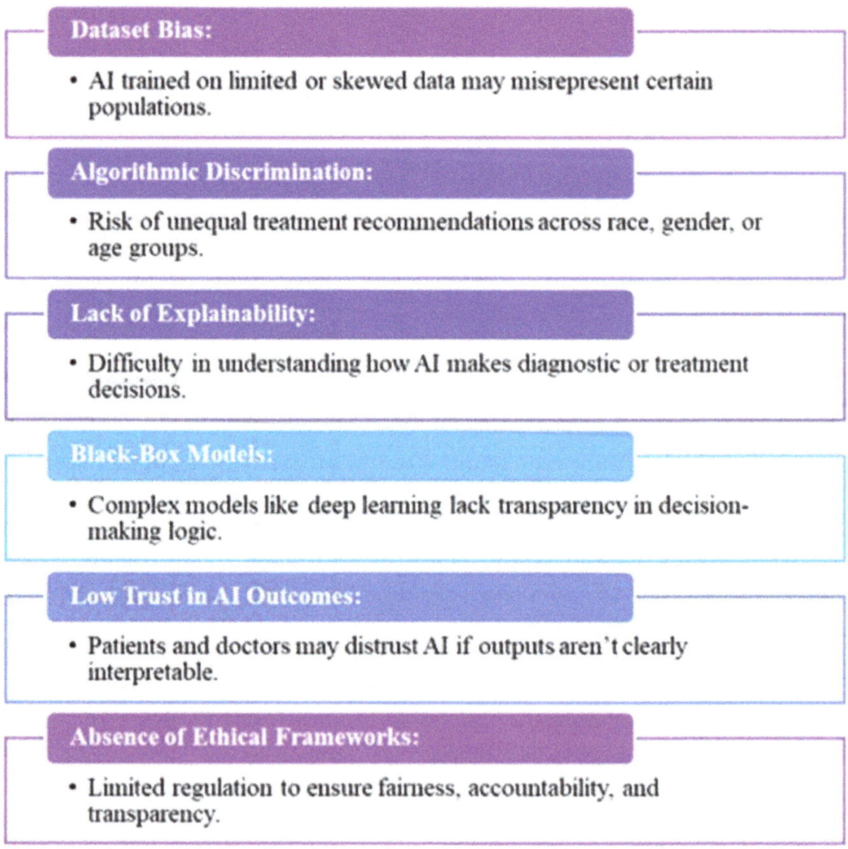

Figure 5: Possible AI bias and transparency issues.

- **Dataset Bias:** The dataset, when generated with AI models, leads to probabilistic matching information rather than the real information. Probabilistic matching information may be generated based on the historical input data. Real population data have the discriminant information with respect to the individual feature inputs. AI-generated data through Large Language Models (LLM) produces skewed (left or right) data.
- **Algorithmic Discrimination:** Some automated AI/ML algorithms produce unfair outcomes based on improper training. This results in predicting diseases better for white tone people and fair prediction for dark-toned people. Algorithms may also use neutral data variables that may strongly correlate with the characteristics of least significance. This leads to unequal treatment recommendations across race, gender, or age groups.
- **Lack of Explainability:** Unlike real doctors, AI models can't provide the explainability to the patients about the diseases, symptoms, disease curing process, and preventive measures. This leads to the lack of explainability and makes it difficult to understand how AI makes diagnostic or treatment decisions.
- **Black-box Models:** Neural network-based Expert systems work multi-dimensionally with multiple layers of information. Complex algorithms like deep learning, which work on large image datasets, lack transparency in decision-making logic.
- **Low Trust in AI Outcomes:** Doctors and patients always suspect that the results generated through AI are prone to errors, and they may not rely completely on the data generated. This creates a trust issue with the AI models.
- **Absence of Ethical Frameworks:** There is a limited regulation available to verify the fairness of the results generated with AI. Also, the accountability and transparency are moderately lacking with AI-generated data.

7.6 Need for Updated Regulations in Immersive Digital Healthcare

Healthcare services progress through the advancements in the integration of the metaverse with AI, ML, VR/AR, and IoT. Existing legal frameworks must be reframed and restructured to address the technological advancements and the complex ethical, legal, and operational challenges that arise. Table 1 shows the areas where the regulatory needs to be focused more.

- **Metaverse-ready Legacy Laws:** Traditional regulations like the Health Insurance Portability and Accountability Act (HIPAA, USA), the General Data Protection Regulation (GDPR, European Union), Insurance Regulatory and Development Authority (IRDA, India), and other countries' regulatory bodies must be restructured to fill the gap that occurs in integrating modern technologies. These regulatory bodies were designed only for 2D digital interactions. These laws must be restructured to be implemented in 3D immersive, cross-border, and determined environments.

Table 1: Regulatory Needs in Immersive Digital Healthcare

S. No.	Area	Current Gap	Metaverse Concern	Regulatory Need	Example
1	Data Privacy	Outdated data laws	3D biometrics and behavior data	New definitions for sensitive data	Eye-tracking in VR therapy
2	Consent	One-time, static	Real-time dynamic data flow	Continuous consent mechanisms	AR-based mental health sessions
3	Licensing	Nation-specific	Cross-border consultations	Global virtual licensing rules	Indian doctor treats US patient
4	AI Regulation	Minimal oversight	AI avatars giving advice	Ethical AI usage codes	AI doctor bots in virtual clinics
5	Identity Verification	Weak or no verification	Avatar impersonation	Strong digital ID frameworks	Fake avatars posing as physicians
6	Record Keeping	Text/audio logs only	VR/AR interactions untracked	VR-enabled interaction logs	Logging gestures during therapy
7	Platform Standards	Disparate protocols	Incompatible data formats	Unified interoperability rules	Wearable syncing with a VR app
8	Liability	Human-centered	Shared responsibility: AI + Healthcare professional	Hybrid liability models	AI misdiagnosis in VR consultation
9	Audit and Compliance	Periodic manual audits	Real-time, immersive operations	Continuous compliance tracking	Auto-checks in VR hospitals
10	Data Ownership	Often unclear	Cloud-based shared data	Patient-centric data ownership	Patient decides who sees VR data

- **Cross-jurisdiction Treatments:** Metaverse-enabled healthcare practitioners who treat their patients across the globe should meet the requirements of the unique licensing regulations followed by each country. Two questions must be answered while treating international patients with the metaverse-enabled platform:
    1. Which type of law will be applied during virtual consultation?
    2. In case of malpractice, which country takes the responsibility to punish the stakeholders?
- **Digital identity and consent changes:** New techniques, when used with new identities such as avatars, biometrics, and virtual reality animated objects, require advanced consent verification mechanisms. This kind of consent change raises concerns about the authenticity of identity, consent for data usage and AI interaction, and privacy concerns of non-verbal behavioural signs.
- **Ethical Use of AI and Simulated Personas:** Designed regulations need to address a few important aspects, such as how and in what ways the AI avatars will provide medical advice, whether the digital twins of doctors or patients are allowed in the treatment process, and whether AI is suggesting the same replicative suggestions for all the patients with the same type of symptoms without considering the individual medical history. These kinds of issues should be considered in building regulations for the AI-simulated applications.

8. Future Directions and Challenges Ahead

8.1 The Role of Blockchain in Securing Medical Data in the Metaverse

Blockchain technology provides a decentralized and tamper-proof ledger system. These advanced encryption-based techniques can be used for **securing sensitive medical data** within the integration of the Metaverse [16]. Key benefits of the integration of blockchain with the metaverse:

- **Data Integrity:** This integration ensures that the health records of patients will be encrypted and stored in a secure ledger. This makes sure that once the health records are created, they cannot be altered without proper authentication mechanisms.
- **Patient Ownership and Consent:** Individual patients can sign a smart contract, and they can empower their data control. This gives them complete access and ownership over their personal data.
- **Secure Identity Verification:** Blockchain integration offers two-step authentication, one at the user end and the other from the administrator end. This strengthens the digital identity through blockchain-based credentials and an authentication mechanism.
- **Auditability:** Blockchain enables a transparent history of who accessed the data by maintaining the interlinks for each record stored in the cloud. This

interlink maintains the transactional history of when and for what purpose the data is accessed.

- **Data Sharing:** Secure data sharing of electronic health records across all the decentralized metaverse platforms is possible with the blockchain integration.

8.2 Possible Challenges of Blockchain and Metaverse Integration

- **Scalability:** High storage space is required to store the video avatars generated in the metaverse. Smart ledgers require greater processing power to process the real-time 3D/AR/VR medical data.
- **Legal Uncertainty:** Global regulations, intellectual property rights, and smart contract enforceability must be focused more on blockchain implementation in healthcare.
- **Interoperability:** Blockchain networks face difficulties when integrated with traditional text-based patient healthcare databases.

8.3 Interoperability between AI Systems and Metaverse Platforms

Integrating AI and Metaverse systems is an essential prerequisite when it comes to providing seamless and immersive experiences in terms of advanced digital healthcare. The wide range of data sources that start this interoperability include wearable devices that can constantly measure vital health indicators (heart rate monitor, blood pressure monitor, glucose levels, oxygen saturation (SPO_2), etc.). Modern wearable devices produce real-time and patient-specific data, which is the foundation of personalized care. Digital EHRs maintain the properly aligned patient history, diagnoses, methods followed, medications provided, and future treatment plans according to the medical history. Owing to the visual nature of the medical imaging hardware, including MRI and CT scanners, the volume of visual data they create is essential when it comes to AI-oriented diagnostics. In addition, the voice and chatbot interaction of a teleconsultation or a digital assistant also considers patient concerns, emotional tone, and behavioural responses, where the findings are qualitative. This process flow is given in Fig. 6.

Data collected from the wearable sources is then fed to the AI systems, which are the intelligent engine of the healthcare-metaverse interface. Advanced NLP engines are used to understand the spoken and written language, both by patients and health care specialists, and thus achieve intuitive and conversational interaction conclusions. Radiological and pathological diagnostic AI systems are used in extracting medical images to diagnose unusual conditions like the presence of tumours inside the human body or fractures in the bone with high accuracy. The predictive analytics models are used to recognize the patterns of past and real-time data, which can be used to predict disease progression or the complications that may occur. At the same time, virtual health assistants complement the consistent

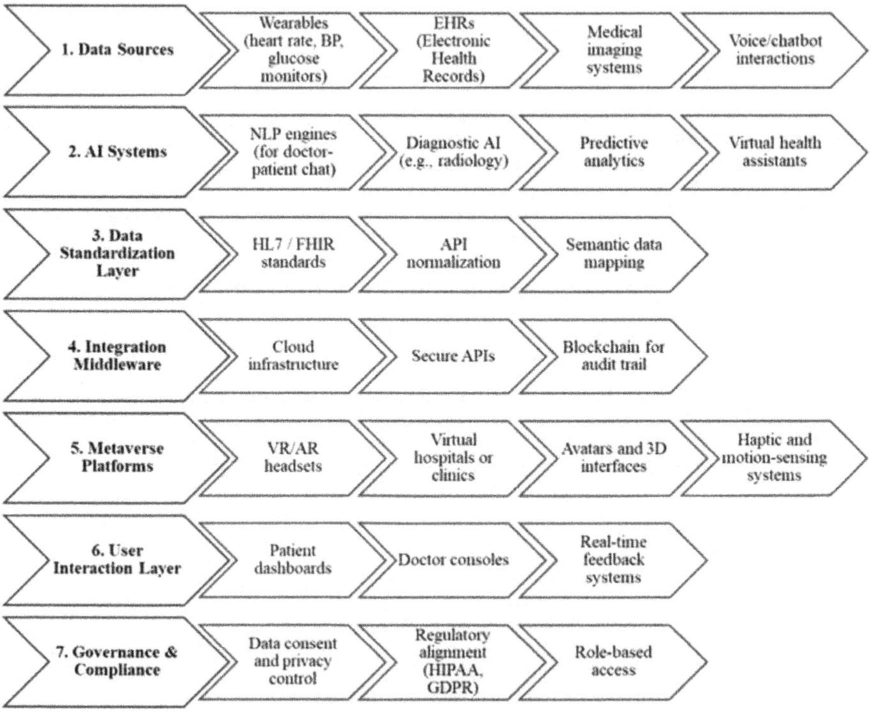

Figure 6: Process flow for interoperability between AI systems and metaverse platforms.

support to remind the patient about medications, conduct follow-ups, and respond to repetitive questions.

The modern developed AI systems require a data standardization layer to make the whole process seamless with conversing with all sorts of immersive platforms, which consist of AI, ML, IoT, Blockchain, and metaverse. It defines this level by standards used globally in healthcare, such as HL7 (Health Level Seven) or FHIR (Fast Healthcare Interoperability Resources), to obtain a high degree of uniformity in the forms of exchanging data. Integration middleware serves as the body of this infrastructure by facilitating how the data, intelligence, and immersive visualization connections take place. The layer provides support for scalable data storage and real-time processing using the cloud infrastructure, secure APIs that allow interactions through all systems, and blockchain technology should be used to keep audit trails of data access, consent, and modifications tamper-proof. Blockchain introduces an element of transparency, especially in transnational or multi-partner health connections.

Metaverse-enabled healthcare systems featuring VR/AR headsets create a virtual hospital environment as per the user's aesthetic choice. This also includes avatars of doctors, nurses, and other medical professionals involved in the treatment process. Haptic and motion sensing systems provide the ability that imitate touch/movement and increase the level of realism when training surgeons or conducting physiotherapy.

All this comes through user user-interactive user interface where the customers receive dashboards with health metrics, health monitoring visualizations, and real-time 3D monitoring through an AI-driven approach. The governance and compliance make the whole process executed smoothly and seamlessly. This includes privacy consent management, regulatory alignment, and providing role-based access to the data.

The next decade will witness a weighty transformation in the healthcare sector with the integration of advanced technologies like AI, the Metaverse, Internet of Things (IoT), blockchain, and quantum computing. This trend will completely redefine the entire process from finding a doctor, fixing an appointment, waiting for the turn, getting treatment, post-treatment follow-up, and other aspects. Figure 7 shows the traditional approach and the advanced modern approach in healthcare.

Traditional approach	Aspect	Future Digital Health Convergence
Reactive (treat after illness)	Care Approach	Proactive & Preventive (predict and prevent illness)
Limited to clinic visits	Patient Involvement	Continuous, real-time engagement via wearables & apps
Siloed, paper/EHR-based	Data Management	Interoperable, real-time, blockchain-secured data sharing
Physical clinics/hospitals, location-dependent	Access to Care	Virtual clinics in the Metaverse, global access
Manual, time-consuming	Diagnosis	AI-assisted, faster and more accurate
Generalized treatment protocols	Treatment Personalization	AI-driven personalized medicine using digital twins
Scarce and stigmatized	Mental Health Support	AI-powered emotional support via empathetic bots and avatars
Sole decision-maker	Doctor's Role	AI-augmented clinician with decision support systems
Centralized, less transparent	Security & Consent	Patient-controlled data via blockchain & smart contracts
Access varies based on geography & wealth	Health Equity	Tech-enabled equity, inclusive platforms for rural & marginalized communities

Figure 7: Traditional vs modern approaches.

9. Conclusion

Digital health will shift from the traditional reactive treatment to proactive care systems based on continuous data monitoring through wearable devices. These systems will try to find any abnormality present in the human body and suggest to him/her the seriousness of taking medications. AI systems also help to find emotional intelligence by allowing systems to understand the sentimentality of patients affected with psychological diseases, their stress levels, and behavioural patterns. Apart from regular AI chatbots and suggestive medical approaches, the next groundbreaking advancement will be the development of digital twins. Digital twins are the virtual replicas of patients built from medical history, genomics, and lifestyle data. These avatar-like models will allow doctors to demonstrate how the surgeries are going to be carried out, predict curing time, and get information from the patients and customize the therapies as per the patient's choice in virtual environments. The use of blockchain will become the key to maintaining patients' health data decentralized and safe. In the future, patients will also have an option to donate their data, and they can earn from that. The patients will gain complete authority over their data by providing roles and security levels by monitoring who and how long the data is used, and what aspect of their data is used in the digital health platforms.

References

1. Esteva, A., Kuprel, B., Novoa, R. A., et al. (2017). Dermatologist-level classification of skin cancer with deep neural networks. *Nature*, 542(7639), 115–118. https://doi.org/10.1038/nature21056
2. Topol, E. (2019). High-performance medicine: The convergence of human and artificial intelligence. *Nature Medicine*, 25(1), 44–56. https://doi.org/10.1038/s41591-018-0300-7
3. Ryu, S., and Heo, E. Y. (2022). Data governance issues in the healthcare metaverse: Opportunities and challenges. *Healthcare Informatics Research*, 28(4), 291–297. https://doi.org/10.4258/hir.2022.28.4.291
4. Zikas, P., Antonis Protopsaltis, Nick Lydatakis, Mike Kentros, Stratos Geronikolakis, Steve Kateros et al. (March-April 2023). MAGES 4.0: Accelerating the world's transition to VR training and democratizing the authoring of the medical metaverse. *IEEE Computer Graphics and Applications*, 43(2), 43–56, doi: 10.1109/MCG.2023.3242686.
5. Bansal, G., Rajgopal, K., Chamola, V., Xiong, Z., and Niyato, D. (2022). Healthcare in metaverse: A survey on current metaverse applications in healthcare. *IEEE Access*, 10, 119914–119946.
6. Al-Saud, L. M., Mushtaq, F., Allsop, M. J., Culmer, P. C., Mirghani, I., Yates, E. et al. (Nov. 2017). Feedback and motor skill acquisition using a haptic dental simulator. *Eur. J. Dental Educ.*, 21(4), 240–247.
7. Ullah, H., Manickam, S., Obaidat, M., Laghari, S. U. A., and Uddin, M. (2023). Exploring the potential of metaverse technology in healthcare: Applications,

challenges, and future directions. *IEEE Access*, 11, 69686–69707, doi: 10.1109/ACCESS.2023.3286696.

8. Popov, V., Mateju, N., Jeske, C., and Lewis, K. O. (2024). Metaverse-based simulation: A scoping review of charting medical education over the last two decades in the lens of the 'marvelous medical education machine'. *Ann Med.*, 56(1), 2424450. doi: 10.1080/07853890.2024.2424450. Epub 2024 Nov 13.
9. Hollander, J. E., and Carr, B. G. (2020). Virtually perfect? Telemedicine for Covid-19. *New England Journal of Medicine*, No. PG-NEJMp2003539-NEJMp2003539, doi: 10.1056/NEJMp2003539.
10. Y. C. L. B.-A. Othmane Nait Hamoud Tayeb Kenaza and M. Ouaked, (2023). Implementing a secure remote patient monitoring system. *Information Security Journal: A Global Perspective*, 32(1), 21–38, doi: 10.1080/19393555.2022.2047839.
11. Koebe, P. (Jun. 2025). How digital technologies and AI contribute to achieving the health-related SDGs. *International Journal of Information Management Data Insights*, 5(1), 100298, doi: 10.1016/J.JJIMEI.2024.100298.
12. UNCTAD. (2025). Data Protection and Privacy Legislation Worldwide. https://unctad.org/page/data-protection-and-privacy-legislation-worldwide. Accessed: Aug. 02, 2025 [Online].
13. Baskar, S., Ramar, K., and Shanmugasundaram, H. (2021). Data security in healthcare using blockchain technology. In: *2021 International Conference on Decision Aid Sciences and Application* (*DASA*), pp. 354–359. doi: 10.1109/DASA53625.2021.9682300.
14. Huynh-The, T., Pham, Q. V., Pham, X. Q., Nguyen, T. T., Han, Z., and Kim, D. S. (Jan. 2023). Artificial intelligence for the metaverse: A survey. *Eng Appl Artif Intell*, 117, 105581, doi: 10.1016/J.ENGAPPAI.2022.105581.
15. Raman, R., Kautish, P., Siddiqui, A., Siddiqui, M., and Nedungadi, P. (2025). The role of metaverse technologies in energy systems towards sustainable development goals. *Energy Reports*, 13, 4459–4476, doi: https://doi.org/10.1016/j.egyr.2025.04.012.
16. Thakur, G., Kumar, P., Chen, C.-M., Vasilakos, A. V., Anchna, and Prajapat, S. (2023). A robust privacy-preserving ECC-based three-factor authentication scheme for metaverse environment. *Comput. Commun.*, 211, 271–285 [Online]. Available: https://api.semanticscholar.org/CorpusID:263202292

CHAPTER

2

Virtual Hospital in the Metaverse: The Future of Healthcare Delivery

Rathna Kumari[1*], C. Arun[1], B. Hariharan[1], Abhiraj Bhowmick[1] and Blessing N.R. Wilfred[2]

[1] Department of Computational Intelligence, School of Computing, SRM Institute of Sciences and Technology, Kattankulathur, Chennai, India

[2] College of Computing and Information Sciences, University of Technology and Applied Sciences-IBRI, Sultanate of Oman

The healthcare metaverse represents a convergence of virtual reality (VR), augmented reality (AR), mixed reality (MR), and supporting technologies to create immersive digital environments for medical applications. This chapter examines the current state and future potential of metaverse technologies in healthcare, analyzing market projections, technological infrastructure, clinical applications, and implementation challenges. With market valuations projected to reach between $125.64 billion and $219.1 billion by 2035, the healthcare metaverse shows promise across multiple domains, including telemedicine, surgical planning, medical education, mental health therapy, and rehabilitation. While early research demonstrates positive outcomes in usability and patient engagement, significant challenges remain in technological maturity, data security, regulatory compliance, and maintaining human connection in virtual care. This review synthesizes current evidence and identifies key considerations for the ethical and effective implementation of metaverse technologies in healthcare delivery.

1. Introduction

Picture a future where your doctor's office isn't a building but a virtual space you enter from your living room, or in which physical therapy is a form of gentle play.

*Corresponding author: madukurr@srmist.edu.in

DOI: 10.1201/9781003679370-2

A realm of holography where surgeons rehearse intricate operations before ever cutting into a patient. Today, we're taking a deep dive into this interesting and rapidly changing intersection of the metaverse, these immersive, participatory, virtual reality-based environments, with healthcare. We'll be looking at some actual feasibility, early efficacy signals, some key design considerations, and finally, the myriad ways these are emerging in health [1, 5, 6].

By the metaverse, we're essentially talking about an all-encompassing virtual universe. It's driven by a trio of technologies: virtual reality, augmented reality, and mixed reality—or what's known as XR, for extended reality [6, 7]. It's like the future internet, a persistent digital layer on which people can move around from virtual space to virtual space using these XR technologies and feel like they're there. Today, immersive, collaborative virtual environments, or ICVEs, are multi-user spaces in the metaverse, where multiple people can be present, engaged, and feel like they are potentially "together" in that virtual space.

1.1 Evolution of Virtual Reality Technology

The first VR headset was developed in the 1960s by Ivan Sutherland, and later innovations like graphical user interfaces (GUIs) made it possible for increasingly lifelike and interactive scenes to appear. With Tim Berners-Lee's invention of the World Wide Web in 1989, the foundation was laid for a worldwide structure of digital interactivity, the necessary stepping-stone for the connected spaces we know were soon to be part of the metaverse [6].

In the late 1990s and early 2000s, persistent virtual worlds began to worm into popular culture and life on the Internet. Environments such as MUDs and early MMOGs like Ultima Online and World of Warcraft were early versions of shared worlds where thousands of users could play in the same space at the same time. That was in 2003, and Second Life remains a milestone in the development of the metaverse, weaving together social media and a 3D world, and serving as a testing ground for virtual societies and economics. In time, Roblox, Minecraft, and Fortnite built on those principles, creating worlds users could tinker with and vast digital communities to share their creations.

1.2 Current Drivers of Adoption

Researchers link this sudden boom of metaverse-related domains to a push-pull phenomenon. The push is coming from continuous, rapid advancements in XR hardware and software itself. Headsets are getting smaller, lighter, and more powerful, and the pull is coming from clients and healthcare providers themselves. They're actively looking for interventions that are more effective, more accessible, and more tailored to individual needs.

The COVID-19 pandemic significantly accelerated this whole trend. It laid bare the limitations of our healthcare systems in no uncertain terms, and at the same time created an overwhelming spike in demand for non-face-to-face services. Telehealth took off, but users wanted more. If you're looking forward, what the metaverse might enable is essentially managing some of these several large challenges, things like escalating health care costs; infrastructure, that cost; rapidly ageing populations—we're running out of young people to look after so many old people—and shortages of health care personnel [5, 6]. The goal is to shift types of care traditionally delivered in crowded hospitals—and now, during a pandemic, particularly risky due to their risk of exposure to the coronavirus—right to people's living rooms

1.3 Market Analysis and Projections

The healthcare metaverse market is experiencing unprecedented growth, with multiple research firms projecting exponential expansion over the next decade. According to Grand View Research, the market was valued at $3.36 billion in 2022 and is expected to grow at a compound annual growth rate (CAGR) of 42.6% through 2030. Precedence Research provides even more robust projections, estimating the market at $11.75 billion in 2024, expanding to $125.64 billion by 2034 with a CAGR of 26.74%. Most optimistically, Roots Analysis projects growth from $14.6 billion in 2025 to $219.1 billion by 2035, representing a CAGR of 31.1% [1, 6].

Healthcare metaverse market size projections from multiple research firms, showing exponential growth potential from 2022 to 2035, are depicted in Fig. 1. These projections reflect the increasing adoption of immersive technologies across healthcare institutions globally. The rapid development of augmented reality (AR), virtual reality (VR), and artificial transformation of the healthcare sector, enabling the creation of immersive and realistic healthcare experiences

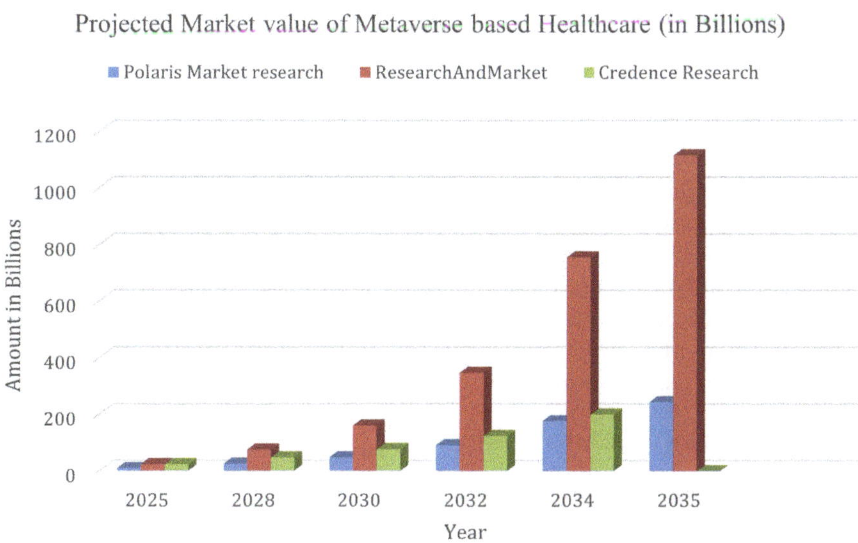

Figure 1: Projected healthcare metaverse market size.

that revolutionize patient care, medical training, and diagnostics. North America currently leads market adoption due to rapid healthcare infrastructure development and integration of AR and VR platforms, while Asia-Pacific is expected to grow fastest during the forecast period. The healthcare industry involves a wide range of stakeholders, including healthcare providers, insurers, patients, and medical researchers. For the metaverse to be fully utilized in healthcare, there must be interoperability between different platforms, systems, and devices, allowing for seamless data exchange and collaboration between stakeholders [12]. The potential enhancement in healthcare through the metaverse, depicted in Fig. 2.

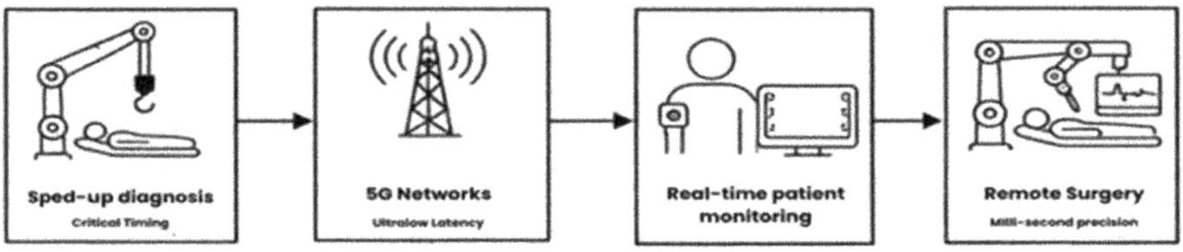

Figure 2: Healthcare enhancement through the metaverse.

2. Technological Infrastructure

2.1 Extended Reality (XR) Technologies

The healthcare metaverse is built upon a sophisticated technology stack that integrates multiple cutting-edge innovations. Extended reality or XR, is the big umbrella term for virtual reality (VR), augmented reality (AR), and mixed reality (MR) [6, 7].

- **Virtual Reality (VR)** is where one is completely immersed. Consider headsets like the Oculus Quest 2; they transport you and shut you out of your physical surroundings.
- **Augmented Reality (AR)** enhances your real world. It superimposes digital information, images, and video data onto your view of reality. Apple Vision Pro is a key example where one can see digital stuff floating in your room, like adding a layer.
- **Mixed Reality (MR)** is the true hybrid; it lets you interact with both real and virtual objects in the same space seamlessly. For example, one could be looking at a virtual heart model, but still, reach out and grab your real coffee mug off your real desk, and the system understands both.

2.2 Supporting Technologies

Artificial Intelligence (AI) and Machine Learning (ML) are fundamental. They're used to simulate human thinking, enhancing immersive experiences and making virtual services smarter. AI enables domains like natural language processing (NLP) that enhance natural conversation with the system or avatars, like talking to a virtual assistant, but more integrated and much more deeply embedded [13]. Computer Vision (CV) is for identifying objects, tracking facial expressions, and understanding movement accurately. The key emerging technologies, associated devices, and challenges associated with them are provided in Table 1.

Table 1: Key Emerging Technologies in the Healthcare Metaverse

Technology	Devices/Examples	Advantages	Challenges
Virtual Reality	Oculus Quest 2, HTC Vive	Full immersion, enhanced learning	Cyber sickness, expensive
Augmented Reality	Apple Vision Pro, AccuVein	Real-time overlay assists in surgery/vein find	Limited FOV, environment dependency
Mixed Reality	Microsoft HoloLens, Magic Leap	Real + virtual blend, interactive simulation	High cost, steep learning curve
Haptic Feedback	GeoMagic Touch, Simodont	Realistic training, touch sensation	Equipment cost, hardware limitations
AI/ML	NLP tools, Virtual assistants	Intelligent responses, smart triage	Algorithmic bias, data quality concerns
Blockchain	Decentralized EMRs, Smart contracts	Secure records, patient-controlled access	Technical complexity, regulatory questions

Network Infrastructure: High-speed networks like 5G and eventually, 6G facilitate super-low latency and high bandwidth for real-time transmission of complex 3D virtual items and services. For domains like remote surgery, there cannot be any ground for lag, especially where milliseconds genuinely matter. Complementing the networks are cloud and edge computing. The Cloud offers scalable storage and processing power for the massive amounts of data generated, while edge computing processes data closer to the source, like on your headset or a local device [2, 5, 6].

Blockchain Technology: Think of it like a secure, distributed, digital ledger. Everyone involved can see the entries, but nobody can secretly change them. Once they're recorded, it's immutable. It enhances the healthcare services, which are decentralized, transparent system for secure record keeping. It enhances data security and privacy in the metaverse, stops data tampering, and empowers patients to control who accesses their health info [2, 6, 15].

Digital Twins: Are essentially real-time, virtual replicas of physical things or even processes. Clinical applications include Mayo Clinic's patient-specific tumor models that enable oncologists to simulate different treatment options before administration, minimizing trial-and-error approaches in cancer therapy. Stanford University has developed digital twin models of the human heart to simulate and study cardiovascular diseases, helping cardiologists assess treatment strategies and improve intervention precision [1, 5, 6, 17].

Haptic Technology: This adds the sense of touch, force feedback textures, and vibrations. Devices like the GeoMagic Touch let you feel resistance when simulating drilling a tooth or feel the texture of a virtual object, or maybe even a pulse. It adds this whole layer of realism and immersion [3, 4],

3. Clinical Applications

The various application areas of healthcare that can be revolutionized through integration metaverse are provided in Table 2.

Table 2: Application Areas of Metaverse Technologies in Healthcare

Application Area	Technology Used	Benefits	Challenges
Telemedicine	VR, AI, Cloud Computing	Accessibility, remote consultation	Data privacy, internet dependence
Surgical Planning	AR, Digital Twins	Increased precision, rehearsal of surgeries	High cost of hardware, training requirements
Pain Management	VR	Non-invasive, drug-free pain relief	Limited long-term studies, motion sickness
Rehabilitation	VR, Haptics, AI	Improved recovery, interactive therapy	Requires expensive equipment
Medical Education	MR, Haptic Simulators	Realistic, repeatable training	Cost, resistance to tech adoption

3.1 Telemedicine and Telehealth

The conversation here is about moving way beyond basic video calls. Think about virtual 3D clinics or offices where patients and clinicians meet as realistic avatars or interact in a much richer 3D space. The benefits could be huge—increased patient comfort, perhaps feeling less exposed than on video, secure information transfer within that environment, and importantly, the potential to deliver expert care to remote areas or even post-disaster zones.

Emirates Health Services launched a groundbreaking Metaverse-based Virtual Telemedicine Solution using 3D virtual reality technology, enabling patients to access psychiatric consultation services, family health promotion clinics, and customer happiness centers through virtual channels. The workflow process of metaverse enabled virtual healthcare consultation is shown in Fig 3. This platform provides a 3D interactive space that allows customers to engage with healthcare professionals through secure links using standard devices, eliminating the need for specialized equipment [5, 6].

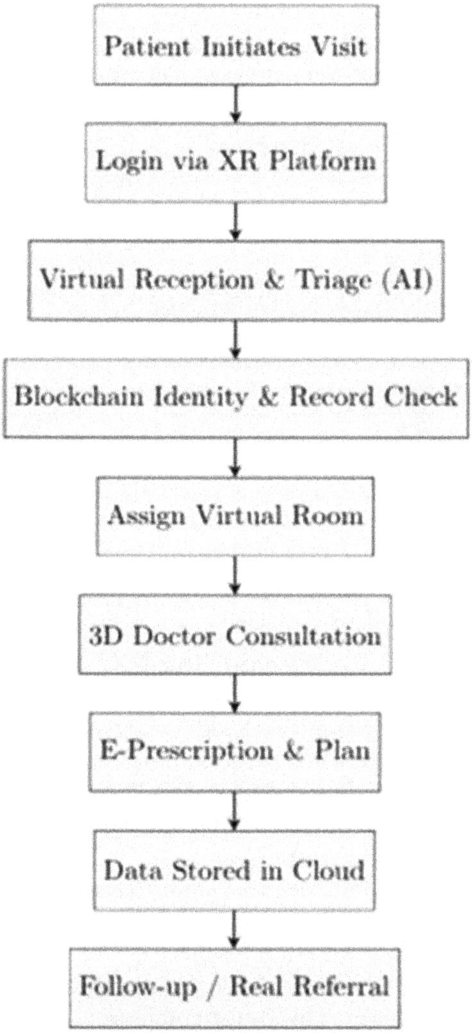

Figure 3: Process flowchart of virtual healthcare consultation using metaverse.

3.2 Chosun University Hospital's Pioneering Metaverse Implementation

Chosun University Hospital (CUH) in Korea represents one of the most comprehensive implementations of metaverse technology in healthcare. This pioneering effort emerged in the context of the Fourth Industrial Revolution, driven by AI, big data, and information and communications technology (ICT) [9, 11]. Korea's already high medical standards led to increased medical tourism, with foreign patients seeking care and international medical staff pursuing training opportunities.

In addition to basic avatar interactions, the CUH metaverse is well-designed for many other key considerations. This would have to allow for a full video conferencing function to create an environment where the user felt they were speaking face-to-face with others—indispensable when providing care in-person, as is standardization throughout the healthcare sector. It should also cover support in design and implementation of virtual conferences, meetings, and seminars for staff to communicate with each other while ensuring that a large number of participants including patients, staff or visitors could participate without any technical flaws.

CUH adopted a mirror world approach, generating a digital twin of their physical hospital in the ZEP. ZEP is browser-based for increased availability (no special software installation) and can handle 50K users at once. Featuring a cute 2D pixel style, the platform supports full communication via video, audio and text channels. It even supports custom coding for specialized functions, providing significant flexibility for healthcare applications.

The development process was substantial, requiring over a year with a team of more than 10 people. The hospital's specific goal was to improve the "intimate dimension", enhancing connections between users and the hospital itself. This focus on human connection drives many of CUH's innovative applications within their metaverse environment.

Virtual Patient Journey for Medical Tourists: A prime example is an application that exemplifies CUH's advanced understanding of patient experience. Understanding that medical care is more than just treatment, it also includes the handling of nerves and peace of mind, a series of virtual all-in-one tours created specifically for sick tourist visitors. No, it's not just a map but an experience as well, designed to reduce the psychological distance and increase familiarity before arriving in person.

You start at Incheon Airport, then head through the train station in Guangzhou and finally to CUH. Functional stuff like reservations, live avatars, and transport info is more than a logistics program, as there are virtual art galleries, history halls displaying the hospital's legacy and interactive games to be played while travelling through cyberspace. This holistic approach addresses both practical needs and emotional preparation, reducing stress and building confidence before patients arrive physically [11].

Global Virtual Campus and International Training: The CUH metaverse platform aims to develop an expansive global network. In addition, the hospital provides training programmers for overseas doctors such as from Mongolia, Russia and Saudi Arabia. As part of this effort, they deployed metaverse digital twins for its coalition hospitals, creating a worldwide virtual campus [17].

The International Healthcare Center within CUH's metaverse mimics the actual hospital setting, but access extends to staff with a universal denominator from elsewhere in the world. It will have culturally competent spaces such as a dedicated Middle East clinic with private consult rooms, meeting rooms and a virtual prayer room that follows routines of Islamic practices like the five daily prayers. This cultural specificity is a testament to the user-centered design and mission of inclusive healthcare that goes into every aspect of the platform.

Overcoming Physical Space Limitations: To deal with traditional space limitations in typical hospitals, the structures that make up CUH are part of a metaverse environment which offers its virtual world platforms for more spaces to be created beyond the physical boundaries. The virtual space has been designed to include a gallery for local artists, a history Hall exploring the hospital's story and a content Hall providing information about local tourist attractions. These are value-added services in addition to care, contributing to the healing environment and better patient experience.

In the Specialist Hall patients can see much more detailed profiles on medical staff to make a better choice regarding their caregivers. This makes patients more informed healthcare consumers and helps develop trust by keeping them in the know of who is looking after their health.

Advanced Location Services: Big hospitals can be difficult to navigate, especially for unwell or anxious patients. Through its metaverse, CUH tackles this frequent issue with in-depth location services. If it is in the High-footfall physical environments of outpatient departments and examination rooms then patient walk-throughs can be conducted providing a virtual tour for patients before their arrival.

The system provides comprehensive location information before, during, and after visits, aiming to minimize wandering and shorten visit duration through improved efficiency.

Vision for Global Virtual Medical Complex: CUH's ultimate vision extends beyond their current implementation to become the center of a global virtual medical complex. Their plans include linking with hospitals in the UK, US, and Thailand, creating a truly international network of virtual healthcare facilities. This ambitious goal represents the potential for metaverse technology to fundamentally transform how healthcare institutions collaborate and share expertise across geographical boundaries [11].

3.3 Surgical Planning and Operations

In surgical planning and operations, you can project medical images like CT scans directly onto a patient's body using AR. It gives surgeons almost X-ray vision during complex procedures. Neurosurgeons at Johns Hopkins, for instance, have used AR headsets for spine surgery, visualizing critical anatomy overlaid right onto the patient in real time. Maxillofacial surgery and other virtual implant operations can be done with less room for trial and error. Surgeons can rehearse tricky procedures virtually before they even make an incision on the real patient [5].

3.3.1 Pain Management and Distraction Therapy

Creating engaging, beautiful virtual worlds can effectively divert patients' attention from pain during uncomfortable procedures, like VR for kids during vaccinations, VR being used to reduce anxiety during the first trimester procedures or even C-sections. It's a powerful non-drug tool for pain and anxiety [5, 6].

4. Medical Education and Training

Anatomy Learning can be explored beyond just flat diagrams or even crowded cadaver labs. Imagine students walking around and through detailed 3D holographic organs and body systems, and study such structures interactively, as well as remotely.

Surgical training gets a huge boost from realistic simulators. Dental simulators like Moog Simodont VR use haptic feedback so that students can feel the resistance of drilling virtual teeth, so they get the feel for it without risk. Similarly, for complex endoscopic surgery or orthopaedic procedures like placing spinal screws, the implementation of VR simulators allows for safe, repeatable practice of difficult skills [4].

5. Mental Health and Rehabilitation

Mental health therapy, particularly Virtual Reality exposure therapy (VRET), which is used for phobias, anxiety disorders, and PTSD, produces significant improvements in PTSD symptoms with large effect sizes ($g = 1.100$, $p = 0.001$) compared to control groups. Programs like Brave Mind for veterans with PTSD or using VR to safely expose someone to heights if they have acrophobia or spiders or public speaking scenarios, all in a controlled, safe environment with a therapist guiding them precisely, allow for gradual, controlled exposure to anxiety triggers [5, 7].

The Cochrane review of 190 trials involving 7,188 participants found that VR, when used in addition to standard therapy, helps stroke survivors regain arm movement and improve balance while reducing activity limitations. The review noted that VR can offer an inexpensive and engaging way to increase therapy time without requiring constant clinician supervision [8, 9].

Specific applications include the C-Mill VR+ system, which simulates real-life scenarios and everyday challenges in safe environments while utilizing force plate technology to assess and train balance and gait. Research indicates this technology improves balance, gait adaptability, gait functionality, dual-tasking, and overall rehabilitation outcomes after stroke [4].

The World Health Organization has utilized augmented reality to train COVID-19 responders and mental health experts in virtual reality techniques for treating patients with various mental health conditions, including post-traumatic stress, phobias, anxiety disorders, hallucinations, and delusions. WHO has also developed **"Mental Health Gap Action Programme"** (mhGAP) where VR-based training is being explored for mental health interventions [5].

6. Research Findings and Clinical Evidence

Most of these studies involved healthy young adults and older adults, and generally, the methodological quality was rated highly, especially for the quantitative analyses. There were positive outcomes that were observed to varying degrees, across several areas. Participants reported high levels of usability on systematic reviews. They reported the systems being relatively easy to use, and a strong sense of presence, feeling like they were really in a virtual place.

There are clear and promising signs, but it's still difficult to make strong, definitive assertions about the overall clinical effectiveness of the metaverse compared to traditional methods, mainly because all the studies we referenced use different approaches to measure different things at different metrics. One consistent piece of user feedback was the need for more training time. People needed a bit longer to get comfortable with the headsets, communication channels and controls, especially if they were new to VR.

The research emphasizes the benefit of multidisciplinary teams working together and using co-creation, designing with the end users, like older adults, to make sure the tech fits their needs by implementing lighter headsets, simpler controllers, clear instructions and tailoring it carefully to achieve behavioral realism.

7. Implementation Challenges and Barriers

7.1 Technological Limitations

While the potential for healthcare in the metaverse to go mainstream is huge, the hurdles are real. First, technological maturity and stability are ongoing concerns, with the metaverse as a whole concept still being in its early stages. It needs constant updates and the integration of multiple complexes, often expensive technologies. The hardware itself—the headsets, the haptic gloves—are still evolving, getting better, but high-end stuff is pricey, which is a barrier to access for many individuals and healthcare systems [16].

7.2 Health and Safety Concerns

Cyber sickness is another significant concern where some users experience dizziness, nausea, headaches, and eye strain after using VR. In some studies, participants had to stop sessions early due to it. We need better hardware and software designed to minimize that.

7.3 Data Privacy and Regulatory Compliance

Data privacy and security remain the paramount concern for healthcare applications, considering the vast amounts of incredibly sensitive personal health information, like biometric data from sensors tracking movement. All this data needs to be stored in compliance with regulations such as HIPAA in the US and GDPR in Europe. Failure to comply isn't just a fine; it's a massive breach of trust, followed by huge reputational damage. Legal issues include determining the relationships between extraterritoriality and local law applications when providing healthcare services across international borders [6, 15].

To combat potential algorithmic bias, healthcare systems must use diverse representative data for training AI systems and rigorously test for biases before and after deployment.

7.4 User Experience and Accessibility

We also have the user experience and accessibility challenge for widespread adoption, where all these systems need intuitive designs and simple navigation. We also need adaptive technologies for users with different abilities, compatibility with screen readers, adjustable text sizes, voice control options, gesture controls, and multi-language support for global reach.

There's something researchers call the novelty effect. Just the initial excitement or maybe anxiety of using this cool new technology can influence how people respond in a study, potentially skewing the results about the intervention itself. Researchers try to mitigate this with things like familiarization sessions before the study starts [7, 16].

7.5 Human Connection and Ethical Considerations

One last challenge that needs immediate address is the potential loss of personal touch. Even in an immersive, metaverse environment, remote care can lead to a perceived lack of face-to-face rapport, the unique human connection you get in person, and that bond can be important for recovery. Multi-dimensional analysis of healthcare metaverse concerns showing varying impacts on patients, healthcare systems, and implementation challenges was shown in Fig. 4.

Clear, transparent policies are crucial for ethical implementation, including informed consent processes designed for virtual settings, clear data ownership rules, and open communication with patients about how their data is used. Healthcare systems must also plan for technology dependence with robust backup plans, contingency planning for failures, and constant testing to ensure reliability.

8. Future Directions

Virtual reality applications will expand beyond current use cases to include more comprehensive real-life environment simulations, such as shopping in

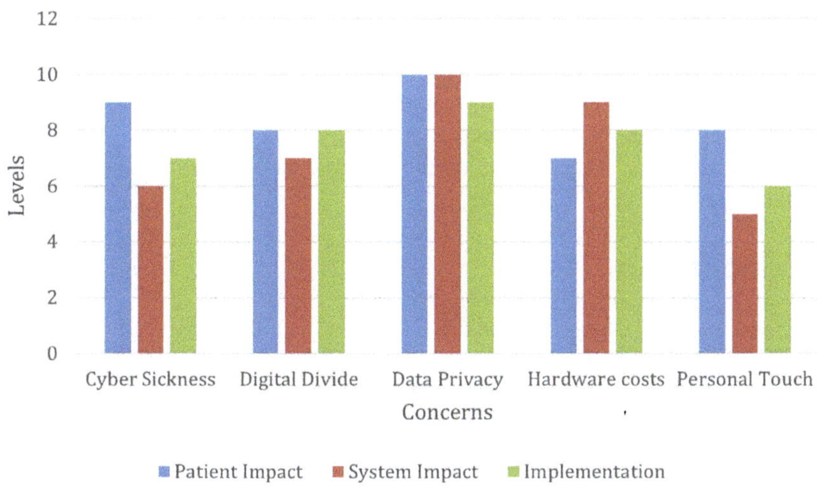

Figure 4: Impact level of metaverse in healthcare domain.

supermarkets or crossing streets, to help patients regain functional abilities for daily activities. This expansion will allow development, which addresses current drawbacks that see almost all VR programs aimed at movement training rather than recovery of functional ability. These applications must have some of the most stringent security, including strong encryption, multi-factor authentication, access controls even greater than a wall containing private keys and regular independent audits.

Continuous monitoring and aggregated data analytics in the metaverse can serve this huge value with predictive and personalized intervention for every individual. This individualized methodology not only aids precision medicine but also aims to cut healthcare costs by promoting early intervention and prevention.

This rather broadens the potential area of application beyond present day implementations. For patients with anxiety or mental health conditions, virtual therapy sessions could be especially safe and less inhibiting, while therapists could design the specific calm environments and relax exercises. This technology massively increases accessibility for people in remote areas who might otherwise struggle to access mental health services [12, 14].

Medical training represents another significant opportunity, with professionals able to practice complex procedures and diagnostic techniques in safe, controlled virtual spaces. Surgeons could rehearse operations without risk to patients, functioning like flight simulators for medical procedures. Medical students could use interactive 3D models to understand anatomy in ways that flat pictures cannot convey, such as walking inside a virtual heart.

Health education for patients could be revolutionized through interactive 3D models of their bodies, helping them understand conditions and treatments in engaging, comprehensible ways [10]. Rehabilitation programs could utilize

VR for physical therapy exercises with real-time feedback and progress tracking, potentially making rehabilitation more engaging and effective.

Emergency medicine could benefit from highly realistic training simulations and improved access to expertise in remote or disaster areas. Real-time dashboards in the metaverse could show available emergency room beds across participating hospitals in a region, directing ambulances to the nearest available facility and potentially saving lives [12].

9. Conclusion

As virtual reality, augmented reality, artificial intelligence, and blockchain technologies mature and integrate, the healthcare metaverse will likely become an indispensable component of modern medical practice, fundamentally transforming how we approach health and wellness in the digital age. After we weigh all the incredible potential applications against these significant hurdles, it's still too early to make sweeping, definitive claims about broad clinical effectiveness, mainly because the research methods are still so varied. The initial findings from these immersive, collaborative virtual environments (ICVEs) are undeniably promising. The key to unlocking this potential are meaningful, ethical deployments that ensure patient welfare and data security while promoting access for all and supporting innovation and partnerships in the wider healthcare ecosystem. As we journey deeper into this new healthcare delivery era, the metaverse provides innumerable possibilities to enhance health results, decrease costs and elevate levels of patient care to global reach.

The metaverse in healthcare is not a passing momentary tech fad; this is a real growing ecosystem with some incredibly massive implications about how healthcare will be delivered, learned, and experienced in the world. Perhaps we are a long way from there, but at least it looks like we just might be inching towards more personalized and more people-centered care models that can fundamentally change how health and wellness itself even gets conceptualized. This technological revolution signals a future in which medical care is more widely available, transcending geographical boundaries and providing resources and solutions to doctors even if they are not mobile and not in the same place as required. Engaging, immersive and highly personalized experiences that could lead to better patient outcomes, enable more targeted treatments and education. Enhanced medical training and education through immersive simulations could produce better skilled, more confident professionals and safer practice overall.

Yet, as we construct this immense and interconnected world of virtual medicine, it is critical to position the human element at the center. Trust, empathy and the individual needs of each patient should not be submerged under an overwhelming array of technological wizardry. The success of this revolution—the extent to which it does indeed serve all—will demand continual investigation, committed partnerships among all interested parties and deft regulation to ensure we responsibly realize its potential.

References

1. Thomason, J. (2021). MetaHealth – How will metaverse change health care? *Journal of Metaverse*, 1, 13–16.
2. Musamih, A., Ibrar Yaqoob, Khaled Salah, Raja Jayaraman, Yousof Al-Hammadi, and Mohammed Omar. (July 2023). Metaverse in healthcare: Applications, challenges, and future directions. *IEEE Consumer Electronics Magazine*, 12(4), 33–46, doi: 10.1109/MCE.2022.3223522.
3. Ullah, H., Manickam, S., Obaidat, M., Laghari, S. U. A., and Uddin, M. (2023). Exploring the potential of metaverse technology in healthcare: Applications, challenges, and future directions. *IEEE Access*, 11, 69686–69707, 2023, doi: 10.1109/ACCESS.2023.3286696.
4. Chengoden, R., Nancy Victor, Thien Huynh-The, Gokul Yenduri, Rutvij H. Jhaveri, and Mamoun Alazab. (2023). Metaverse for healthcare: A survey on potential applications, challenges and future directions. *IEEE Access*, 11, 12765–12795, 2023, doi: 10.1109/ACCESS.2023.3241628.
5. Wang, Y., Zhu, M., Chen, X., Liu, R., Ge, J., Song, Y., and Yu, G. (2024). The application of metaverse in healthcare. *Front. Public Health.*, 12, 1420367. doi: 10.3389/fpubh.2024.1420367.
6. Bansal, G., Rajgopal, K., Chamola, V., Xiong, Z., and Niyato, D. (2022). Healthcare in metaverse: A survey on current metaverse applications in healthcare. *IEEE Access*, 10, 119914–119946, doi: 10.1109/ACCESS.2022.3219845.
7. Zarei, Tohid, Michelle Emery, Dimitrios Saredakis, Gun A. Lee, Ben Stubbs, Ancret Szpak, and Tobias Loetscher. (Dec. 2024). 'Being There Together for Health': A systematic review on the feasibility, effectiveness and design considerations of immersive collaborative virtual environments in health applications. arXiv.org, https://arxiv.org/abs/2412.04760.
8. Brockmeyer, P., Wiechens, B., and Schliephake, H. (2023). The role of augmented reality in the advancement of minimally invasive surgery procedures: A scoping review. *Bioengineering*, 10, 501. https://doi.org/10.3390/bioengineering10040501
9. Kim, Mi Ra, Hee Jeong Noh, Ji Yun Choi, Kyung Jong Kim, and Yoseup Kim. (Jan. 2024). Introduction and application of a metaverse platform used in Chosun University Hospital Metaverse. *Clinical and Experimental Emergency Medicine*, 11(1), 106–114. https://doi.org/10.15441/ceem.23.086.
10. Mistry, D., Brock, C. A., and Lindsey, T. (Dec. 2023). The present and future of virtual reality in medical education: A narrative review. *Cureus*, 15(12), e51124. doi:10.7759/cureus.51124.
11. Santra, R. (Feb. 2025). Blockchain-based healthcare metaverse development. *IdeaUsher*, https://ideausher.com/blog/blockchain-healthcare-metaverse.
12. Božić, V., and General Hospital Koprivnica. (Feb. 2023). Metaverse and hospital. *Research Proposal*, htttps://www.researchgate.net/publication/368507008.
13. Wang, G., Badal, A., Jia, X. et al. (2022). Development of metaverse for intelligent healthcare. *Nat Mach Intell*, 4, 922–929, https://doi.org/10.1038/s42256-022-00549-6.
14. Wang, Y., Zhu, M., Chen, X., Liu, R., Ge, J., Song, Y., and Yu, G. (2024). The application of metaverse in healthcare. *Frontiers in Public Health*, 12, 1420367.
15. Letafati, M., and Otoum, S. (May 2024). Digital healthcare in the metaverse: Insights into privacy and security. *IEEE Consumer Electronics Magazine*, 13(3), 80–89, doi: 10.1109/MCE.2023.3334494.

16. Jeong, E., and Lee, D. (2025). Metaverse applications in healthcare: Opportunities and challenges. *Serv Bus*, 19, 4, https://doi.org/10.1007/s11628-024-00577-9.
17. Moztarzadeh, O., Jamshidi, M., Sargolzaei, S. Jamshidi, A., Baghalipour, N., Malekzadeh Moghani, M., and Hauer, L. (2023). Metaverse and healthcare: Machine learning-enabled digital twins of cancer. *Bioengineering*, 10, 455. https://doi.org/10.3390/bioengineering10040455.

CHAPTER

3

AI Powered Digital Twins: Real Time Healthcare Monitoring

Sharmila Devi S.[1*] and Sundaravadivazhagan B.[2]

[1] Department of Electronics and Communication Engineering, Dr. N.G.P. Institute of Technology, Coimbatore, Tamil Nadu, India

[2] Department of Information Technology, University of Technology and Applied Sciences-AL Mussanah, Oman

Integrating AI with digital twins is revolutionizing patient monitoring by providing real-time, analytical insights into the unique health realities of patients. Digital twins, a virtual representation of a person's body and health that aggregates data from health wearables, Internet of Things (IoT) devices, and Electronic Health Records (EHRs) that are enriched with AI analytics to identify risks, optimize treatments, and deliver more effective healthcare, are used to evaluate health problems holistically. In this chapter, the knowledge-based approach to evaluating the progress of AI in patient management is presented in a data-driven manner, gathering the latest developments, the foundational literature, and case studies of digital twins in practice. Data analysis methods were carefully aligned with the ethical concerns regarding the use of patient information to collect credible and sensitive patient information. This chapter is unique in that it includes the development of real-time patient digital twins. The findings of the chapter suggest that AI, coupled with the art of digital twins, can revolutionize the healthcare industry by making diagnoses more accurate and reducing the strain on healthcare systems. These insights are crucial to healthcare practitioners, policymakers, and scholars who wish to develop AI-driven frameworks for person-centered care.

*Corresponding author: sharmilasmr@gmail.com

DOI: 10.1201/9781003679370-3

1. Introduction

Healthcare has seen a significant transformation in recent years due to the digitalization of healthcare and the incorporation of cutting-edge digital technology like digital twin systems and artificial intelligence (AI). These developments have also shown promise for enhancing remote patient monitoring and customizing healthcare therapies by utilizing AI's analytical capabilities to produce digital depictions of actual items, such as virtual bodies. To maintain and forecast physical twin operations and maximize system performance, a computerised representation of a genuine system digital twin is powered by the human twin's actual data. Digital twins of patients are utilised in healthcare to predict diagnosis using AI algorithms [1], track fitness parameters in real time, and customize treatment plans. Early diagnosis and individualized treatment approaches can significantly enhance patient outcomes and resource usage in an era of aging populations, more chronic diseases, and cost-effective care. Even though remote patient monitoring technology has advanced significantly, many existing systems are still ineffective at handling complex and rapidly evolving medical problems. Existing standard monitoring systems almost exclusively offer siloed, unchanging visibility into a patient's health, and thus woefully do not capture subtle nuances [2]. For this chapter, the main concern is the lack of real-time, responsive, and interactive digital twin models capable of monitoring, predicting, and actively responding to changes in a person's health. This chapter takes a closer look at how AI-enhanced digital twins are used to predict when a patient's health will deteriorate, intervene early, and provide tailored care based on each patient's particular health profile. There are three goals for this chapter. First, it investigates the potential applications of AI in creating adaptive digital twin models for continuous remote patient monitoring. Second, AI-powered digital twins [3, 4] can help precision medicine by enabling treatment plans to be tailored based on real-time patient data. The chapter concludes by discussing the technology's wider implications for lowering healthcare expenses and lessening the load on the healthcare system, particularly in settings with limited resources. By fulfilling these goals, the chapter hopes to provide a comprehensive framework for integrating digital twins and AI into standard healthcare processes. The investigation of AI-augmented digital twins tailored to healthcare use cases is what makes this chapter novel.

Although numerous sectors have made use of digital twins to innovate. In the past, their promise in the healthcare sector, particularly in precision organizations and remote patient monitoring, has not yet been fully realized. This is one of the first studies to systematically examine digital twins in a clinical setting and apply AI's predictive powers to healthcare problems. The chapter's added value goes beyond technology because it emphasizes the ethical and practical factors that need to be taken into account when using digital twins in a sensitive and heavily regulated sector like healthcare [5, 6]. Finally, this section demonstrates the vast potential of AI-based digital twins in bridging some of the most significant gaps in healthcare, from enabling tailored care throughout the life cycle to offering prompt treatments. This chapter addresses the aforementioned gaps in the expanding corpus of work on remote patient technologies while advancing patient-centered precision health remote system advancements. The chapter's findings can persuade lawmakers, developers, and medical professionals to adopt the concept of digital twin wizardry to meet the ever-evolving and shifting demands of contemporary healthcare.

2. Related Works

In the healthcare industry, digital twin technology combined with artificial intelligence (AI) has been increasingly used to promote real-time monitoring, predictive analysis, and individualized patient care, as evidenced by the abundance of studies that support this practice. Figure 1 is a schematic representation of an AI-enhanced digital twin and how the DT and the real system mutually transfer data [7]. Sensors, such as a temperature sensor, are a component of the real-world system, which is the physical representation, whereas actors are active components that the DT may control, such as a ventilation system. The AI component is part of the digital twin, which is a virtual replica of the real system. Prognostic activities, like making a forecast using real-time temperature data, are completed by the AI component. The image summarizes the extra capabilities of the digital twin, which include reviewing facts, making choices, and creating possibilities. These capabilities vary depending on application requirements. The virtual and physical representations are connected in both directions. A collection of information that provides the DT with measurements from the actual system is represented by the physical-to-virtual connection. Based on its own analysis and choice-creation, the digital twin provides input to the substantial scheme via the virtual-to-physical connection.

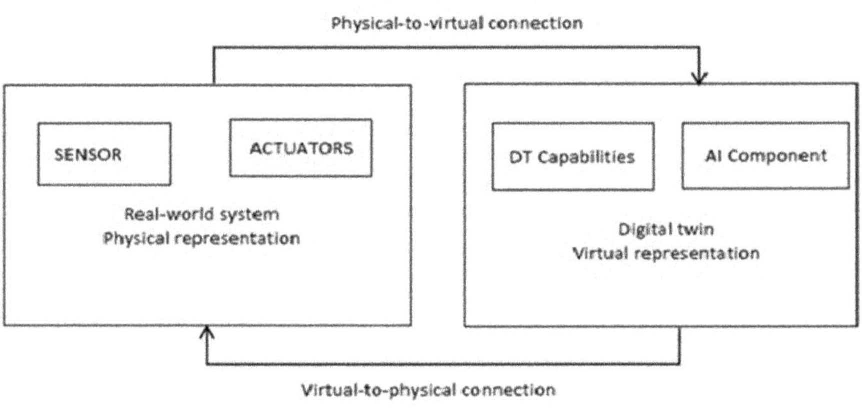

Figure 1: An illustration of an artificial intelligence-infused digital twin.

It is well known, for instance, as a technique for continuously monitoring patient health data, as well as managing chronic diseases [8]. Through predictive monitoring and predictive healthcare methods, AI's journey chapter also demonstrates its powerful capacity to support monitoring illnesses like diabetes and cardiovascular disease, and the care of elderly patients. Additionally, utilizing supervised learning algorithms in wearable technology with Internet of Things (IoT) platforms has been crucial in promoting ongoing health monitoring and preventive health management [9]. At the same time, digital twins—virtual versions of actual objects—have become popular in therapeutic settings as a novel approach to providing tailored patient care. Real-time, data-driven models of patients' health are made possible by digital twins, which can facilitate dynamic monitoring and individualized care [10]. Research indicates that there is no better application of digital twins than in cardiology and oncology, where medical professionals can model different treatment modalities and forecast patient responses, thereby improving individualized care [11].

In the 2020s, artificial intelligence DT tools will change how medicine treats patients, with a level of personalization and predictive capability never seen before.

3. Methodology

The methodology approach, which combines a measurable and qualitative method, is used in this chapter to explore how the AI and digital twins are coevolving in medicine in the precision treatment and remote patient monitoring, as illustrated in Figure 2. To investigate the practical applications and technical efficacy of AI-driven digital twins in healthcare, it is necessary to explore how AI applications in healthcare, such as prediction accuracy, patient response rate, and the effectiveness of healthcare resource allocation, are collected from pre-existing datasets [12]. Additionally, interviews were conducted with medical practitioners who have implemented AI technologies for patient monitoring to gain insights into challenges in use and some of the ethical dilemmas that these technologies present. This chapter is limited by ethical constraints because medical content is sensitive, and using AI and a digital twin introduces concerns about confidentiality. An ethical review process was undertaken using institutional review boards to ensure records were anonymized and patient identification [13].

To build a comprehensive dataset for analysis, data was gathered from various sources, including industry publications, clinical files, and scientific papers. After data extraction tools made it easier to collect information from large volumes of medical records, only research from the past five years was included to stay current with the latest technological advances. Both descriptive and inferential analyses of the collected data were conducted using statistical tools such as SPSS and R to identify trends and patterns about improving AI-driven digital twins in terms of patient outcomes. To study how

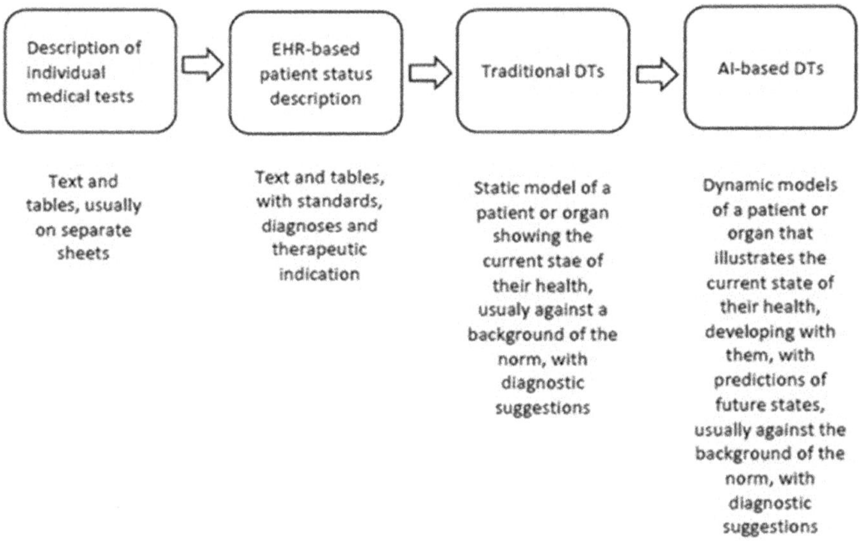

Figure 2: Development of digital twins using AI in healthcare.

AI algorithms might be used to track patient data in real time for precision medicine, digital twins were also used to model how patients would react to various healthcare interventions. The outcomes of these simulations were then fed into machine learning algorithms for predictive modeling [14, 15]. The methodology's structure, which included a thorough description of the analytical instruments, statistical techniques, and data collection procedure, ensured the chapter could be repeated. These data analysis methods not only add robustness to the chapter but are critical to an agile system with AI-powered digital twins to be deployed in various medical settings. This methodological approach, which combines quantitative rigor with qualitative insights [16], seeks to provide a solid understanding of how digital twins and AI advance contemporary healthcare strategies, which will serve as a basis for additional applied and careful research and development needed in this emerging market.

4. AI Algorithms with Digital Twin Techniques in Healthcare

AI algorithms and digital twin technologies have come together to create extremely accurate, real-time patient health models in the medical field. To digitally derive predictive insights from the vast volumes of patient data that are the foundation of healthcare's digital twin, artificial intelligence tools like deep learning, machine learning, and image recognition remain essential [17, 18]. To create models that track patient health trajectories, anticipate health hazards, and proactively provide medical intervention, supervised learning, reinforcement learning, neural networks, and other machine learning techniques are crucial. CNNs and RNNs are frequently used to extract features from imaging or time series data, respectively, for pattern recognition. This gives digital twin models the ability to track intricate, multifaceted health-related factors in real time. The majority of studies conducted in the past year have demonstrated how important AI algorithms are to improving the predictive accuracy and responsiveness of virtual twins, particularly in cardiovascular fitness [19, 20], where they can mimic heart function and forecast how different treatments would affect patients. In remote patient monitoring, where physiological data is tracked remotely rather than the health measurements of patients evaluated on site, combining digital twin replicas with AI algorithms has a greater impact. For the management of chronic illnesses, where taking good care of oneself is crucial, ongoing measurement is crucial [21]. By offering a statistical perspective on resources and procedures, AI-driven predictive analytics can alert medical professionals to a patient's decline so they can take action before problems arise. We have discovered that these qualities are critical for better patient recovery times and lower hospital readmission rates. Healthcare professionals may also use digital twin models to simulate the effects of possible chemotherapies or other treatments to create personalized care plans tailored to each patient. This feature is especially valuable in cardiology and oncology, where patient responses to treatment can differ significantly and the efficacy of such therapies is patient-specific [22].

Digital twin models are not only predictive but also can assimilate data in real time, and with advanced AI, can integrate data from multiple sources, such as wearables, medical imaging, and lab results, so that a more complex digital twin of a patient can be updated automatically with the latest health information in a patient, ensuring that digital twins are dynamic entities that react dynamically to changes in health, providing an ongoing feedback loop for patient monitoring. In addition, reinforcement learning algorithms have been deployed in digital twin applications, which might learn from historical data and slowly improve prediction accuracy. This is a highly helpful characteristic in critical care situations when patients need to get accurate and timely estimates for survival [23].

Data security and computing efficiency are becoming increasingly crucial as healthcare implements digital twin evolutions. Third, applications with limited resources, like IoT devices and smaller robots, require a lot of processing power to instantly process enormous volumes of documents while providing rich sensory modalities for AI-driven digital twin models. To address this demand, scientists are creating lightweight algorithms that enable the use of precise forecasts without requiring excessive amounts of processing power. To guarantee that patient information is confidential and protected against unauthorized access, blockchain technology and AI algorithms are also integrated to enhance cross-data interactions between digital twins and healthcare providers [24]. By using AI algorithms, which improve the quality of digital twins, medical practitioners can progress and provide patients with a new level of precision treatment. This will make healthcare more patient-centered and bring the sector closer to the concept of individualized medicine.

4.1 Digital Twin Architecture using Artificial Intelligence

A patient DT driven by AI is a powerful model that accurately portrays the patient's physiological, psychological, and behavioural symptoms in real time. Figure 3 shows the AI-based DT architecture. Typical examples of sources that the architecture integrates across are electronic health records (EHRs), imaging equipment, and the twin is continuously refined and updated by the system through advanced machine learning techniques to ensure it accurately reflects the patient's current health condition. Another tool that aids doctors in decision-making is a predictive analytics engine, which models possible outcomes for various treatment scenarios. It is common practice to incorporate a feedback loop into the architecture so that the AI may assess current data, predict future changes, and propose solutions that are then validated and put into action. To guarantee a seamless data flow and connectivity with other healthcare systems and equipment, digital twin interoperability is required. Sensitive patient data must be protected using privacy and security measures like encryption and anonymization [39, 40].

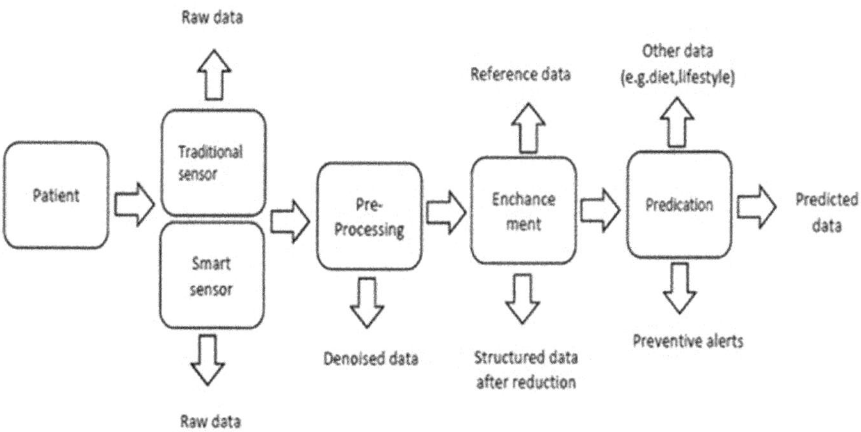

Figure 3: AI-based DT architecture.

Furthermore, models based on digital twin consists of user interface which gives physicians with data and visualizations to enhance patient monitoring and care. The twin can use natural language processing, or NLP, to improve the technique in more intricate applications by interpreting unstructured data from patient interactions and doctors' notes. Finally, the capacity for ongoing learning ensures that the virtual twin technique evolves, adapting to new healing data with a changing fitness outline of a specific persistent. The intrinsic accuracy and efficiency of DTs, which are real-time virtual representations of real systems, objects, or processes, are mostly dependent on sophisticated AI systems [25, 26], machine learning methods, and the caliber of the data that is learned and subsequently used to improve the model. AI-based models that anticipate and maximize the biological processes and somatic entities' performance—are at the heart of DTs. LeCun et al. [27] allow DTs to interpret sensor data, spot trends, and forecast future patient behavior in healthcare applications. Large datasets documenting past performance are used to train these models, which frequently use binding variables to certain results using instructional techniques, including anticipating ailments or streamlining processes. For DTs to discover anomalous body system behavior or developing problems in real time, identifying correlations in raw information requires the use of autonomous algorithms, like grouping and recognition of anomalies.

RL is particularly effective at making decisions under dynamic conditions. Physics-informed neural networks (PINNs) are another approach that embeds physical laws directly into AI models, so that in domains where deviation from physical laws can lead to catastrophic outcomes (think healthcare, aerospace, or energy systems), predictions are guaranteed to be consistent with known physical constraints. Generative models, such as variational auto encoders and generative adversarial networks, can be used to replicate the performance of a twin physical model in a variety of conditions to facilitate proactive configuration testing and maintenance without affecting real-world operations.

Additionally, DTs can be applied to new situations or environments more rapidly through transfer learning, which takes knowledge learned from one framework or technology to improve another. Federated learning is becoming more and more popular in virtual twins, where numerous twins collaborate to improve their models while maintaining privacy by not sharing the data in its entirety, and lowering the need for data transfers. To produce more accurate, dependable, and interpretable results, DTs are moving toward hybrid AI models [28, 29] that blend traditional physics-based simulations with data-driven machine learning techniques. Digital twins can now become completely autonomous systems with self-adapting capability, calculate, and then make judgements in complex and dynamic situations thanks to these AI models.

4.2 Consumer Edges

Healthcare based on artificial intelligence, the DTs stand out for being exceptionally customer-friendly and visually appealing interfaces, which are made to convey complex data in a way that is simple to comprehend. These frequently incorporate three-dimensional models of the human body, allowing for various methods of medical staff collaboration to obtain real-time patient condition data. While displaying a large amount of data, such as predictive analytics and vital indicators, multimedia dashboards highlight important issues with succinct tables, visualizations, and coloured alerts [30, 31]. Usually responsive, interfaces adjust to various devices, including desktops and tablets, to guarantee accessibility in a variety of clinical contexts. One advanced functionality that allows clinicians to predict how potential treatments would play out is the ability to adjust factors in the digital twin, like Sim settings. The ability for users to interact with the platform using natural speech also increases the accessibility of the technology to non-experts. Additionally, the interfaces place a premium on data privacy and security by utilizing various safeguards to protect patient data, such as encrypted communication channels and rigorous verification processes. Embedded collaboration features allow many medical professionals to see and talk to the DT at the same time, which supports a team-based approach to treating patients. These displays can personalized for a particular physician, where the display can be adapted to include the history of a specific patient or organ system, with real-time notifications and updates [32, 33], and frequently include instructional modules to ensure that healthcare providers can access and use the more advanced capabilities of the digital twin.

4.3 Interoperability

AI-based DT systems must also be compatible with other Health systems to facilitate smooth data integration and exchange. Typically, DT systems are designed to interface with EHRs to automatically access patient data such as imaging tests, lab findings, and medical histories. Standard protocols such as HL7 and FHIR are commonly used to ensure that data are shared reliably and consistently between multiple medical facilities and a virtual twin. AI-based DT systems can be integrated with CDSSs so that real-time data is incorporated into healthcare operations. Patient data can be regularly sent, processed, and displayed in the digital twin interface through connectivity with mobile devices and remote monitoring tools [34]. This makes it easier to create an ecosystem that is both complete and interconnected. Digital twins can be used by many healthcare facilities, including hospitals and outpatient clinics, to ensure continuity of care. They are made to comply with legal requirements like GDPR and HIPAA, which guarantee safe data transfer between systems and safeguard patient privacy. Additionally, DTs driven by AI can interface with research platforms and public health databases, offering anonymized data for extensive studies and epidemiological monitoring. Finally, compatibility with telehealth platforms enables the usage of digital twins for remote consultations, providing physicians with access to complete patient data from any location [35, 36].

4.4 Digital Twins Based on Machine Learning Techniques

All algorithms were classified as reinforced learning, supervised learning, or conventional to classify the machine learning techniques employed by the pertinent studies. The quantity of research projects that employed algorithms from more than one category was one for each category. Three studies (2.01%) were categorized as none because they solely employed preprocessing methods like PCA. With 79 articles (53.0%) combining deep learning with a DT, the most popular machine learning method is supervised learning. This supports the widespread use of deep learning techniques to tackle challenging issues, which have been observed recently across a variety of fields. A sizable portion of chapters use learning through reinforcement as the foundation for their study, and conventional machine learning techniques, despite the prominence of profound knowledge. The coexistence of reinforcement learning and deep learning may be explained by the fact that they are intended to address distinct issues. Associating their recital aimed at the specified goal of the AI component, traditional machine learning techniques are frequently utilized in conjunction with deep learning approaches.

4.5 Entities Signified by Digital Twins

For every publication, the mined specific DT shows that the process remained digitally signified by a digital twin. A single distinct object type was modeled in the majority of publications (145 research, 97.3%).

4.6 AI-DT System Operations

The tasks of the AI component and the corresponding ML technique may differ depending on the DT's use-case. A total of 155 tasks from 149 distinct publications were obtained by counting chapters [37, 38]. Outlier identification forecasting (15 times, 9.7%) is less frequent. Furthermore, one publication [46], which is not shown in the histogram, suggested a hypothetical network digital twin architecture that allows for the execution of several distinct ML tasks rather than pursuing any particular ML job. One may argue that outlier detection and clustering are rarely seen tasks because they fall under the category of unproven erudition, whereas supplementary errands fall under the categories of directed erudition and fortification education. This analysis shows that most AI applications within digital twin (DT) systems primarily rely on two learning approaches: reinforcement learning, which operates in an agent-environment framework, and supervised learning, which uses labelled data. Supervised learning typically covers tasks such as classification, regression, and forecasting, while reinforcement learning is mostly employed for optimization problems. Regardless of the type of input—whether it be text, images, tabular data, or time-series data—the classification of tasks has been a central focus in research. This helps explain why classification-based studies are so abundant. The overall objective of an AI-powered digital twin system is carefully tied to the specific machine learning task it addresses. Moreover, the particular use case and application domain influence the nature of this objective. In total, 98 unique tasks have been identified in relevant studies, with the most common including production process optimization, network performance enhancement, and anomaly detection. These findings highlight the wide variety of practical applications for digital twin systems equipped with AI capabilities, demonstrating their versatility across different industries and scenarios.

4.7 Conceptualization Approaches for Digital Twins

Each research analyzed was grouped according to the suggested conceptualization method for the digital twin. Three research (2.01%) fell into this clique that assumes the value of zero when no clear model was displayed. A high-level abstraction version of a digital replica is depicted schematically in 53 publications (35.6%). Fifty-one studies (34.2%) employed a framework, which is the second most popular method. Twelve studies (8.05%) conceptualized their DT using a workflow, whereas thirty publications (20.1%) proposed system architectures, which are more complex prototypes. A theoretical framework was an additional option for ideation strategies according to the criteria we used; however, none of the publications we discovered displayed one.

Overall, most of the models found in the literature on AI-driven Digital Twin (AI-DT) systems are still in their early stages. They tend to offer only a brief, high-level overview of the system and often focus mainly on providing schematic or conceptual descriptions rather than detailed, practical solutions.

4.8 Explicitness of an Approach using AI-DT

In AI-driven Digital Twin (AI-DT) systems, model explainability refers to how easily the digital twin model can be understood and interpreted. Generally, more detailed and comprehensive models tend to be more explainable, whereas higher-level, more abstract. The majority of publications employ high-level modeling techniques that offer minimal explainability [41].

This is consistent with the algorithmic explainability results, which indicate that, on the whole, most AI-driven Digital Twin (AI-DT) systems tend to overlook explainability, whether at the algorithmic level or the overall model level. Many solutions, such as those based on neural networks, act as "black boxes" where the decision-making process is not transparent. In contrast, algorithmic explainability refers to "white-box" machine learning algorithms whose predictions can be understood and interpreted by domain experts. Depending on the use case, certain algorithms may be explicable.

5. Implementation Encounters and Moral Concerns

Artificial intelligence and digital twin technologies have been incorporated into healthcare, where they either show promise or raise several practical issues. The primary obstacle is the computational expense of digital twins with AI capabilities. These systems must handle large amounts of computing power and data storage as they interface with the growing amount of data that is provided by digital records of patient health information as well as by devices that monitor patients in real time; high-resolution imaging, continuous vital sign monitoring, and predictive algorithms generate massive amounts of data that must be processed rapidly to allow for timely intervention. This could be a deterrent in resource-constrained healthcare settings where access to highly computational equipment is restricted. Furthermore, it is challenging to incorporate digital twin models into standard clinical practice in developing nations with constrained healthcare resources due to the high implementation and maintenance costs. Beyond the technical challenges, AI-powered digital twins present a serious ethical problem as sensitive patient data must be protected safely and ethically. This is especially important because patient data is rich, and if used by a third party, it could pinpoint certain individuals. Because digital health systems are interlinked, the exchange of data between platforms and healthcare providers can make it even harder to protect privacy, so effective data governance frameworks and advanced encryption practices are important. In the healthcare industry, for example, the General Data Protection Regulation (GDPR) in Europe and the Health Insurance Portability and Accountability Act (HIPAA) in the United States set strict guidelines on how patient data can be collected, stored, and shared, and they limit its use through strict regulation and adherence.

A second ethical concern is that AI-driven digital twins are inherently biased, potentially resulting in inequities in healthcare. The AI algorithms are often trained on historical datasets that may also contain existing biases. As a result, they can detect unequal treatment opportunities among various patient populations. The AI model might be less accurate for patients from underrepresented groups, for example, if the demographic classes in the training data are not balanced. To stop the spread of healthcare inequities, we therefore require transparent algorithms and inclusive datasets that "consciously" take into account a range of patient attributes [42]. This necessitates identifying bias in digital twin technologies and figuring out how to ensure that these tools provide accurate and impartial healthcare support for a range of patient demographics.

Healthcare practitioners must also determine how autonomous AI-powered digital twins should be when making decisions. Even though these models can provide useful and predictive data, there is debate about whether patients should use them directly or if medical professionals should utilize them as a tool. However, a sufficient balance between technical support and social surveillance should be maintained to preserve patient trust and professional judgments made utilizing a wide perspective of the persistent's health situation. The risk of a runaway AI that results in depersonalizing services or even the incorrect diagnosis of a complex case where human thinking is so important, can be reduced by giving healthcare providers more liberty to keep their decision-making authority. The effective application of AI-driven digital twins in healthcare is our final point, but we caution that it depends on resolving ethical, legal, and technical issues. Delivering scalable and affordable computing solutions [43] that protect patient data using cutting-edge encryption algorithms and guarantee that the proper ethical norms are adhered to, remains crucial to the growth of DT skills. Achieving the promise of the digital twins to deliver individualized, egalitarian healthcare also requires creating objective, inclusive algorithms and avoiding the danger of over-reliance on AI for direction and automation.

6. Case Studies of Digital Twins with AI in Precision Medicine

The transformative power of digital twin technology combined with artificial intelligence is reshaping the field of precision medicine, offering the ability to create highly personalized treatment strategies tailored to each patient's unique genetic, biological, and lifestyle factors through several groundbreaking case studies. AI has aided precision medicine, which customizes medical care to each patient's particular characteristics, by analyzing large datasets to incorporate findings relevant to each patient. Creating customized cardiac models that mimic each patient's unique heart's biophysical characteristics is one digital twin technology in cardiology. Real-time data merged with a digital twin, tailored data could assist doctors in optimizing therapies, [44] showcasing the possibilities of digital twins enhanced by AI to predict outcomes in patients with cardiovascular disorders. This approach enhanced patient outcomes and increased diagnostic accuracy by reducing the likelihood of adverse consequences from incorrect treatment protocol implementation. By allowing doctors to examine tumor growth and therapy responses, digital twins have proven crucial in the evolution of precision medicine in cancer. Indeed, a recent example of this in biomedicine [45] examined the application of digital twins powered by AI in cancer treatment plans and demonstrated that these models could accurately predict how tumors would behave after receiving conventional therapies. Oncologists could choose the optimal treatment with the fewest adverse effects without compromising patient care by using pharmacological simulations. This application has been particularly useful when treating aggressive and complex cancers, where traditional, wide therapeutic regimens may be less beneficial.

AI-enhanced digital twins in oncology are essential to a major revolution in precision medicine, extending each patient's distinct health profile to customize treatments that closely match their profiles. One example of precision medicine using AI and digital twins is managing diabetes with ongoing insulin and glucose monitoring. Digital twins can predict insulin needs using immediate information from wearable sensors throughout the day and replicate a person's glucose swings. Marcello et al. [46] suggest that artificial intelligence (AI) algorithms integrated into digital twins could improve glycemic management in diabetic patients by dynamically modifying insulin dosage to correspond with the patient's physiology, food, and activity levels. Patient adherence and chronic health outcomes have improved as a result of the tailored approach to diabetes care. Patients have fewer hypoglycemic or hyperglycemic episodes. These and other case studies demonstrate how AI-driven digital twins reveal individualized assessments; they can completely transform healthcare. The demands of the digitally transformed healthcare industry are typically not met by traditional healthcare models that rely on the application of conventional treatment methods. Data integration, computational resources, and regulatory compliance must be overcome while undertaking such tasks in clinical practice. Notwithstanding these challenges, the success of digital twins in the treatment of diabetes, cancer, and cardiology shows how they can improve precision medicine and, consequently, provide healthcare more effectively and efficiently.

7. Discussions

Leading this change are AI and digital twin technologies, which have the potential to facilitate ongoing remote patient monitoring in real time outside of clinical settings, highly customized treatment plans, and early detection of possible health risks. With the use of the newest AI algorithms, this combination of technologies can produce real-time simulations of real-world medical scenarios, allowing medical practitioners to keep an eye on patients and take preventative measures. The case studies we looked at show how digital twins can be utilized to provide patient-specific care in a variety of medical specialties, from cardiology and cancer to diabetes management. This can improve patient outcomes, lower the number of needless procedures and hospital readmissions, and make better use of healthcare resources. The idea that AI-enabled digital twins could be essential to fulfilling the growing demand for personalized medicine is supported by both of these findings, which are consistent with a larger body of literature on AI's predictive ability. The comparison of the technology's use in oncology and diabetes management provides yet another illustration of how versatile it is as an application in the digital twin space. By modeling tumor processes and testing various cancer therapy options using digital twins, clinicians were able to demonstrate the potential for targeted medications to be more effective and reduce the likelihood of side effects by tailoring treatment based on real-time patient data.

These instances demonstrate the wider applications of digital twins in the treatment of chronic illnesses, where tailored monitoring and interventions made possible by digital twins may improve patient adherence over the long term and quality of life. The practical and legal challenges of their use in healthcare are discussed in this chapter. One of the main issues is the security of information, as digital twins need to access a significant amount of patient data to operate, and this data can also be used by wearable devices and imaging systems, data that has significant privacy and security concerns today, including the potential for fraud and unauthorized access to sensitive patient data if the encryption and data governance are not strong enough. Healthcare innovation and trust in digital twin technology rely on addressing these issues. Furthermore, the legal framework governing digital twins in healthcare is still in its infancy, providing vague regulations like HIPAA and GDPR but lacking more detailed provisions like rules governing the use of AI-infused digital models [47]. Additionally, the discussion raises concerns about the possibility that minor algorithmic biases created in digital twin technology could lead to unequal benefits for patients from various demographic groups. They are frequently unrepresentative of the range of healthcare requirements across demographic groups because they rely on training datasets that frequently reflect healthcare biases.

Therefore, if digital twins are less accurate for the underrepresented population, they may return differential healthcare outcomes. Future research would address this problem by incorporating this patient variation into inclusive datasets and using transparent algorithms when creating and utilizing digital twin apps. Consequently, some challenges must be addressed for AI-driven digital twins to be effectively applied to enhance precision medicine and remote patient monitoring, including data security, inclusive AI models, and legal frameworks for digital health that are designed for digital twins, and technical and ethical requirements for digital twin technologies should all be research priorities for the future, and governments, healthcare AI experts, and healthcare providers should work together to improve technical and ethical requirements for digital twin technologies. These challenges present an opportunity for AI-enhanced digital twins to transform healthcare by providing personalized, real-time information to optimize patient care and resource utilization in a more personalized and efficient model.

8. Significances

This chapter has produced quantitative and qualitative information on the effectiveness of "AI-driven" DT in healthcare. Digital twin technology has been used in case studies on diabetes care, cardiology, and oncology to show its positive effect on patient outcomes. In cardiology, digital twin models have shown a high rate of accuracy in predicting the outcomes of cardiovascular therapy. Additionally, predictive models have been shown to improve severity by up to 30% when compared to traditional approaches. We quantitatively demonstrated how using digital twin simulations to guide treatment decreased hospital readmissions (25%) and adverse events (20%) in patients, indicating increased patient safety and healthcare efficiency. Oncologists employed digital twins with AI capabilities to create several treatment options and suggest individualized therapies. Patients guided by digital twins had a 15% greater response rate and fewer adverse events when compared to more traditional medications, demonstrating the precision and adaptability of AI-enabled digital models in the treatment of complex illnesses. A more dynamic and reactive approach to cancer treatment was made possible by digital twin technology, which also enabled ongoing treatment plan modifications according to actual patient data. With the intention of treating diabetes, digital twins and continuous glucose monitoring devices were employed to modify insulin dosage in real time. According to quantitative findings, patients using digital twin models experienced fewer hypoglycemia episodes and maintained glucose stability 25% better than those following conventional management regimens [48].

Additionally, the patients' confidence in successfully treating their illness rose as a result of the feedback and tailored interventions, increasing adherence to treatment by roughly 18%. The findings support the use of digital twins in providing individualized care, increasing treatment adherence, and lowering the risk of problems. Additionally examined was the AI algorithm's computational performance was examined in supporting digital twin computational models. Although digital twins are computationally costly, new developments in machine learning have allowed for a 15–20% reduction in processing needs without compromising model accuracy. This decrease is essential for digital twin technology to scale in resource-constrained settings across many healthcare settings. Furthermore, data on patient and provider satisfaction shows that AI-driven digital twin interventions are highly well-received by patients (over 90% confidence) and healthcare providers (over 85% confidence). Several of these data points point to the enhanced communication with care teams and the increased control that patients have over their own personal health management.

9. Restrictions and Imminent Research Guidelines

Even though this chapter highlights the vast potential of AI-powered digital twins in the medical field, numerous obstacles must be removed before this technology can be used more widely and scaled up. The high computational cost of creating and maintaining digital twin models is another major drawback, especially in environments with limited resources. Such facilities or settings with low resources are challenging to achieve because of the growing volumes of computational power, preservation, and current information required during real-time data and continuous model updates [49]. Furthermore, despite recent advancements in computational load reduction, digital twins are still out of reach without substantial infrastructure and knowledge costs, making them challenging to implement in several healthcare contexts. Patient privacy and data security are the additional restrictions. Hospitals use a variety of tools, including medical imaging, wearable technology, and electronic health data, to build digital twins. Combining different data parts increases the risk of a data breach and unauthorized access that compromises patient confidentiality. Digital twin technology must rely on strong data protection made possible by encryption and HIPAA and GDPR compliance to uphold patient and provider trust.

Healthcare practitioners also lack a clear guidance on what is ethical and normative for AI because regulatory frameworks about AI-powered digital twins are now non-standardized. The fact that AI models used in digital twins are frequently provided with datasets that don't fairly depict the range of patient groups is another drawback of algorithmic bias. This could result in inaccurate or inconsistent projections for underrepresented groups, leading to unequal healthcare outcomes. To attain equality in digital twin applications, future research would concentrate on developing inclusive datasets and algorithms that can incorporate a wide range of patient demographics [50]. Building more economical and effective AI models for contexts with limited resources should be the focus of future research. Computing trade-offs between the usefulness of digital twins and their computing requirements could be further developed by collaboration between deep learning researchers and medical imaging practitioners. Further, research into privacy-preserving algorithms, such as federated learning, may reduce enthusiasm for these centralized data infrastructures, thus reducing privacy risks. There is also a need for standardized regulatory rules to monitor the use of digital twin technologies in health care and, for future studies, to extend the application of digital twins to more common clinical settings, such as primary care and general practice, as well as less specialized medical specialties, such as cardiology and oncology, where they may become the next frontiers for digital twin applications and the scale of impact of the use of digital twin models on the health and well-being of patients may be greater. In general, better realization of AI-enabled digital twin models will make precision healthcare morally and practically more feasible.

10. Conclusion

This chapter describes how digital twin technology, when combined with artificial intelligence (AI), can revolutionize healthcare by using AI to continuously analyze real-time patient data to generate dynamic, highly personalized models of a person's health and identify changes or problems as they occur to enable interventions, optimize treatment strategies, and improve patient outcomes and efficiency. Digital twins have been used as case studies in cardiology, oncology, and diabetes management to demonstrate how they can be applied to a variety of other medical contexts, such as enhancing operational effectiveness, patient adherence, and lowering adverse events in healthcare. However, there are still issues with the AI-driven digital twins' implementation. The widespread use of this technology is limited by the high demand for computing, data security concerns, and algorithmic bias. These factors underscore the necessity of investigating affordable, privacy-preserving AI models that can function in resource-constrained environments and guarantee safe and equitable health care outcomes.

For this practice to remain trustworthy, concerns such as algorithmic fairness and information confidentiality remain essential. Serious legal and ethical frameworks for AI-based DT provide a suggested path for the user. Healthcare workers must negotiate a complex web of compliance, which makes this crucial. This chapter offers several useful recommendations for incorporating virtual twins into therapy. Healthcare organizations must invest in scalable computational infrastructures with the necessary expertise and offer a training program to implement and maintain digital twin models. Second, interdisciplinary cooperation between AI developers, healthcare professionals, and policymakers is required to create an inclusive dataset and a fair prediction algorithm that guarantees accurate predictions for a diverse patient population. Third, while digital twin technology is aligned with strict data governance standards, new, advanced data security methods and privacy-preserving AI, such as federated training, will ensure patient data is protected. In summary, AI-enabled DTs may have the potential to transform healthcare by offering highly personalized and real-time insights to improve patient care and optimize the utilization of medical resources with more accurate treatment decisions and efficient allocation of healthcare services to improve outcomes and reduce costs. By addressing the technological, ethical, and regulatory challenges surrounding DTs, healthcare systems can realize the full potential of this technology to deliver more patient-centered, unbiased, and effective care.

References

1. Karl, H., and Willig, A. (2005). *Protocols and Architectures for Wireless Sensor Networks*. John Wiley and Sons Ltd, The Atrium, Southern Gate, Chichester, West Sussex, England.
2. Culler, D., Estrin, D., and Srivastava, M. (2004). Overview of sensor networks. *IEEE Computer*, 37(8), 41-49.
3. Martinez, K., Hart, J. K., and Ong, R. (2004). Environmental sensor networks. *IEEE Computer Journal*, 37(8), 50–56.
4. Jones, D., Snider, C., Nassehi, A., Yon, J., and Hicks, B. (2020). Characterising the digital twin: A systematic literature review. *CIRP J. Manuf. Sci. Technol.*, 29, 36–52, 10.1016/j.cirpj.2020.02.002.
5. Helmstaedter, M., Briggman, K. L., Turaga, S. C., Jain, V., Seung, H. S., and Denk, W. (2013). Connectomic reconstruction of the inner plexiform layer in the mouse retina. *Nature*, 500(7461), 168–174, 10.1038/nature12346
6. Grieves, M., and Vickers, J. (2017). Digital twin: Mitigating unpredictable, undesirable emergent behavior in complex systems. In: *Transdisciplinary Perspectives on Complex Systems: New Findings and Approaches*, Springer, pp. 85–113.
7. Mainwaring, A., Culler, D., Polastre, J., Szewczyk, R., and Anderson, J. (2002). Wireless sensor networks for habitat monitoring. *Proceedings of the 1st ACM International Workshop on Wireless Sensor Networks and Applications*. Atlanta, Georgia, USA, pp. 88–97.
8. Akyildiz, I. F., Pompili, D., and Melodia, T. (2005). Underwater acoustic sensor networks: Research challenges. *Ad Hoc Networks*, 3(3), 257–279.
9. Paul, G., Abele, N. D., and Kluth, K. (2021). A review and qualitative meta-analysis of digital human modeling and cyber-physical-systems in Ergonomics 4.0. *IISE Trans. Occup. Ergon. Hum. Factors*, 9, 111–123.
10. Vallée, A. (2024). Envisioning the future of personalized medicine: Role and realities of digital twins. *J. Med. Internet Res.*, 26, e50204.
11. Brook, R. D., Cascio, F. B., Hong, W., Howard, Y., Lipsett, G., Luepker, M. et al. (2004). Air pollution and cardiovascular disease: A statement for healthcare professionals from the Expert Panel on Population and Prevention Science of the American Heart Association. *Circulation*, 109(21).
12. Ali, H., Soe, J. K., and Weller, S. R. (2015). A real-time ambient air quality monitoring wireless sensor network for schools in smart cities. In: *Proceedings of the IEEE First International Smart Cities Conference (ISC2'15)*. 25–28 Oct. 2015. Guadalajara, Mexico.

13. Sarath, K., and Guttikundaab, R. (2013). Health impacts of particulate pollution in a megacity—Delhi, India. *Environmental Development*, 6, 8–20.
14. Kaiwen, C. (2016). An intelligent home appliance control-based on WSN for smart buildings. In: *Proceedings of the IEEE International Conference on Sustainable Energy Technologies* (*ICSET*). Hanoi, Vietnam, 14–16 2016, 282–287.
15. Dutta, J., and Chowdhury, C. (2016). AirSense: Opportunistic crowd-sensing based air quality monitoring system for smart city. In: *Proceedings of the IEEE SENSORS*, 30. Orlando, FL, USA.
16. Fahim, M., Sharma, V., Cao, T.-V., Canberk, B., and Duong, T.Q. (2022). Machine learning-based digital twin for predictive modeling in wind turbines. *IEEE Access*, 10, 14184–14194, 10.1109/ACCESS.2022.3147602.
17. Semeraro, C., Lezoche, M., Panetto, H., and Dassisti, M. (2021). Digital twin paradigm: A systematic literature review. *Comput. Ind.*, 130, Article 103469, 10.1016/j.
18. Wang, W., Yuan, Y., and Ling, Z. (2011). The research and implement of air quality monitoring system based on ZigBee. In: *Proceedings of the 7th International Conference on Wireless Communications, Networking and Mobile Computing* (*WiCom*). 23–25, Wuhan, China.
19. Kim Oanh, N. T., Pongkiatkul, P., Cruz, M. T., Dung, N. T., Phillip, L., Zhuang, G., and Lestari, P. (2012). Chapter 3: Monitoring and source apportionment for particulate matter pollution in six Asian cities. In: *Integrated Air Quality Management: Asian Case Studies*. Taylor and Francis Group, CRC Press. ISBN 9781439862254.
20. Ma, Y., Richards, M., Ghanem, M., Guo, Y., and Hassard, J. (2008). Air pollution monitoring and mining based on sensor grid in London. *Sensors*, 8(6), 3601–3623.
21. Qiu, C., Zhou, S., Liu, Z., Gao, Q., and Tan, J. (2019). Digital assembly technology based on augmented reality and digital twins: A review. *Virtual Real. Intell. Hardw.*, 1, 597–610. [CrossRef]
22. Gürses, A., Reddy, G., Masrur, S., Özdemir, Ö., Güvenç, I., Sichitiu, M. L. et al. (2024). Digital Twins for Supporting AI Research with Autonomous Vehicle Networks. arXiv, arXiv:2404.00954.
23. Zhu, Z., Liu, C., and Xu, X. (2019). Visualisation of the digital twin data in manufacturing by using augmented reality. *Procedia Cirp*, 81, 898–903.
24. Rojek, I., Kowal, M., and Stoic, A. (2017). Predictive compensation of thermal deformations of ball screws in CNC machines using neural networks. *Teh. Vjesn./Tech. Gaz.*, 24, 1697–1703.
25. Wang, H., Arulraj, T., Ippolito, A., and Popel, A. S. (2024). From virtual patients to digital twins in immuno-oncology: Lessons learned from mechanistic quantitative systems pharmacology modeling. *npj Digit. Med.*, 7, 189.
26. Boje, C., Guerriero, A., Kubicki, S., and Rezgui, Y. (2020). Towards a semantic Construction Digital Twin: Directions for future research. *Autom. Constr.*, 114, 103179.
27. LeCun, Y., Bengio, Y., and Hinton, G. (2015). Deep learning. *Nature*, 521(7553), 436–444, 10.1038/nature14539
28. Al-Zyoud, I., Laamarti, F., Ma, X., Tobón, D., and El Saddik, A. (2022). Towards a machine learning-based digital twin for non-invasive human bio-signal fusion. *Sensors*, 22(24), 9747, 10.3390/s22249747
29. Alamin, K.S.S., Chen, Y., Macii, E., Poncino, M., and Vinco, S. (2022). A machine learning-based digital twin for electric vehicle battery modelling. *2022 IEEE International Conference on Omni-Layer Intelligent Systems*, IEEE, pp. 1–6, 10.1109/COINS54846.2022.9854960

30. Boulfani, F., Gendre, X., Ruiz-Gazen, A., and Salvignol, M. (2020). Anomaly detection for aircraft electrical generator using machine learning in a functional data framework. *2020 Global Congress on Electrical Engineering*, GC-ElecEng, IEEE, pp. 27–32, 10.23919/GC-ElecEng48342.2020.9285984
31. Li, M., Gao, J., Zhou C., Shen X., and Zhuang W. (2022). Digital twin-driven computing resource management for vehicular networks. *GLOBECOM 2022-2022 IEEE Global Communications Conference*, IEEE pp. 5735–5740, 10.1109/GLOBECOM48099.2022.10001032
32. Miao, J., and Zhang, P. (2022). UAV visual navigation system based on digital twin. *2022 18th International Conference on Mobility, Sensing and Networking*, MSN, IEEE, pp. 865–870, 10.1109/MSN57253.2022.00140
33. Li, B., Liu, Y., Tan, L., Pan, H., and Zhang, Y. (2022). Digital twin assisted task offloading for aerial edge computing and networks. *IEEE Trans. Veh. Technol.*, 71(10), 10863–10877, 10.1109/TVT.2022.3182647
34. Wang, Z., Gupta, R., Han, K., Wang, H., Ganlath, A., Ammar, N., and Tiwari, P. (2022). Mobility digital twin: Concept, architecture, case study, and future challenges. *IEEE Internet Things J.*, 9(18), 17452–17467, 10.1109/JIOT.2022.3156028
35. Chhetri, S. R., Faezi, S., Canedo, A., and Faruque, M. A. A. (2019). QUILT: Quality inference from living digital twins in IoT-enabled manufacturing systems. *Proceedings of the International Conference on Internet of Things Design and Implementation*, pp. 237-248, 10.1145/3302505.3310085
36. Mozo, A., Karamchandani, A., Gómez-anaval, S., Sanz, M., Moreno, J. I., and Pastor, A. (2022). B5GEMINI: AI-driven network digital twin. *Sensors*, 22(11), 4106, 10.3390/s22114106
37. Hassard, G., Ghanem, M., Guo, Y., Hassard, J., Osmond, M., and Richards, M. (2005). Sensor grids for air pollution monitoring. In: *Proceedings of 3rd UK e-Science All Hands Meeting*, 2004.
38. Ghewari, M. U., Tejaswini Mahamuni, Pooja Kadam, and Anupama Pawar. (2018). Vehicular pollution monitoring using IoT. *International Research Journal of Engineering and Technology*, 5(2), 1734–1739.
39. Liu, J.-H., Chen, Y.-F., Lin, T.-S., Lai, D.-W., Wen, T. H., Sun, C.-H. et al. (2011). Developed urban air quality monitoring system based on wireless sensor networks. In: *Sensing Technology, 2011 Fifth International Conference on IEEE*, pp. 549–554.
40. Kavita Surannavar, Mansurabegum Tatwanagi, Saniya Patel Nadaf, Basavaraj Hunshal, Daneshwari Patil. (2017). Vehicular pollution monitoring system and detection of vehicles causing global warming. *International Journal of Engineering Science and Computing*, 7(6), 12611–12614.
41. Zhang, Y., Wang, Y., Gao, M., Ma, Q., Zhao, J., Zhang, R. et al. (2019). A predictive data feature exploration-based air quality prediction approach. *IEEE Access*, 7, 30732–30743.
42. Xia, L., and Shao, Y. (2005). Modelling of traffic flow and air pollution emission with application to Hong Kong island. *Environmental Modelling & Software*, 20(9), 1175–1188.
43. Sharmila Devi, S., Kaviarasu, N., Kiruthikram, P. P., and Praveen Kumar, K. (2023). Air pollution prevention using wireless sensors. *IEEE International Conference on Advancements in Electrical, Electronics, Communication, Computing and Automation*, pp. 1–5.

44. Arroyo, P., Lozano, J., Suárez, J. I., Herrero, J. L., and Carmona, P. (2016). Wireless sensor network for air quality monitoring and control. In: *Chemical Engineering Transactions*, pp. 217–222.
45. Arun Kumar, Pushpendu Kar, Rakesh Warrier, Aditi Kajale, and Sanjib Kumar Panda. (2017). Implementation of smart LED lighting and efficient data management system for buildings. *Energy Procedia*, 143, 173–178.
46. Marcello, A., Gómez Maureira, D. O., and Livia Teernstra (2011). ThingSpeak—An API and Web Service for the Internet of Things. LIACS, Leiden University.
47. Ming Zhao, and Arun K. Kumar. (2017). Machine-to-machine communication and research challenges: A survey. *Wireless Personal Communications*, 97(3), 3569–3585.
48. Arun Kumar, Kai, H. Y. S., Wong, J., and Chong, P. H. J. (2017). Location-based routing protocols for wireless sensor networks: A survey. *Wireless Sensor Network*, 9(1), 25–72.
49. Wang, S.-L., Chen, Y. L., Kuo, A. M-H., Chen, H.-M., and Shiu, Y. S. (2015). Design and evaluation of a cloud-based Mobile Health Information Recommendation system on wireless sensor networks. *Computers & Electrical Engineering*, 49, 221–235, DOI:10.1016/j.compeleceng.2015.07.017.
50. Brunelli, D., and Rossi, M. (2014). Enhancing lifetime of WSN for natural gas leakages detection. *Microelectronics Journal*, 45(12), 1665–1670.

CHAPTER

4

MetaDiagnostics with AI-Powered Healthcare beyond Reality

Ashwini A.[1*], D. Karthika Priya[2], Balasubramaniam S.[3] and Seifedine Kadry[4]

[1] Department of Electronics and Communication Engineering, Vel Tech Rangarajan Dr. Sagunthala R&D Institute of Science and Technology, Avadi, Chennai, Tamil Nadu, India

[2] Department of Artificial Intelligence and Data Science, Easwari Engineering College, Ramapuram, Chennai, India

[3] School of Computer Science and Engineering, Kerala University of Digital Sciences, Innovation and Technology (Formerly IIITM-K), Digital University Kerala, Thiruvananthapuram, Kerala, India

[4] Department of Computer Science and Mathematics, Lebanese American University, Beirut, Lebanon

The sphere of modern diagnostics is being revolutionized under the influence of Artificial Intelligence (AI) and Metaverse, which has widened the boundaries of Suppose Howard Healthcare to the field of immersive, intelligent, and patient-centered innovations. MetaDiagnostics is an ideal representation of a futuristic paradigm where the AI-supported algorithms are integrated into a form of virtual and augmented reality-based environments to deliver real-time, quality, and interactive experiences in diagnostic instances. This type of transformation is more than an ordinary clinic-oriented assessment, as it enables medical workers to provide accurate assessments with the help of a simulated digital environment driven by the analytical abilities of AI. These deep learning, computer vision, and natural language processing-based devices in the Metaverse will be able to combine multiple diagnostic modalities and decide regarding the presence of medical conditions. In this type of immersion, a visual, interactive, and information-rich environment can be used for remote consultation, early disease diagnosis, and continuous patient monitoring. By integrating patient digital twins

*Corresponding author: a.ashwinivel@gmail.com

DOI: 10.1201/9781003679370-4

into predictive modeling, MetaDiagnostics could allow clinicians to virtually simulate the results of treatment and receive an individual approach to care at a previously impossible level of accuracy. The second opportunity provided by the Metaverse is the ability for experts from all over the world to assess virtual cases and have real-time discussions on diagnosis. However, the matter of data privacy, standardization of diagnostic procedures in a virtual environment, and ethical inclusion of AI are also a top priorities. To the new frontier, MetaDiagnostics marks the opening of a new era—towards networked, more intelligent and fair healthcare systems—where there is no longer a limitation to the delivery of diagnostics that are the best in the world.

1. The Evolution of Diagnostics: From Analog to AI

Medical diagnostics have shifted from the tactile intuition of analog methods to the data-driven selectivity of Artificial Intelligence, as shown in Figure 1. The pre-digital world diagnosis greatly depended on the senses, experience, and limited instruments of a doctor, which included stethoscopes, thermometers, and X-rays. Although these tools represented revolutionary advances at the time, they were inherently limited by their subjective nature and lacked data [1]. Practitioners often reached different diagnostic conclusions, and the lack of high-resolution real-time information caused delays and even led to generalized treatment. Despite these limitations, this period established the fundamental concepts of clinical reasoning and pattern recognition that still form the basis of modern diagnostic frameworks.

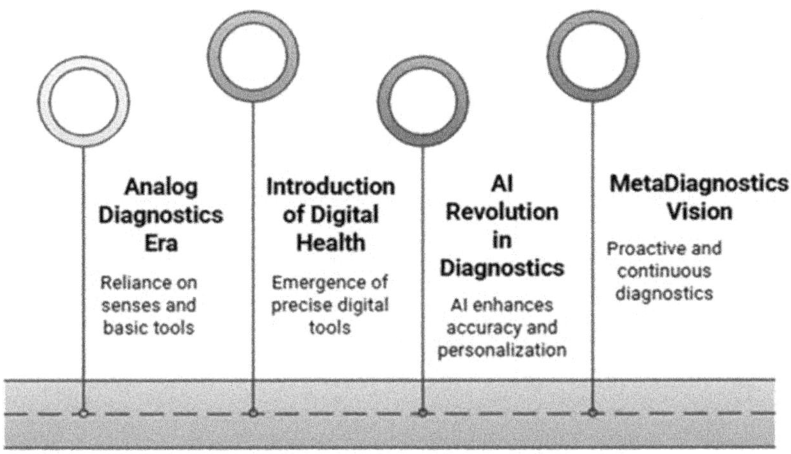

Figure 1: Evolution of medical diagnostics.

Once digital health technologies emerged, diagnostics began to evolve quickly. More precise, reproducible, and quantitative assessments were introduced by computerized tomography (CT), magnetic resonance imaging (MRI), and digital pathology. The factual revolution, on the other hand, has come in the form of the introduction of artificial intelligence [2]. Not only are AI-endowed diagnostics making accuracy more accurate, but they are defining a different possible understanding of diagnostic intelligence. Beyond traditional diagnostics through observation, diagnostics have shifted to diagnosis through prediction and personalization, as seen in deep learning models that detect small anomalies in radiological scans and AI algorithms that interpret genomic data to assess disease risks. MetaDiagnostics—an integration of AI, big data, and cognitive computing—represents an evolution where diagnostics become proactive, continuous, and integrated with real-time patient data [3]. In this context, AI is not just a tool but a collaborator in clinical reasoning, ushering in a new era of healthcare that is focused on the future rather than the present.

2. The Role of AI in Modern Diagnostics

Artificial Intelligence (AI) is transforming the field of diagnostics by enhancing computationally precise clinical decision-making, as in Figure 2. Previously, the process of making diagnoses was linear and reactive, a process of running tests based on hypotheses and limited by the mental capacity of the clinician

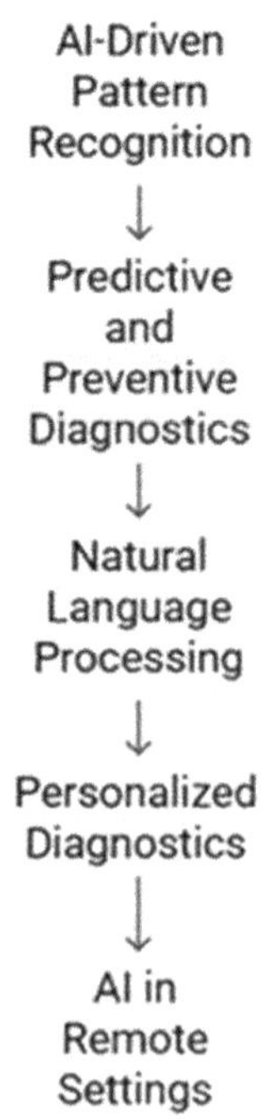

Figure 2: AI in modern diagnostics.

[4]. Currently, AI is evolving toward more proactive, real-time, and highly personalized diagnostics, where data from various sources can be quickly combined to enable faster and more accurate disease identification. This transition forms the foundation of MetaDiagnostics, a new field that transforms healthcare into a connected, intelligent, and self-improving domain.

2.1 AI-Driven Pattern Recognition and Image Analysis

Medical imaging is a significant impact of AI in diagnostics. Other deep learning models, including convolutional neural networks (CNNs), have been shown to surpass human ability in recognizing patterns in radiology, dermatology, and pathology images. AI systems are used in radiology to identify cancers, microcalcifications, or hemorrhages at an early stage of imaging scans with new levels of speed and accuracy. For example, Artificial Intelligence, such as Google LYNA, has demonstrated greater than 90 percent sensitivity in the detection of metastatic breast cancer through lymph node biopsies [5]. In addition to detection, AI can measure the size of lesions, give the status of the tumor, and identify inconsistencies among imaging modalities. What it leads to is a radical advance in not just the degree of accurate diagnoses, but also in lessening latency in diagnosis, hence rendering earlier intervention and more fruitful results.

2.2 Predictive and Preventive Diagnostics

AI can enable diagnostics to stop at the current symptoms and extend into the realms of prediction. ML models that receive longitudinal data on patients would predict the likelihood of developing an illness (e.g., cardiovascular disease, diabetes, or Alzheimer's) years before people show clinical symptoms based on the longitudinal data (electronic health records (EHR), genomics, and lifestyles) to guide preventive behaviors. This predictive quality enables preventive diagnostics, where intervention is not only aimed at treating the disease but also at preventing it entirely. These systems become learning and adjusting, so the risk profiles of people are dynamic. Diagnostics evolve into continuous processes with AI, capable of detecting pre-disease conditions and supporting preventive medicine, which is a vital pillar for healthcare powered by AI, extending beyond current practices limits.

2.3 Natural Language Processing and Clinical Decision Support

Medical records are often unstructured, and valuable information may be concealed within the free-text clinical forms. The subfield of AI known as Natural Language Processing (NLP) makes this data discoverable by scraping, sorting, and decoding written information. Based on NLP algorithms, it is feasible to identify meaningful diagnostic indicators, warn regarding possible comorbidities, and even identify mismatches between symptoms and medical plans. AI, when combined with a decision support system, provides clinicians with real-time diagnostic recommendations, alerts, and triage prioritization. This enhanced form should by no means substitute physicians but serve to allow them to operate with quicker access to relevant information, particularly in the stressful work setting of an emergency room or an intensive care department.

2.4 Personalized Diagnostics through Multi-Omics Integration

The linchpin of personalized medicine is AI because it enhances the ease of working with enormous and intricate data. In a fashion, multi-omics data (such as genomics, proteomics, metabolomics, and microbiomics) can be incorporated into the entire landscape of a diagnosis [6]. The main problem with this is that AI algorithms have the potential to tell not only which disease someone has, but also which one, along with its specific features, is distinctive of the individual. As an example, in oncology, AI systems have the potential to identify a tumor genotype with the most promising immunotherapy approach, warranting diagnostic precision, which is individualized to a particular patient on a molecular level. Such a movement to personalization is one of the main pillars of MetaDiagnostics, as the so-called one-size-fits-all approach will be replaced with individualized diagnostic pathways.

2.5 AI in Remote and Resource-Limited Settings

The AI advantage also includes making diagnostics more accessible. In rural or underserved areas where medical specialists are scarce, AI-powered diagnostic tools, often embedded in smartphones or handheld devices, can fill the gap. AI chatbots, mobile imaging software, and cloud-based decision-support systems can help community health workers carry out accurate diagnostics directly under the supervision of specialists. These solutions are particularly effective in cases of global crisis, such as the pandemic, where diagnostics of a scalable, automated, and distance-based nature are required. In that regard, AI is no longer a technological innovation but also an international health issue.

3. Integration of AI with Immersive Environments

With the transcendence of medicine's addiction to traditional modalities, the combination of Artificial Intelligence (AI) and immersive technologies such as Virtual Reality (VR), Augmented Reality (AR), and Mixed Reality (MR) is fast redefining diagnostic experiences. That convergence takes the passive reading of data and converts it into an active, three-dimensional, and interactive exploration, real, allowing what we call MetaDiagnostics: a paradigm of diagnostics that works at the threshold of reality and simulation [7]. In this case, AI is no longer an assistive tool but a perception engine, enhancing all immersive tools with real-time, intelligent assistance to clinicians and patients.

The combination of AI and immersive environments marks a shift from observational diagnostics to experiential diagnostics. Doctors can now enter, communicate with, and calculate digital copies of patient anatomy, and AI is providing real-time guidance, meaning, and optimization of that communication. This leads to a combination of radicalized intuition in diagnostic landscapes, a design that presents emergent information that is neither merely visualized but felt, and does not only reinvent the spatial, cognitive, but also the temporal context of medicine.

3.1 Immersive Visualization Powered by AI

One of the most significant advancements in the field is AI-enhanced 3D medical visualization. Conventional imaging methods, like CT and MRI, provide volumetric data, but viewing this information on a 2D screen limits spatial perception. AI allows automatic segmentation, labeling, and refinement of anatomical structures to turn raw scan data into high-fidelity immersive 3D models in VR or AR. These models may be rotated, dissected, and zoomed, revealing pathologies never seen before. As an example, the brain MRI scan could be pre-analyzed with an AI model, with the areas of interest highlighted, followed by a volumetric reconstruction in VR, allowing a neurologist to walk through a brain and view a lesion from different angles. This enhances spatial awareness, diagnostic confidence, and interdisciplinary collaboration dramatically.

3.2 AI-Guided Training and Decision Support in Immersive Platforms

AI-integrated immersive simulations are effective training simulators in clinical education and diagnostics (Figure 3). AI-powered VR platforms can produce imperfect simulations whose outcomes are based on how the user acts. Trainees can practice diagnostic procedures, such as detecting the tumor margin, reading an EKG, or diagnosing rare diseases, using an AI-powered system that allows

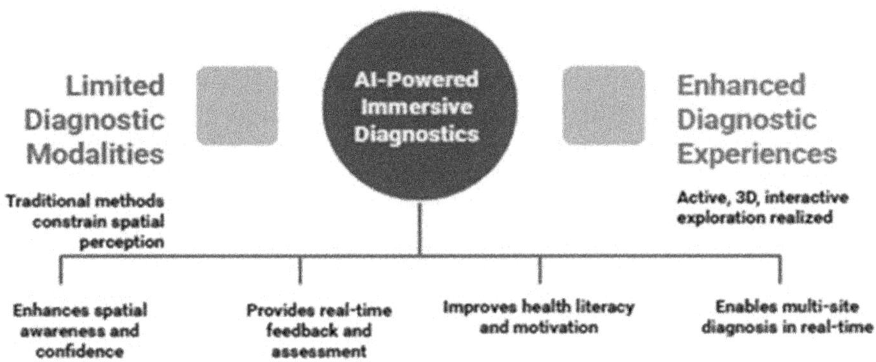

Figure 3: Revolutionizing diagnostics with AI and immersive tech.

them to receive practice opportunities and real-time feedback, performance assessment, as well as contextual information [8].

More importantly, real-time AI-guided decisions are supported by these environments. As an example, in remote tele-diagnostic sessions, clinicians wearing an AR headset can get annotations by AI, which overlay directly on a patient feed or imaging (Cabo and McCurdy, 2020) or even on a patient's body, providing probabilities, recommended tests, or diagnosis. This spatial augmentation is used to simplify difficult decision-making and delivers actionable intelligence right to the clinician's line of sight.

3.3 Patient-Centered Immersive Diagnostics

AI-enhanced immersive experiences provide an anamorphically custom-tailored patient experience. Using AR/VR, a patient will have a chance to engage with his or her health data in understandable and liberating ways. An example is an AI-powered application that can create an illusion of a virtual model of the pancreas in a patient with diabetes and, in real-time, show how the disease develops and what changes in lifestyle cause it. This will enhance health literacy, motivation, and compliance with the treatment.

Telemedicine is becoming a sympathetic diagnostic tool. AI-enhanced VR consultation, where the well-being of the patient is tracked by means of emotion analysis, speech recognition, and tracking of biosignals, allows measuring the physical and emotional balance of a patient in a more full-fledged way in comparison with a video call [9]. This results in more detailed diagnostics, particularly in the area of mental health, chronic pain, or neurodegenerative diseases, where the symptoms are multi-modal and subtle.

3.4 Remote Collaboration and Global Diagnostics

By combining AI and collaborative immersive technologies, healthcare providers would be capable of conducting multi-site diagnosis even at the user level. A cardiologist in Tokyo and a radiologist in London could simultaneously interpret a patient's heart model in mixed reality, with an AI assistant providing real-time interpretation and explanations. They enable multi-specialist decision-making so that diagnostic silos are reduced, and interdisciplinary consensus is gained faster. AI can act as a common cognitive layer, which can help eliminate human expertise and language barriers, as well as time zones. Globalized real-time diagnostics is a feasible reality.

3.5 Challenges in Merging Intelligence with Immersion

The combination of immersive environments and AI faces several obstacles, regardless of the impact and value it can have. The accuracy of the data and the speed of transmission are crucial in real-time diagnostic immersion; AI models need to run on high-resolution data with a low ratio of latency rate to be clinically efficient. The issue of standardization and interoperability in the interaction of imaging systems, AI engines, and XR platforms is not fully developed, which precludes scalability.

Furthermore, the ethical issues to consider include patient data privacy, informed consent in the immersive environment, and the psychological effects of hyperrealistic diagImmersivenostics [10]. The immersive AI should be transparent, inclusive, and give users a clear sense of direction, where clinicians and patients retain control over the diagnostic process.

3.6 The Future of MetaDiagnostics: Reality Reconstructed

Integration of AI and immersive environments is one of the fundamentals of the MetaDiagnostics environment—a place where diagnostics are not limited by screens, stationary data, or idle viewing. Diagnostics in this space are dynamic, spatially intelligent, and aware of context. AI does not merely explain data, but remakes reality to the cognitive and clinical requirements of the user. AI will continue to sever the boundary between bio-initiated and synthetic senses as brain-computer interfaces, haptic feedback, and hologram projection develop. In the future, diagnosis will no longer be limited to hospitals or labs, but can be done anywhere, personalized, continuous, and highly intensive. This is the beginning of a diagnostic metaverse, where medicine does not only do more than it used to, but also what we previously believed was possible.

4. Digital Twins and Synthetic Patients for Diagnosis Simulation

The development of the AI-driven world of healthcare has led to a revisit of the idea of digital twins and synthetic patients, which refine the simulative environment and forecasts of the diagnostic process by emphasizing personalization. In old practice, a diagnosis would be made by visible symptoms and analysis of retrospective data. That is why, today, when a combination of AI, real-time data, and high-fidelity modeling becomes a reality, we can create a virtual identity of human physiology, one that resembles patients with startling similarities [11]. These digital beings, a blend of simulation and sentient models, are becoming diagnostic and anticipatory, transforming how diagnostics are conducted by viewing them as part of observation and shifting towards an anticipatory approach that involves simulation.

The very basis of this transformation is the emergence of what can be called MetaDiagnostics—a paradigm in which diagnostic intelligence can act in silico before it reaches the human body. Digital twins and synthetic patients are more than analysis tools: they serve as living laboratories to predict and test disease progression, interventions, and enhance treatments in virtual space, along with its demo-reality and even beyond.

4.1 Digital Twins: Living Mirrors of Patient Physiology

The live, constantly updated virtual model of a particular patient, created through the use of multi-source data streams, wearable devices, and medical imaging, genomics, and EHRs, is called a digital twin. These virtual equivalents adapt to the patient. They change as physiological parameters, lifestyle, and even environmental situation change. With diagnostics, digital twins allow clinicians and AI models to plan different diagnosis scenarios prior to any invasive measures. So, when a patient has an issue with their heart, specifically a blockage of their arteries, a digital twin of the affected arteries could be used to simulate the effects of the blockage progressing, the various outcomes and effects of any stent operations, and streamline the process of the diagnosis, without actually using a real person in real life.

The twin AI engine is constantly updated with new data and simulated results to improve its accuracy in predicting the future. The scope of the implications is impressive: mistakes will be avoided, unnecessary tests will be prevented, and guesswork and diagnostics will be replaced with precise simulation. Additionally, digital twins enable long-term patient monitoring, allowing them to forecast future health trajectories by analyzing current physiological and behavioral signals.

4.2 Synthetic Patients: Training Grounds for AI and Clinicians

Synthetic patients are fully developed models created by AI, whereas digital twins are simply simulations of actual people. That is why these synthetic constructs, with the help of generative AI models, are being built to represent the full range of human variability, including rare genetic disorders and complex comorbidities, creating a scalable solution to the data scarcity and ethical issues related to the use of real patient data.

Artificial patients play a central role in diagnostic AI training and testing. Instead of access only to biased or incomplete clinical data, developers would be able to train algorithms on very large numbers of synthetic patients, making the performance of the test more equitable, generalizable, and robust. In medicine, medical trainees can interact with web-based synthetic patients to test diagnostic hypotheses during immersive simulations, in a consequence-free system. For example, an AI-based system designed to diagnose conditions like autoimmune diseases could be trained on millions of artificial profiles that vary slightly in symptom complexity and responses to diagnostics [12]. This builds an open, dynamic, scattershot type of laboratory in which the formulation of diagnostics might be developed in an iterative and ethically responsible way.

4.3 Diagnosis Simulation: A New Clinical Reality

Together, digital twins and synthetic patients enable a completely new approach to diagnosis simulation. Imagine a clinical platform where a doctor can generate diagnostic hypotheses for a digital twin of a patient and then compare them with synthetic data from the entire population. This allows for a population-based diagnosis and outcome prediction supported by AI. Such simulation-based methods may also be very important in the field of differential diagnosis, where symptoms are either complex or overlapping and may contribute to improper diagnosis [13]. The use of AI-driven simulations would enable thousands of diagnostic permutations to be evaluated in silico and reduce the range of possibilities, highlighting rare conditions that could otherwise have remained unnoticed.

Simulations have the potential to speed up triage in emergency or critical care. The digital twin of a patient could be pre-assessed by AI, enabling it to simulate diagnostics for all vital systems before a physician enters the room and to provide real-time feedback and alerts for potential complications. This forward-looking, synthetic diagnostic logic introduces new safety and speed in making critical decisions.

5. Real-Time Data Collection and Processing in Virtual Spaces

The incorporation of the practices involved in real-time data updating and processing into virtual settings is one of those landmark achievements in the discipline of MetaDiagnostics. With the shift of healthcare into the immersive and interactive digital sphere of virtual reality (VR), augmented reality (AR), and mixed reality (MR), the potential to capture, transmit, and analyze patient data in real time has become core to the field. And augmenting these immersion platforms using the capabilities of IoT-enabled biosensors, wearables, and AI algorithms can continuously track a broad range of physiologic and behavioral data: heart-rate and respiration, eye-movement, neural-signals, gait-patterns, facial micro-expressions, and even stress-indicator measures. The virtual medium becomes a diagnostic laboratory where all interactions, gestures, and information can be fed into a smart system that is designed to monitor health status in real time.

It is essential that this data can be processed immediately during the course of these immersive environments to provide applicable diagnostics and decision-making. Artificial intelligence is critical in making sense of these humongous streams of data with minimal latency, especially the edge AI and cloud-based deep learning models [14]. As another example, the vocal tone and facial expressions of a patient can be analyzed in real-time with the help of a virtual consultation, allowing for the identification of an emotional state or the initiation of the onset of a neurological disease. Likewise, a clinician examining a digital twin of a patient organ system can detect anomalies in real-time, scan data within a patient population context, and even recommend the next course of diagnosis, all within the same virtual view. Not only does this make the process of diagnosis quicker and more accurate, but it also allows for proactive action in a manner that the delayed diagnostic approaches found in more traditional processes do not.

Additionally, the combinatory effect of real-time data with immersive space establishes a closed-loop biofeedback/diagnostic reinforcement system. Patients who undergo VR treatment for PTSD, stroke rehabilitation, or chronic pain can be supervised in real time, and AI can adapt the environment to the results of physiological changes. This kind of malleability transforms virtual spaces into living diagnostics—constantly sensing, learning, and developing based on the user [15]. A more advanced approach where diagnostics are performed through the body, rather than with the body, by seamlessly blending real-world and virtual intelligence, is the direction we are heading. It is a substantial milestone in achieving the MetaDiagnostic vision: healthcare that is beyond passive observation and evolving into dynamic, real-time, and highly personalized insight.

6. AI-Based Virtual Radiology and Pathology Labs

The rise of AI-powered virtual radiology and pathology labs has sparked a revolution in diagnostic medical space, with an emphasis on the use of equipment, transitioning to smart cloud-driven elastic environments, as shown in Figure 4. These labs utilize the strength of artificial intelligence, high-resolution digital imaging, and virtual interface to carry out diagnostics at a speed, precision, and scale never imagined. In radiology, AI algorithms can automatically examine X-rays, MRIs, CT scans, and PET scans in real time, detecting anomalies of various types (including tumors, fractures, hemorrhages, and degenerative changes) with master-level accuracy. When used in virtual environments, these functionalities allow the radiologist to remotely access, modify, and view diagnostic images in an immersive 3D space, often utilizing haptics and spatial computing.

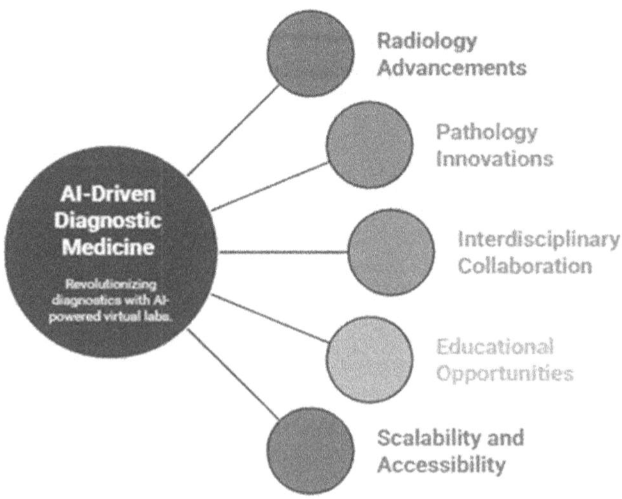

Figure 4: Unveiling the dimensions of AI-driven diagnostic medicine.

Likewise, virtual pathology laboratories use whole-slide imaging, AI-driven histopathological analysis, and cloud-connected databases to digitize the entire microscopic process [16]. High-resolution tissue samples are digitized and analyzed carefully using convolutional neural networks to identify minor cellular anomalies in cases of cancer, infection, or autoimmune disease. On a virtual platform, pathologists will have the opportunity to investigate tissue morphology in 3D, zooming into areas of interest, and receive recommended diagnoses, probability heat maps, and cross-referenced annotations by millions of previous cases, all recommended by the AI [17]. This significantly increases the speed, consistency, and diagnosis, particularly in poorly resourced areas where access to pathology expertise is often limited.

Interdisciplinary collaboration and worldwide accessibility are also improved by the virtualization of these diagnostic specialties. A radiologist in New York and a pathologist in Mumbai can access patient data simultaneously with the help of AI systems, which leverage their collective knowledge through shared virtual labs. The two platforms not only enable second opinions and consensus diagnoses but also import real-time training scenarios of medical students and junior specialists via simulation using synthetically generated cases and interactive simulations. As such, AI-driven labs continue their evolution [18]. They are becoming the central element of the MetaDiagnostics paradigm, enabling faster, more accurate, and more accessible diagnostics that are scalable and resistant to global health demands.

7. Accessibility to Underserved and Remote Regions

Timely, correct, and cost-effective diagnostics are a continuing challenge in underserved areas and remote parts of the world. Shortage of medical facilities, access, competent personnel, and diagnostic devices, also known as healthcare deserts, remains one of the major causes of late-stage disease diagnosis, avoidable loss of lives, and excess disease burden. Conventional diagnostic platforms are dependent on large-scale laboratories, expensive imaging devices, and skilled workers who are, in most cases, unavailable to deprived groups. Nevertheless, the scenario is fast changing due to AI-based MetaDiagnostics, which is being administered through a virtual and decentralized platform.

MetaDiagnostics presents a completely new approach to diagnostic processes by integrating artificial intelligence, mobile connection, edge computing, and cloud-based platforms [19]. Such innovations reduce the need for physical infrastructure and human expertise because diagnostic services reach the patient directly, regardless of whether they are in a remote village, a war-torn area, or an underserved urban slum. The meeting of virtual diagnostics with AI presents an important transformation—the switch from clinic-centered to community-based, patient-empowered diagnostics.

7.1 AI-Powered Mobile Diagnostics: Care without Borders

Among the most effective implementations of MetaDiagnostics, one can distinguish the implementation of AI-empowered mobile diagnostic units. These units support point-of-care machines, portable scanners, and diagnostic wearables to gather patient information and analyze it in situ with AI aid. Whether it's using smartphone-based retinal scanners for diagnosing diabetic retinopathy or handheld ultrasound devices with AI to manage pregnancy and maternal health, these tools will help integrate community health workers as local diagnostic agents, with AI systems offering real-time guidance.

Such AI algorithms, trained on large, heterogeneous data sets, can identify diseases such as tuberculosis, pneumonia, malaria, cervical cancer, and anemia, with a high level of accuracy even without trained doctors. Additionally, these systems switch to offline mode due to edge AI, allowing diagnostics to continue uninterrupted during rare connectivity scenarios [20]. And once connectivity is regained, the data can be transferred to the cloud for further review by centralized teams or AI, establishing a distributed diagnostic network that is both resilient and scalable.

7.2 Virtual Consultation and Diagnostic Platforms

Telemedicine and virtual reality are additional tools used by MetaDiagnostics to reduce the expertise gap between underserved areas and those with diagnostic expertise. Diagnostic tools can be provided cloud-based and used by patients or local healthcare providers, with an opportunity to upload the results of imaging or biosignal scanning and have reports analyzed by AI with suggested clinical steps. Remote pathology or radiology labs (which have already been mentioned) are virtual environments that can connect a health facility in a small local community with specialists thousands of kilometers away, combined with AI, allowing prompt triage and prioritizing cases when there is an emergency.

Also, immersive diagnostic surroundings are designed and built to support distant casework. For example, diagnostic goggles powered by AR can help a rural nurse perform a procedure, while an AI manages step-by-step feedback and monitors the patient's vitals. When human supervision is required, a holographic or VR consultation can project a specialist remotely and mark a new era of long-distance care that is interactive, immersive, and intelligent.

7.3 Cultural and Linguistic Inclusivity through AI

The second strength of AI-based MetaDiagnostics is overcoming cultural, linguistic, and literacy barriers that commonly become an obstacle in care delivery to remote or underserved populations. The regional dialects and language-trained natural language processing (NLP) systems can be used to communicate with the local population and the AI systems. Chatbots and voice-based diagnostic assistants can generate culturally specific language and formats to provide patients with protocols related to symptom-checking, adherence to medication, and follow-up.

Globally, AI-powered interfaces with visual displays, non-SAT rigorous health education tools, and audio instructions can dynamically adjust user literacy levels to make diagnostic information more accessible and easier to manage [21]. Such an inclusive design will also provide the chance that no population will be left behind, and the world will experience the true democratization of diagnostics.

7.4 Economic Affordability and Scalability

One of the best impediments to quality diagnostics in low-resource settings has been cost. The cost of care delivery is dramatically reduced by using the AI-based MetaDiagnostics, since the construction of infrastructure is unnecessary, tedious analysis can be automated, and the supply chain can be optimized. Improved operational efficiency and lower costs are also linked to cloud-based diagnostics and remote analytics in health systems. Additionally, mobile-first services mean less patient travel, less time off work, and lower out-of-pocket expenses.

For public health, more so, this scalability is essential. AI-led diagnostic initiatives can be introduced to entire regions without massive logistical costs, provided by governments and non-profit-making organizations. As an example, in the case of outbreaks involving infectious disease, the immediate response could be AI-based testing and contact tracing to prevent the accidental extension of its domains, thus offering a prophylactic shield leveraging smart diagnostics [22]. MetaDiagnostic has a long-term goal of establishing self-sustaining autonomous diagnostic ecosystems in underserved areas: systems that unite local health workers and the AI systems and decentralized labs to work in concert in providing continuous, adaptive care. The ecosystems can be combined with blockchain to guarantee safe storage of health records, digital twins that simulate longitudinal care, and supply chain systems powered by AI to ensure access to diagnostic equipment and prescribed medicines remains satisfactory.

Even the most remote areas will be able to tap into international diagnostic intelligence as the connectivity of infrastructure, such as the low-Earth orbit internet (e.g., Starlink), grows. It is not vague at all: there are no far-fetched places, no forgotten communities. The future of AI-based MetaDiagnostics means that the place of residence will no longer define healthcare destiny.

8. Simulated Diagnostic Walkthroughs with Avatars and Digital Tools

Simulated diagnostic walkthrough in a digital environment is transforming how clinicians, students, and even patients experience the process of a diagnostic pathway in the new MetaDiagnostics world. Such simulations are based on a combination of extended reality (XR), artificial intelligence, and interactive digital environments, which make re-creating clinical scenarios as awe-inspiring as possible. On these platforms, the user is guided through a hospital, lab, or even a patient's rooms by a customizable avatar [23]. A user can connect each of these avatars to synthetic patients, medical equipment, and AI programs to simulate the entire diagnostic process for an actor who will take a patient history, order examinations, analyze test results, and make conclusions.

This modality not only offers particular diagnostic accuracy but also helps to facilitate easy learning and the acquisition of skills in Figure 5. Trainees are provided with an opportunity to work with various conditions—they can be pediatric, emergency, infectious disease, and oncology—and have high-fidelity diagnostic cases and receive real-time feedback information provided by AI tutors that monitor their actions, reasoning, and consequences. Symptoms can be dynamically presented depending on the diagnostic decisions made by the user, and this difference also shows a cause-and-effect knowledge that cannot be learned in a static textbook. Moreover, in an avatar, it is possible to set a specific set of physiological, genetic, and behavioral backgrounds, and potential simulations of rare diseases or unusual phenomena, which are required to increase diagnostic acuity in an absolutely safe setting, can be performed.

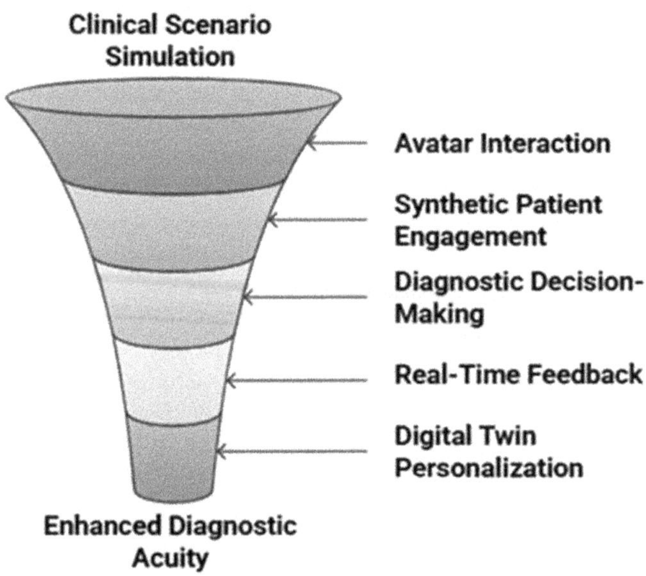

Figure 5: AI-driven diagnostics through simulation.

Besides, digital twin technology is being merged more and more with simulated walkthroughs, allowing real-time personalization. A doctor will be able to interact with a digital twin of a real-life patient that includes biometric data, images, and develop clinical parameters to conduct parallel diagnosis, but without risking the patient or testing the effect of different interventions [23]. This not only enhances precision medicine but also acts as a reference space in which various healthcare professionals can participate in a co-diagnosis or co-treatment process, even when remote in terms of geographic location, represented by their avatars. The more that AI learns during these interactions, the more intelligent the tools created in the simulations grow, and the more they become sensitive and even more specific to clinician and patient requirements.

These simulated diagnostic platforms are going to change diagnostics in that they change the diagnostic process, which is a matter of procedure, into a matter of experience, change, and concurrence. Having both avatars as the erudite assistant or individualized patient proxy and having computer equipment with flexible diagnostic facilities, healthcare providers have the potential to iterate, refresh, and reinstate techniques of diagnosis. This strategy does not merely improve competence and confidence but foretells a certain future in which diagnostic prowess will be formed as much through virtual experience as actual exposure.

9. Real-World Use Cases of Metadiagnostics Platforms

The concept of MetaDiagnostics, which combines AI, immersive space, and real-time data into a new generation of a more advanced diagnostic ecology, may seem futuristic, as in Table 1. However, several practical stages in real life are already being based on the transition to a new paradigm of diagnosis. An example is how Project ECHO (Extension for Community Healthcare Outcomes) has transformed from it was designed as a telemedicine program into an online collaborative diagnostic platform. In this case, the use of AI-powered dashboards and case-based discussions meets the need to focus on improving diagnostics in such fields as hepatitis C, cancer, and mental health by linking expert hubs and healthcare providers in remote settings [24]. Though not completely immersive, the model proves that distributed intelligence and AI assistance can make diagnostic expertise decentralized over geographies.

Another notable one is PathAI, which utilizes the power of AI-based pathology diagnostics and helps clinicians interpret digital biopsy slides. As applied in hospitals and in clinical trials around the world, the platform offered by PathAI enhances the accuracy of diagnosis, shortens turnaround time, and is cloud-friendly or can be used on an edge system, important aspects of the MetaDiagnostics vision. In radiology, there are Aidoc and Zebra Medical Vision, which offer real-time AI analysis of medical images (e.g., CT and MRI) that automatically point out abnormal results: intracranial hemorrhage, lung nodules, etc. Examples of these platforms are already embedded into hospital workflows in the U.S., Europe, and Asia, showing that AI-enhanced diagnostics have become a part of reasonable practice.

Table 1: AI- MetaDiagnostics with Region Deployment

Application/ Platform	Description	AI Role/MetaDiagnostics Relevance	Region/ Deployment
Project ECHO	Originally a telemedicine initiative, now an online collaborative diagnostic platform	AI dashboards + expert-driven case discussions enable decentralized, remote diagnostics	Global (especially remote healthcare settings)
PathAI	AI-based pathology diagnostics used for interpreting digital biopsy slides	Enhances diagnostic accuracy, reduces turnaround time, cloud and edge compatible	Hospitals and clinical trials worldwide
Aidoc & Zebra Medical Vision	Real-time AI analysis of radiological images (CT, MRI)	Automatically detects anomalies (e.g., hemorrhages, lung nodules); integrated into hospital workflows	U.S., Europe, Asia
Digital Twin Initiatives	Patient-specific digital models integrating imaging, genomics, and EHR	Models disease progression and supports precise diagnosis and treatment	Mayo Clinic, Mount Sinai (USA)
Oxford Medical Simulation & SimX	XR-based immersive training and diagnostic simulation platforms	AI-enhanced simulations with real-time data, biosensor inputs for education and diagnostics	Medical education globally
Babylon Health & Ada Health	Mobile apps using AI for symptom assessment and preliminary diagnostics	Use of knowledge graphs, probabilistic reasoning engines for quick diagnostics in underserved areas	Africa, Asia, Latin America

It is being found in the real medical environment that digital twins save the day. Researchers at such institutions as Mayo Clinic and Mount Sinai are working on the development of patient-specific digital models that combine imaging, genomics, and EHR data to model disease progression and to ensure the most accurate proposal for diagnosis and treatment [26]. In addition, XR-based platforms (such as Oxford Medical Simulation and SimX), facilitating immersive training and diagnostic experiences, will be used to educate healthcare professionals by immersion in immersive training and diagnostic exercises lifelike, AI-enhanced diagnostic walkthroughs. These learning environments permit teams to practice complicated diagnostic situations in simulated surroundings heavily augmented with real-time information feeding, including wearable or simulated biosensors.

Babylon Health and Ada Health provide AI-based mobile applications to assess symptoms and preliminary diagnostics with the help of knowledge graphs and probabilistic reasoning engines in resource-limited environments. Millions of people in underserved communities around the world, in Africa, Asia, and Latin America, have accessed these tools and demonstrated that MetaDiagnostics is not just about elegant high technology, but about democratic access to intelligent diagnostic support globally [26]. Such real-world applications indicate a transition to the analysis of diagnostics through a fragmented approach of specialists to integrated, intelligent, learning, adapting, and scalable analytics. With mergers and the upcoming meta-technologies, MetaDiagnostics will cease to be a far-fetched idea in the future; rather, it will be the new paradigm of precision, accessibility, and personalization of healthcare in the global arena.

10. Data Privacy and Cybersecurity in the Metaverse

Data privacy and cybersecurity are not just an option in the ever-growing world of the metaverse, as they join the ranks of an emerging frontier in diagnostics, patient care, and health data permissions. Sensitive health data is being created, exchanged, and conceptualized continuously in the context of interdependent machine intelligence, avatars, wearable computing, and cloud computing components in the MetaDiagnostics settings. Whether the digital twins are a copy of real-time physical biometrics or the diagnostic results are parsable by AI, every layer of interaction induces possible points of attack [27]. It is no doubt a tremendous task to consider how such an immersive and interconnective system can ensure the confidentiality, integrity, and availability of patient data and requires reassessment of conventional healthcare data protection systems.

The metaverse-based diagnostics have a larger surface area exposed to cyber risks such as identity theft, identity breaches, deepfake manipulation, AI model poisoning, and unauthorized visits to virtual clinics systems. Security solutions that can highlight these risks are a new breed of solutions: architected using decentralized identity protocols like blockchain, threat detection engines using AI, and privacy-preserving computing like federated learning and homomorphic encryption. Such data regulations as HIPAA, GDPR, and the new data regulations in the metaverse should be modified to control biometric data, virtual behavior patterns, and AI inference data in such new environments [28, 29]. After all, assurance in MetaDiagnostics platforms will rely not just on clinical accuracy but on the security of cybersecurity infrastructures that secure all the virtual interactions, so that both patients and providers can travel to the new reality with sophistication and without fear.

11. Cross-Border Virtual Diagnostics and Policy Considerations

The emergence of cross-border virtual diagnostics has been possible due to the ascent of MetaDiagnostics, which is AI-enhanced and developed in immersive technologies. This is when patients in one country can get diagnostic assessments provided by the professionals or an AI system in another. The possibilities for this worldwide diagnosis are enormous; the speed of second opinions or having access to specialists with rare diseases, providing equal delivery of care, even in areas with limited high-order healthcare infrastructure. Radiology, digital pathology, and teleconsulting platforms can now work across borders without any difficulties with service delivery: they expand the capacity of local health systems as well as geographical and financial access to high-quality diagnostics. Nevertheless, this novel paradigm creates numerous legal and regulatory issues, as well as ethical considerations, which should be covered to provide safe and standard care.

Policy-related issues involve data sovereignty, such that patient data sourced in one region can be stored or processed in another, potentially creating privacy, ownership, and separation of local applicable regulatory enactments like HIPAA, GDPR, and location-specific health data systems. All these issues require international interoperability standards, mutual recognition of digital credentials, and strong cross-border data-sharing agreements that should observe ethics and legal protection. As MetaDiagnostics grows, a coordinated policy response internationally will be necessary so that virtual care between countries is not only technically viable but also legally acceptable, ethically appropriate, and culturally acceptable.

12. Conclusion

Diagnostic evolution is undergoing an era of transition: in a new frontier, artificial intelligence, immersive technologies, and data-based innovation combine to create a new field—MetaDiagnostics. This chapter has discussed the trends of how diagnostics are moving outside the confines of traditional clinical environments to dynamic, interactive, and smart environments enabled by AI, virtual reality, digital twins, and cross-border platforms. A once very analogue and siloed set of specialist tools is increasingly becoming an ecosystem of real-time, personal, predictive diagnostic experiences that are geography-less, presence-free, even biology-free. MetaDiagnostics is not a simple concept of a technological upgrade, but a re-imagination of what the process of healthcare diagnostics means, what it can be, and what form it can be processed into. It allows clinicians to practice complicated conditions using avatars and digital technologies, provides avenues to bring world-level expertise to underserved populations, and paves the way for forever diagnostics through an immersive environment and robot companions. However, these opportunities also come with important responsibilities: one should guarantee data privacy, establish the idea of fair policies, address cybersecurity risks, and support international cooperation. Going forward, innovation will no longer be sufficient to achieve success in MetaDiagnostics, but the ethical, inclusive, and sustainable constructs around it. Here, there is a convergence of reality and virtuality, and it is MetaDiagnostics that reminds us of a future where diagnostics go beyond traditional boundaries, assumptions, and ultimately, reality.

References

1. Bilski, P., and Wojciechowski, J. (2014). Artificial intelligence methods in diagnostics of analog systems. *International Journal of Applied Mathematics and Computer Science*, 24(2), 271–282.
2. McKeon, A., and Wakeling, A. (1989, August). Fault diagnosis in analogue circuits using AI techniques. In: *Proceedings. 'Meeting the Tests of Time', International Test Conference*, pp. 118–123. IEEE.
3. Cadamuro, J. (2021). Rise of the machines: The inevitable evolution of medicine and medical laboratories intertwining with artificial intelligence—A narrative review. *Diagnostics*, 11(8), 1399.
4. Aamir, A., Iqbal, A., Jawed, F., Ashfaque, F., Hafsa, H., Anas, Z., ... and Mansoor, T. (2024). Exploring the current and prospective role of artificial intelligence in disease diagnosis. *Annals of Medicine and Surgery*, 86(2), 943–949.
5. Alotaibi, F. M., Almazam, A. A., Emam, A. M., Alqahtani, N. S., Alheggi, A. I., Alshahranl, W. N., ... and Alharbi, N. H. M. (2020). Exploring the impact and applications of artificial intelligence in advancing modern medical diagnostic practices – Role of healthcare providers. *International Journal of Health Sciences*, 4(S1), 114–131.
6. Khalifa, M., and Albadawy, M. (2024). AI in diagnostic imaging: Revolutionising accuracy and efficiency. *Computer Methods and Programs in Biomedicine Update*, 100146.
7. Bekteshi, L. (2025). Education in the era of AI and immersive technologies: A systematic review. *Journal of Research in Engineering and Computer Sciences*, 3(1), 01–14.
8. Wang, D., and Huang, X. (2025). Transforming education through artificial intelligence and immersive technologies: Enhancing learning experiences. *Interactive Learning Environments*, 1–20.
9. Ahmad, M. K., & Rana, R. S. V. (2025). Integrating virtual reality with artificial intelligence for immersive learning. *International Journal of Web of Multidisciplinary Studies*, 2(2), 15–20.
10. Padoan, A., and Plebani, M. (2024). Dynamic mirroring: Unveiling the role of digital twins, artificial intelligence and synthetic data for personalized medicine in laboratory medicine. *Clinical Chemistry and Laboratory Medicine (CCLM)*, 62(11), 2156–2161.
11. Łukaniszyn, M., Majka, Ł., Grochowicz, B., Mikołajewski, D., and Kawala-Sterniuk, A. (2024). Digital twins generated by artificial intelligence in personalized healthcare. *Applied Sciences*, 14(20), 9404.
12. Kaul, R., Ossai, C., Forkan, A. R. M., Jayaraman, P. P., Zelcer, J., Vaughan, S., and Wickramasinghe, N. (2023). The role of AI for developing digital twins in healthcare: The case of cancer care. *Wiley Interdisciplinary Reviews: Data Mining and Knowledge Discovery*, 13(1), e1480.
13. Kayser, K., Kayser, G., Radziszowski, D., and Oehmann, A. (2004). New developments in digital pathology: From telepathology to virtual pathology laboratory. *Studies in Health Technology and Informatics*, 105, 61–69.
14. Kayser, K., GĂśrtler, J., Bogovac, M., Bogovac, A., Goldmann, T., Vollmer, E., and Kayser, G. (2009). AI (Artificial Intelligence) in histopathology – From image analysis to automated diagnosis. *Folia Histochemica et Cytobiologica*, 47(3), 355–361.

15. Parwani, A. V., and Amin, M. B. (2020). Convergence of digital pathology and artificial intelligence tools in anatomic pathology practice: Current landscape and future directions. *Advances in Anatomic Pathology*, 27(4), 221–226.
16. Bell, N., Hung, P., Lòpez-De Fede, A., and Adams, S. A. (2023). Broadband access within medically underserved areas and its implication for telehealth utilization. *The Journal of Rural Health*, 39(3), 625–635.
17. Hewitt, S., McNiesh, S., and Fink, L. (2019). Barriers to primary care access in rural medically underserved areas: Immediate care: A simple solution to a complex problem. *Online Journal of Rural Nursing and Health Care*, 127–155.
18. Wenang, S., Schaefers, J., Afdal, A., Gufron, A., Geyer, S., Dewanto, I., and Haier, J. (2021). Availability and accessibility of primary care for the remote, rural, and poor population of Indonesia. *Frontiers in Public Health*, 9, 721886.
19. Azeta, J., Omeche, T. T., Daniyan, I., Abiola, J. O., Daniyan, L., Phuluwa, H. S., and Muvunzi, R. (2025). Artificial intelligence and robotics in predictive maintenance: A comprehensive review. *Frontiers in Mechanical Engineering*, 11, 1722114.
20. Lippitsch, A., Steglich, J., Ludwig, C., Kellner, J., Hempel, L., Stoevesandt, D., and Thews, O. (2024). Development and evaluation of a software system for medical students to teach and practice anamnestic interviews with virtual patient avatars. *Computer Methods and Programs in Biomedicine*, 244, 107964.
21. Hirumi, A., Kleinsmith, A., Johnsen, K., Kubovec, S., Eakins, M., Bogert, K., ... and Cendan, J. (2016). Advancing virtual patient simulations through design research and interPLAY: Part I: Design and development. *Educational Technology Research and Development*, 64, 763–785.
22. Carey, B. (2022). Simulation and virtualization technologies, artificial intelligence diagnostic tools, and metaverse healthcare systems in 3D immersive environments. *American Journal of Medical Research*, 9(2), 9–24.
23. Wetli, D. J., Bergauer, L., Nöthiger, C. B., Roche, T. R., Spahn, D. R., Tscholl, D. W., and Said, S. (2022). Improving visual-patient-avatar design prior to its clinical release: A mixed qualitative and quantitative study. *Diagnostics*, 12(2), 555.
24. Fiaz, F., Sajjad, S. M., Iqbal, Z., Yousaf, M., and Muhammad, Z. (2024). Metassi: A framework for personal data protection, enhanced cybersecurity and privacy in metaverse virtual reality platforms. *Future Internet*, 16(5), 176.
25. Parlar, T. (2023). Data privacy and security in the metaverse. In: *Metaverse: Technologies, Opportunities and Threats* (pp. 123–133). Singapore: Springer Nature Singapore.
26. Rather, A. H., Haq, I. U., and Walia, N. K. (2025). Privacy and security in the metaverse. In: *Leveraging Metaverse and Analytics of Things (AoT) in Medical Systems* (pp. 189–207). Academic Press.
27. Towett, G., Snead, R. S., Grigoryan, K., and Marczika, J. (2023). Geographical and practical challenges in the implementation of digital health passports for cross-border COVID-19 pandemic management: A narrative review and framework for solutions. *Globalization and Health*, 19(1), 98.
28. Saliba, V., Legido-Quigley, H., Hallik, R., Aaviksoo, A., Car, J., and McKee, M. (2012). Telemedicine across borders: A systematic review of factors that hinder or support implementation. *International Journal of Medical Informatics*, 81(12), 793–809.
29. Pham, T. (2025). Ethical and legal considerations in healthcare AI: Innovation and policy for safe and fair use. *Royal Society Open Science*, 12(5), 241873.

CHAPTER

5

MetaCare Revolution in AI-Driven Personalized Medicine in the Virtual World

Ashwini A.[1*], Joel Livin A.[2] and Balasubramaniam S.[3]

[1] Department of Electronics and Communication Engineering, Vel Tech Rangarajan Dr. Sagunthala R&D Institute of Science and Technology, Avadi, Chennai, Tamil Nadu, India

[2] Engineering Department (Electrical Section), University of Technology and Applied Sciences, Ibra, Sultanate of Oman

[3] School of Computer Science and Engineering, Kerala University of Digital Sciences, Innovation and Technology (Formerly IIITM-K), Digital University Kerala, Thiruvananthapuram, Kerala, India

The intersection of artificial intelligence (AI), personalized medicine, and virtual environments is ushering in a new era of healthcare—one where treatment is not just reactive, but predictive, precise, and immersive. In the emerging metaverse environment, AI helps medical specialists to present hyper-personal medical treatment to suit the specifics of the genetics, physiology, and lifestyle of a user. This integration is transforming the traditional clinical experience by using digital avatars, intelligent wearables, and immersive simulations to create personalized therapeutic plans, all of which can be easily accessed within the virtual world. Metaverse engages AI algorithms to process real-time, large-scale biomedical and behavioral data in the healthcare context to enable smart diagnosis, precision regimens, and continual virtual care supervision. Using digital twins as virtual representations of patients allows clinicians to observe procedure outcomes and assess treatment effectiveness in a virtual environment before applying it in real life. Ranging from distant virtual medical visits with AI-supported virtual physicians to the retailing of custom drug formulations by metaverse pharmacies, AI is front and center in changing the locations and

*Corresponding author: a.ashwinivel@gmail.com

DOI: 10.1201/9781003679370-5

modalities of healthcare delivery. Along with clinical interventions, such an AI-driven metaverse model can enhance patient autonomy and engagement through virtual wellness programs, behavior modeling, and mental health management, combined with natural language processing and emotion detection technologies. Nonetheless, the present transformation throws up serious concerns about the privacy of data, regulatory capability, digital equity, and the ethical application of AI within virtual care. This chapter explores these concerns while examining the potential of AI to transform personalized health within a metaverse context.

1. Introduction to the Metaverse in Healthcare

The healthcare industry, expanding quickly worldwide, is the foundation of the metaverse, a persistent and immersive online space where people can explore digital worlds and interact through digital avatars in real time [1]. The metaverse was originally understood to be a game and socialization tool, but is now known as a more transformative platform that virtual medical environments could operate around, where patient care, education, simulation, and health monitoring would occur within an interconnected, self-encompassing environment. As healthcare continues to digitalize, the metaverse is offering new potential solutions to overcome geographical barriers, access issues, and resource limitations.

The metaverse is a collection of technologies like augmented reality (AR), virtual reality (VR), artificial intelligence (AI), blockchain, and the Internet of Medical Things (IoMT) used to create a smart and interactive ecosystem in healthcare [2]. Such virtual ecosystems would allow patients to communicate with doctors through realistic avatars, participate in therapy, practice surgical procedures, or even interact with a virtual replica of their own biology. The hospitals and clinics are conceptualized as so-called smart virtual clinics where, due to sensors and built-in diagnostic tools, as well as treatment suggestions and patient education, they are integrated into immersive interfaces, enhancing participation, customization, and response.

Personalization and preventive medicine have also become an opportunity for mastering the metaverse in the medical field. Ongoing data streams through wearables, biosensing, and AI analytics will enable patients to receive real-time feedback and early warnings about potential health risks in a virtual environment that feels tangible and accessible [3]. In the case of chronic conditions, care for mental health, physical rehabilitation, or even recovery after surgery, the metaverse provides adaptive, interactive, and gamified treatment methods that make treatment more accessible and efficient. With this digital revolution, privacy, ethical, interoperability, and infrastructure challenges must be addressed to unlock the potential of the metaverse as a key component of future healthcare delivery, as demonstrated in Figure 1.

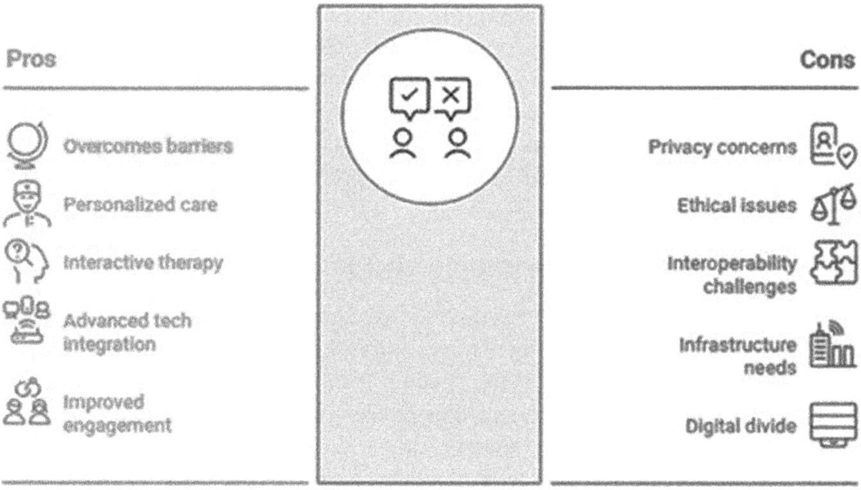

Figure 1: Metaverse in healthcare.

2. The Evolution of Personalized Medicine

Unlike the traditional one-size-fits-all approach, precision medicine, also known as personalized medicine, represents a shift toward more specialized healthcare tailored to individual genetic, environmental, and lifestyle factors. It can be traced to the developments in genomics and molecular biology of the late 20th century (especially since the end of the Human Genome Project in 2003). This monumental success paved the way for learning how personal genetic differences can be used to alter the risks of diseases, response to drugs, and influence drug reactions [4].

2.1 Traditional Medicine – The One-Size-Fits-All Era

When modern healthcare was still in its infancy, medicine worked on a generalized model in which treatments were formulated using overall population averages. Physicians treated patients with pharmacological therapies and interventions, often with a limited understanding of individual variability, relying on trial and error to find what worked best for each patient. Although this method was useful when treating most normal diseases, heredity, metabolism, or pathogen specificity, a patient was not considered. This inefficiency of treatment, negative drug interactions, and incorrect diagnosis were sometimes based on the absence of personalization.

2.2 The Genomics Breakthrough – Human Genome Project

The development of personalized medicine went through a revolutionary stage with the introduction and subsequent completion of the Human Genome Project

(1990–2003). The project successfully mapped the entire human genome, showing that scientists could understand the genetic makeup of the human body [5]. Scientists have been able to identify the specific genes responsible for certain illnesses and understand how genetic variation affects an individual's response to drugs for the first time. This discovery laid the foundation for personalized care, which is based on an individual's DNA profile, and it has changed many lives forever.

2.3 Rise of Pharmacogenomics and Targeted Therapies

The rise of the genomics revolution resulted in the development of pharmacogenomics, which explores how genetic variation affects an individual's response to drugs. It helped develop specific forms of therapy, such as creating cancer-specific therapies, because specific cancer-related genetic mutations could be identified and remedied by specific drugs. As an example, HER2-positive breast cancer patients were already aided by such treatments as Trastuzumab, which targets the HER2 gene specifically. This transition allowed clinicians to develop a less generalized chemotherapy regimen and instead focus on direct treatment of poorly implemented regulations.

2.4 Integration of Big Data and Electronic Health Records (EHRs)

Medical technology has improved, leading to an increase and diversification of patient data. The availability of electronic health records (EHRs) and massive health databases allowed clinicians and researchers to monitor how people with the disease improved or worsened and how the pattern of health varied with time in the population [6]. This data, in combination with statistical and machine learning tools, offered more insight into the behavior of patients, risk factors, and outcomes. Personalized medicine began by consisting of genetic information, lifestyle, environmental, and comorbidity-related factors to create a more holistic approach to treatment.

2.5 Artificial Intelligence and Predictive Analytics

The use of artificial intelligence (AI) has become another step in making personalized medicine a reality. Machine learning algorithms, which process complex data, such as genomics, imaging, sensor, and clinical history data, now predict disease risk and identify optimal therapies and recommend preventive interventions. The result is technologies that have enhanced the accuracy of diagnosis and supported the development of proactive and parameter-perfect care [7]. Wearable health monitoring using AI is also used for real-time tracking without visiting a clinic or hospital; they are continuously sends patient-specific data as feedback.

2.6 The Metaverse and Digital Twins – A New Frontier

Modern personalized medicine is advancing us further along the path of transformation toward an immersive metaverse environment where the virtual world, augmented reality, and digital twins are revolutionizing healthcare delivery. Such settings can enable the use of a digital version of a patient-generated profile based on real-world information about a person to model how an individual might respond to various treatments or interventions [8]. In virtual clinics, patients and physicians can communicate through avatars, where AI-based diagnostics and therapy concepts create a dynamic and highly personalized healthcare experience, as shown in Figure 2. Besides making care more accessible and engaging, this step will create a strong platform for simulation, training, and continuous improvement of personalized treatment plans.

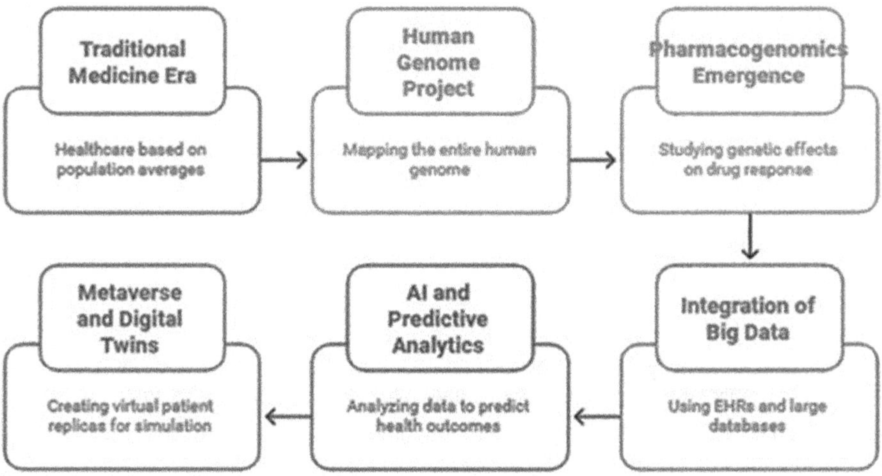

Figure 2: Evolution of personalized medicine.

As the price of genome sequencing decreased, it became more feasible to incorporate genetic and molecular evidence into clinical practice [9]. Personalized medicine was first used most effectively in oncology through tumor genetic profiling, which enabled oncologists to match identified mutations with specific studies. With time, the field of personalized medicine has increased to encompass cardiology, neurology, infectious diseases, and rare genetic disorders, allowing patients to have a specific diagnosis and treatment with a minimum of side effects. Personalized medicine has gained momentum over the past years with the intersection of big data analytics, artificial intelligence, wearable technology, and real-time health monitoring. Genomic, medical imaging, electronic health records, and wearable sensor data could not have been previously utilized, but now AI algorithms can discover underlying patterns in this data, helping to explain and predict an individual's health risks and trajectories. This shift toward proactive and predictive health management has transformed medicine into a more dynamic, personalized, and interactive practice.

In the modern world, the development of personalized medicine in a virtual environment represents the next stage in its evolution, linked to the metaverse. To this end, AI can be used to create digital twins of patients based on real-world health data to allow a response to treatment to be simulated before its actual implementation in the real world [10]. This innovation is sure to elevate precision care to the next level by combining insightful biological knowledge with an intuitive, real-time, and patient-friendly virtual interface. As technology advances, personalized medicine is poised to set new standards of care—ensuring that medical decisions are based on the individual needs of each person rather than relying on population averages.

3. AI's Role in Real-Time Personalized Health Monitoring

Artificial Intelligence is a transformative technology that can enable real-time customized monitoring of health situations, used to provide continuous, data-driven healthcare that is flexible to a specific individual's physiological and behavioral profiles [11]. Unlike traditional conservative health management, which relies on periodic health checks and fixed diagnostics, AI enables dynamic monitoring of vital health indicators and lifestyle habits through a combination of smart devices, wearable motion sensors, and biomedical IIoT. Such systems receive and send an ongoing flow of patient data, which is processed in real-time by AI algorithms that can identify aberrations, forewarn health hazards, and give patients, as well as care providers, advanced cautionary alerts.

Chronic disease management is one of the most significant examples of AI used in real-time monitoring [12]. In diseases like diabetes, hypertension, and heart disease, AI can continuously monitor the results, such as blood glucose levels, heart rate variability, or blood pressure, and recommend personalized adjustments in diet, medication, or exercise. Based on implementations of adaptive learning models, AI can become more accurate as it learns an individual's usual health patterns and then detects subtle changes that could indicate the start of an illness or a shift in their health condition. This increases the clinical outcomes, besides lowering the emergency hospitalizations and health expenditures.

Besides physical well-being, another benefit of AI is shaping mentality by recognizing emotions, analyzing voice, and recording behavior [13]. Virtual assistants based on AI and mobile apps can recognize depression, stress, or anxiety by observing speech patterns, sleep activities, or the user's communication behavior. The latter systems can offer real-time coping techniques, connect the beneficiary to virtual therapists, or signal care providers to take further action. This preventative method can close the mental healthcare access disparity, particularly in organizational or remote locations.

The real-time tracking AI feature is also optimized in virtual medical worlds, such as the metaverse. Within them, digital avatars and twins may be tracked alongside the user, and healthcare practitioners may test reactions to drugs or treatments virtually [14]. AI combines real-life information and virtual behavior to offer interaction and personal insights, including feedback, in a fun, natural-seeming display. Regardless of whether it is applied to telehealth systems, wearable systems, or even metaverse clinics, AI makes sure that individualized health management is not only responsive but also proactive and is indeed the foundation of precision health in the 21st century.

4. Digital Twins and Predictive Simulation Models

Digital twins, the concept of virtual representations of elements of the real world, have quickly become a popular idea in healthcare as a disruptive mechanism for personalized and predictive care. However, digital twins were initially developed for engineering and manufacturing but are now being repurposed to model human biology and patients' health profiles [15]. A healthcare digital twin integrates physiological (e.g., in real-time), health history, genetic, lifestyle, and sensor-based health indicators into a computationally enabled model of the patient, which relates to their body and the effects of their response to interventions. This computer model is constantly updated based on the actual patient, offering an excellent platform for simulating treatment and predicting health outcomes, as shown in Figure 3.

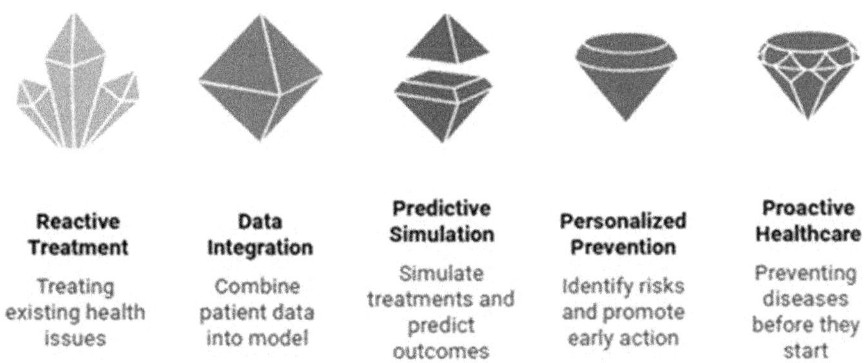

Figure 3: Digital twins in personalized medicine healthcare.

Another use of digital twins that proves to be among the most effective is predictive simulation. The combination of AI and machine learning allows clinicians to use digital replicas to model disease progression, test different treatment scenarios, and predict how a patient might respond to a specific drug before prescribing it in the real world [16]. A case in point in cardiology is that the effects of different surgical procedures or medication treatments can be tested using a digital twin of a patient's heart. The radiology field uses some simulation to virtually optimize the individual treatment plan (in oncology, this can include simulating the potential response of a tumor to cancer therapies (chemotherapy, immunotherapy, or radiation)). Such predictive models not only improve clinical decision-making but also decrease trial-and-error measures, enhance patient safety, and accelerate the recovery processes.

Besides customized treatment, digital twins come in handy whenever it comes to preventative care. Digital twins can detect early indicators of health-related risks or disease by modeling the possible outcomes of future experiences using current data trends. An example is a twin will be able to know of being prone to diabetes or hypertension several years in advance, thus changing his/her lifestyle or undergoing preventative treatment [17]. The nature of this proactive model of care is that it changes the focus from the process of treating a disease to the process of maintaining health.

Digital twins are even more real and experiential when directly integrated into healthcare ecosystems built in the metaverse. These patients and care providers can visualize and interact with their respective biological systems in 3D and receive insights in an abstract, gamified format. Along with AI-powered analytics, such platforms enable real-time simulation, collaboration during treatment planning, and customized education [18]. Digital twins will enhance the future of precision medicine and enter the next stage of development in which each and every decision will be tested remotely, validated, and optimized prior to being sent to the patient.

5. Virtual Avatars and Doctor-Patient Interaction in 3d Spaces

Digital or virtual images of interactive people are referred to as virtual avatars and are redefining the relationship between doctors and patients in immersive health settings. Regarding the metaverse and 3D virtual worlds, avatars serve as the primary means of presence and communication, enabling clinicians and patients to interact within a simulated environment that closely replicates clinical spaces [19]. Combined with the real-time data feed, AI support, and emotion-aware infrastructure, such virtual interactions are enriched with an emotion-enhancing experience, making them both medically informative and emotionally responsive.

Among the main benefits of avatar-based interaction is the elimination of distance [20]. Users in isolation or in underserved areas can log into the virtual clinics with their personal avatars and communicate with medical workers anywhere in the globe. The virtual clinics tend to copy the physical infrastructures, such as consultation rooms, lab facilities, and pharmacies, and present a complete package virtually. Within such an environment, the substance of avatars does not remain rigid: they can represent body postures, facial expressions, and sound projections, increasing the feeling of presence, familiarity, and confidence in doctor-patient interactions.

In addition, real-time biometric and health data can also be linked to virtual avatars, allowing the physician to observe the patient's vital signs, review their previous medical records, and examine their diagnostic images [21]. The built-in health assistants in the metaverse can also act as co-consultants and, in real-time, access evidence-based guidelines, perform risk assessments, and provide patient-specific insights to support the session and enhance interaction. Patients, in turn, can see their personal health-related conditions in interactive 3D models of organs, symptoms, or therapies, which will make them understand their conditions and follow professional recommendations more effectively.

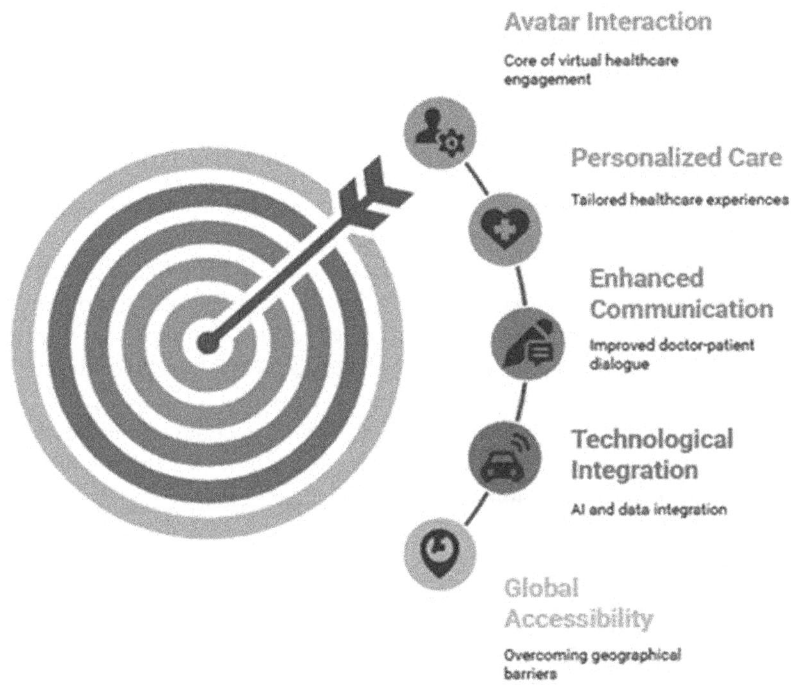

Figure 4: Virtual avatars in healthcare.

Personalized and adaptive education of patients in these 3D spaces is depicted in Figure 4. Avatars can engage in more interactive training sessions related to their condition-specific learning, such as breathing exercises for asthma or lifestyle simulations to manage diabetes [22]. Mental healthcare through the use of avatars is on the increase. Patients participating in therapy sessions with the support of anonymous or expressive avatars offer a safer environment to address sensitive issues as well as a greater ability for emotional expression.

As things are becoming more realistic in terms of virtual avatars and with the advent of AI, their use in telemedicine and telecare is going to increase. Avatar-based interaction changes the meaning of the interactions, as postoperative follow-up sessions or rehabilitation coaching, as well as interdisciplinary consultations, are no longer a team of health professionals and patients but rather consultations between avatars. This outcome is a more relational, involved, and inclusive care experience—a combination of the effectiveness of technology with the human aspect of personalized care.

6. AI-Powered Diagnosis and Therapeutic Planning

AIs are transforming the environment of diagnosis and treatment scheme planning, making clinical decisions much quicker, more accurate, and highly personal. Compared with the traditional diagnostic process which involves a predefined set of steps as well as the intuition of the clinician, an AI system has the capability of processing tremendous amounts of data of a highly heterogeneous nature (e.g., medical imaging, lab results, genomics, and lifestyle records) with the ability to establish patterns and correlations that might otherwise go unnoticed by human observation [23]. This helps in early diagnosis of diseases, including cancer, heart-related illnesses, and neurological disorders, among other rare genetic diseases, to a great extent.

The analysis of medical images is one of the most notable AI-based uses of AI in the field of diagnosis. X-rays, CT scans, MRIs, and histopathology slides can be processed and interpreted to an expert level through deep learning techniques [24]. These systems not only detect abnormalities like tumors and fractures, but also classify them based on severity and predict their progression. Lung nodules at an early stage can be detected more accurately with the help of AI algorithms in radiology and applied as early treatment. In dermatology, AI models help recognize melanoma automatically, provide faster care to patients, and reduce the workload for specialists.

In addition to being used in the diagnosis, AI can also be applied in therapeutic planning. AI can suggest the most effective treatment based on a patient's medical history, genetic makeup, other conditions, and response when these data are combined in large amounts. In oncology, as another example, AI-based platforms can examine tumor genomics and recommend the individual drug program or indicate immunotherapy [25]. Such systems continuously learn and evolve with new data, helping doctors choose the most effective treatments with the fewest side effects. Another type of AI implementation in acute care for clinical decision-making can be seen in intensive care, where AI helps optimize ventilator settings or manage polypharmacy in older patients.

In such virtual environments, clinicians may see 3D models of a patient's anatomy, carry out a virtual surgery, or even model drug effects in a matter of moments [26]. Virtual assistants and digital dashboards can provide real-time AI-generated insights to streamline care pathways and enable collaborative care between geographies. Such a combination of AI and immersive technology will guarantee a more understandable, more effective, and patient-oriented process of healthcare delivery. AI-implemented diagnosis and therapeutic planning can not only increase the capacity of health practitioners but also bring democratization of expert-level care. Once these tools are continually integrated with data and approved by regulatory agencies, they will become important aspects of contemporary, precision-based medicine, as they provide a future in which diagnosing is done faster, medicines are smarter, and patient outcomes are orders of magnitude better.

7. Virtual Pharmacies and Precision Drug Delivery

Virtual pharmacies are becoming one of the most important innovations in the digital healthcare sector, both in the metaverse and the telemedicine development environment. Digital pharmacies work in the same manner as conventional ones, but online, where the patient can access prescription services, drug advice, and medications through avatar-fueled interfaces and automated systems [27, 28]. The first is that patients in virtual settings can connect with licensed pharmacists through avatars, allowing them to discuss their medication plans and get immediate answers about drug interactions, regimen timing, and side effects—all from the comfort of their home.

7.1 Digital Access and Convenience

It is in the form of virtual pharmacies that patients can access medications and advice on pharmaceuticals at any time and from anywhere, in the comfort of their homes. Via web portals, apps, or metaverse experiences, users may order a prescription, replenish medications, and discuss pharmaceuticals with a pharmacist via an avatar or chatbot. This is especially helpful for older adults, rural patients, or those with mobility issues.

7.2 Avatar-Based Consultations

Patients engage with a pharmacist through digital avatars present in immersive virtual spaces that mimic body language and facial expressions [29]. Such interactions are the approximations of real visits to pharmacies, which makes the consultations more personal and involving. In the visually rich world, patients can ask questions, discuss their prescriptions, and get detailed information on how the dosage is applied, possible side effects, and drug interactions.

7.3 AI Integration and Smart Recommendations

Artificial intelligence is also extensively used in virtual pharmacies, where all health records, medication history, and genetic information of patients are analyzed to make personalized recommendations. For example, a patient might be allergic to a certain medication, and the AI system would identify this and suggest alternatives. This is real-time data-based assistance that can reduce the number of mismatched prescriptions and enhance patient treatment.

7.4 Secure E-Prescriptions and Blockchain Verification

To address these challenges, such sites tend to employ blockchain technology in issuing and confirming electronic prescriptions, so that the prescription process is safe, traceable, and tamperproof. Patients will have the assurance that their prescriptions via mobile devices are genuine, and only specified personnel will access them, and the chances of fraud are reduced, thus enhancing compliance [30].

7.5 Automated Logistics and Delivery Systems

Once the prescription is filled virtually, the medication can be delivered directly to the patient's door using automated delivery systems, such as drones or smart lockers. The overall capacity of this industry, where prescribers handle prescription delivery, makes the virtual pharmacy a highly efficient and scalable model within the modern healthcare system.

7.6 Genomic-Based Customization

Precision drug delivery relies on studying the unique genetic makeup to understand how an individual patient metabolizes and responds to certain drugs [31]. The information provided by this pharmacogenomic information assists in identifying the correct medication and dose, decreasing the chances of adverse drug response and maximizing therapeutic success.

7.7 AI-Powered Treatment Planning

Artificial intelligence algorithms are trained to process a combination of patients' characteristics, such as genomics, age, weight, lifestyle, and medical history, to produce the optimal drug delivery plans. These AI models continue to learn and optimize their recommendations based on patient outcomes, and allow a dynamic and flexible method of treatment.

7.8 Digital Twin Simulations

Prior to a drug being administered, clinicians can use a patient's digital twin, a virtual model that is formed using the actual health data that a patient possesses, to actually simulate how their body will react. This forecasting ability enables healthcare professionals to trial various drugs or doses virtually, thus limiting trial-and-error interventions and increasing the safety level.

7.9 Targeted Delivery Technologies

New technologies like nanomedicine, microchips, and smart pills are being employed to take the drugs directly to the desired position in the body (e.g., a tumor or infected part). These are more effective and have fewer systemic effects, which can be called a breakthrough in precision medicine.

7.10 Real-Time Monitoring and Feedback

IoT-based devices and sensors that can be worn can monitor patients receiving precision drug therapy in real time. Holter or any other data on heart rate, blood pressure, glucose levels, or organ function can be fed back to clinicians and AI systems and properly adjusted so that, regardless of circumstances, the best results are achieved.

The particular feature of virtual pharmacies within a metaphorical healthcare ecosystem is that they are connected to real-time health data and customized treatment plans. AI-powered systems analyze a patient's entire medical history, including their genomic makeup, allergies, and medications they have taken, to automatically suggest or confirm that a specific medicine is being prescribed based on the individual's biological profile. This is the essence of precision drug delivery: ensuring the right drug is used at the right time, in the right amount, for the right person [32]. These individualized regimens reduce adverse drug reactions and enhance the therapeutic outcome, particularly with patients having chronic diseases or complex multiple diseases.

Moreover, blockchain technology and smart contracts will continue to be integrated into virtual pharmacies to guarantee safe, transparent, and auditable tracking of prescriptions. Patients can receive a digital prescription, which is authenticated, tamper-proof, and traceable through decentralization, thus minimizing potential prescription fraud or medication abuse. This also involves some logistics platforms using drones or automated systems to physically deliver drugs ordered in this virtual space, thus completing the cycle of virtual consultation, prescription, and physical access to the medication.

More advanced systems also use virtual pharmacies to simulate drug efficacy through the use of digital twins. A digital twin of a patient can predetermine how his or her body will behave when being exposed to a specific drug or a specific dose. Such an ability becomes essential when it is utilized in experimental drugs, complex pharma genomic reactions, and individual oncology drugs. Virtual pharmacies are a combination of immersive technology, real-time analytics, and predictive simulation, and change the way drugs are prescribed, ordered, or delivered, making delivery both safer, smarter, and more efficient.

8. Mental Health and Behavioral Modeling in Virtual Spaces

The process of including mental health care in the virtual and immersive environment is opening new horizons in diagnosis, therapy, and continuous monitoring of behavior. In virtual space, patients will be able to access therapy sessions, self-help interventions, and emotional wellness programs with the help of avatars, interactive environments, and with the assistance of AI-based support systems [33]. Such platforms grant not only accessibility and confidentiality but also enable citizens to communicate in a way that would not be available in such traditional, in-person therapy. It is particularly useful for individuals with social anxiety and PTSD or depression, or individuals in a geographically isolated world with little or no access to mental health experts.

This digital mental health experience becomes more powerful through the use of AI and machine learning in behavioral modeling that continuously analyzes the user based on their actions, speech, facial expressions, and interaction history. Passive data can also be collected during sessions on a virtual platform, including voice tone, response delays, eye-tracking, and avatar behavioral patterns; this should measure emotional states, stress levels, and intellectual interest. [34]. Such insights also help therapists better understand a patient's mental health development and create more personalized, solution-focused treatment plans. Indicators of depressive relapse or increasing anxiety may also be observed early on, such as the example when there are subtle signs of the same even before they are evident even to the patient, as shown in Table 1.

More sophisticated applications include AI-based conversational agents (also known as virtual therapists) being incorporated within the metaverse area spaces so that they can provide mental health assistance 24/7. These agents use natural language processing (NLP) and emotional computing to interact with users through conversation, providing cognitive behavioral therapy (CBT) codes and mindfulness, along with stress-reduction techniques. These agents have fully immersive and calming environments (including nature scenes or guided meditation rooms) in which users can spend time and reap the therapeutic benefits of such experiences, promoting emotional resilience.

Additionally, behavioral modeling can be done collaboratively in virtual spaces, such as having family members, caregivers, or support group members participate in a session or a simulated environment to enhance social skills, emotional regulation, or coping strategies. It is downright useful for those with an autism spectrum disorder (ASD), ADHD, or social phobias. Individualized simulations can help patients practice real-life interactions, such as job interviews or conflict-resolution scenarios, in a safer, controlled environment to improve their ability to interact in the real world [35]. To sum things up, the use of virtual spaces enabled by AI and behavioral modeling options in design essentially offers a transformational method of mental healthcare, helping to make it more accessible, personalized, and proactive. With such systems under development, there is the possibility of not just treating mental illness but also the possibility of enhancing holistic mental well-being among different people.

Nonetheless, it is in the integration of such technologies that thorny ethical, legal, and regulatory issues become incorporated, which should be closely managed. The subjects of data privacy, transparency of algorithms, and fair access must also be taken into account to ensure that the future of healthcare is not only smart but also non-discriminative and reliable. Using the example of our current standing on the edge of this digital healthcare shift, the unmatched potential of AIs, personalized medicine, and virtual platforms within it is obvious, as we can expect it to bring improved health outcomes, a higher level of patient experience, and a new paradigm of what modern medicine is capable of achieving.

Table 1: Behavioral Modeling in Virtual Spaces

Component	Description	Key Benefits
Virtual Therapy Sessions	Avatars and interactive environments allow patients to attend mental health sessions in immersive virtual settings.	Accessible, private, and reduces stigma; ideal for individuals with PTSD, depression, or social anxiety.
AI-Based Behavioral Modeling	Real-time analysis of speech, behavior, facial expressions, and interaction history through machine learning.	Enables early detection of emotional distress, relapse prediction, and customized therapy planning.
Passive Data Collection	Collects tone, speech delay, eye movement, and avatar behavior during virtual sessions without active input.	Helps assess emotional state, stress levels, and cognitive engagement subtly and continuously.
Conversational AI Agents	Virtual therapists using NLP and emotional computing to conduct CBT, mindfulness training, and emotional support.	24/7 mental health assistance; provides therapy on demand in calming, immersive environments.
Immersive Wellness Environments	Virtual natural landscapes, meditation rooms, and calming scenes are integrated into therapy platforms.	Enhances emotional resilience and supports mental recovery through environmental simulation.
Collaborative Behavioral Modeling	Involves family, caregivers, or peer groups in therapeutic simulations and skill-building sessions.	Improves emotional regulation, social skills, and coping, especially useful for ASD, ADHD, and phobias.
Simulated Real-Life Scenarios	Virtual rehearsals for job interviews, conflict resolution, or social interaction simulations tailored to individual needs.	Boosts confidence and real-world functionality in a safe, supportive environment.
AI-Enhanced Personalization	Uses aggregated behavioral data to customize treatment paths dynamically based on individual patient needs and progress.	Provides highly personalized care pathways; improves therapy effectiveness and engagement.
Holistic Mental Wellness Design	Combines therapy, behavioral training, AI insights, and virtual spaces for a complete mental wellness ecosystem.	Enables prevention, treatment, and long-term emotional well-being at scale.

9. Ethical, Legal, and Regulatory Challenges

9.1 Ethical Challenges

The use of AI and virtual environments in personalized healthcare raises important ethical issues, particularly regarding patient autonomy, consent, and digital equity. Immersive environments, such as the metaverse, where patients interact with virtual avatars, AI agents, and digital twins, challenge the boundaries of informed consent. Some patients might not be aware of the whole extent of the utility of their data as it is used, run, or simulated through virtual reality settings [36]. Moreover, there are ethical questions concerning the use of AI in making a diagnosis or treatment suggestions (and, more particularly, where they override or shape human clinical assessment). Another pressing challenge is the digital divide, the uneven access to digital infrastructure, devices, or skills that could exclude vulnerable groups from accessing advanced virtual healthcare models.

9.2 Legal Challenges

The world of technology constantly changes, and legal regulation still lags; the extremely fast development of AI-based virtual healthcare has yielded a high number of legal uncertainties. The second issue is liability attribution: if an AI system or virtual assistant misdiagnoses or issues a faulty prescription, it's unclear who would be responsible—the software developer, the healthcare provider, or the platform operator. Additionally, legal responsibility becomes complex due to factors such as ownership of intellectual property generated by AI insights in medical applications, cross-border transfer of medical services, and the location of entities in the metaverse. The issue of applying law across national borders arises when virtual consultations happen worldwide, and a patient in one country is treated by a virtual doctor in another.

9.3 Regulatory Challenges

At the regulatory level, virtual healthcare platforms and AI tools must comply with healthcare requirements and data regulations, although existing rules often lack consistency and are somewhat incompatible with an immersive, borderless online environment. Regulatory agencies such as the FDA, EMA, and CDSCO have begun working on standards to regulate medical devices and software based on AI, but the introduction of virtual reality, digital twins, and avatar-based communication can complicate the situation. The requirements of data security, AI validation, and the standardization of virtual consultation will require novel regulatory measures. Furthermore, health-related sensitive information is highly likely to be collected and processed in real-time in virtual worlds, increasing the risk of non-compliance with data privacy regulations like GDPR or HIPAA when virtual worlds cross jurisdiction boundaries.

10. Conclusion

The emerging technology where AI, specialized medicine, and immersive virtual reality come together is transforming the landscape of the medical industry. The futuristic concept of digitized medicine becomes a tangible reality when artificial intelligence-based diagnostics, teleconsultations, and precision treatments are seamlessly integrated within virtual ecosystems. With the availability of real-time data, intelligent algorithms, and an interactive user interface, the healthcare profession can take hyper-personalized care to the next level, making it proactive, predictive, and participatory, and at the core of this is the paradigm shift from treating people in a generalized manner to an individualized approach to wellness. The metaverse and other virtual worlds offer a novel and revolutionary framework to reconsider the patient's experiences with the healthcare system in a new way. These innovations are creating a healthcare ecosystem that is more surgical with digital twins that model treatment reactions, avatars that assist with mental health treatment, and virtual pharmacies to personalize medication distribution. Notably, AI serves as the intelligent foundation of such a system, which makes it possible to deploy perpetual surveillance and real-time decision support, along with flexible learning that grows along with the individual profile of a patient.

References

1. Adil, M., Song, H., Khan, M. K., Mastorakis, S., Farouk, A., and Jin, Z. (2025). Metaverse in health care: Security challenges and pathways for future research. *IEEE Systems, Man, and Cybernetics Magazine*, 11(1), 95–106.
2. Vashishth, T. K., Sharma, V., Sharma, K. K., Kumar, B., Chaudhary, S., and Panwar, R. (2025). Data-driven healthcare: Leveraging AoT and metaverse for better diagnosis. In *Leveraging Metaverse and Analytics of Things (AoT) in Medical Systems* (pp. 41–60). Academic Press.
3. Sujatha, R., Sarlinraj, M., Mohanraj, S., and Subash, T. (2025). Integration of metaverse and AoT into the healthcare system. In: *Leveraging Metaverse and Analytics of Things (AoT) in Medical Systems* (pp. 15–39). Academic Press.
4. Ashwini, A., Shamini, G. I., Prathaban, B. P., and Balasubramaniam, S. (2025). MultiSense diagnosis: Navigating disease diagnosis with metaverse multimodal interaction. In: *Applying Metaverse Technologies to Human-Computer Interaction for Healthcare* (pp. 235–253). Auerbach Publications.
5. Yingngam, B., Khumsikiew, J., and Netthong, R. (2025). Digital twins for telemedicine and personalized medicine. In: *Digital Twins for Smart Cities and Villages* (pp. 295–325). Elsevier.
6. Nakayama, K., Ishibashi, T., Ishikawa, M., and Kyo, S. (2025). Recent clinical and molecular findings in low-grade serous ovarian carcinoma including prospects for personalized medicine using cancer organoids. *Academia Oncology*, 2(1).

7. Guo, Y., Waisberg, E., Ong, J., Kumar, R., and Lee, A. G. (2025). A future of personalized medicine for astronauts: Considering genetic variability and biologic sex-based differences in space medicine. *Acta Astronautica*, 228, 527–531.
8. Yadav, S., and Kaur, J. (2025). Personalized communication: AI-driven solutions for enhanced collaboration. In: *Convergence of Antenna Technologies, Electronics, and AI* (pp. 269–294). IGI Global.
9. Ozobu, C. O., Adikwu, F. E., Cynthia, O. O., Onyeke, F. O., and Nwulu, E. O. (2025). Developing an AI-powered occupational health surveillance system for real-time detection and management of workplace health hazards. *World Journal of Innovation and Modern Technology*, 9(1), 156–185.
10. Thirupathi, L., Kaashipaka, V., Dhanaraju, M., and Katakam, V. (2025). AI and IoT in mental health care: From digital diagnostics to personalized, continuous support. In: *Intelligent Systems and IoT Applications in Clinical Health* (pp. 271–294). IGI Global.
11. Ashwini, A., Kavitha, V., Balasubramaniam, S., and Kadry, S. (2025). MetaHealth: Transforming healthcare through AI integration. *Applying Metaverse Technologies to Human-Computer Interaction for Healthcare*, 121.
12. Recharla, M., Chakilam, C., Kannan, S., Nuka, S. T., and Suura, S. R. (2025). Harnessing AI and machine learning for precision medicine: Advancements in genomic research, disease detection, and personalized healthcare. *American Journal of Psychiatric Rehabilitation*, 28(1), 112–123.
13. Li, X., Loscalzo, J., Mahmud, A. F., Aly, D. M., Rzhetsky, A., Zitnik, M., and Benson, M. (2025). Digital twins as global learning health and disease models for preventive and personalized medicine. *Genome Medicine*, 17(1), 11.
14. Basaure, V. (2025). Models in medicine: The digital twin for health. *Serie Selección de Textos*, 10, 3–16.
15. Faisal, S. M., Ishrat, M., and Khan, W. (2025). Digital twins in healthcare: Revolutionizing patient care and medical operations. In: *Digital Twins for Smart Cities and Urban Planning* (pp. 69–89). CRC Press.
16. Vengathattil, S. (2025). Advancing healthcare systems with generative AI-driven digital twins. *International Journal of Innovative Science and Research Technology*, 10(4), 1678–1688.
17. Vyas, S., Gupta, S., and Tyagi, A. (2025). Metaverse and its applications. In: *Meta-Health: Understanding Metaverse for Healthcare* (pp. 1–25). Singapore: Springer Nature Singapore.
18. Morone, G., Ciancarelli, I., Calabrò, R. S., Cerasa, A., Iosa, M., and Gimigliano, F. (2025). MetaRehabVerse: The great opportunity to put the person's functioning and participation at the center of healthcare. *Neurorehabilitation and Neural Repair*, 39(3), 241–255.
19. Sharma, A. (2025). Introduction to metaverse for healthcare. *Metaverse Technologies, Security and Applications for Healthcare*, 1-35.
20. Jauniaux, B., Burke, J., and Harji, D. (2025). Healthcare metaverse in surgery: Scoping review. *BJS Open*, 9(2), zrae155.
21. Panahi, O., and Panahi, U. (2025). AI-powered IoT: Transforming diagnostics and treatment planning in oral implantology. *J Adv Artif Intell Mach Learn*, 1(1), 1–4.
22. Ajayi, R. (2025). AI-powered innovations for managing complex mental health conditions and addiction treatments. *Int Res J Modern Eng Technol Sci*, 7(1), 87.

23. Alavinejad, M., Shirzad, M., Javid-Naderi, M. J., Rahdar, A., Fathi-Karkan, S., and Pandey, S. (2025). Smart nanomedicines powered by artificial intelligence: A breakthrough in lung cancer diagnosis and treatment. *Medical Oncology*, 42(5), 134.
24. Al-Raeei, M. (2025). The role of artificial intelligence in enhancing breast disease management: Early detection and prognostic innovations. *Archives of Medicine and Health Sciences*, 10-4103.
25. Bernatoniene, J., Plieskis, M., and Petrikonis, K. (2025). Pharmaceutical 3D printing technology integrating nanomaterials and nanodevices for precision neurological therapies. *Pharmaceutics*, 17(3), 352.
26. Sakalli, İ. (2025). Integral role of physics in advancing pharmacy education and research. *EMU Journal of Pharmaceutical Sciences*, 7(3), 122–132.
27. El-Tanani, M., Satyam, S. M., Rabbani, S. A., El-Tanani, Y., Aljabali, A. A., Al Faouri, I., and Rehman, A. (2025). Revolutionizing drug delivery: The impact of advanced materials science and technology on precision medicine. *Pharmaceutics*, 17(3), 375.
28. Kim, J. Y., Marshall, V. D., Rowell, B., Chen, Q., Zheng, Y., Lee, J. D., and Yang, X. J. (2025). The effects of presenting AI uncertainty information on pharmacists' trust in automated pill recognition technology: Exploratory mixed subjects study. *JMIR Human Factors*, 12, e60273.
29. Torous, J., Linardon, J., Goldberg, S. B., Sun, S., Bell, I., Nicholas, J. and Firth, J. (2025). The evolving field of digital mental health: Current evidence and implementation issues for smartphone apps, generative artificial intelligence, and virtual reality. *World Psychiatry*, 24(2), 156–174.
30. Panok, V., Shevchenko, A., Nazar, M. M., Starkov, D., Mescheryakov, D. S., and Shevtsov, A. (2025). Methodological principles of educational and psychological chatbot development. *Information Technologies and Learning Tools*, 2(106), 76–93.
31. Wang, Y., Wang, L., and Siau, K. L. (2025). Human-centered interaction in virtual worlds: A new era of generative artificial intelligence and metaverse. *International Journal of Human–Computer Interaction*, 41(2), 1459–1501.
32. Sokołowska, E., Sokołowska, B., Chrapusta, S. J., and Sulejczak, D. (2025). Virtual environments as a novel and promising approach in (neuro) diagnosis and (neuro) therapy: A perspective on the example of autism spectrum disorder. *Frontiers in Neuroscience*, 18, 1461142.
33. Singh, R. R., Kumar, S., Pandey, A., Tripathi, S. K., Yadav, P. K., and Pathak, V. (2025). The role of the metaverse in emergency medicine and its legal implications: A systematic review. *Toxicology*, 19(1).
34. Pasa, B., Bernes, A., Gaggioli, A., Tuccari, E., Zollo, F., Vulpiani, G., and Cerasa, A. (2025). LawVerse: The legal framework for clinical metaverse content. *Journal of Medical Extended Reality*, 2(1), 13–19.
35. Goswami, S. A., Patel, K. C., Dave, S. A., Patel, K. D., & Darji, D. A. (2025). Metaverse and virtual healthcare opportunities and challenges. *Defending the Metaverse*, 304–318.
36. Bansal, D., and Bhattacharya, N. (2025). Metaverse in healthcare: Potential applications and challenges. *Exploring the Metaverse*, 31–43.

CHAPTER

6

Smart Scalpel: The Triple Revolution Transforming Precision Surgery in Metaverse Healthcare Ecosystems

Ashwini A.[1*], Jeya S. Shemona[2], Balasubramaniam S.[3] and Seifedine Kadry[4]

[1] Department of Electronics and Communication Engineering, Vel Tech Rangarajan Dr. Sagunthala R&D Institute of Science and Technology, Avadi, Chennai, Tamil Nadu, India

[2] Department of Electronics and Communication Engineering, Sree Sakthi Engineering College (autonomous), Karamadai, India

[3] School of Computer Science and Engineering, Kerala University of Digital Sciences, Innovation and Technology (Formerly IIITM-K), Digital University Kerala, Thiruvananthapuram, Kerala, India

[4] Department of Computer Science and Mathematics, Lebanese American University, Beirut, Lebanon

With the advancement of the Smart Scalpel, precision surgery is transforming due to the collaboration of AI, robotics, and virtual environments. Because of this triple revolution, surgeons now achieve superior accuracy, are given on-demand support for decisions, and human mistakes become less likely because of AI. AI and robotics enable precise control at the microscopic level, and AI tools also forecast the outcomes of procedures and assist the doctor's actions based on each patient's needs. Merging these technologies has transformed traditional operating rooms into intelligent spaces that enhance surgical accuracy and patient safety. The main part of this change is bringing precision surgery into systems that use virtual reality for healthcare. With these virtual systems, surgeons have access to simulated surgeries, can practice in groups, and perform remote operations using virtual copies of the patients. Surgeons can practice difficult surgeries in virtual environments that closely resemble real tissues and organs because of extended reality (XR) and haptic feedback systems. This technology helps surgeons improve their skills and provides access to

*Corresponding author: a.ashwinivel@gmail.com

DOI: 10.1201/9781003679370-6

high-quality care for people who might not receive it otherwise, regardless of where they live or their income. The smart scalpel is important beyond surgery, supporting a patient-centered approach to healthcare. AI monitors patients after surgery, rehabilitation takes place virtually, and staying engaged with patients in the metaverse means they do not stop receiving care. Information from surgical procedures is used to update AI systems, which help improve surgery techniques. By developing interoperability and personalizing healthcare, integrating smart surgical tools, AI, and meta-verse technology enables greater safety, intelligence, and accessibility in precision surgery everywhere.

1. Introduction to Smart Scalpel and Triple Revolution

Smart robotics has brought lasting changes to various fields, especially healthcare, where accuracy, efficiency, and adjustability are most important. The term "Scalpel" stands for the transformation of surgical tools from simple hand tools to complex machines controlled by robots that require less help from surgeons [1]. This type of system uses sensors, actuators, and artificial intelligence (AI) to manage complex tasks flawlessly. Robot technology ensures that surgeons achieve more accurate results, make surgeries less invasive, and help patients recover speedily.

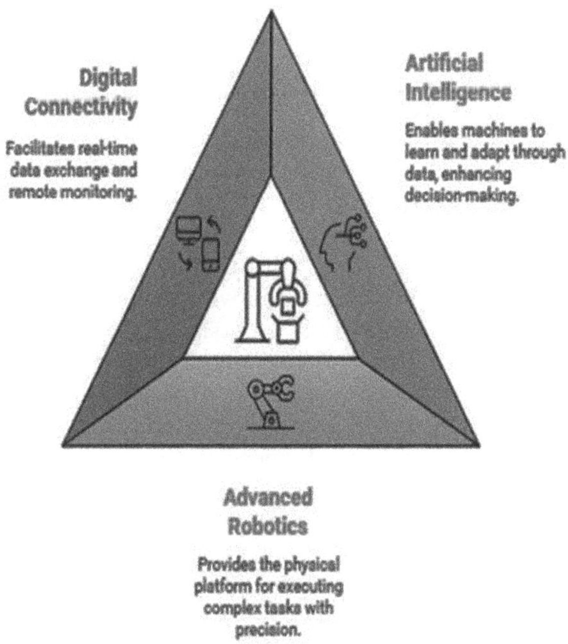

Figure 1: Foundation of smart robotics.

This transformation occurs mostly because of the Triple Revolution, which combines Artificial Intelligence, Advanced Robotics, and Digital Connectivity, as shown in Figure 1. Machines use AI technology to study data, which supports predicting outcomes and managing tasks without human direction. Robotics allows machines to carry out difficult tasks and, thanks to new technology like 5G, cloud computing, and IoT, we can now share data in real time, monitor situations remotely, and even conduct surgeries remotely [2]. All three are transforming the medical world, enabling procedures to use data, be carried out remotely, and rely less on where they happen or who carries them out.

Besides healthcare, smart robots are used in manufacturing, the military, space activities, and to help people in daily life. Even so, the "Scalpel and Triple Revolution" concept shows that these technologies are completely revolutionizing critical systems, because the consequences of any error are especially severe. There are many advantages, but ethical problems, worries about data privacy, system reliability issues, and the requirement for effective regulations are still present. However, having robots assist with critical systems takes us a step closer to having intelligent machines help humans face, optimize, and solve difficult problems together [3].

2. The Rise of Precision Medicine in Virtual Healthcare Ecosystems

Healthcare can be tailored to each person using precision medicine, which studies a person's genes, daily habits, the environment they live in, and medical history. Doctors in conventional medicine use the same practices for many patients, but precision medicine looks for treatments that are right for each individual and are less likely to have unwanted effects [4]. Because of genomic, bioinformatics, and machine learning technologies, clinicians are now better able to identify who stands at risk of disease, manage its ongoing course, and direct appropriate therapies, as in Figure 2.

Virtual healthcare is speeding up this transformation by introducing telemedicine platforms, devices people can wear, online health records, and AI for helping with decisions. They make it possible for patient health data to be checked in real time, so that problems can be caught and managed early. By using virtual platforms, patients can reach healthcare professionals more easily, require fewer hospital visits, and get medical advice and follow-up care without leaving home [5]. This makes it easier and cheaper for laboratories, and it ensures that precise treatment plans can be delivered quickly to many patients.

With the progress of healthcare, more benefits are being discovered from the relationship between big data and precision healthcare. Algorithms for AI can process a variety of health data. For example, patients' past medical records, DNA sequences, and lifestyle data, to discover useful patterns and suggest the most appropriate treatment. Not only does this boost how decisions are made, but it also motivates researchers and innovators. Yet, using precision medicine on

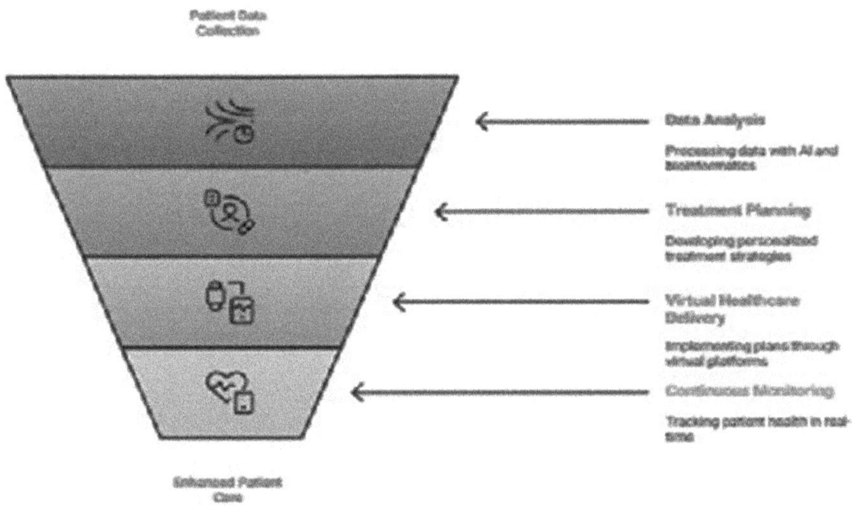

Figure 2: Precision medicine in virtual healthcare.

the internet creates serious problems [6]. For example, issues with data security, asking for patients' permission, making sure everyone is digitally capable, and ensuring equal access. Getting past these problems helps ensure that precision medicine in digital healthcare becomes inclusive, personalized, and more effective for everyone.

3. Artificial Intelligence and Machine Learning in Surgical Outcome Prediction

When the metaverse, artificial intelligence (AI), and machine learning (ML) come together, it could bring major changes to how surgical planning, procedures, and outcomes are handled. Since it is a virtual, interactive, and immersive digital environment, the metaverse shows promise for preoperative simulation, surgical education, and involving patients. Combining AI and ML with digital surgery brings about extremely accurate, information-driven models meant for surgeons, who can test surgeries, predict the outcomes, and gauge risks without harming a patient [7]. From real-time data and health records, these virtual patients are built, and in them, surgeons can practice and optimize their procedures using predictions, as in Figure 3.

Simulations are dependent on the use of artificial intelligence and machine learning. With massive patient data, including scans, pathological information, genes, and past operation outcomes, ML tools provide accurate information about complications, the time needed for recovery, and the possible outcome of surgeries. In the metaverse setup, such predictions are presented visually, allowing surgeons and their teams to see and explore what different decisions might result

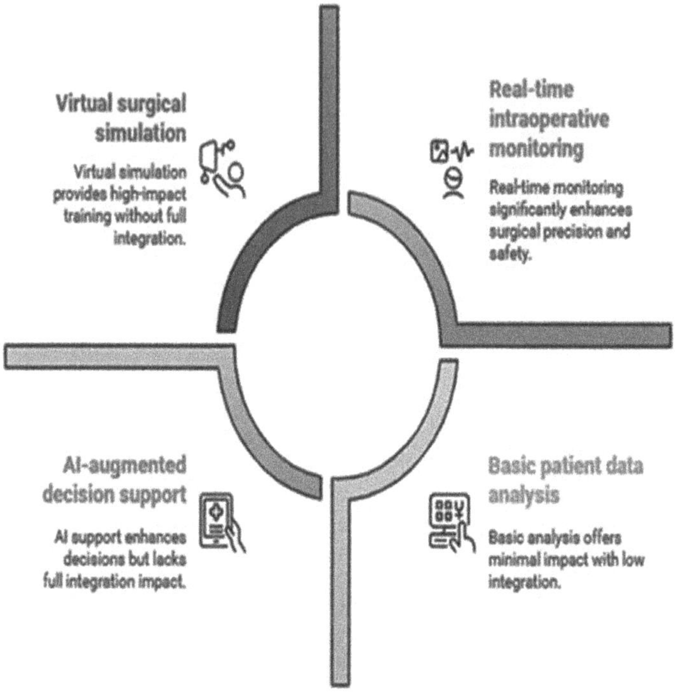

Figure 3: AI and ML in surgical prediction.

in. It supports a new way of caring for patients by encouraging virtual discussions and demonstrations that help patients and doctors choose appropriate treatment.

3.1 Virtual Surgical Simulation and Digital Twins

Using 3D modeling and patient records (MRI, CT scans, EHRs) in the metaverse, it is possible to build highly accurate digital copies of a patient's body. Surgeons practice surgical techniques in the virtual environment by experiencing and observing how surgeries are done from inside the body [8]. Using historical and patient data, AI and machine learning help to predict the amount of blood that might be lost, the chances of complications, and the possible success of various surgical approaches. Simulation games help guide decisions about the actual surgery by sharing useful data first.

3.2 Predictive Analytics for Risk Assessment

Machine learning systems analyze large datasets from previous surgeries, patient details, and outcomes afterwards. They try to predict post-surgical problems by examining a patient's risk factors, such as infections after an operation. In the metaverse, predictions can be displayed visually, allowing surgeons and healthcare teams to experiment with various scenarios, evaluate different treatment options, and make more informed decisions. It aids in personalizing care based on what is predicted about a patient's individual risk profile.

3.3 AI-Augmented Decision Support Systems

With AI, doctors can receive advice during or before surgery, including the best approach, essential tools, and potential challenges. With the metaverse, these systems give surgeons a chance to use interactive and immersive controls and get tips, warnings, and instructions on a 3D platform. It simplifies planning and procedures, mainly for rare or risky cases, and aids decision-making with data and models in real time.

3.4 Real-Time Intraoperative Monitoring

AI and ML models run on real-time information coming from tools, robots, cameras, and the vital signs of the patient during surgery. The system's findings can be used in augmented reality (AR) within the metaverse, helping surgeons identify unexpected changes like abnormal bleeding or decreased oxygen levels. When surgeons get this real-time support, they can make quick changes that improve the patient's safety and the outcome of the procedure [9]. The way the data is displayed makes sure the key data can be viewed easily and does not get in the surgeon's way.

3.5 Immersive Surgical Training and Skill Assessment

Traditional surgical training is being improved by bringing in virtual operating rooms as well. By using simulations, doctors can practice in simulated surgeries and get ideas on how to improve from AI. Using analysis of movements, thinking, and speed, ML models decide on proficiency and point out what areas should be worked on. Arranging training this way makes learning paths fit the students' needs, helps them master skills results and avoids using bodies or dangerous live training.

3.6 Postoperative Recovery Monitoring and Prediction

Most patients after surgery are provided with devices that measure their heart rate, temperature, and how much they move. Computers continuously analyze data to forecast issues like infections or delays in injury healing. The combination of the metaverse with healthcare means patients can use virtual spaces, communicate with doctors, see improvement, and get advice on rehabilitation from AI. Virtual check-ins encourage patients to participate and allow doctors to act early, which cuts down on hospital readmissions and helps patients heal faster [10].

Additionally, collaboration between AI mentors and real-time guidance in the metaverse can assist with learning new procedures and providing help during operations. Those learning surgery can try complex procedures in simulation, and experienced doctors can perfect their skills using AI-assisted future results. On the other hand, using many tools can still be challenging due to inconsistent methods for joining and sharing data, security risks online, and the fact that not everyone can access these web applications. Issues involving data privacy, getting proper consent in online spaces, and fairness in algorithms should also be considered. Nevertheless, the connection between the metaverse, AI, and ML marks a big change, making surgery safer, smarter, and more predictable.

4. Real-Time AI Guidance During Surgery

Integrating AI into a surgeon's virtual environment during procedures is the next major step toward smart healthcare. This way, the metaverse offers an interactive and real-time platform where AI helps by visualizing and analyzing data from the surgery, for improved accuracy in decision-making [11]. Surgical teams can understand current and potentially developing issues, work with actual visualizations of the patient's organs, and get guidance from the system as needed, all during the surgery.

Inside the metaverse surgical suite, AI units are gathering and processing data coming from tools such as intraoperative MRIs, CT scans, robots, and patient sensors. Next, it overlays highlights that identify tumors, blood vessels, or cutting locations, and this is projected into the surgeon's line of sight through either headsets or smart displays. They are always displaying the latest and most relevant images as steps are performed in the surgery. An example of this is when the AI system spots a major artery or discovers unusual tissue, it immediately informs the surgeon. This helps prevent mistakes. Medical specialists from other parts of the world joining the surgery online can provide helpful advice or second opinions in real-time.

Also, real-time guidance from AI in the metaverse makes training and teamwork easier. Soon, surgical trainees will be able to witness live cases on a screen and follow AI-guided interpretation of what happens as it takes place. In the metaverse, surgeons can save and replay their operations, examine the choices they have made, and improve their skills with the help of AI metrics [12]. Latency, concerns about cybersecurity, partnership with hospital systems, and government permission are some of the obstacles this technology deals with. Once these hurdles are addressed, metaverse AI assistance during operations will greatly improve how surgeries are conducted in terms of intelligence, cooperation, and accuracy.

5. Benefits of Robotic Surgery: Precision, Stability, and Reduced Fatigue

Metaverse AI robotic surgery improves accuracy in surgery by uniting virtual reality and advanced AI. Surgeons use tools in the metaverse to visualize patient organs in three dimensions and special overlays from AI point out important structures such as blood vessels, nerves, and tumors. Such practical instructions allow surgeons to perform very fine actions safely and without any risk to nearby healthy tissues. The surgeon directs the robotic arms, which perform precise and steady actions that are very helpful for surgeons doing minimally invasive surgeries. Combining these tools gives doctors better results in surgery, reduces risks for patients, and helps clients recover faster [13].

Unmatched Precision

Robotic surgery provides the highest level of precision, by allowing surgeons to use advanced 3D visuals and AI-supported maps of body organs, which help them identify important sites and perform careful, detailed procedures that minimize damage to healthy tissues.

Tremor-Free Movements

With robotic aid, natural hand movements are eliminated, enabling the surgeon to handle instruments more evenly and with greater control, which is key for small and delicate surgeries.

Real-Time Predictive Feedback

While performing surgery, AI observes the data to detect possible difficulties and advises surgeons on how to prevent risks and safeguard patients.

Enhanced Dexterity

Robotic arms can move more than human wrists; surgeons are able to reach difficult body areas with confidence [14].

Compensation for Patient Movement

AI technology watches over the patient during surgery and changes the position of instruments so they do not move and stay stable the whole time.

Ergonomic Operating Environment

Surgeons use ergonomic devices in the metaverse. They can handle procedures for a longer time, without feeling tired or strained.

Reduced Cognitive Load

AI helps complete routine jobs, which lowers the mental stress for surgeons and lets them pay more attention to challenging and key parts of surgery.

Improved Reaction Times

Due to less tiredness and mental stress, surgeons can react more swiftly and attentively to any intraoperative emergency, which helps ensure the procedure is safe.

Lower Risk of Surgeon Injury

Being in a warm environment and having fewer physical demands than in regular surgery makes musculoskeletal problems less likely for surgeons over the years.

Better Patient Outcomes

Surgical patients experience fewer mistakes, heal more quickly, face fewer risks, and have better patient outcomes.

Metaverse AI robotic surgery leads to better precision, greater stability, and less exhaustion for the surgeon, as in Figure 4. Surgeons in traditional surgery must keep their arms and bodies in difficult positions and work for a long time, which can cause stress and tiredness for them [15]. Being inside a comfortable virtual environment using a robotic console allows surgeons to sit and support their bodies while viewing the surgical site more clearly.

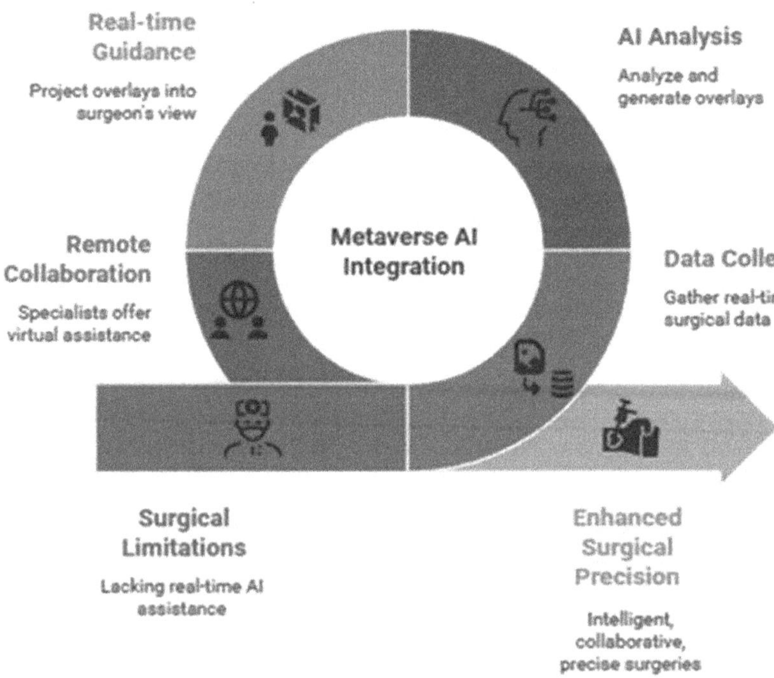

Figure 4: Benefits of smart robotics surgeries.

6. Overlaying 3d Anatomical Models in Real-Time Metaverse

Superimposing 3D models of anatomy on a live meta-versatile platform is now giving surgeons a big breakthrough in how surgeries are planned and understood. It allows surgeons to see exact 3D views of the patient's organs and blood vessels, which are shown either on the patient or inside the surgeon's view during surgery. They are built from preoperative imaging data such as MRI, CT scans, or ultrasounds, and the real-time facts during surgery keep the models updated [16]. By combining these models within the metaverse, surgeons have sharper spatial awareness, which helps them correctly navigate difficult body parts and perform safer procedures.

Doctors can spot important anatomical features that may be hidden in standard imaging or hard to see during direct observation by using 3D models. Blood vessels, tumors, and nerves can be easily identified in different colors or textures, which helps surgeons prevent mistakes during surgery. Additionally, with the interactivity of the metaverse, surgeons can rotate, zoom in, and dig through the digital layers to see the patient's special anatomy and make their plans for surgery. Because these technologies interact in real-time, there is less uncertainty, procedures are completed faster, and patients often recover better.

6.1 Patient-Specific Modeling

Doctors and surgeons use 3D models of the human body in the metaverse, based on patient images like MRI, CT scans, or ultrasound. These virtual replicas are created based on each patient's internal anatomy, allowing surgeons to perform procedures with precise targeting for that person.

6.2 Real-Time Updates

Real-time metaverse overlays change as new data is fed from within the operating room. By observing these changes, surgeons can follow tissue movement, organ position, and any bleeding that occurs during the procedure.

6.3 Interactive Visualization

In the metaverse, surgeons can use 3D models and adjust their view by zooming, rotating, or slicing parts of the model [17]. Using this technology, surgeons can study different body parts from multiple directions, which supports their understanding of difficult relationships during surgery.

6.4 Augmented Reality Integration

Using augmented reality (AR) devices in the metaverse, surgery teams can see inside a patient's body even though the skin is intact. Being able to switch between different views helps the surgeon navigate and perform accurate surgery.

6.5 Highlighting Critical Structures

With AI, 3D models clearly show the blood vessels, nerves, and tumors in a building using special textures. Because the organs are easy to tell apart, surgeons can decrease the possibility of making a mistake and ensure safety.

6.6 Preoperative Planning

Surgeons practice their surgeries, map out where to make incisions, and decide on the best route for each case by using 3D anatomical models in the metaverse before beginning surgery. Organizing the details ahead adds to the surgeon's confidence and decreases the time for decisions during surgery.

6.7 Collaborative Surgery

Many surgeons or specialists from anywhere can zoom in on and interact with the same 3D model in the metaverse. This allows healthcare staff to talk, help one another, and make decisions together as the procedure happens.

6.8 Training and Education

For surgeons in training, being inside the metaverse with 3D models is a valuable way to learn. They can perform simulations that mimic real surgeries and see how their actions would affect patients.

6.9 Enhanced Precision and Safety

The use of real-time 3D models, surgical tools, and robotics in the metaverse helps doctors focus only on the affected areas and avoid harming the healthy tissues [18]. As a result, surgeons can perform procedures that are more secure and effective than before.

6.10 Postoperative Analysis

Post-surgery, healthcare professionals can check the surgery in the metaverse to assess outcomes and review their actions, as well as any challenges. It helps ensure surgical care always gets better.

7. AR for Surgical Navigation and Immersive Visualization

Surgery can now be guided by Augmented Reality (AR), displaying digital visualizations directly in the surgeon's line of sight. This technology in headsets or smart glasses delivers an exact representation of the blood vessels, tumors, or nerve pathways of the patient as seen by the surgeon. With this guidance, surgeons can navigate difficult operating areas more confidently and precisely, especially when visibility is limited [19]. Enhancing how doctors see space around them in AR helps avoid harming any healthy tissues during delicate or minimally invasive surgical procedures.

Augmented reality allows surgeons to look at 3D models specific to patients during surgery, as in Figure 5. They can be turned around, enlarged, or cut virtually, so people can better understand the links between structures and common diseases. Being interactive enables surgeons to adjust their approach as the procedure progresses, which aids in making better decisions [20]. It is also possible for AR to interact with robotic surgical equipment, so that the virtual planning helps to improve the accuracy and speed of real surgery.

Characteristic	Navigation	Visualization	Collaboration	Training
Enhancement	Real-time data overlay	Interactive 3D model manipulation	Remote specialist support	Realistic hands-on experience
Benefit	Increased surgical accuracy	Better decision-making support	Improved access to expertise	Controlled learning environment
Technology	AR headsets/smart glasses	Integration with robotic tools	Virtual presence in operating room	Immersive visualization support

Figure 5: Foundation of smart robotics.

AR makes it possible for surgeons to collaborate from afar. Augmented reality allows surgeons in different places to virtually attend the operation, guide the surgeon, and advise in real time. In unusual or difficult cases that need medical expertise, this feature becomes very useful. Besides, using AR in surgery allows students and new surgeons to practice backed by precautionary measures and real-life situations [21]. In general, using augmented reality for surgery and advanced visualization greatly enhances safety, precision and treatment results, indicating a major shift in precision medicine.

8. Impact on Surgical Training and Integrated Systems

Using augmented reality, virtual reality, artificial intelligence, and robotics in surgical practice has significantly transformed how people train for surgery. Learning from a virtual environment gives new professionals the opportunity to practice challenging procedures as much as they need before attempting them in real life with patients [22, 23]. Using true-to-life simulations, surgeons-in-training can recognize different body structures and handle surprises, so they learn faster and become better surgeons overall.

When AI, robotics, and meta-versatile platforms are combined within systems, the learning and working experience becomes smooth and continuous. AI algorithms provide personalized feedback, check your progress, and suggest ways to improve. Multiple users, such as students, trainers, and surgeons, can use the metaverse to help each other from different locations in real time. In this way, people in underdeveloped areas can access top-notch surgical training, promoting equality in surgical education worldwide.

The use of AI, 3D overlays, and robotic skills smooths the process of using new techniques in actual surgery [24]. As technologies evolve, they will keep changing how surgery is taught and practiced, ensuring that surgeons are more skilled, accurate, and assisted by advanced online tools.

9. Improved Accuracy and Reduced Complications

The introduction of AI, AR, and robots into surgery has greatly increased the accuracy of surgeries. Thanks to detailed and live images as well as precise instruments, surgeons can more precisely reach diseased areas without harming nearby healthy tissues. Such AI-powered graphics and 3D versions of the human body highlight important areas such as nerves and vessels to protect surgeons from making mistakes [25]. More precise surgery means there are fewer mistakes, and patients do better after surgery.

In addition, performing surgeries with robotic assistance is less invasive for the patient, which helps lower the chances of infections, bleeding, and longer recovery periods. Instruments that monitor during the surgery can detect and solve issues early, which minimizes the risks [26]. The stability that robotic arms give helps remove hand tremors and keeps movements steady, which is vital for precise surgery. Because of this, better accuracy, thanks to advanced surgical tools, reduces the risk of complications after surgery, allows patients to heal faster, and reduces the amount of time spent in the hospital. People who get minimally invasive operations face less pain, can resume normal life more quickly, and have better long-term results [27]. By using AI, AR, and robotics, surgery is now safer, more dependable, and produces better results than in the past.

10. AI-Driven Autonomous Surgical Robots using Metaverse Simulations

Using AI, new surgical robots now perform many surgical duties without needing significant guidance from a doctor. By using sophisticated artificial intelligence algorithms, these robots assess tough surgical settings, decide what action to take, and perform detailed actions. In combination with simulations powered by the metaverse, they are trained and improved in fully immersed virtual environments based on real anatomy and surgery settings [28]. Here, robots use training in the metaverse to look through extensive data of surgery cases, practice many "if this, then that" situations, and boost their abilities before carrying out a real operation.

Using metaverse simulations, robots for surgery can improve their performance through practice on models that show complex patient anatomy and changing body conditions. With ongoing learning and virtual practice, robots gain an understanding of the properties of human tissues, what complications may occur, and the best surgical approach. Because of this training, robots perform delicate or simple repetitive tasks consistently, with a much lower risk of making errors that people can make.

10.1 Learning and Training Robots via Metaverse Simulations

Before actual surgery, robots are taught to perform tasks in virtual reality through the metaverse. Many patient scenarios and sample robots in the simulations make it easier for the robot to learn the best practices, anticipate surprises, and improve its decision-making skills by going through numerous virtual surgical experiences [29]. Working through situations in these controlled environments allows them to make independent decisions.

10.2 Robotic Assistants with Partial Autonomy

For this robotic method, robots make precise movements such as suturing, cutting tissues, and guiding instruments; the surgeon is responsible for important decisions. Using metaverse simulations, these assistants become better at their tasks and support human team members for good teamwork and quick achievements.

10.3 Fully Autonomous Surgical Robots

AI systems can perform complex surgeries independently while continuously assessing information about the patient as they operate. With knowledge gained from many metaverse simulations, they can carry out complex operations, manage differences in body structure, and respond to anything new that happens in surgery.

10.4 Real-Time Adaptive Robots

In this category, robots regularly alter their surgical plan based on ongoing information from the surgery, such as how the tissue feels or how the patient is doing. With the simulation, robots repeatedly train, adjusting and responding safely to unexpected circumstances, helping improve how procedures are performed.

10.5 Collaborative Robots in Remote Surgery

Remote surgeons work together with the robots, providing instructions that change what the robots do in real time. Via the metaverse, experts can "enter" the surgical area and step in or offer advice when needed, helping people in many regions receive important medical care.

10.6 AI-Enhanced Diagnostic Robots

Some autonomous robots make use of AI-powered diagnostics to review images and information happening during surgery within the Metaverse [30]. Such robots allow surgeons to see and mark tumor-surrounding tissues, unusual tissues, and blood vessels, which helps ensure the procedure is carried out with more accuracy.

10.7 Robots for Minimally Invasive Procedures

Specialized autonomous robots designed for laparoscopic and endoscopic surgeries learn to operate in confined spaces through simulations in the metaverse. The slim design of the tools allows for painful procedures to be performed with only small cuts and quick recovery times healing.

10.8 Robotic Systems with Multi-Modal Feedback

They use feedback from various sensors—visual, touch, and force—and AI to enhance how surgeons perform surgeries. These simulations help robots interpret what they see, which makes it safer for them to handle organs and surgical equipment.

10.9 Reinforcement Learning-Based Robots

They are provided with reinforcement learning algorithms, which help them learn how to perform better through their actions in the meta-versatile world. While practicing surgery many times, they improve their techniques without any danger to living patients.

10.10 Predictive and Preventive Robots

The robots rely on simulations in the metaverse to predict surgical problems and change their conduct accordingly. Doctors sometimes slow down or change how they operate close to sensitive tissues to help protect their patients.

The metaverse, integrated with autonomous AI-powered robots, enables distant surgeons to operate on patients overseas. While surgeons manage emergencies remotely, the computer handles the basic activity throughout the surgery. Combining these technologies is expected to make surgery more effective and efficient, shorten the length of surgeries, and lower costs because of fewer complications. Improvements in research and technology mean that AI-assisted robots trained in metaverses could completely change global surgical practices and patient care.

11. The Metaverse Transformative Impact on Healthcare Systems

Healthcare systems could benefit a lot by having patients, healthcare workers, and devices communicating smoothly inside digital environments. The change results in healthcare that is easier to use, more suited to individuals, and more efficient [31]. With virtual reality and augmented reality, patients can conduct remote consultations, join therapy sessions, and access health information in innovative ways that break down distance and time barriers. It makes it easier for underserved populations to see a doctor quickly, and monitoring their health can be done remotely with assistance from digital devices connected within the metaverse, as in Table 1.

Table 1: Impact of Metaverse on Healthcare Systems

Area of Impact	Description	Benefits
Remote Consultations	Virtual clinics and 3D avatars for patient-doctor interactions	Increased access, convenience, reduced travel and wait times
Surgical Training & Simulation	Immersive VR-based surgery practice with real-time feedback	Safer training, skill improvement, no risk to real patients
Collaborative Surgery	Real-time virtual collaboration among surgeons globally	Expert guidance, better outcomes, global knowledge sharing
AR/VR-Assisted Procedures	Overlaying digital anatomical data on real-world surgical fields	Enhanced precision, reduced errors, improved spatial awareness
Patient Education	Interactive 3D models to explain procedures and conditions	Better understanding, improved decision-making by patients
Mental Health Therapy	Virtual reality environments for stress, PTSD, and phobia treatments	Safe, immersive, and controlled therapeutic experiences
Tele rehabilitation	Virtual physiotherapy and motion tracking for recovery	Continual support, improved patient compliance
AI Integration & Data Analysis	Real-time health monitoring and predictive analytics in virtual platforms	Early diagnosis, personalized treatment, proactive care
Medical Conferences & Training	Immersive, 3D educational events and virtual labs	Cost-effective, global participation, hands-on learning
Digital Twins in Healthcare	Virtual replicas of organs or full-body systems for simulation and monitoring	Personalized medicine, surgery planning, and improved outcomes

The metaverse greatly improves the work of healthcare workers. People involved in healthcare, regardless of their location, can join and share resources in virtual spaces to develop critical plans, simulate surgeries, and perform complex procedures. Advanced simulations and 3D models of the human body help surgeons practice and decide more wisely, which in turn helps them avoid mistakes and achieve better results [32]. Healthcare is being transformed by the metaverse, which enables the integration of smart medical tools, robotics, and

AI. With automated care, on-the-spot diagnostics, and AI-provided care advice, the load on healthcare staff is lowered. A result of digital transformation is lower cost, wiser use of resources, and better focus on patients' needs.

12. Conclusion

Modern healthcare is being reshaped by the rising use of the metaverse, artificial intelligence, machine learning, and robotics. Due to these advances, medical diagnosis, treatment, and surgical procedures are now more precise, more efficient, and accessible than ever before. Integrating these technologies supports detailed surgical training, face-to-face guidance, autonomous robots, and specialized patient care, all aimed at achieving better results. Beyond that, the metaverse is a perfect tool for remote teamwork, education, and healthcare, giving equal access to quality medical experts to communities worldwide. With their ongoing changes, they should help to avoid mistakes, allow patients to recover quickly, and improve the way resources are managed in healthcare worldwide. Healthcare is being transformed by the collaboration of meta-versatile technologies with robots and analytics, which is also making medicine more precise, concerned about patients, and focused on equality. Welcome this shift to embrace the full impact digital health can have and benefit people everywhere.

References

1. Lampridis, S. (2023). From scalpel to robot: The evolving landscape of diaphragmatic plication. *Video-Assisted Thoracic Surgery*, 8.
2. Dario, P., Hannaford, B., and Menciassi, A. (2003). Smart surgical tools and augmenting devices. *IEEE Transactions on Robotics and Automation*, 19(5), 782–792.
3. Alotaibi, M. I. R., Albargi, A. A. B., Alrashdi, M. I. H., and Alsheddi, M. S. (2024). The future of specialized surgery and minimally invasive procedures. *Tec Empresarial*, 6(2), 1096–1110.
4. Valencia-Garcia, R., Martinez-Bejar, R., and Gasparetto, A. (2005). An intelligent framework for simulating robot-assisted surgical operations. *Expert Systems with Applications*, 28(3), 425–433.
5. Denicolai, S., and Previtali, P. (2020). Precision medicine: Implications for value chains and business models in life sciences. *Technological Forecasting and Social Change*, 151, 119767.
6. Mbunge, E., Muchemwa, B., Jiyane, S. E., and Batani, J. (2021). Sensors and healthcare 5.0: Transformative shift in virtual care through emerging digital health technologies. *Global Health Journal*, 5(4), 169–177.
7. Ginsburg, G. S., & Phillips, K. A. (2018). Precision medicine: From science to value. *Health Affairs*, 37(5), 694–701.
8. Hassan, A. M., Rajesh, A., Asaad, M., Nelson, J. A., Coert, J. H., Mehrara, B. J., and Butler, C. E. (2023). Artificial intelligence and machine learning in prediction of

surgical complications: Current state, applications, and implications. *The American Surgeon*, 89(1), 25–30.
9. Pettit, R. W., Fullem, R., Cheng, C., and Amos, C. I. (2021). Artificial intelligence, machine learning, and deep learning for clinical outcome prediction. *Emerging Topics in Life Sciences*, 5(6), 729–745.
10. Senders, J. T., Staples, P. C., Karhade, A. V., Zaki, M. M., Gormley, W. B., Broekman, M. L., ... and Arnaout, O. (2018). Machine learning and neurosurgical outcome prediction: A systematic review. *World Neurosurgery*, 109, 476–486.
11. Nespolo, R. G., Yi, D., Cole, E., Wang, D., Warren, A., and Leiderman, Y. I. (2023). Feature tracking and segmentation in real time via deep learning in vitreoretinal surgery: A platform for artificial intelligence-mediated surgical guidance. *Ophthalmology Retina*, 7(3), 236–242.
12. Dasgupta, P., and Raison, N. (2025). AI in surgery. In: *Artificial Intelligence in Urology* (pp. 237–248). Academic Press.
13. Protserov, S., Hunter, J., Zhang, H., Mashouri, P., Masino, C., Brudno, M., and Madani, A. (2024). Development, deployment and scaling of operating room-ready artificial intelligence for real-time surgical decision support. *npj Digital Medicine*, 7(1), 231.
14. Campetella, M., Ragonese, M., Gandi, C., Bizzarri, F. P., Russo, P., Foschi, N., ... and Sacco, E. (2025). Surgeons' fatigue in minimally invasive and open surgery: A review of the current literature. *Urologia Journal*, 92(1), 161–168.
15. Jiang, S., Naito, K., and Liverneaux, P. (2025). Advantages in precision, safety, and aesthetic outcomes of robot-assisted minimally invasive techniques in peripheral nerve microsurgery: A narrative review. *Advanced Technology in Neuroscience*, 2(3), 122–127.
16. Nicolosi, F., de Laurentis, C., Giussani, C., Marcus, H. J., Spena, G., and Ammar, A. (2024). Mixed reality and metaverse. In: *Ethical Challenges for the Future of Neurosurgery* (pp. 141–159). Cham: Springer Nature Switzerland.
17. Choi, S. Y., Choi, D. H., Cho, S. H., Ahn, S. H., and Han, S. H. (2025). Anatomy education potential of the first digital twin of a Korean cadaver. *PLOS One*, 20(3), e0305679.
18. Afrose, N., Chakraborty, R., Hazra, A., Bhowmick, P., and Bhowmick, M. (2025). Implementation of metaverse for healthcare system modeling. *Metaverse Technologies, Security and Applications for Healthcare*, 325–350.
19. Choi, H., Cho, B., Masamune, K., Hashizume, M., and Hong, J. (2016). An effective visualization technique for depth perception in augmented reality-based surgical navigation. *The International Journal of Medical Robotics and Computer Assisted Surgery*, 12(1), 62–72.
20. Hettig, J., Engelhardt, S., Hansen, C., and Mistelbauer, G. (2018). AR in VR: Assessing surgical augmented reality visualizations in a steerable virtual reality environment. *International Journal of Computer Assisted Radiology and Surgery*, 13, 1717–1725.
21. Chen, X., Xu, L., Wang, Y., Wang, H., Wang, F., Zeng, X., ... and Egger, J. (2015). Development of a surgical navigation system based on augmented reality using an optical see-through head-mounted display. *Journal of Biomedical Informatics*, 55, 124–131.
22. Shahrezaei, A., Sohani, M., Taherkhani, S., and Zarghami, S. Y. (2024). The impact of surgical simulation and training technologies on general surgery education. *BMC Medical Education*, 24(1), 1297.

23. Parsons, B. A., Blencowe, N. S., Hollowood, A. D., and Grant, J. R. (2011). Surgical training: The impact of changes in curriculum and experience. *Journal of Surgical Education*, 68(1), 44–51.
24. Azadi, S., Green, I. C., Arnold, A., Truong, M., Potts, J., and Martino, M. A. (2021). Robotic surgery: The impact of simulation and other innovative platforms on performance and training. *Journal of Minimally Invasive Gynecology*, 28(3), 490–495.
25. Ashwini, A., Shamini, G. I., Prathaban, B. P., and Balasubramaniam, S. (2025). MultiSense diagnosis: Navigating disease diagnosis with metaverse multimodal interaction. In: *Applying Metaverse Technologies to Human-Computer Interaction for Healthcare* (pp. 235–253). Auerbach Publications.
26. Roos, L. L., Stranc, L., James, R. C., and Li, J. (1997). Complications, comorbidities, and mortality: Improving classification and prediction. *Health Services Research*, 32(2), 229.
27. Moulton, J. S., and Moore, P. T. (1993). Coaxial percutaneous biopsy technique with automated biopsy devices: Value in improving accuracy and negative predictive value. *Radiology*, 186(2), 515–522.
28. Perkins, J. (2022). Immersive metaverse experiences in decentralized 3D virtual clinical spaces: Artificial intelligence-driven diagnostic algorithms, wearable internet of medical things sensor devices, and healthcare modeling and simulation tools. *American Journal of Medical Research*, 9(2), 89–104.
29. Checcucci, E., Verri, P., Amparore, D., Cacciamani, G. E., Rivas, J. G., Autorino, R., ... and Porpiglia, F. (2023). The future of robotic surgery in urology: From augmented reality to the advent of metaverse. *Therapeutic Advances in Urology*, 15, 17562872231151853.
30. Ashwini, A., Kavitha, V., Balasubramaniam, S., and Kadry, S. (2025). MetaHealth: Transforming Healthcare through AI integration. *Applying Metaverse Technologies to Human-Computer Interaction for Healthcare*, 121.
31. Campbell, D. H., McDonald, D., Araghi, K., Araghi, T., Chutkan, N., and Araghi, A. (2021). The clinical impact of image guidance and robotics in spinal surgery: A review of safety, accuracy, efficiency, and complication reduction. *International Journal of Spine Surgery*, 15(s2), S10–S20.
32. Qiu, C. S., Majeed, A., Khan, S., and Watson, M. (2022). Transforming health through the metaverse. *Journal of the Royal Society of Medicine*, 115(12), 484–486.

CHAPTER

7

Mental Health in the Metaverse: AI-Driven Virtual Therapies

Abinaya M.[1*] and Vadivu G.

Department of Data Science and Business Systems, School of Computing, SRM Institute of Science and Technology, Kattankulathur, Chennai – 603203

This chapter examines the intersection of mental health, artificial intelligence, and the Metaverse, emphasizing how immersive technologies are redefining psychological care in a digital era. It highlights the rise of mental health challenges driven by urbanization, climate anxiety, technology overexposure, and systemic disparities, and explores the limitations of traditional therapy. The discussion focuses on the potential of AI-driven interventions, including virtual therapists, chatbots, and VR-based exposure therapies, to provide scalable, personalized, and accessible support that transcends geographical, social, and economic barriers. The chapter also considers real-world applications, case studies, and the advantages of immersive, culturally adaptive care environments. At the same time, it underscores ethical and practical concerns, such as data privacy, clinical validation, algorithmic fairness, and dependency on technology. By presenting both opportunities and risks, the chapter positions AI-enabled virtual therapies as a transformative yet complex frontier in mental healthcare, where innovation must be balanced with equity, human dignity, and ethical responsibility.

1. Introduction

1.1 Background and Motivation

Mental illness has become a major public health concern in the 21st century, affecting people across all demographic, geographical, and socioeconomic

*Corresponding author: am0150@srmist.edu.in

DOI: 10.1201/9781003679370-7

backgrounds. The World Health Organization (WHO) states that in 2019, nearly 970 million people worldwide were living with a mental disorder, a number that has continued to rise, especially after the COVID-19 pandemic [1]. The crisis triggered unprecedented levels of anxiety, depression, and psychological distress, exposing systemic failures within global mental health systems. Traditional mental health services, which rely on face-to-face consultations, were disrupted, delayed, or became inaccessible during lockdowns and healthcare system pressures. At the same time, the pandemic sped up the adoption of digital health technologies, leading to a significant shift in how healthcare, particularly mental healthcare, is delivered, accessed, and experienced [2]. One of the most ground-breaking advancements is the emergence of the Metaverse, a vast, immersive, and ubiquitous virtual environment that combines virtual reality (VR), augmented reality (AR), artificial intelligence (AI), blockchain, and social networking technologies. Originally developed for gaming and entertainment, the Metaverse has rapidly evolved into a multifaceted platform for learning, commerce, social interaction, and, more recently, healthcare. In this rapidly evolving digital landscape, mental health care is transforming. By integrating AI algorithms into 3D immersive spaces within the Metaverse, it is possible to create scalable, interactive, and personalized mental health interventions. AI-powered chatbots, emotionally intelligent agents, and virtual therapy settings enable new forms of therapy that cross geographical, economic, and social barriers that have long limited access to mental health care [3]. These innovations include offering anonymity, 24/7 availability, and adaptive, culturally-sensitive therapy tailored to an individual's emotional profile and history.

Additionally, the combination of AI and the Metaverse offers a potential solution to the shortage of trained mental health professionals, especially in low- and middle-income countries. When developed responsibly and ethically, AI technologies can enhance the effectiveness of human therapists, broaden the scope of care delivery, and facilitate large-scale monitoring of emotional states. Technologies such as natural language processing (NLP), sentiment analysis, behavioral pattern recognition, and affective computing enable AI to recognize and respond to human emotions with a level of empathy and contextual understanding that surpasses current computer systems [4]. At the same time, this technological advancement also poses extremely serious concerns about privacy, data protection, clinical effectiveness, and ethical boundaries. The reliance on machine-driven diagnosis and treatment protocols calls for strict validation, algorithmic decision-making transparency, and strict regulation to prevent abuse or injury. This chapter aims to explore the intersection of mental health, artificial intelligence, and the Metaverse to examine the potential for innovation and the complex challenges that lie ahead. The aim is to present a comprehensive analysis of how virtual therapy powered by AI can revolutionize psychological care in a fast-digitalizing world. Through empirical evidence, theoretical arguments, and practical applications, this chapter emphasizes the importance of developing future-proof, human-centered, and morally grounded mental health solutions for the Metaverse [5].

1.2 Scope and Objectives

This chapter aims to:

- Define the intersection of AI, the Metaverse, and mental healthcare.
- Review emerging technologies like **virtual therapists and emotional AI**.
- Examine the benefits and risks of digital mental health platforms.
- Provide insights into ethical and policy considerations.

2. Understanding the Metaverse and AI Integration

2.1 Defining the Metaverse

The Metaverse is a paradigm break with how humans are using the internet, not as a flat 2D surface of click-through screens, but as a spatial, experiential, and immersive virtual reality. It is commonly described as a persistent, synchronous, shared 3D digital world where humans interact with each other and digital objects using avatars. The concept is based on science fiction (e.g., Snow Crash by Neal Stephenson, Ready Player One by Ernest Cline), but it is now emerging as a real, multi-dimensional digital infrastructure made possible by several different technologies converging. Basic Technologies that played a vital role in the metaverse [6]:

Virtual Reality (VR) and Augmented Reality (AR)

VR creates immersion by replacing the user's world with a world generated by a computer, accessed through headsets (e.g., Oculus Quest, HTC Vive). AR, on the other hand, places virtual objects into the real world, often through smartphones or smart glasses (e.g., Microsoft HoloLens). They combine to provide the foundation for spatial computing in which users can "be" present in a virtual world [7].

Artificial Intelligence (AI)

AI provides intelligent behavior for virtual actors (such as NPCs or bots), predicts user actions, generates adaptive content, and supports personalization. It provides real-time speech recognition, natural language understanding, and emotion recognition in avatars, thus simulating near-human interactions in virtual space. Blockchain and Web3 Technologies Blockchain also enables decentralization of transactions, ownership, and identity in the Metaverse. It is supportive of Non-Fungible Tokens (NFTs), virtual assets, and user-owned platforms. This offers interoperability, transparency, and digital ownership within an otherwise monopolistic digital space [8].

Cloud Computing and Edge Computing

The Metaverse is founded on massive, distributed, real-time computing capacity. Cloud infrastructures like AWS, Azure, and Google Cloud offer virtual worlds and serve real-time interactions. Edge computing offers low-latency performance needed for immersive user experiences [9].

Implications for Mental Health

Therapeutic presence: People may assume avatars to interact with therapists or support groups in a virtual environment, simulating face-to-face interaction.

Safe environments: Phobic patients with PTSD, or anxious individuals, may be exposed to virtual stimuli in a controlled environment in exposure therapy [10].

Cognitive and affective engagement: Interactive components increase the patient's engagement and affective processing and hence improve the effectiveness of therapy.

2.2 AI Role in the Metaverse

Artificial Intelligence (AI) is the cognitive and operational foundation of the Metaverse. Though technologies such as VR and AR produce immersive environments, it is AI that makes these virtual worlds intelligent, personalized, responsive, and interactive. For mental healthcare, AI converts static digital landscapes into adaptive therapeutic environments that can recognize, analyze, and respond to users' emotional and psychological conditions in real time [11].

AI as the Cognitive Engine

AI software drives the smart agents and adaptive interfaces that characterize the user experience in the Metaverse. These agents are able to interact with users through natural dialogue, analyze their mental state, and provide therapeutic recommendations. This turns the Metaverse into a cognitively augmented environment where interactions are not just entertaining but also therapeutic and meaningful [12]. AI provides three key functions in mental health software in the Metaverse:

1. **Emotional Insight with Natural Language Processing (NLP):** Natural Language Processing makes it possible for AI to analyze human emotions, ideas, and mental states from users' speech, text, or chat activity. During a virtual counselling session or chatbot exchange, AI-driven NLP engines can:
    - Identify emotional tone, stress, and sentiment polarity.
    - Recognize mental health warning signs (e.g., depressive speech, suicidal thoughts, markers of anxiety).
    - Monitor longitudinal trends in mood and language use patterns over time.

- These observations can be utilized to tailor therapeutic responses, warn human clinicians if needed, and ensure contextual appropriateness and emotional responsiveness of the intervention.
- NLP-powered AI chatbots such as Wysa and Woebot provide Cognitive Behavioral Therapy (CBT)-inspired responses. When embedded in VR-based avatars, they enact human-like therapeutic conversations in immersive environments [13].

2. **Personalized Therapy Suggestion and Predictive Behaviour:** Metaverse AI systems can create and constantly update a psychological user profile based on analyzing:

   - Historical patterns of behavior and emotional trends
   - Therapy session histories
   - Biometric and physiological data such as heart rate, eye movement, and voice stress

By using machine learning algorithms, the system can personalize therapy sessions based on the individual's cognitive style and emotional needs. Provide intervention recommendations, e.g., mindfulness, exposure, and narrative therapy, based on dynamic needs. Forecast psychological threats, like burnout or emotional deterioration, and actively recommend coping mechanisms or refer users to human therapists. Such personalization increases effectiveness and motivation, particularly in populations underserved or averse to seeking formal care.

Example: Sites like Tess by X2AI apply AI to provide individualized emotional support at scale, which adjusts to every user's language style and emotional reaction in real-time [14].

3. **Realistic Human Interaction Simulation with Generative Models:** Advances in Generative AI (e.g., large language models such as GPT-4, text-to-speech synthesis, and avatar animation) allow for the simulation of virtual therapists, support group leaders, or even therapy companions that:

   - Have natural conversation flow, empathy, and adaptive questioning.
   - Have realistic non-verbal communication through avatar facial expressions and gestures.
   - Mimic therapy situations, like social interactions for individuals with social anxiety, bereavement counselling, or trauma work. Such realism closes the gap between computer and in-person therapy, with virtual sessions coming across as more true-to-life and emotionally impactful [15].

Use Case: An AI avatar therapist leveraging VR might take a user with PTSD through graded exposure therapy while modulating tone, pace, and content in response to real-time biometric cues (e.g., accelerated heart rate or voice tremble).

4. **Integrative Feedback Loop:** AI in the Metaverse doesn't happen in a vacuum; it learns perpetually through feedback loops:
    - **Input:** Voice, gestures, eye movement, and physiological monitoring.
    - **Processing:** AI models process data, identify emotional/cognitive patterns.
    - **Response:** The system provides tailored therapeutic material or adapts the setting.
    - **Adaptation:** AI revises the user's mental health profile for further optimization.

This closed-loop personalization process guarantees that therapy is not fixed but dynamically changes with the user, a key benefit over traditional one-size-fits-all models of therapy.

3. Mental Health Challenges in the Digital Era

3.1 Rising Mental Health Issues

The contemporary age has seen a catastrophic increase in mental health disorders prompted by a set of social, economic, environmental, and technological advancements. The World Health Organization (WHO) states that more than 970 million individuals across the globe were living with mental health disorders in 2019, with depression and anxiety disorders being among the leading causes of disability. This figure has increased considerably during the COVID-19 pandemic, which interrupted social networks, aggravated loneliness, and added new stressors across populations [16].

Urbanization and Social Fragmentation

Urbanization at a speedy rate, especially in developing countries, has been responsible for social disintegration and rising stress. While cities provide improved access to resources, they also subject citizens to a high cost of living, alienation, stressful working conditions, pollution, and erosion of usual support systems. All these tend to result in elevated rates of depression, anxiety, and disorders related to stress, particularly among adolescents and the aged [17].

Climate Anxiety and Existential Stress

The climate crisis is also becoming a mental health crisis. Heightened awareness of global environmental decline, extreme weather, and loss of biodiversity is giving rise to "eco-anxiety, an ongoing fear of ecological apocalypse". Young people, in particular, express feelings of despair, guilt, and helplessness regarding the future of the planet. These psychological impacts are often followed by a perceived absence of systemic response by the powers, with the resulting disillusionment and psychological exhaustion [18].

Technology Addiction and Digital Overexposure

Ironically, as they bring people together around the world, digital platforms are also a breeding ground for growing mental unease. Prolonged use of screens, algorithmic content exposure, and social comparison online have been associated with heightened levels of anxiety, depression, cyberbullying, and sleep disorders. Social media platforms' dopamine-fuelled design fosters addictive use, culminating in dependency, attention fragmentation, and emotional dysregulation. Children and teens are most at risk because their cognitive and emotional systems are still in development [19].

Socioeconomic and Cultural Disparities

Mental health is not similarly impacting all groups. Marginalized groups like ethnic minorities, LGBTQIA+, refugees, and poor populations are disproportionately impacted by mental health due to structural discrimination, violence, poverty, and the availability of culturally appropriate care. These populations are likewise hindered from accessing help by institutional mistrust, cultural stigma, or language barriers, widening the treatment gap [20].

3.2 Barriers to Traditional Therapy

While mental illnesses have grown more common, the conventional systems of mental healthcare continue to be overwhelmed, underfinanced, and sometimes unavailable, especially in low- and middle-income nations (LMICs). Multiple systemic obstacles hinder patients from receiving timely and effective treatment.

Stigma and Shame

One of the most common barriers is societal stigma. In most societies, mental illness continues to be regarded as a manifestation of individual weakness, religious failure, or moral corruption. This causes people to deny their symptoms, be late in getting treatment, or refuse therapy altogether. Not only does stigmatization impact public attitude, but it is internalized by the patients themselves, generating self-stigma that aggravates psychological distress.

Example: In rural India, studies reveal that more than 60% of people with mental illness do not access care for fear of stigma or social exclusion.

High Costs and Time Constraints

Conventional mental health treatment, particularly in private clinics in cities, is usually unaffordable. Psychotherapy and psychiatric treatment involve frequent sessions, which may be financially burdensome for patients who lack insurance or social assistance. Moreover, extensive waiting lists, inflexible scheduling, and strict office hours discourage regular attendance, especially among those with jobs or caregivers.

Lack of Skilled Mental Health Workers

There exists a critical shortage of licensed mental health professionals worldwide. The WHO estimates that over 50% of countries have fewer than one psychiatrist per 100,000 people. In many rural or underserved areas, psychologists, counsellors, or social workers may be absent, forcing patients to travel long distances or forego treatment. This "mental health desert" phenomenon creates a vast service gap, particularly in LMICs.

Fact: In Sub-Saharan Africa, the mean mental health worker ratio is 0.1 per 100,000 population, while in most high-income countries, it is 10+ per 100,000 [21].

3.3 Need for Innovation

Understandably, given these obstacles, there is a need to innovate outside traditional mental healthcare systems. Digital technologies, specifically AI-powered platforms and immersive experiences in the Metaverse, can provide solutions to breach these systemic blockages.

24/7 Access and On-Demand Support

AI-driven solutions can provide round-the-clock support, enabling users to reach out for mental health support at their most vulnerable moments, whether alone, in the dark, or amid a crisis. Digital solutions are unencumbered by time and place, unlike conventional therapists who work within set hours and geography.

Example: Chatbots such as Wysa and Tess offer 24/7 CBT-inspired support with real-time therapeutic activities, mood monitoring, and journaling functions.

Bridging Geographic and Socioeconomic Gaps

Digital mental health tools can transcend physical borders, reaching remote populations that lack local services. Mobile-based platforms can operate in low-bandwidth conditions, making them suitable for rural or resource-constrained areas. Furthermore, digital platforms can be cost-effective compared to in-person therapy, democratizing access for economically disadvantaged individuals.

Case Study: In Kenya, AI-based SMS-based counselling services have reached over 100,000 teenagers with minimal psychoeducation and crisis support at low infrastructure cost.

Anonymity and Decreased Stigma

Virtual therapy software, particularly that embedded in avatar-based platforms or chat interfaces, offers user anonymity, which can greatly lower social stigma. People are more likely to reveal their mental health issues in judgment-free spaces, and this will boost help-seeking behaviour and emotional honesty.

Insight: A new Stanford study revealed users shared 30% more personal information with AI chatbots than they did with human therapists in introductory sessions, a sign of trust bred through anonymity.

Cultural and Linguistic Personalization

AI-powered platforms can be trained on culturally unique, multilingual datasets, providing customized therapy experiences that connect with users across different backgrounds. This is especially useful in plural societies where universal models do not work. Tone, content, and strategies may be adjusted by AI according to user values and contexts [22].

4. AI-Driven Virtual Therapies

The use of artificial intelligence (AI) in mental healthcare is opening up a new avenue of digitally mediated, scalable, and personalized therapy interventions. These AI-based therapies are not a replacement for human clinicians but to augment and extend the reach, continuity, and efficacy of psychological treatments, particularly in immersive settings such as the Metaverse. This section examines the various forms of AI-based treatments for mental health, their operational mechanisms, therapeutic applications, and the utilization of virtual and immersive worlds to deliver them [23].

4.1 Types of AI-Based Interventions

AI-driven therapies for mental health fall under three functional categories:

Rule-Based Chatbots

Rule-based systems rely on set scripts or decision trees, normally based on proven models of therapy like Cognitive Behavioral Therapy (CBT) or Dialectical Behavioral Therapy (DBT). They apply if-then statements to answer user input, so they are predictable and safe to use to provide psychoeducation, mindfulness reminders, and simple coping skills.

Example: Woebot, created by Stanford psychologists, is a CBT-derived chatbot that gives brief daily discussions. Emotionally intelligent conversations are used to enable users to monitor their mood, recognize cognitive distortions, and learn to reframe thoughts.

Strengths

- Clinically informed
- Low possibility of erratic responses
- Straightforward to deploy and scale

Limitations

- No adaptability or profound personalization
- Not flexible in responding to intricate user emotions or crises [24]

Machine Learning-Driven Emotional Assistants

These systems leverage machine learning (ML), more specifically natural language processing (NLP), sentiment analysis, and affective computing, to recognize and react to user emotions in real-time. They learn from user interactions continuously and update their models to improve therapeutic effectiveness [25].

Features

- Recognize shifts in emotional tone over time
- Forecast stress or depressive conditions based on user input
- Adjust therapy based on feedback in terms of behavior

Example: Tess, an empathetic AI developed by X2AI, employs NLP to engage emotionally with users across 15+ languages. It is scalable for use in clinical and non-clinical environments and has been implemented in schools, refugee camps, and hospitals.

VR-Based Guided Exposure Therapy

Virtual Reality (VR) worlds enable patients to practice simulated situations that could provoke phobic, traumatic, or anxiety responses in the real world. The worlds are directed by artificial intelligence (AI) software that modulates difficulty, tracks user reactions (e.g., biometrics, voice stress), and offers graduated exposure therapy with low risk.

Example: Oxford VR provides social anxiety exposure therapy through job interviews, public speaking, or group conversation simulations. AI is employed on the platform to track physiological responses and lead users through progressively difficult situations.

4.2 Virtual Therapists and Chatbots

Virtual therapists are based on a connection to AI, which imitates the actions of trained experts via avatar-mediated dialogue, voice interfaces, or text-based interaction robots. These technologies are based on psychological paradigms and respond dynamically to [26]:

Real-Time Sentiment Detection

- User history and preferences
- Engagement metrics and therapeutic objectives

Fundamental Therapies Supported

- **Cognitive Behavioral Therapy (CBT):** Recognition of negative thought patterns and reframing them.
- **Motivational Interviewing (MI):** Building user motivation to alter behavior (addiction, procrastination).

- **Mindfulness-Based Interventions (MBIs):** Providing guided meditations, breathing, and grounding.

Technical Features

- Emotion detection from speech/text
- Multimodal inputs (speech, gaze, biometric signals)
- Detection of crises and escalation to human therapists

The University of Southern California's Institute for Creative Technologies has shown through research that patients tend to feel more at ease sharing sensitive information with virtual humans than they do with real humans, particularly during initial therapeutic interactions.

4.3 Personalized Mental Health Solutions

The main benefit of AI-based mental health treatments is personalization. In contrast to conventional models based on generalized protocols, AI allows for hyper-personalized therapy via data convergence and ongoing learning.

Dynamic Learning Systems

These systems apply artificial intelligence, reinforcement learning, and user modelling to:

- Learn an individual's emotional patterns
- Adapt the intervention to the user's progress or regressions
- Personalize the length, difficulty, and wording of therapy
- Integration with EHR and Clinical Data
- AI platforms with Electronic Health Records (EHRs) provide:
  - Overall perspectives of a patient's mental and physical well-being
  - Multimodal interventions informed by medication, diagnoses, and therapy history
  - Smooth transition between virtual and real-world care
- Multilingual and Culturally Adaptable Interfaces
- Using multilingual NLP models and culturally nuanced AI training data, computer-based therapies can:
  - Treat linguistically diverse groups
  - Observe cultural conventions in therapeutic style and guidance
  - Decrease attrition in cross-cultural therapy sessions

Example: AI platforms such as Wysa handle more than 10 languages and provide therapy adjusted to users from various cultural backgrounds based on region-specific wording and analogies [27].

4.4 VR Environments for Emotional and Cognitive Therapy

Immersive Virtual Reality (VR) environments offer transformative potential in both emotion regulation and cognitive reconstruction.

Controlled Exposure and Desensitization

Virtual Reality (VR) driven by AI can simulate real-life triggers like crowded trains (for social anxiety), heights (for acrophobia), or settings related to trauma within a controlled and modifiable setting. This provides:

- Repeated exposure without actual-world ramifications
- Monitoring of user stress signals in real-time
- AI-driven progress from low to high intensity exposure
- Biofeedback and Emotional Regulation

Through the combination of wearables and biometric sensors, VR therapies can:

- Monitor heart rate, skin conductance, and pupil dilation
- Identify stress in the user in real time
- Provide relaxation cues, such as guided visualization or deep breathing, as required

Example: The BehaVR platform utilizes biofeedback-augmented VR therapy to treat stress, anxiety, and chronic pain by modifying the environment according to real-time physiological signals.

Virtual Nature and Mindfulness Environments

VR modules can mimic tranquil natural settings waterfalls, forests, and beaches, which have been proven to decrease cortisol and boost parasympathetic activity. Coupled with AI-guided voice directions, these spaces promote:

- Mindfulness exercises
- Grounding exercises
- Cognitive defusion and emotional distancing [28]

5. Advantages of Virtual Therapies in the Metaverse

The combination of artificial intelligence and immersive virtual space in mental healthcare offers revolutionary potential for accessibility, engagement, and social acceptance. The Metaverse, when augmented with AI-powered therapeutic platforms, can close the treatment gap, diminish stigma, and broaden inclusiveness by providing flexible, smart, and emotionally attuned care experiences.

This section explains how virtual therapies in the Metaverse support mental health services in three main areas: accessibility, real-time tracking, and stigma reduction.

5.1 Accessibility and Inclusivity

Traditional mental healthcare is still limited by geography, expense, time, and systemic disparities. Metaverse-based AI therapies break down most of those barriers by opening up care to anyone who has an internet connection and a supported device.

24/7 Multi-Device Availability

Virtual therapy platforms, unlike conventional clinics, operate continuously across time zones, providing support during off-hours, emergencies, or when traditional services are unavailable (e.g., rural settings, lockdown periods, conflict zones). They are accessible via:

- VR headsets (e.g., Oculus, HTC Vive)
- Smartphones and tablets
- Desktop interfaces with AR or 3D components

This asynchronous, non-linear model of therapy provides users with control over when and how they engage, increasing the likelihood of adherence and long-term psychological benefits.

Example: An insomniac user might log on to a virtual forest for guided meditation at 2:00 AM and get immediate AI-based CBT-driven coaching to cope with intrusive thoughts.

Multilingual and Customizable Platforms: Most AI-based mental health platforms have natural language processing models learned from many languages and dialects. This allows:

- Therapy in users' native language, increasing emotional resonance
- User accessibility in linguistically diverse areas such as India, Africa, and Southeast Asia
- Avatar, voice, environment, and content format customization (e.g., visual aids for hearing-impaired individuals)
- Cultural, linguistic, and neurodiversity adaptation makes the experience more inclusive and efficient [29].

Adapted Support for Neurodivergent and Disabled Groups

The Metaverse provides adaptive interfaces that are easily customizable to fit neurodiversity people (e.g., those with autism, ADHD, or sensory processing disorder) and physically impaired users. These are:

- Low-sensory spaces for hypersensitive users
- Text-to-speech and speech-to-text functions
- Eye-tracking and gesture-based controls for motor-impaired users
- Gamified behavioural therapy modules for learning-disabled children

University of Cambridge research points out that neurodivergent patients exhibit greater emotional investment and lower levels of stress in gamified VR therapy environments than traditional talk therapy.

5.2 Real-Time Support and Monitoring

Possibly the most significant strength of AI-powered therapy in the Metaverse is its ability to undertake real-time monitoring and intervention, a key benefit over traditional static models of therapy.

- Emotional Drift Monitoring
- AI agents embedded in virtual worlds can constantly monitor:
- Linguistic affect (tone, word selection, tempo)
- Body language and facial expressions (through avatar behavior mapping)
- Speech characteristics (e.g., tremor, pause length, pitch)

This enables the system to identify emotional drift, the very subtle change in affect that leads to crises or relapse, and react by:

- Dynamic content alteration (e.g., slowing down conversation, initiating a mindfulness module)
- Suggesting grounding exercises
- Triggering escalation protocols

Wearables and Biofeedback Integration

Virtual therapy platforms often combine with smart rings (e.g., Oura Ring), wristbands (e.g., Fitbit), or EEG headsets compatible with VR, allowing for real-time physiological monitoring. Measures like:

Heart Rate Variability (HRV)

- Galvanic skin response
- Pupil dilation and eye movement
- Respiratory rates are processed using AI models to detect levels of stress, anxiety, fear, or relaxation. This real-time biofeedback loop allows context-aware delivery of therapy, providing personalized breathing exercises, meditative cues, or de-escalation instructions at the very moment users require them.

Crisis Identification and Escalation: In extreme instances of suicidal thoughts or panic attacks, the system can:

- Identify high-risk language or biometrics
- Trigger emergency alerts
- Route the user to a human therapist, helpline, or emergency contact
- Log securely for post-crisis clinical analysis

The AI-based mental health application Koko, embedded within VR environments, employs emotional classifiers and keyword triggers to intervene in cases of suicide ideation by routing users towards live support in seconds [30].

5.3 Reducing Stigma

Social stigma is one of the most deeply rooted barriers to mental health treatment, especially in collectivist societies where talking openly about emotional pain is seen as shameful. The Metaverse provides strong means to overcome this stigma through anonymity, avatar representation, and participation in virtual communities.

Anonymity and Masking of Identity: People in the Metaverse interact through avatars, computer representations that can be non-identifiable, genderless, culturally neutral, or symbolic. This psychological distancing:

- Lessens fear of exposure or judgment
- Fosters greater emotional expression
- Assists early-stage seekers who would otherwise not seek therapy at all [31]

Group Therapy without Physical Presence: The Metaverse facilitates avatar-based group sessions, led by AI or human therapists. The virtual group environments:

- Mimic typical support groups (e.g., for addiction, bereavement, PTSD)
- Make participants comfortable sharing without being seen.
- Establish a community through shared space and emotional identification.

Removing visual identity is thought to minimize social comparison and defensiveness, maximizing receptiveness to group therapy.

Mental well-being activities in the Metaverse can be integrated into gamified environments, virtual art therapy, narrative quests, and meditation challenges. This makes mental health discussions part of everyday digital habits and makes therapy less clinical and more interactive.

Case Study: Mind Quest VR integrates therapeutic activity with game-like quests where users can work on trauma recovery through narrative-based interactions in a safe space [32].

6. Challenges and Ethical Issues

While the use of AI and immersive technologies in mental health holds great promise, it also presents enormous challenges that need to be tackled through multidisciplinary practice, policy guidelines, clinical standards, and ethical regulation. In a field as sensitive as psychological wellness, any mistake, bias, or harm can have widespread impacts on individual health, public trust, and fairness within systems. Here, four main areas of concern are discussed: data privacy, clinical validation, algorithmic fairness, and user dependency, and provide measures to avert these risks.

6.1 Data Privacy and Security

Security of personal information is probably the most urgent ethical issue with virtual mental health services. Patients using Metaverse-based therapy websites or apps disclose intimate information, ranging from mood diaries and trauma stories to biometric and behavioural patterns. Such sets of data, if compromised or exploited, may result in identity theft, social stigmatization, or psychological damage.

Major Risks

- Unsecured avatar sessions or virtual rooms result in eavesdropping.
- Third-party monetization of data (e.g., selling behaviour data to advertisers).
- Location and movement tracking using VR/AR devices.
- Hacked biometric data (e.g., stolen from smart rings or eye trackers).

Required Safeguards

- **Zero-Trust Architectures:** Presume breach and authenticate each access request.
- End-to-End Encryption (E2EE): All communications—text, voice, video, and biometric need to be encrypted in transit and at rest.

Decentralized Identity Systems: Deployment of blockchain-based identity verification without central storage.

Privacy-by-Design Frameworks: Integration of privacy protections into each layer of system design. A research article in Nature Digital Medicine highlighted the necessity for regulatory agencies such as HIPAA (USA) or GDPR (EU) to adapt to include immersive and AI-facilitated mental health interfaces, which are partially not covered under existing regulations [33].

6.2 Therapeutic Efficacy and Validation

Though most virtual and AI-based therapies are novel, their clinical verification tends to be behind their technological progress. The mental health sector requires evidence-based treatments.

Existing Gaps: Insufficient randomized controlled trials (RCTs) comparing the efficacy of VR/AI therapy vs. regular therapy. Dominance of short-term pilot research with little evidence regarding long-term effects. Challenges in measuring therapeutic alliance, a strong determinant of success for conventional talk therapy. Underrepresentation of minority populations in the existing digital therapy literature and concerns regarding generalizability.

Solutions and Research Imperatives

- Fund and make cross-disciplinary clinical trials (psychologists + data scientists) a priority.
- Create standardized outcome metrics for virtual therapeutic rapport (e.g., engagement, trust, responsiveness).
- Add longitudinal outcome measurement (6 months to 3 years).
- Create independent ethics review boards for AI mental health technologies before public release.

The NIH has just started to fund studies to assess the clinical effectiveness of AI-created CBT modules in avatar-based VR systems, a first step toward mainstream medical acceptance [34].

6.3 Bias and Fairness in AI

AI systems are no more equitable than the data and design principles they are constructed. In mental health, bias can lead to misdiagnosis, exclusionary material, and perpetuation of structural inequities.

Danger Vectors: Bias in training data: If AI models are trained on highly Western, English-language, neurotypical data, they might:

Misunderstand linguistic subtleties in other cultures

Miss depression or psychosis in underrepresented populations
Algorithmic opacity: Unclear decision-making contributes to distrust and regulatory challenges.

Mitigation Strategies

Bias Audits: Perform routine checks throughout training and after deployment.
Inclusive Data Sets: Gather diverse, multilingual, and representative data on which to train AI models.
Explainable AI (XAI): Make sure systems can explain why they made a diagnosis or therapy suggestion.
Community Co-Design: Engage marginalized user communities in the design and testing process.

Case Study: Researchers discovered that some initial suicide prevention chatbots incorrectly interpreted passive expressions of distress in African American Vernacular English (AAVE), which revealed a severe cultural gap in AI training [35].

6.4 Dependency and Overreliance on Technology

AI-based therapy is convenient and scalable, but overdependence on human-less interactions carries psychological and behavioral dangers.

Potential Problems

- Avoidance of real-life social engagement results in heightened loneliness.
- AI-synthesized empathy can produce emotional bonding with avatars, obscuring distinctions between authentic and artificial support.
- Self-diagnosis or dismissal of red-flag signs, being misled by superficial responses of AI.
- Risk of treatment delay, postponing face-to-face care for severe disorders in reliance on AI platforms.

Suggested Precautions

- **Hybrid Approaches:** AI assistance must support, not displace, licensed practitioners.
- **Scheduled Human Monitoring:** Periodic meetings with a human clinician or therapist.

- **Digital Hygiene Practices:** Instill breaks, mindfulness outside the digital space, and "digital detox" habits.

Usage Limits and Feedback Alerts: Install session time limits and AI notifications encouraging users to seek human services as needed.

Ethical Note: Individuals with serious psychotic symptoms or suicidal thinking should never depend exclusively on AI therapy; systems should alert for such conditions and escalate them right away [36].

7. Real-World Applications and Case Studies

7.1 Existing Platforms and Initiatives

The potential of AI-based treatments in the Metaverse is already being realized in a few early pioneering applications and clinical uses. These early efforts show the manner in which virtual worlds, chatbots, and biometric response systems are transforming the provision of mental health care.

Wysa

Wysa is an artificial intelligence-powered chatbot offering text-based mental health treatment using Cognitive Behavioral Therapy (CBT), mindfulness, and journaling. Its uniqueness lies in the possibility of escalating up to human coaching, blending AI scalability with the human touch. It is available in more than 30 countries and has more than 100 million conversations, offering low-cost depression, anxiety, and stress therapy.

Effect: Studies show that Wysa increases emotional regulation, especially among youth, and may be a useful first-line intervention tool.

OxfordVR

OxfordVR, developed by researchers at the University of Oxford, brings virtual reality immersion to the treatment of social anxiety, psychosis, and agoraphobia. Oxford offers exposure-based cognitive therapy in safe, virtual settings that simulate public speaking, crowded environments, or social interaction. These are AI-driven avatars that adapt based on patient performance.

Example: In 2021, a report was made that over 50% of patients who were receiving VR therapy for psychosis indicated clinically significant improvement in confidence and social behavior.

BehaVR

BehaVR combines behavioral psychology, neuroscience, and in-VR biometric feedback. Participants are led through emotion regulation training, psychoeducational information, and mindful exercises while their physiological data (heart rate, skin conductance) are monitored in real-time to adapt therapy.

Application: Utilized in addiction treatment and chronic pain clinics, BehaVR drives personalized stress relief modules from real-time user feedback [37].

7.2 Success Stories and Constraints

There is increasing empirical evidence supporting the effectiveness of such platforms. For example, a study by Stanford University revealed that VR therapy reduced symptoms of social anxiety by 20% after six weeks of guided, avatar-supported exposure therapy. Such gains were sustained on follow-up, suggesting long-term behavior change.

Challenges

- **Low Digital Literacy:** Especially among rural or older populations, low exposure to VR/AI tools hinders adoption.
- **Language and Cultural Barriers:** Most AI systems are English-centric, leaving out non-English speakers or culturally dissimilar users.
- **Infrastructural Deficiencies:** LMICs could be short of bandwidth, devices, or support infrastructure to handle high-performance AI or VR applications.
- **Skepticism and Resistance:** Some clinicians and consumers are uneasy about employing non-human agents for psychiatric or emotional therapy. Promising early platforms, but to scale globally, be inclusive, and integrate hybrid with existing mental health systems, all these issues need to be addressed [38].

8. Future Opportunities and Innovations

The next decade holds the promise to transform mental health care with converging technologies, namely, AI, VR, wearable sensors, and decentralized governance models.

8.1 AI and VR Developments

Generative AI Therapists: With the progress of large language models (LLMs) like GPT-4 and the next, AI-powered avatars are becoming increasingly capable of:

- Having empathetic, dynamic, and realistic conversations
- Offering therapy akin to human methods (CBT, DBT, MBCT)
- Matching tone, body language, and dialog complexity with user needs
- These hyper-realistic therapists can mimic human rapport, enhancing emotional connection in therapeutic relationships.

Emotional Intelligence and Affective Computing: Affective computing allows avatars to identify and respond to human emotions in real-time by processing:

Facial expressions and tone of voice

- Biometric information (e.g., skin temperature, breathing patterns)

- Posture and gaze monitoring: These avatars are capable of modulating feedback according to the user's emotional and physiological state, and this makes the virtual therapy richer and more profound [39].

8.2 Wearable Technology and Biofeedback Integration

Future platforms for therapy will increasingly be informed by real-time information that is collected using wearables and smart devices. This information includes:

- **Heart rate variability (HRV):** Uncovers stress or relaxation
- **Electrodermal activity (EDA):** Measures emotional arousal
- **Posture monitoring:** Identifies fatigue, disengagement, or distress
- **Pitch and voice fluency:** Monitor cognitive workload or anxiety

These physiological indicators will be interpreted by AI engines to deliver adaptive therapy, slowing down, module switching, or calling for mindfulness when needed.

8.3 Vision for the Future

DAOs (Decentralized Mental Health Ecosystems)

Emergent blockchain frameworks suggest Decentralized Autonomous Organizations (DAOs) to manage digital mental health platforms:

- Community ownership and control
- Clear funding and resource allocation
- Patient data sovereignty

This model offers ethical, open, and user-driven innovation in mental health services.

Cross-Border Digital Therapy Regulations: With therapy becoming international via the Metaverse, there is a necessity for:

- Pre-standardized data protection laws
- Cross-licensing of virtual therapists
- Global teletherapy laws that safeguard both consumers and clinicians
- Worldwide mental health policy needs to adapt to the acceptance of such digitally transcendent care models.

AI as Emotional Co-Pilots: In the future, not just will AI offer therapy, it will track mental health in daily life:

- Offering nudges, affirmations, or reminders about stress
- Recommendation of social interaction, diet, or regimen
- As an emotional well-being anticipatory ally, instead of intervening only during crisis moments
- This is a shift from reactive to proactive mental health treatment.

9. Conclusion

This chapter emphasized the way Metaverse-based virtual therapy using the power of AI represents a paradigm shift in global mental healthcare. Immersive platforms and AI scale mental health services to underserved and hard-to-reach groups. Virtual environments reduce stigma, language barriers, and time constraints, personalizing treatment to the actual emotional, behavioral, and physiological state. Technological potential, privacy of data, bias, and clinical efficacy issues must be strictly regulated. Implement global AI standards on bias, explainability, and transparency. Enforce informed consent and user control over data sharing. Conduct Clinical Validation. Prioritize RCTs, longitudinal studies, and ethnographic evaluations. Support open science and open reporting of AI models. Integrate digital mental health education into community and school programs. Provide affordable hardware and access to the underserved. The Metaverse is not just a playground for tech but a new psychological frontier. Virtual AI-powered therapies could democratize psychiatric treatment, reduce stigma, and deliver compassionate, intelligent, and responsive support systems across borders and cultures. Technology has always been in the service of human dignity, though, with ethical principles prioritizing equity, privacy, and well-being. The future of mental health is not human vs machine, but human with machine, with empathy leading us, data improving us, and with ethics guiding us.

References

1. Health, T. L. G. (2020). Mental health matters. *The Lancet. Global Health*, 8(11), e1352.
2. Ralston, A. L., Andrews III, A. R., and Hope, D. A. (2019). Fulfilling the promise of mental health technology to reduce public health disparities: Review and research agenda. *Clinical Psychology: Science and Practice*, 26(1), 60.
3. Altaf Dar, M., Maqbool, M., Ara, I., and Zehravi, M. (2023). The intersection of technology and mental health: Enhancing access and care. *International Journal of Adolescent Medicine and Health*, 35(5), 423–428.
4. Yuan, W. (2022). Identifying the effect of digital healthcare products in the metaverse on mental health: Studying the interaction of cyberchondria and technophobia. *American Journal of Health Behavior*, 46(6), 729–739.
5. Mazzolenis, M. V., Mourra, G. N., Moreau, S., Mazzolenis, M. E., Cerda, I. H., Vega, J., ... and Thérond, A. (2024). The role of virtual reality and artificial intelligence in cognitive pain therapy: A narrative review. *Current Pain and Headache Reports*, 28(9), 881–892.
6. Cheng, S. (2023). Metaverse. In: *Metaverse: Concept, Content and Context* (pp. 1–23). Cham: Springer Nature Switzerland.

7. Muñoz-Saavedra, L., Miró-Amarante, L., and Domínguez-Morales, M. (2020). Augmented and virtual reality evolution and future tendency. *Applied Sciences*, 10(1), 322.
8. Kalasampath, K., Spoorthi, K. N., Sajeev, S., Kuppa, S. S., Ajay, K., and Angulakshmi, M. (2025). A literature review on applications of explainable artificial intelligence (XAI). *IEEE Access*, 13.
9. Sun, Y. (2025). Cloud and edge computing as effective trends in business model innovation: A bibliometric review. *Journal of Software: Evolution and Process*, 37(1), e2754.
10. Im, S., Jo, D., and Lee, S. M. (2024). Exploring the impact of therapeutic presence on working alliance in metaverse counseling. *The Counseling Psychologist*, 52(5), 698–724.
11. Ibrahim, A. (2024). The role of artificial intelligence in the metaverse. *Arts and Design Studies*, 110.
12. Saghiri, A. M. (2020, April). A survey on challenges in designing cognitive engines. In: *2020 6th International Conference on Web Research (ICWR)* (pp. 165–171). IEEE.
13. Shetty, N. P., Singh, Y., Hegde, V., Cenitta, D., and K, D. (2025). Exploring emotional patterns in social media through NLP models to unravel mental health insights. *Healthcare Technology Letters*, 12.
14. Wahyudi, E., Windianto, N. E., Ananda, G. F., Solaeman, A., and Setiawan, W. (2024). Personalized medicine meets artificial intelligence: Beyond "hype", towards the metaverse. *Informatics for Health and Social Care*, 49(2), 149–152.
15. Achenbach, J., Waltemate, T., Latoschik, M. E., and Botsch, M. (2017, Nov.). Fast generation of realistic virtual humans. In: *Proceedings of the 23rd ACM Symposium on Virtual Reality Software and Technology* (pp. 1–10).
16. Srivastava, K., Das, R. C., and Chaudhury, S. (2014). Virtual reality applications in mental health: Challenges and perspectives. *Industrial Psychiatry Journal*, 23(2), 83–85.
17. Szabo, C. P. (2018). Urbanization and mental health: A developing world perspective. *Current Opinion in Psychiatry*, 31(3), 256–257.
18. Wu, J., Snell, G., and Samji, H. (2020). Climate anxiety in young people: A call to action. *The Lancet Planetary Health*, 4(10), e435-e436.
19. Das, A., Sharma, M. K., Thamilselvan, P., and Marimuthu, P. (2017). Technology addiction among treatment seekers for psychological problems: Implication for screening in mental health setting. *Indian Journal of Psychological Medicine*, 39(1), 21–27.
20. Miranda, J., McGuire, T. G., Williams, D. R., and Wang, P. (2008). Mental health in the context of health disparities. *American Journal of Psychiatry*, 165(9), 1102–1108.
21. Wuthrich, V. M., and Frei, J. (2015). Barriers to treatment for older adults seeking psychological therapy. *International Psychogeriatrics*, 27(7), 1227–1236.
22. Jauhiainen, J. S. (2024). The metaverse: Innovations and generative AI. *International Journal of Innovation Studies*, 8(3).
23. Mazzolenis, M. V., Mourra, G. N., Moreau, S., Mazzolenis, M. E., Cerda, I. H., Vega, J., ... and Thérond, A. (2024). The role of virtual reality and artificial intelligence in cognitive pain therapy: A narrative review. *Current Pain and Headache Reports*, 28(9), 881–892.
24. Aggarwal, A., Tam, C. C., Wu, D., Li, X., and Qiao, S. (2023). Artificial intelligence–based chatbots for promoting health behavioral changes: Systematic review. *Journal of Medical Internet Research*, 25, e40789.

25. Bansal, H., Aryan, A., Pathak, H. A., and Shukla, S. D. (2024, Dec.). An AI-powered mental health assistant for personalized and adaptive care. In: *2024 International Conference on Progressive Innovations in Intelligent Systems and Data Science (ICPIDS)* (pp. 67–74). IEEE.
26. Torous, J., Bucci, S., Bell, I. H., Kessing, L. V., Faurholt-Jepsen, M., Whelan, P., ... and Firth, J. (2021). The growing field of digital psychiatry: Current evidence and the future of apps, social media, chatbots, and virtual reality. *World Psychiatry*, 20(3), 318–335.
27. Kabudi, T., Pappas, I., and Olsen, D. H. (2021). AI-enabled adaptive learning systems: A systematic mapping of the literature. *Computers and Education: Artificial Intelligence*, 2, 100017.
28. Takac, M., Collett, J., Conduit, R., and De Foe, A. (2023). A cognitive model for emotional regulation in virtual reality exposure. *Virtual Reality*, 27(1), 159–172.
29. De Clara, L. (2024). Accessibility and inclusivity in mental health: New perspectives on immersive psychotherapy. In: *Inclusivity and Accessibility in Digital Health* (pp. 1–12). IGI Global.
30. Villegas-Ch, W., García-Ortiz, J., and Sánchez-Viteri, S. (2024). Towards intelligent monitoring in IoT: AI applications for real-time analysis and prediction. *IEEE Access*, 12.
31. Yadav, V., and Dhanda, N. (2024). The metaverse and mental health: The future. *Decentralized Systems and Distributed Computing*, 337–354.
32. Giosan, C., Popoviciu, C. M., Zhamaliyeva, S., Zaborot, I., and Deac, G. (2024). Evaluating the efficacy of support groups in the metaverse for Ukrainian refugees: A protocol for a randomized clinical trial. *Trials*, 25(1), 697.
33. De Clara, L. (2024). Accessibility and inclusivity in mental health: New perspectives on immersive psychotherapy. In: *Inclusivity and Accessibility in Digital Health* (pp. 1–12). IGI Global.
34. Buragohain, D., Khichar, S., Deng, C., Meng, Y., and Chaudhary, S. (2025). Analyzing metaverse-based digital therapies, their effectiveness, and potential risks in mental healthcare. *Scientific Reports*, 15(1), 1–21.
35. Mehrabi, N., Morstatter, F., Saxena, N., Lerman, K., and Galstyan, A. (2021). A survey on bias and fairness in machine learning. *ACM Computing Surveys (CSUR)*, 54(6), 1–35.
36. Zhai, C., Wibowo, S., and Li, L. D. (2024). The effects of over-reliance on AI dialogue systems on students' cognitive abilities: A systematic review. *Smart Learning Environments*, 11(1), 28.
37. Lepore, S. J., and Helgeson, V. S. (1998). Social constraints, intrusive thoughts, and mental health. *Journal of Social and Clinical Psychology*, 17(1), 89–106.
38. Zhou, B., Huang, M., Li, C. L., and Xu, B. (2022). Leisure constraint and mental health: The case of park users in Ningbo, China. *Journal of Outdoor Recreation and Tourism*, 39, 100562.
39. Usmani, S. S., Sharath, M., and Mehendale, M. (2022). Future of mental health in the metaverse. *General Psychiatry*, 35(4), e100825.

CHAPTER

8

Virtual Reality in Rehabilitation: Redefining Patient Recovery with AI

Vanajaroselin Chirchi[1*], Emmanvel Raj M. Chirchi[2], Lokabhiram Dwarakanath[1], Sangeeta Urankar[1] and Ciro Rodriguez R.[3]

[1] Department of ISE, Dayananda Sagar Academy of Technology and Management (DSATM), Bengaluru – 560082

[2] CSE(AIML), East West Institute of Technology, Bengaluru – 560091

[5] Department of Software Engineering, Universidad Nacional Mayor de San Marcos UNMSM, Peru

The convergence of Artificial Intelligence (AI) and Virtual Reality (VR) is transforming the landscape of rehabilitation, offering novel, patient-centered approaches that enhance recovery outcomes. This chapter explores how AI-augmented VR environments are redefining traditional rehabilitation paradigms by enabling immersive, adaptive, and data-driven interventions for patients recovering from neurological, musculoskeletal, and cognitive impairments. We examine the role of AI in personalizing VR therapy sessions through real-time biomechanical and behavioural feedback, dynamic difficulty adjustments, and predictive analytics for patient progress monitoring. Through case studies spanning stroke rehabilitation, orthopaedic recovery, and neurocognitive therapy, we illustrate how these intelligent systems foster patient engagement, improve motor and cognitive functions, and provide clinicians with actionable insights. Furthermore, the chapter discusses the technical architecture, challenges, and ethical considerations of integrating AI and VR in healthcare, including data privacy, accessibility, and clinician training. By presenting emerging trends and future directions, we argue that AI-driven VR rehabilitation is not merely an adjunct to conventional therapy but a paradigm shift towards more interactive, precise, and effective patient care.

*Corresponding author: dr.vanajaroselin-ise@dsatm.edu.in

DOI: 10.1201/9781003679370-8

1. Introduction

Virtual reality is no longer just used for gaming and entertainment. It's quietly establishing a role in rehabilitation, especially for people recovering from physical injuries or nervous system damage. Patients can now participate in interactive sessions where the therapy feels more like an activity than a chore. These sessions focus on movements that matter in real life. Lately, there's been a shift in how researchers see VR. It's now being used to recreate everyday tasks in a way that feels real but is still safe. That matters, especially early on when recovery is just starting. These realistic simulations allow people to practise safely, which in turn helps the brain form new connections after injury. This rewiring, also known as neuroplasticity, is important to many recovery strategies. Stroke patients often benefit the most from this kind of targeted repetition [1]. There's also growing evidence that VR can help children with physical difficulties [2]. Some have improved movement and even a reduction in discomfort by using VR for rehabilitation [3].

Of course, not all virtual therapy works equally well. A lot depends on how real the environment feels, how quickly it responds, and how closely the content matches the person's situation. The feeling of being "present" in the virtual setting plays a big role. If people feel like they're really there, they're more likely to stay focused and keep at it [4]. Adding artificial intelligence into the mix helps, too. With AI, therapists can adjust the session while it's happening. They can make things harder or easier based on how someone is doing, keeping the experience just within reach [5]. The theoretical foundations of VR in rehabilitation, as described by [6], are described in Figure 1.

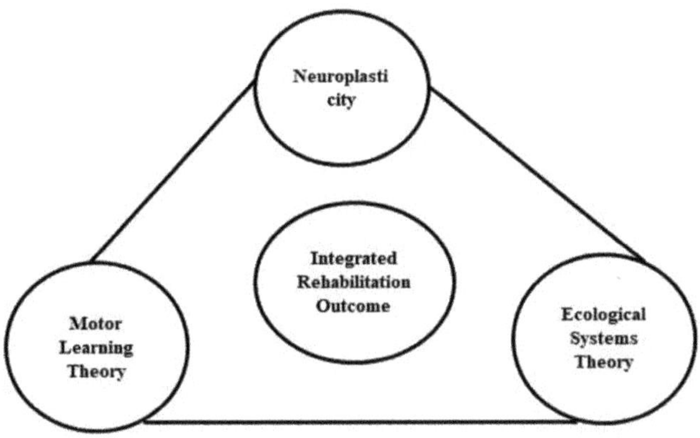

Figure 1: Theoretical foundations of VR in rehabilitation.

This chapter brings together theory, research, and real examples to show how VR and AI together might shape the future of therapy. It explores how artificial intelligence can be added to that experience, making therapy more flexible and effective, especially for conditions like stroke or Parkinson's. It also examines what still needs to be fixed before these tools can become part of everyday use care.

2. Virtual Reality In Rehabilitation

VR is changing how therapy gets delivered. It builds digital worlds that people can move through, interact with, and respond to in real time. For someone recovering from an injury, this means useful exercises, not abstract ones. The movements are practical. They match up with actions a person needs in daily life [7]. Doing those movements repeatedly in a structured setting helps the brain rewire itself [8]. It also lets therapists provide treatment that's more tailored to the person in front of them.

Immersion is one of the big advantages. When people feel like they're really part of the virtual scene, they tend to put in more effort and stay motivated. This is especially important in stroke recovery, where sensory feedback and attention make a real difference [9]. Tools like headsets, motion trackers, and touch-based gear work together to create an environment that feels surprisingly close to real life [9]. All of that helps people not only practise movement but also remember it better [10]. Therapists, meanwhile, can adjust the pace or complexity as they go [11].

The instant feedback in VR also matters. Unlike traditional exercises that might feel repetitive or come with a delay before feedback, VR gives people immediate cues. They see and hear how well they're doing right then and there. This can help correct mistakes and reinforce better habits [12]. When the system is powered by AI, it can go a step further. It adapts based on user performance. For stroke patients, this can lead to better control of the hand and arm. In Parkinson's therapy, it helps with walking and balance by setting up realistic but safe challenges [13].

VR in therapy pulls from a mix of fields like movement science, psychology, and brain research. The main idea is that doing a task over and over in different settings helps build skill. That's something VR can deliver, often using game-style challenges and goal-oriented tasks [14]. Some existing rehab methods are also finding new life here. For example, constraint-induced therapy, where the stronger limb is limited so the weaker one gets used more, can now be simulated through virtual characters [15]. Mirror therapy, which was once done with actual mirrors, is now happening through digital limbs that people control in real time [16]. These approaches keep people interested and allow for more flexibility.

VR rehab is being used in many different situations. It has shown positive results for people recovering from strokes, head injuries, spinal cord damage, and diseases like Parkinson's and multiple sclerosis [15, 16]. In stroke recovery, it has helped improve hand movement, walking, and balance, often with better results than traditional care alone [17]. It has also been useful in therapy for children, especially those with coordination or developmental problems. Play-based VR tasks help them with planning movement and building coordination[17, 18]. Because the sessions can be tweaked for age, skill level, and attention span, the technology fits a wide range of users.

Some people feel motion sickness or get tired quickly. Not all clinics have the budget for high-quality equipment [18]. There's also the need for trained staff who can guide the session and interpret the results. Another issue is how realistic the virtual task feels. If it doesn't match real-world movement, what's learned might not carry over. Future work must address these limits, improve usability, and set clear clinical standards.

AI might help fill in those gaps. Smarter systems can keep track of how patients are doing and make changes instantly. This could support therapy outside the clinic, including at home. With AI, sessions can be adjusted on the spot. The system can offer the right level of difficulty and keep people motivated [19]. AI can also collect patterns in progress, giving therapists a clearer view of what's working and what's not. Used together, VR and AI may provide care that is more engaging and informed by real-time data.

In the end, VR-based rehab brings together technology, science, and personalization in a way that could shift the standard approach. It's already showing strong results, and as the tools become easier to use and better connected, the future of therapy may feel more interactive and more centred around the person.

Based on the discussions in previous paragraphs, Figure 2 compares VR Rehabilitation and Traditional Rehabilitation.

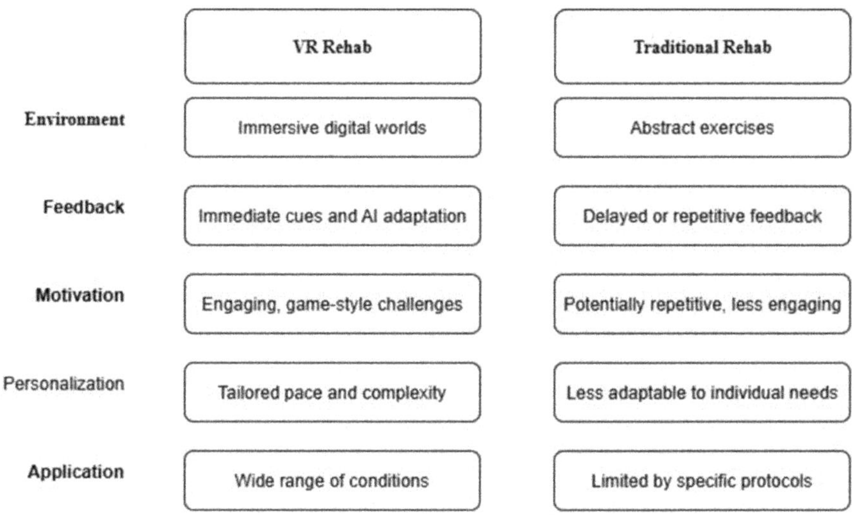

Figure 2: Comparing traditional rehabilitation and VR rehabilitation.

3. Artificial Intelligence in Rehabilitation

Artificial intelligence is starting to change how rehab is done. Instead of sticking to fixed routines or waiting for therapist input, AI is making therapy smarter and more personal. These systems can analyze what a person is doing in real time and adjust the session while it's happening [19]. That's a big shift, especially for neurological conditions like stroke or Parkinson's, where recovery often depends on doing the same movement again and again. AI can work behind the scenes, using data from motion sensors or cameras to track progress and offer feedback that fits the person's pace and ability.

One of the main things AI does well is watch how someone moves and give feedback on the spot. It can notice if an arm is out of line or if a movement isn't quite smooth. This kind of real-time guidance is useful in stroke rehab, where small changes make a big difference [19]. Some VR setups already use AI to check how well a task is being done, whether a movement is fluid, how far a limb reaches, or if the task was finished correctly [20]. The tech doesn't just measure things either. It can spot unusual patterns and help therapists fine-tune what they're doing. These systems often rely on visual models trained to pick up tiny motion details, giving a clearer view than what's possible by eye [20].

Beyond tracking, AI helps make therapy plans more flexible. In the past, patients were often given standard sets of exercises, no matter how they were progressing. But AI platforms can change the plan depending on how the person is doing. If someone is improving, the challenge can increase; if they're tired or struggling, it can ease up [20]. Some systems turn therapy into a kind of game, changing levels based on how well the person is moving or how focused they are. This approach makes therapy less frustrating and helps people stick with it for longer [21].

AI also pulls in information from lots of sources. Wearables, EMG signals, and motion sensors all feed into a single system that builds a full picture of the patient. This lets clinicians catch problems early, like when someone starts compensating with the wrong muscles or getting too tired too quickly [21]. In more advanced setups, like robotic exoskeletons, AI takes control of the movement support itself. The system senses what the body needs and adjusts the help it gives. That's huge for people with paralysis, since it makes the training more natural and less draining [21].

AI isn't only being used in clinics, either. Many systems are being adapted for use at home. With apps and remote tools, patients can do sessions under light supervision without leaving their homes. Some even come with built-in voice assistants or simple chatbots that guide the session, give reminders, or keep motivation up [22]. These tools are especially helpful for older adults or people who live far from rehab centres. They also let families be more involved, which can make a big difference in how often therapy gets done.

Still, there are problems to sort out. One of the big ones is how AI models are trained. Most of the training data comes from ideal lab settings, not real patients. That means the AI might not handle messy, unpredictable movements properly [21,22]. If it gets something wrong, it might give poor feedback or even reinforce bad habits. The solution lies in training with broader datasets and doing more testing in real-life conditions. Getting AI to work smoothly with hospital systems is another hurdle. Many platforms don't connect easily with electronic health records or therapist tools. Without that link, data can be lost or hard to use. Clinics also need staff who understand how to use the systems, which adds cost and training time. Then there's the matter of trust. Therapists and patients need to know how AI makes decisions. If it feels too much like a black box, people might not feel confident using it.

Safety is also key. If the system misreads a signal, it could push a patient too far or give the wrong advice. That's why new tools need to undergo tough testing before being rolled out. They should be checked in proper trials and measured against gold-standard rehab methods [23]. Getting that approval takes time, but it is important to make sure the tools are truly helpful.

The next section will look at how AI and VR work together. When you bring them into the same space, it opens up new ways to make rehab more immersive, responsive, and focused on each person's real progress.

4. AI-Augmented VR Systems: A Synergistic Approach

The experience in rehabilitation drastically alters when virtual reality and artificial intelligence are combined. It's no longer just about doing a task in a digital setting. The AI watches, listens, and learns from how the person is doing. The VR makes the whole thing feel real. The result is a therapy session that adapts, nudges, and sometimes surprises. These systems respond in the moment, shifting to meet the user where they are mentally and physically [20].

The key here is how well AI can read body data while someone moves through a virtual space. These systems are trained on thousands of examples of what normal or abnormal motion looks like. When something seems off, like a shoulder not lifting enough or a step dragging, it notices. It can make the activity easier or tougher, or just pause for a rest. What's great is that this happens quietly in the background. The person just keeps going, often not even realizing that the task is shifting based on what they're doing [6]. For therapists, this means getting real data, not guesswork about how joints are moving or whether a task is being done properly [13].

In stroke recovery, where repeating meaningful movements is a core part of regaining control, these platforms have shown solid results. People using VR that adjusts based on how they're doing tend to stick with it longer. They also often regain more hand and arm function than with traditional rehab alone [1]. The AI doesn't just track progress. It changes the "game" as the person gets better. If they're doing well, the task gets harder. If they're tired or frustrated, it dials things down a bit [11]. It's a kind of responsive therapy that feels almost like being coached in real time.

These VR setups can also blend physical movement with mental challenge. That's helpful for conditions like Parkinson's or brain injuries, where just walking or standing still isn't the whole story. People must think, solve problems, and stay balanced. In these systems, the virtual world might ask them to climb stairs while avoiding obstacles or carry out a task in a crowded room. All the while, the AI is monitoring how steady they are, how quickly they react, and whether they're improving [17]. It's this mix of body and brain that makes recovery more complete. The richness of the virtual world encourages the brain to rewire more effectively [9].

Another powerful feature is that these systems don't always need to be used in a clinic. Because the AI tracks progress remotely, people can continue sessions at home. The data goes into the cloud, where therapists can check in later. If something's not right, they'll see it. Wearables and even smart exoskeletons send information back to the system, and AI algorithms adjust what the patient sees or feels next [2, 8]. This means fewer trips to the hospital, more freedom, and, importantly, no drop in the quality of care. Of course, there are challenges. One of the big ones is that not all AI models work well outside of test labs. If they've only been trained on a narrow set of people, they might give strange feedback to others. A system that understands a 35-year-old athlete recovering from an injury might not be helpful for an 80-year-old stroke survivor [20]. The more varied the training data, the better these systems will become.

Another concern is trust. If a rehab tool tells someone to repeat a movement or stop for a rest, it should be clear why. Right now, many AI decisions feel like they happen in a black box. That's fine in a video game, but not when it affects someone's health. Both patients and clinicians need to understand why the AI is recommending something [10]. That's how confidence builds.

There's also the problem of cost and complexity. These systems need to fit into real clinical life, not just research settings. That means linking up with hospital data systems, working with therapist software, and having an interface that doesn't require hours of training [11]. If they're too hard to use or don't fit how therapists work, they won't last. To make the most of AI in VR rehab, tech teams need to work closely with healthcare professionals. Systems need to speak the same language as therapists, show results in useful ways, and give feedback that makes sense. It's not just about the technology; it's about the care that wraps around it.

The next part will explore actual cases and studies showing how this blend of VR and AI is already being used in stroke recovery, Parkinson's therapy, and even home-based care. These real-life stories help make the potential of this technology easier to understand.

5. Case Studies and Applications

In recent years, virtual reality and artificial intelligence have started making their way from labs and pilot projects into real therapy rooms. What used to be seen as experimental is now slowly becoming part of daily rehab for stroke survivors, children with coordination issues, and people living with Parkinson's or spinal injuries. What stands out in these cases isn't just the technology, it's how people respond to it. Patients feel more involved. Therapists get better data. And outcomes often improve.

Take the example of stroke rehab. [1] looked at how VR helped people regain function after a stroke. One man, 62 years old, had an ischaemic stroke that affected movement in his upper body. Instead of just doing exercises with a physio, he used a VR program for six weeks. It mimicked daily tasks, reaching for things, holding objects, and moving with purpose. What made the difference was that the AI inside the program kept adjusting the difficulty based on how he was doing each day. Over time, his Fugl-Meyer Assessment score went up by 35 percent. He also said he felt more motivated. The sense of progress was clearer. That's often what helps people keep going.

In another example, [3] built a VR-based system to help stroke patients regain control of their arms and shoulders. It used deep learning to track how people moved and then changed how tough the exercises were. In a small trial of 20 people, the system tweaked shoulder and elbow exercises depending on how well someone was doing. At the end of four weeks, most of them could move with a better range and control. More importantly, they stuck with the program. The personalization seemed to matter not just physically, but mentally.

Parkinson's is another area where these tools are showing promise. [17] ran a study with 40 participants. Half did standard therapy. The other half used a VR game system that challenged them to stay balanced while doing different tasks like walking or turning. These weren't just random games. The system was built to recreate tricky situations from everyday life. And it gave instant feedback. Over eight weeks, the group using VR did better on balance tests, including the Berg Balance Scale and Timed Up and Go. That's crucial for Parkinson's patients, where balance loss can lead to falls. What helped was the AI gently increasing the difficulty just enough to keep people on edge, but not past it.

VR and AI aren't just for adults. Children with motor skill issues are also benefitting. [9] worked with kids who struggled with movement planning and coordination, like those with developmental coordination disorder. A nine-year-old boy was experiencing difficulties with fine motor skills, including handwriting. The team created a 10-week VR program that let him interact with digital drawings and simple tasks using his hands. By the end, his test scores on the MABC-2 had improved, and he found the sessions fun. That's key in paediatric therapy. If it feels like play, they'll come back. Later versions of that setup have added AI that tweaks the challenges on the fly based on how the child is doing [20]. The tech is even helping in cases of spinal cord injury. [1] described a case where a 32-year-old woman, paralysed from the waist down after a spinal cord injury, trained with a smart exoskeleton and VR program. The AI interpreted muscle signals and adjusted how much help the exoskeleton gave. Over 12 weeks, she started regaining some voluntary movement in her legs. That's not something many expect in long-term paralysis. But the repetition, feedback, and engagement made a difference.

In rural areas or for people who can't easily travel, this technology is starting to close gaps. A model developed by [8] and later improved now allows people to do VR therapy at home while their therapist tracks progress from afar. One woman, aged 67, recovering from a mild stroke, used such a system at home for 10 weeks. The AI helped guide her through exercises, and her therapist adjusted her goals based on what the system reported. By the end, her ability to do daily tasks had improved by 25 percent. She also said she felt more in control of her recovery.

Even in areas like pain management, where physical change is hard to measure, VR and AI are showing benefits. Mirror therapy, once done with real mirrors to trick the brain into seeing a missing limb, has now moved into VR. [24] laid the groundwork, but more recent work has added AI-powered feedback and haptic cues. One man, aged 47, dealing with phantom limb pain, spent six weeks interacting with a virtual version of his missing arm. The system responded to his real-time input, showing him a moving, responsive limb. His pain dropped by half, and the effect lasted after therapy ended [6].

These case studies aren't isolated. They point to a shift where therapy becomes more responsive, more portable, and often more effective. Patients feel seen. Progress is clearer. And the experience, while still hard work, feels less clinical and more personal. The next section will step back and look at the limits of this approach. What still needs fixing? What barriers keep this technology from reaching more people? These are the questions that shape the next phase of development.

5.1 Clinical Case Study and Evidence

Table 1 presents four notable case studies that exemplify the successful integration of VR and AI technologies in diverse rehabilitation settings. Each case showcases a unique patient group, specific technological implementation, and measurable therapeutic outcomes:

- **MIDAS (Mild stroke – Hand rehabilitation):** Combined VR and exoskeleton technologies with AI feedback to support hand function recovery in mild stroke patients. Reported high patient engagement (96%) and no adverse effects.
- **Acute Stroke Rehab:** Utilized VR environments and AI analytics for early-stage ischemic stroke recovery. Patients demonstrated measurable improvements in the NIH Stroke Scale and Barthel Index scores.
- **Reh@City (Chronic stroke – Cognitive rehab):** Designed to improve cognitive deficits post-stroke, particularly in activities of daily living (ADLs). AI-adapted VR tasks to enhance executive and visuospatial abilities.

- **ParkiVR (Parkinson's disease rehab):** Focused on gait and balance training for Parkinson's patients. The system integrated AI to analyze gait patterns and adjust VR exercises accordingly. Outcomes included improved postural stability and reduced fall incidence, making it a valuable tool for mobility rehabilitation in neurodegenerative disorders.

Table 1: Case Study with Its Outcome

Case Study	Patient Group	Technology Used	Key Outcomes
MIDAS	Mild stroke (hand rehab)	VR + exoskeleton + AI	96% engagement, no side effects
Acute Stroke Rehab	Ischemic stroke patients	VR + AI analytics	Improved NIHSS and Barthel Index
Reh@City	Chronic stroke (cognitive)	VR + AI for ADLs	Enhanced executive and visuospatial function
ParkiVR	Parkinson's disease patients	VR balance training + AI gait tracking	Improved balance, gait coordination, and reduced fall risk

5.2 Case Study: AI-VR in Parkinson's Disease Rehabilitation

Background

Parkinson's Disease (PD) is a progressive neurodegenerative disorder characterized by motor symptoms such as tremors, bradykinesia (slowness of movement), rigidity, and postural instability. Non-motor symptoms include cognitive decline and mood disturbances. Traditional physiotherapy, although effective, is limited by low engagement and difficulty in replicating real-life movement contexts.

Intervention Approach

An interdisciplinary team developed a **VR-based motor and cognitive training system** integrated with **AI-driven motion analysis**. The setup included:

- **VR headset** with simulated environments (e.g., city navigation, object grabbing)
- **Motion sensors and wearable trackers**
- **An AI module** that analyzed motor symptoms (tremors, gait) in real-time
- **Feedback system** to adjust task difficulty and pace

"Patients performed virtual walking tasks while AI continuously monitored gait symmetry, stride length, and tremor frequency."

Patient Profile

- Name: Mr. A.B. (pseudo-anonymized)

- Age: 62
- Diagnosis: Idiopathic Parkinson's (Hoehn & Yahr Stage II)
- Symptoms: Left-side rigidity, resting tremor, mild cognitive impairment
- Previous Therapy: 6 months of conventional physiotherapy with slow progress

Treatment Plan

- Duration: 8 weeks (3 sessions/week, 45 minutes/session)
- Tasks: Virtual cycling, obstacle navigation, memory games
- Progression: AI-adapted movement sensitivity and added visual/auditory challenges as performance improved

Outcomes

Table 2: Pre- and Post-Therapy Clinical Outcomes of Parkinson's VR-AI Rehab Program

Metric	Pre-Therapy	Post-Therapy
Gait Stability (m/s^2)	0.45	0.68
Tremor Severity (UPDRS)	3.5	2.0
Task Completion Rate (%)	62%	91%
Patient Engagement Score	Low	High

Patient Feedback

"For the first time, therapy didn't feel like therapy. It felt like I was in a game—but I could tell my legs were getting better."

Conclusion

The AI-VR hybrid rehabilitation significantly improved motor control and patient motivation in a patient with Parkinson's. AI's ability to track nuanced movement deterioration and adapt therapy in real time proved essential. This case demonstrates the potential of tech-driven rehabilitation in managing chronic neurodegenerative conditions.

5.3 Comparison of Traditional and VR Methods

This table outlines key differences between conventional rehabilitation methods and emerging AI-VR-based rehabilitation approaches, highlighting how modern technology addresses the limitations of traditional systems:

1. **Feedback**
   - **Traditional Rehab:** Feedback is typically provided by a therapist after observing performance, which may be delayed or subjective.
   - **AI-VR Rehab:** Feedback is real-time and automated, as sensors and AI algorithms instantly analyze motion, posture, and interaction, enabling immediate corrections.

2. **Personalization**
   - **Traditional Rehab:** Often follows a generic program with minimal individual tailoring, leading to suboptimal outcomes.
   - **AI-VR Rehab:** Uses AI to deliver personalized therapy, adapting intensity and content based on the patient's current status and progress.
3. **Motivation**
   - **Traditional Rehab:** Exercises can be repetitive, leading to boredom and reduced patient compliance.
   - **AI-VR Rehab:** Incorporates gamification, immersive environments, and interactive tasks, making sessions enjoyable and improving patient engagement.
4. **Monitoring**
   - **Traditional Rehab:** Progress is manually observed and recorded by therapists, which may lack accuracy or consistency.
   - **AI-VR Rehab:** Enables continuous monitoring through motion tracking and data analytics, offering precise performance metrics and progress visualization.
5. **Accessibility**
   - **Traditional Rehab:** Requires physical presence at healthcare facilities, which limits access for patients in rural or remote areas.
   - **AI-VR Rehab:** Supports tele-rehabilitation, allowing patients to access therapy from home using portable VR and AI tools, thus improving accessibility and convenience.

Table 3: Comparison Table between Traditional Rehab vs AI-VR Rehab

Feature	Traditional Rehab	AI-VR Rehab
Feedback	Manual and infrequent	Real-time and automated
Personalization	One-size-fits-all programs	AI-driven adaptive protocols
Motivation	Repetitive and passive	Engaging gamified sessions
Monitoring	Therapist-dependent	Continuous, data-driven tracking
Accessibility	Limited by geography	Tele-rehab and remote access

6. Technical Challenges and Ethical Considerations

Even with all the advances, using artificial intelligence and virtual reality in rehab isn't as simple as plugging in new tech and watching results roll in. The tools might be smart, but they're only as good as the systems and people using them. There are still hurdles, some technical, others ethical, that slow things down or raise concerns. Until these are addressed properly, the full potential of AI-augmented rehab might stay just out of reach.

One of the biggest technical issues is how AI models are trained. Many rely on data gathered in clean, controlled lab settings. But people in real-life rehab don't move like test subjects. Stroke survivors, for example, often show irregular, non-linear patterns that confuse models trained on healthy bodies [6]. When an algorithm struggles to read this, it might give the wrong feedback or even reinforce poor habits. To avoid that, we need much more varied data, more diverse bodies, ages, and movement types. Validation across different patient groups should become the norm, not the exception.

Integration with healthcare systems is another sticking point. A lot of VR setups work well in research labs, but struggle when moved into hospitals or clinics. The problem often lies in compatibility. Most hospitals already have complex electronic health records (EHRs) and strict routines. If the rehab system can't "talk" to those records, therapists end up duplicating effort, or worse, skipping key data. According to [11], many platforms still lack common formats, clinician-friendly dashboards, or reliable analytics. Fixing that takes more than coding. It needs cross-disciplinary teamwork engineers, doctors, and administrators, all working together.

There's also the question of upkeep. These aren't one-time purchases. VR headsets, sensors, and AI software all need regular updates, maintenance, and sometimes hardware upgrades. For large clinics, that's a logistical problem. For smaller centres or rural setups, it might be a deal breaker.

But the challenges don't stop with hardware and software. The ethical side of this shift is just as complex and sometimes harder to navigate.

To start with, there's the matter of consent and privacy. AI-powered systems often collect detailed movement, voice, and even biometric data. Who owns that data? Who sees it? And what happens if it's breached? Patients need to know exactly what's being collected and how it's used, especially when that data is stored on the cloud or shared across systems.

Algorithmic bias is another worry. Just like in other areas of AI, rehab algorithms can inherit bias from the data they're trained on. That might mean less effective results for people from underrepresented backgrounds. If left unchecked, it risks widening gaps in care instead of closing them.

Long-term exposure to virtual environments also raises psychological questions. [23] pointed out that not everyone responds well to immersive therapy. Elderly patients, or those with cognitive impairments, might feel disoriented or overwhelmed. While VR is often seen as engaging, it isn't one-size-fits-all. More research is needed to understand when, how often, and for how long it should be used.

Another major concern is fairness in access. These systems are expensive. A good headset, motion tracking gear, and supporting software can cost thousands. That puts them out of reach for many community clinics and for families trying to support therapy at home. Unless developers focus on lowering costs or offering basic versions, there's a real risk that only wealthier groups benefit. [1] warn that, without action, the gap in care could widen rather than close.

Finally, there's regulation. While countries are starting to create rules for AI in healthcare, many grey areas remain. Who's responsible if a system gives poor guidance and someone gets hurt? How should these platforms be tested before they go live? And how do we track long-term results in the real world? Current systems of approval designed for drugs or standard devices often fall short. According to [8], regulatory bodies will need to rethink their frameworks if they want to keep up.

In short, the potential is huge, but so are the challenges. Getting this right means thinking beyond the excitement of new tools. It means asking hard questions, listening to patients, and building systems that work not just in theory but in real-world clinics. Only then can AI and VR become more than experimental solutions and truly change how rehab is delivered.

7. Emerging Trends and Future Directions

As artificial intelligence and virtual reality keep evolving, new trends are starting to reshape how we think about rehab. These developments aren't just add-ons to existing systems; they're signs that digital rehabilitation is moving into its next phase. Some of these changes are already underway, while others are just starting to show promise. What's clear is that the future of therapy is going to feel very different, both in the clinic and at home.

One area gaining serious momentum is the pairing of VR with wearable sensor systems. Devices like smart garments, EMG bands, and motion trackers are now able to collect a steady stream of data on how a person moves, how their muscles fire, and even how their heart responds to effort [15]. This information gives a much fuller picture of progress, not just in terms of motion, but also physical strain, fatigue, and muscle coordination. As more feedback tools are added, like vibration, pressure, or resistance, it becomes possible to simulate real-world textures or effort, which adds another layer of realism to rehab tasks.

Another major shift is the growth of tele-rehabilitation. More people are doing therapy from home now, especially since the pandemic changed how care is delivered. Cloud-based platforms make this possible. These systems track performance, give users tailored prompts, and send updates back to therapists. The result is less need for in-person sessions, but still enough supervision to keep therapy on track [16]. As internet access improves, especially in rural or low-resource areas, these kinds of setups may help close the gap for patients who can't easily reach a clinic.

Alongside that, there's growing interest in explainable AI, or XAI. Right now, many AI systems are seen as "black boxes." They spit out recommendations, but it's hard to tell why. That's not ideal in rehab, where therapists need to understand how decisions are made. XAI is working to fix this by offering clearer feedback on what the system is doing. For example, it might show that a patient's shoulder angle was too tight, or that task difficulty was lowered due to signs of fatigue [10].

Making AI more transparent could improve clinical trust and also help patients better understand their own progress.

Another trend is a move toward patient-centred design. Rather than building systems based only on what's technically possible, developers are starting to ask what patients actually want and need. This includes how the VR world looks, how fast things move, and what kind of feedback is easiest to process. Games, storylines, and even social features are being added to keep people engaged. That matters for kids, who might get bored easily, but also for older adults who might feel intimidated by new technology [9]. Some platforms are also starting to use voice control, eye tracking, or brain-computer interfaces so that even users with limited mobility can take part.

Looking ahead, the key to all of this is collaboration. No single field can do this alone. It takes input from engineers, therapists, neuroscientists, designers, and ethicists to build systems that are not only powerful but also safe, fair, and usable. Long-term studies are also needed. Many current trials run for just a few weeks or months. But to truly understand the value of these tools, we need to track outcomes over years, across different settings and populations.

If these pieces come together with more natural interfaces, clearer AI decisions, wider access, and better testing, then AI-augmented VR might move from an experimental option to a mainstream part of rehab. The shift is already underway. What comes next will depend on how well we balance the technology with the human side of recovery.

8. Conclusion

The combination of artificial intelligence and virtual reality is changing how rehabilitation is done. It's not just about adding new tools to the same old routines. These technologies make it possible to shape therapy around the person and what they need, how they move, and how they respond in real time. Whether it's recovering after a stroke, dealing with Parkinson's, or rebuilding function after an injury, AI and VR are opening doors that didn't exist before. AI helps make therapy more personal. It watches how people move, picks up on patterns, and adjusts the session without needing a therapist to be there every second. VR, on the other hand, makes therapy feel more like an activity than a medical task. It brings in game-style challenges, real-world simulations, and settings that keep people involved for longer. Together, they shift the focus from one-size-fits-all care to something that feels more alive and more human. There are still hurdles. The tech can only be as good as the data it's trained on, and most of that comes from very controlled lab settings. It doesn't always reflect the messiness of real-life recovery. Then there's the issue of access. Not everyone can afford the gear, and not every clinic is ready to plug these systems into their daily work. There's also the human side to consider. People need to trust what the system tells them. If they don't understand how or why decisions are made, they're less likely to stick with it.

On top of that, we still need better rules. Regulators are trying to keep up with fast-moving tech, but gaps remain. Questions about data privacy, system safety, and who's responsible if something goes wrong aren't fully answered yet. Without clear guidelines, some clinics might be hesitant to leap.

Even so, the signs are promising. Trends like wearable sensors, at-home therapy platforms, and explainable AI are helping to fill in the gaps. The next big step will be to blend all these parts into systems that work not only in trials, but in everyday rehab. For that to happen, engineers, therapists, researchers, and patients will need to work together to shape the future of care. If done well, this shift could mean a rehab process that feels more engaging, more adaptive, and more in tune with each person's journey. It's not just about smarter machines. It's about smarter recovery that meets people where they are and helps them get where they want to go.

References

1. Aderinto, N., Olatunji, G., Abdulbasit, M. O., Edun, M., Aboderin, G., and Egbunu, E. (2023). Exploring the efficacy of virtual reality-based rehabilitation in stroke: A narrative review of current evidence. *Annals of Medicine*, 55(2), 2285907. https://doi.org/10.1080/07853890.2023.2285907
2. Ahmed, A., El-Sayed, H., Islam, S., Biswas, K., Sundarasekar, R., and Manogaran, G. (2023). AI and IoT-enabled smart exoskeleton system for rehabilitation of paralyzed people in connected communities. In: *Proceedings of the ACM International Conference* (pp. 1–10).
3. Bai, X., Li, R., Zhang, Y., Jiang, Y., and Zhao, L. (2022). Artificial intelligence limb rehabilitation system on virtual reality platform. *Computational and Mathematical Methods in Medicine*, 2022, Article ID 2688003. https://doi.org/10.1155/2022/2688003.
4. Brassel, S., Power, E., and Campbell, A. (2021). Recommendations for the design and implementation of virtual reality for acquired brain injury rehabilitation: Systematic review. *Journal of Medical Internet Research*, 23(7), e26344. https://doi.org/10.2196/26344
5. Capacci, G., Biffi, E., Ferrario, V., Gandolla, M., Beretta, E., Pedrocchi, A., and Lunardini, F. (2021). Learning to assess the quality of stroke rehabilitation exercises using machine learning. *IEEE Access*, 9, 123456–123467. https://doi.org/10.1109/ACCESS.2021.3103456
6. Deb, S., Rahman, M., and Haque, A. (2022). Deep learning models for movement analysis in VR-based rehabilitation. *IEEE Transactions on Neural Systems and Rehabilitation Engineering*, 30, 456–467. https://doi.org/10.1109/TNSRE.2022.3141592
7. Dockx, K., Bekkers, E. M. J., Van den Bergh, V., Ginis, P., Rochester, L., Hausdorff, J. M., Mirelman, A., and Nieuwboer, A. (2016). Virtual reality for rehabilitation in Parkinson's disease. *Cochrane Database of Systematic Reviews*, (12). https://doi.org/10.1002/14651858.CD010760.

8. Faria, A. L., Andrade, A., Soares, L. I., and Badia, S. B. (2016). Benefits of virtual reality based cognitive rehabilitation through simulated activities of daily living: A randomized controlled trial with stroke patients. *Journal of NeuroEngineering and Rehabilitation*, 13(1), 96. https://doi.org/10.1186/s12984-016-0196-z
9. Giglioli, I. A. C., Raya, M. A., and Riva, G. (2018). The past, present, and future of virtual and augmented reality research: A network and cluster analysis of the literature. *Frontiers in Psychology*, 9, 2086. https://doi.org/10.3389/fpsyg.2018.02086
10. Jeyaraman, M., Khurana, P., Khurana, A., Gupta, R., and Sharma, A. (2024). Ethical considerations in AI-driven rehabilitation systems. *International Journal of General Medicine*, 17, 45–58. https://doi.org/10.2147/IJGM.S453903
11. Khalid, M. U., Javaid, M., Haleem, A., Singh, R. P., and Suman, U. (2024). Impact of AI-powered solutions in rehabilitation process: Recent improvements and future trends. *International Journal of General Medicine*, 17, 945–960. https://doi.org/10.2147/IJGM.S453903
12. Laver, K. E., Lange, B., George, S., Deutsch, J. E., Saposnik, G., and Crotty, M. (2017). Virtual reality for stroke rehabilitation. *Cochrane Database of Systematic Reviews*, (11). https://doi.org/10.1002/14651858.CD008349.
13. Lee, M. H., Siewiorek, D. P., Smailagic, A., Bernardino, A., and Badia, S. B. I. (2021). Learning to assess the quality of stroke rehabilitation exercises. In: *Proceedings of the 24th International Conference on Intelligent User Interfaces* (pp. 218–228). https://doi.org/10.1145/3441852.3441876
14. Levin, M. F., Snir, O., and Liebermann, D. G. (2012). Virtual reality versus conventional treatment of reaching ability in chronic stroke: Clinical feasibility study. *Neurology and Therapy*, 1(1), 1–15. https://doi.org/10.1007/s40120-012-0005-5
15. Liu, X., Zhang, Y., Wang, J., Chen, Z., and Sun, Q. (2025). Multimodal data fusion in AI-driven rehabilitation systems. *Sensors*, 25(2), 1234. https://doi.org/10.3390/s25020123
16. Neo, P. J., Tan, Y., and Koh, G. (2024). Tele-rehabilitation platforms powered by AI and VR: Expanding access to care. *Journal of Medical Systems*, 48(1), 12. https://doi.org/10.1007/s10916-023-02067-2
17. Pazzaglia, C., Imbimbo, I., Tranchita, E., Minganti, C., Ricciardi, D., Lo Monaco, R., Parisi, A., and Padua, L. (2020). Comparison of virtual reality rehabilitation and conventional rehabilitation in Parkinson's disease: A randomised controlled trial. *Physiotherapy*, 106, 36–42. https://doi.org/10.1016/j.physio.2019.07.003
18. Proffitt, R. M., and Lange, B. (2015). Considerations in the efficacy and effectiveness of virtual reality interventions for stroke rehabilitation: Moving the field forward. *Physical Therapy*, 95(3), 441–448. https://doi.org/10.2522/ptj.20130571
19. Rand, D., Kizony, R., and Weiss, P. L. (2008). The virtual mall: A functional virtual environment for stroke rehabilitation. *Annual Review of Cybertherapy and Telemedicine*, 3, 193–198.
20. Rahman, M., Sarker, S., Haque, A. K. M. N., Uttsha, M. M., Islam, M. F., & Deb, S. (2023). AI-driven stroke rehabilitation systems and assessment: A systematic review. *IEEE Transactions on Neural Systems and Rehabilitation Engineering*, 31, 192–207. https://doi.org/10.1109/TNSRE.2022.3219085
21. Reda, F., Ahmed, M., Hassan, A., and Khan, S. (2018). Integration of AI in healthcare workflows: Challenges and opportunities. *Journal of Biomedical Informatics*, 85, 102–112. https://doi.org/10.1016/j.jbi.2018.08.007

22. Rose, T., Attree, D. A., Brooks, B. M., Cotton, S. C., and Wilson, B. (2018). Immersion of virtual reality for rehabilitation Review. *Applied Ergonomics*, 69, 153–161. https://doi.org/10.1016/j.apergo.2017.12.008
23. Stoll, J., Mulligan, K., & Rankin, J. (2021). Psychological impact of immersive virtual environments in rehabilitation: A review. *Cyberpsychology, Behavior, and Social Networking*, 24(4), 234–242. https://doi.org/10.1089/cyber.2020.0435
24. Subramanian, S. K., Knaut, C. S., and McComas, J. (2008). Arm pointing movements in a three-dimensional virtual environment: Effect of two different viewing media. In: *Virtual Rehabilitation* (pp. 181–185). https://doi.org/10.1109/ICVR.2008.4625191

CHAPTER

9

AI-Powered Wearables and Continuous Health Monitoring: Innovations, Challenges, and Future Prospects

Selvam Durairaj[1*], Suseela Sellamuthu[1], K Uma Maheswari[1] and Malik Mohamed Umar[2]

[1] School of Computer Science and Engineering (SCOPE), Vellore Institute of Technology, Chennai Campus – 600127, Tamil Nadu, India

[2] National Space Science & Technology Center (NSSTC), United Arab Emirates University (UAEU), Al Ain, 15551, Abu Dhabi, UAE.

The healthcare industry is entering a revolutionary era due to the combination of wearable technology and artificial intelligence (AI), which enables continuous, real-time health monitoring with previously unattainable levels of precision, responsiveness, and personalization. Heart rate, blood oxygen levels, sleep patterns, and physical activity are just a few of the physiological signals that may be recorded by AI-powered wearables. These devices allow the early identification of ailments such as diabetes, respiratory disorders, and cardiovascular diseases by using ML algorithms and data analytics to identify even the most minor changes in vital signs. This chapter examines the state of wearable technology with AI integration, emphasizing chronic illnesses, improving patient engagement and adherence, and proactive health management. The main frameworks of this system that support wearable data in AI models, communication protocols, smartwatches, and biometric trackers, remote wearable monitors, and sensor-integrated data design are also examined in this chapter. The final outlines of future research initiatives, including explainable AI, prioritizing explainable and transparent AI, improved power efficiency and edge AI integration, smooth integration with the healthcare infrastructure, federated learning, and next-generation biosensors, moving away from reactive treatment models and toward proactive, individualized, and preventative care systems that wearable AI enables.

*Corresponding author: selvam.d@vit.ac.in

DOI: 10.1201/9781003679370-9

1. Introduction

The healthcare industry is on the brink of a revolutionary era with the integration of wearable technology and AI, providing continuous, real-time health monitoring with unmatched accuracy, adaptability, responsiveness, and flexibility. Heart rate, blood oxygen saturation, sleep, and activity are some physiological signals AI-based wearables monitor, ranging from AI-based trackers to innovative biosensors. These wearables facilitate early detection of diseases such as diabetes, respiratory disorders, and condition-based breathing through ML-based algorithms and data analytics to monitor even small changes in vital signs. This chapter considers the wearable technology with AI probability of incorporation scenario, its capability to monitor chronic disease, enhance patient engagement and adherence involvement, and provide healthcare supervision and preventive healthcare management. The underlying technology platforms enabling these systems, including computational AI models, communication network protocols, and sensor and new device design, are examined in this chapter.

Despite the encouraging trends, there are some issues with expanding the medical space. The battery's life, compatibility, integration, confidentiality of data, and predictive bias are significant issues in mass adoption. The ethical issues of extensive monitoring and information acquisition are balanced with cautious reservation. Notwithstanding overall encouraging behavioural patterns, there are still specific challenges. The ethical implications of ubiquitous scrutiny and data retention should be carefully weighed. Even with these promising trends, there are some challenges.

Continuous health monitoring also shifts healthcare from reactive to anticipatory and preventive care. AI-based wearables enhance chronic disease management, reduce hospitalization, and facilitate interventions, distance monitoring, and real-time feedback.

During international public health crises, like the COVID-19 pandemic, these technologies have been extremely helpful in enabling remote care and decreasing the number of clinic visits. However, other obstacles must be overcome before AI can be used in wearable medical equipment. Data privacy and security, algorithm transparency, model bias, device interoperability, and user compliance continue to be challenges.

In companies, regulatory frameworks have yet to evolve to meet the ethical and legal concerns of having intelligent monitoring devices in daily life. This chapter provides an overview of the current state of wearable technology incorporating artificial intelligence for healthcare monitoring and where it is going. It reviews the most important developments shaping the industry, considers barriers to wider take-up, and considers possible future research areas that could make these technologies' impact even greater. The chapter reviews how AI wearables can make healthcare delivery a more participative, personalized, and pre-emptive process, considering the possible advantages and limitations.

Combining AI and wearable technology is one of the most revolutionary developments in modern healthcare. With the shift in healthcare towards patient-centred, data-informed, and preventive treatment, wearables with AI capabilities have become a new changer for continuous health monitoring in the AI-based systems. Often beyond the scope of traditional clinical diagnostics, advanced technologies enable the AI collection, processing, and analysis of multimodal physiological information in real-time, with real-time feedback on a person's health trajectory. Current wearable technology can track vital indicators such as heartbeat, saturation of oxygen (SpO_2), heartbeat (ECG), glucose, lung temperature, and calories burned when combined with biomedical sensors and enhanced by AI-driven analytics. They can use machine learning and deep learning algorithms to interpret high-frequency data in real-time to identify notable dynamic risk scores, detect anomalies, and also for disease prognosis prediction.

These systems extend the reach of healthcare beyond hospital ceilings, allowing comprehensive ambient intelligence in everyday situations. By integrating with AI, wearable devices enable edge computing and cloud infrastructures to safeguard durability and scalability simultaneously, encouraging low-latency decision-making for chronic disease management for diabetes, hypertension, cardiovascular disease, and neurodegenerative conditions. AI wearables offer pharmacological reminders, continuous psychological feedback, and individually designed interventions that substantially improve the results. Aggregated and categorized wearable data can enhance epidemiological research, individual medication, community health monitoring, and public healthcare policies. AI algorithms trained on these datasets can track the spread of illnesses, spot new health trends, and help healthcare organizations optimise their use of resources in monitoring and tracking.

There are still several significant obstacles to their transformative potential. The wider integration of these technologies is limited by problems including algorithmic bias, lack of interoperability, form factor and battery limitations, data protection laws (such as GDPR and HIPAA), and the requirement for clinical validation. The main idea of Careful thought is also given to ethical conundrums involving data ownership, informed consent, and ongoing biometric monitoring. This study addresses the emerging designs, core technologies, and practical applications of artificial intelligence-based wearable healthcare systems. Aimed at generating a push towards increased reliability, usability, and ethical use of smart wearables in digital healthcare environments, it examines the existing shortcomings, investigates transdisciplinary solutions, and maps the future research directions.

2. Literature Review

Research in digital healthcare is now focused on integrating AI into wearable medical equipment. Augmented with machine learning algorithms, wearable devices have advanced beyond fitness tracking, now offering real-time diagnostics, personalized health recommendations, and early detection capabilities.

Thanks to recent advances in machine learning, wearables can now analyze intricate physiological information. Demonstrated a wearable ECG device based on DL that can precisely identify cardiac arrhythmias. Their convolutional neural network (CNN) model learned temporal patterns from unfiltered signal input, excelling traditional rule-based methods. A deep neural network for classifying ventricular fibrillation was also proposed by [10], and it was implemented similarly to board-certified cardiologists.

Integrating AI into wearable healthcare gadgets has gained substantial attention in digital healthcare research. With ML algorithms, wearable technology has advanced beyond simple health monitoring of fitness to allow for timely detection, specific health recommendations, and immediate form diagnostics. Because of the latest developments in ML, wearable technology was at the forefront of movement analysis of complex physiological information. A DL-based ECG wearable device, able to consistently detect cardiac rhythm disturbances in the heart, was demonstrated by [7]. Their convolutional neural network (CNN) model learned time-dependent trends from unstructured signal data, beating traditional rule-based methods.

Wearables incorporating AI features demonstrated the potential in addressing the management of chronic problems [3]. The management of respiratory disorders, including hypertension, was examined using intelligent wearables. This study demonstrated how continuous monitoring combined with AI-based feedback could improve quality of life and reduce hospitalization rates. Furthermore, [6] showed that real-time glucose monitoring and predictive alerts significantly reduced the frequency of hyperglycaemia episodes in individuals with diabetes. [1] performed a technical assessment of sensors worn on the body for medical devices. Their test with temperature sensors, accelerometers, photoplethysmography (PPG), and electromyography (EMG) revealed the advantage of sensor fusion in improving precision. They argued that while there is a perception that technology counts, the value of wearables is in the combination of sensors and AI algorithms [9].

Researchers have explored hybrid AI models, as wearable technology has processing power and energy efficiency limitations. For wearable systems, [11, 24, 25] proposed an edge–cloud collaboration architecture in which deep analysis is performed in the cloud, and lightweight inference is carried out on-device. Federated learning, which protects user privacy while facilitating cooperative model training across dispersed nodes, was employed by [12] to expand this model further. Privacy, surveillance, and data misuse are now significant concerns due to the increasing availability of personal health data. [13, 26, 27] controlled data collection and sharing, emphasizing the essentials of AI transparent systems within an ethical framework. They recommended using differential privacy, secure multiparty computation, and blockchain-based audit trails to increase trust. Additionally, if algorithmic bias is not addressed, [8] cautioned that it could exacerbate healthcare inequities.

Table 1: AI-Powered Wearable Survey

Author(s)	Objective	AI-Powered Wearable	Innovation	Limitations	Challenges
Bhamidipaty et al. (2025) [14]	To explore the transformative role of AI sensors in healthcare	Sensor-integrated smart wearables	Generative AI integration in biomedical monitoring	Data privacy concerns	Noise in biosensor data, real-time processing
Etli et al. (2024) [15]	Examine AI-driven wearables for real-time monitoring and predictive analytics	Smartwatches and biometric trackers	Personalized health predictions using AI	Limited generalizability	Battery life and sensor accuracy
Lyroi et al. (2024) [16]	Transforming remote patient monitoring using AI wearables	Remote wearable monitors	Improved chronic care via real-time analytics	Connectivity dependency	Regulatory compliance
Kumar (2022) [17]	Continuous monitoring for chronic disease prevention	AI wearables for chronic care	Automated alerts for critical vitals	Limited sensor interoperability	Data standardization
Sarker (2025) [18]	Case study on sensor fabrics for chronic health monitoring	AI-powered textile sensors	Non-invasive, fabric-based monitoring	Scalability issues	Durability and washability
Wah & Ng (2024) [19]	Overview of AI-driven health wearables	General AI-enabled health wearables	Emphasis on wellness optimization	Lack of real-world testing	Human factor acceptance
Oluwagbade (2024) [20]	Focus on preventive healthcare using wearable AI	Preventive monitoring tools	Early warning systems for diseases	Cost barrier for mass adoption	Data overload & interpretation
Secara & Hordiiuk (2024) [21]	Personalized systems combining AI and wearables	AI-integrated monitoring platforms	Real-time adjustments in treatment plans	Data inconsistency	Sensor calibration
Paul (2025) [22]	Predictive health monitoring with AI sensors	Wearable biosensors	Early detection of chronic issues	Data security risks	Algorithm transparency
Komalasari (2024) [23]	Personalized wellness via AI wearables	Activity and vitals monitoring wearables	Behavioral insights for wellness	Individual variation in performance	Limited personalization

[4] study on user behaviour revealed that intelligent feedback, gamification, and adaptive interfaces within AI wearables enhanced compliance in the short term. They did mention that long-term use relies significantly on contextual personalization and integration into clinical routines. [5] concurred, arguing that unobtrusive design and seamless interoperability with smartphones and Electronic Health Records (EHRs) are key to long-term engagement. Despite the encouraging results, [1] noted the absence of standardized datasets and clinical validation among devices. [2] emphasized the need to perform more interdisciplinary research and trials to determine the effectiveness of AI-based wearables across various populations, states of disease, and applications, as depicted in Table 1.

3. AI-Powered Wearable Approach

By providing continuous, intelligent health monitoring outside of clinical settings, the combination of wearable technology and AI is transforming the future of healthcare. Real-time data, early intervention, and individualized care are becoming increasingly critical in healthcare models that replace traditional systems, which frequently rely on patient-reported symptoms and routine check-ups. The wearable approach is leading this change, driven by AI. It is an ecosystem of smart devices with sensors that can gather behavioral and physiological data and use AI algorithms to interpret it to provide helpful health insights.

Physical activity is tracked by smart AI-based devices like biosensor patches, smart watches, and fitness trackers. The essential variables, such as heart rate, sleep, blood oxygen, glucose, and exercise, are monitored through AI-enabled wearables. Wearables can utilize machine learning and pattern detection to identify abnormal patterns, forecast health danger, and deliver personalized feedback. This method allows arrhythmia, sleep disorders, and diabetes complications to be detected in the early stages before they cause symptoms. These technologies are data gatherers and clever partners in treating chronic conditions, wellness promotion, and remote patient care. Combining cloud computing, edge AI, and mobile health platforms improves scalability and reactivity, thereby increasing access to individualized treatment. Wearables with AI capabilities present a possible way forward as healthcare systems worldwide are under increasing pressure to become more effective and preventive, turning patients into active participants in their health journey.

Suppose a methodology has critical problems like validation, the fairness of an algorithm, the fairness of a device, and the privacy of data. In that case, these problems should be resolved so that wearable AI technology can be utilized effectively, fairly, and securely with ongoing research and development.

3.1 Sensor-Integrated Smart Wearables

Sensor-integrated smart wearables, or wearable devices that gather and analyze physiological data in real-time, are transforming preventive and personalized healthcare. A variety of biosensors are featured in blood oxygen saturation (SpO_2) sensors, accelerometers, gyroscopes, electrocardiograms (ECG), electroencephalograms (EEG), and body temperature sensors. Important health indicators are continuously tracked by integrating sensors and enabling the identification of subtle physiological changes.

When combined with powerful AI algorithms, deep learning and machine learning wearables perform complex signal processing tasks such as anomaly detection, event classification, and predictive trend analysis. These devices are useful for collecting biometric data; they detect unusual patterns and send real-time alerts, offering insights that can be used immediately. This characteristic makes them particularly helpful when early intervention may prevent adverse outcomes, such as detecting arrhythmias or the early stages of cardiac arrest. In chronic illness, wearables help diabetic patients better and more quickly control their blood sugar levels through continuous glucose level monitoring. Furthermore, fall detection, mobility monitoring, and rehabilitation therapy, particularly in neurologically impaired or elderly patients, are effective with sensor-based activity recognition.

Research today is directed toward enhancing privacy, performance, and usability. Federated learning, enabling decentralized model training without sending private patient information to cloud servers, is increasingly a robust solution to data privacy. With contextual data and information from multiple sensors, multimodal data fusion offers more robust decision-making capabilities, mimicking a broader set of skills, such as those of a human clinician. Further, attempts are ongoing to bring AI algorithms to edge computing platforms, enabling wearable technology to deliver low-power, real-time analytics without reliance on remote servers. These advancements point to the future of patient-centric, AI-based healthcare delivery as highly reliant on sensor-integrated smart wearables, most widely accessible and well-liked wearables with AI capabilities. These everyday consumer products are increasingly crucial for early illness detection and health monitoring. These small, wrist-worn devices have several sensors for monitoring key parameters, including heart rate, sleep, body temperature, blood oxygen saturation (SpO_2), and measurements of physical activity, such as steps, calories, and intensity of movement. A GPS monitors outdoor activity and locates their whereabouts. The integration of cloud platforms and mobile applications enables the real-time synchronization of data collected in the healthcare context, providing timely feedback and remote clinical assessment of long-term health patterns to clients. Numerous tiny, wrist-worn gadget sensors track vital parameters, including heartbeat rate, periods of sleep, body temperature, blood oxygen saturation, and fitness activity measurement such as steps, calories burnt, and action intensity. GPS-enabled devices are frequently used to record external exercise activities and control their whereabouts. In a powered AI system, medical information is designed for real-time synchronization with an effortless interface connected to the cloud environment and mobile apps, enabling separate clinical analysis with long-term wellness patterns and timely client updates response.

AI's capabilities enhance the use of these devices to convert random biometric data into useful health insights by analyzing oxygen levels in the blood, behavioral trends, and heart rate variability modification. ML algorithms are used to forecast medical conditions, which include precursor indicators of ventricular fibrillation, stroke, or chronic stress. Some solutions provide simple and intuitive communication by enabling voice-based health inquiries or symptom reporting using AI-powered NLP. AI is also increasingly utilized in customized health coaching features that adjust fitness programs based on biometric information and specific objectives. Use cases of wearable and physiological monitors include chronic disease management and healthcare prevention. The wearable is appealing for improving the efficiency of health surveillance and fitness workouts, and produces AI-based feedback on how it functions. HRV and EDA data analysis by stress-detecting gadgets to encourage mindful breathing or relaxation. AI-driven sleep stage evaluation offers comprehensive data information on REM, light, and deep sleep stage cycles. It is an additional tool that users use to improve the quality of their sleep.

Research in this area uses a closed-loop to real-time cardiac prediction utilizing single-lead EGG data gathered by wrist-based sensors. Another growing field of research is emotion identification for biosignals because AI can recognize mood swings by analyzing subtle signals and physiological indicators. To improve engagement and adherence, researchers are additionally investigating how adapting an AI model dynamically changes alerts, messages, and actions based on a customer's changing health profiles.

3.2 Remote Wearable Monitors

The independent wearable monitor is one of the increasingly clinically advanced wearables driven by AI, intended to serve patients who require ongoing monitoring of their health away from hospital settings. Regulatory organizations like the United States FDA or the EU CE certification periodically audit these devices, guaranteeing excellent protection of patients, precision of data, and dependability. Remote monitors are specifically designed for applications such as telehealth and treating chronic illnesses, in contrast to generic consumer wearables. Sometimes featured features include respiration rate sensors, wireless ECG patches, pulse oximeters, and blood pressure cuffs. By transmitting patient information instantly to healthcare providers over secure internet connections, these technologies remove the need for physical presence at a medical facility and enable 24/7 analysis and early medical intervention implementation.

AI is being implemented to improve the diagnostic and estimation capabilities and remote wearable monitoring systems. Machine learning and deep learning models look at longitudinal health data to identify aberrations or indicate adverse health consequences like heart failure decompensation, epileptic convulsions, or COPD flare-ups. These algorithms can identify subtle changes above a patient's baseline physiological parameters, enabling early warning systems that allow doctors to intervene before an illness progresses into a medical emergency. AI is also used in ongoing trend analysis to help doctors evaluate the results of recommended remedies and make data-driven modifications over time.

Satellite imagery monitors have extensive medical uses, such as surgical rehabilitation monitoring and the at-home administration of neurological, pulmonary, and cardiovascular conditions. Patients undergoing cardiac surgery, for instance, can wear clothing that tracks their heart rhythm. A medical expert electronically monitors this data and responds in real time during an arrhythmia. Wearable pulmonary function tests can also identify respiratory irregularities and, if necessary, initiate telephone consults to help medicate patients with COPD.

3.3 AI Wearables for Chronic Care

Through intelligent, adaptable, and ongoing health monitoring, AI-supported wearables for extended treatment transform how long-term illnesses are managed. This particular equipment can help patients with neurodegenerative disorders, including Parkinson's disease, hypertension, type-2 diabetes, epilepsy, and other chronic conditions. Chronic care wearables are made to document physiological signals specific to the behavioral patterns of their diseases, as opposed to general-purpose health wearables. The result is that patients and medical personnel can monitor the progression of the illness, revise treatments in real time, and stop unforeseen flare-ups.

These specialized gadgets mainly cater to the demands of patients with chronic disorders, which include hypertension, glucose intolerance, and epilepsy, as well as neurodegenerative illnesses like Parkinson's disease. Chronic care wearables can capture physiological signals specific to illness patterns of behavior instead of general-purpose health wearables. This makes it possible for patients and medical personnel to monitor the progression of the illness, make immediate adaptations to therapies, and stop sudden flare-ups. Chronic care wearables are designed to monitor physiological signals and disease-specific behavioral patterns rather than general-purpose health wearables. They enable patients and healthcare professionals to closely track the progression of illness, make timely changes to treatments, and prevent sudden episodes from occurring.

Wearable glucose monitors, for instance, using AI algorithms can predict increases in blood sugar and suggest adjustments in insulin dosage to reduce the risk of hypoglycaemic episodes. Parkinson's disease patients can also benefit from gait analysis and fall detection features, which utilize motion sensors and deep learning to identify abnormalities in movement patterns and trigger an alarm.

For instance, wearable glucose monitors that use ML algorithms can forecast blood sugar spikes and recommend changes to insulin dosage to lower the potential of hypoglycemic episodes. Gait analysis and recognizing fall features, which use motion detection technologies and deep understanding to detect anomalies in movement patterns and sound an alarm, are also beneficial for people with Parkinson's disease.

These gadgets' AI capabilities forecast possible health emergencies by employing historical and real-time data through advanced predictive modelling. The algorithms used in reinforcement learning can naturally and subtly learn an individual's wellness habits, offering continuous health monitoring with more effective suggestions and alerts to prevent unnecessary treatments and maximize health compliance. This allows hypertensive patients to stay informed about their cardiovascular status without recurrent clinic visits. In this manner, hypertensive patients can stay at the forefront of their cardiovascular status without recurrent clinic visits. Researchers are looking into feedback loops with AI integration to create intelligent systems that automatically respond to patient feedback and adjust treatment plans.

A virtual or digital twin of a patient is another new concept by which one can simulate the progression of a disease and how a treatment will be effective, finally helping doctors to make improved decisions. Emotion-aware AI systems monitor voice, face, or biosignal signals to recommend behavior or drug interventions are also used to explore emotional and psychological states, which are paramount in chronic disease endpoints. These programs provide patients with more autonomy and decrease hospitalization rates to enhance the quality of life in patients with chronic diseases. These programs seek to empower patients and reduce hospitalization rates to enhance the quality of life in patients with chronic diseases.

3.4 AI-Powered Textile Sensors

AI textile sensors are the result of the convergence of wearable health tech and emerging materials science, and they provide a comfortable and inconspicuous way of monitoring health continuously. The flexible, stretchy sensors in these high-tech wearables, integrated into everyday clothing like a shirt, sock, or undergarments, can monitor physiological signals such as temperature, breathing rate, EMG, and ECG. Bright clothes fit the body's movement instead of rigid equipment that is unpleasant or clumsy to wear for hours. Wearing them as part of everyday exercise will not affect comfort. Since they are inconspicuous, they are most appropriate for individuals who need to be monitored all the time and sensitively, such as newborn babies, aged patients, and rehab patients.

These advanced materials are further enhanced by integrating AI chips and embedded computers, which can directly preprocess, filter, and classify biosignals on the garment. Real-time responsiveness improves, latency significantly decreases, and the need for continuous data transfer to external devices is minimized thanks to this on-device intelligence. Additionally, AI-driven compression methods transmit and store large amounts of physiological data effectively without sacrificing accuracy. Due to these features, textile sensors are practical tools for applications such as post-stroke rehabilitation, where monitoring minor muscle responses and mobility metrics over time is necessary, and neonatal and pediatric monitoring, where skin-friendliness and comfort are essential. They offer a new approach to sleep medicine by integrating movement and respiratory tracking into nightwear to diagnose and monitor disorders like sleep apnea. The field is progressing rapidly, with computationally sophisticated pattern recognition and signal processing from textile-based neural networks such as conductive fibre grids and e-yarns, which embed computation into clothing. Energy-autonomous wearables are also being developed by integrating energy harvesting devices like thermoelectric or triboelectric generators to remove battery life limitations and provide continuous data capture. Additionally, unprecedented efforts are being put into creating wash-proof, long-lasting clothing to endure everyday use and washing, which is greatly required for practicality.

4. Application in Healthcare

Wearable AI technology has evolved from slim fitness wearables to sophisticated health monitoring wearables applicable in the clinic. When paired with artificial intelligence and real-time data, wearables can provide varied healthcare requirements, from chronic disease management to emergency interventions. The main areas of application are covered in more detail below.

4.1 Chronic Disease Management

Heart disease, diabetes, and high blood pressure are some of the diseases that must be pre-treated and screened regularly. AI wearables bridge the gap between clinic visits by providing continuous personalized health data.

- Artificially intelligent continuous glucose monitors (CGMs) for diabetic patients can forecast hypoglycemic events and give individualized dietary or insulin advice.
- PPG and ECG sensor wearables can track blood pressure patterns in patients with high blood pressure, identify irregularities, and alert patients and healthcare professionals before problems arise.
- The Apple Watch detects irregular heart rate variability and atrial fibrillation, speeding up early medical assessment with AI technology.
- These technologies enable anticipatory treatment adjustment, decrease emergency visits, and promote illness self-management.

Wearable technology with AI features has come a long way from thin fitness wearables to sophisticated health monitoring wearables that can be applied in the clinic. Wearables can support various healthcare requirements, from managing chronic diseases to facilitating emergency interventions, when combined with artificial intelligence and real-time data. The main areas of application are elaborated further below.

4.2 Remote Patient Monitoring (RPM)

Wearables with AI capabilities are being utilized more and more for Remote Patient Monitoring (RPM), particularly for:

- Post-surgical recovery, where patients can be monitored at home for vital signs, wound healing, or signs of infection.
- Elderly care, where wearable devices help track mobility, sleep, hydration, medication adherence, and signs of cognitive decline or physical deterioration.
- Advanced monitoring frequently includes heart disease, diabetes, and high blood pressure in some conditions. AI wearables bridge the gap between clinic visits by providing continuous personalized health data.

4.3 Fitness and Preventive Care

Lifestyle and wellness management is one of the most popular wearable applications. AI-powered wearables offer:

- Activity tracking (steps, distance, calories burned) using accelerometers and gyroscopes.
- Sleep monitoring, analyzing, and sleep stages and disturbances using movement and heart rate data to offer personalized sleep hygiene recommendations.
- Stress analysis uses measures including skin temperature, electrodermal activity, and heart rate variability (HRV) to identify physiological stress and recommend breathing or relaxation techniques.

These characteristics lower risk factors for chronic diseases, preserve mental health, and enable people to take proactive measures toward healthy living.

4.4 Emergency Response

Wearables' AI software can recognize life-threatening situations in real-time and can therefore be valuable instruments in health emergency scenarios:

- Fall detection programs use motion sensors to detect sudden impact and subsequent inactivity, which benefits older adults living alone.
- Seizure alarm systems can track muscle activity, heart rate, and movement patterns and predict or alert caregivers to an impending epileptic seizure.
- Cardiac anomaly detectors continuously watch out for abnormal heart rhythms, sudden falls in oxygen levels, or other anomalies in ECG or PPG signals and issue instant alarms, even emergency contact procedures.

These capabilities significantly reduce emergency response time, likely saving lives and improving recovery results. Wearable health technologies and AI have enabled several applications of acute, chronic, preventive, and rehabilitative care. AI-enabled wearables with real-time, patient-specific interventions and around-the-clock monitoring are revolutionizing the delivery of more innovative, secure, and patient-centric care.

5. Innovations in AI-Powered Wearables and Continuous Health Monitoring

The wearables industry's AI technology has evolved at an unprecedented rate, transforming the infrastructure of modern medicine. Such technologies bring about a paradigm shift away from reactive, traditional interventions towards proactive, predictive, and preventive care approaches. AI-driven wearable technologies equip clinicians with real-time, personalized health data by creating synergy from innovation in hardware miniaturization, sensorization, edge computing, and personalized analytics.

Sensor data fusion enables the formation of an integrated picture of the person's health. As one illustration, microneedle arrays that glitter can track interstitial glucose without puncturing the body and even deliver insulin, as an easy-to-use supplement to traditional glucose monitoring. Sweat sensors have also been made wearable to monitor hydration levels, electrolytes, and indicators of exhaustion or stress, leading to continuous monitoring.

The second breakthrough is the convergence of on-device computing and Edge AI, now that machine learning models are being integrated into wearable devices. Facilitating real-time analysis and decision-making that is not dependent on cloud connectivity reduces latency, safeguards data privacy, and enhances energy efficiency. Those who live in rural or low-bandwidth areas will especially benefit from this innovation. On-device AI is already used by many smartwatches and fitness trackers today to analyze sleep patterns, identify arrhythmias, and offer personalized health advice.

Learning AI models across large health databases makes prospective and preventative healthcare analytics equally innovative. These types of systems can accurately predict the onset of medical disorders by recognizing subtle changes in health measurements. For example, cardiac attacks can be predicted a few days before using airway pressure variations and heart rate fluctuations. Similarly, wearables that detect postures and gait can help older people assess their fall vulnerability and initiate treatment or precautionary alarms. An additional component of AI wearables is adaptive, personalized feedback loops that change over time based on a person's behavior and physiological baselines for comparison. These gadgets leverage a user's historical events, daily activities, and psychological trends to learn advice rather than generic ones. For instance, sleep monitoring equipment can recommend various bedtimes based on recovery history and a prediction of probable sleep deficit. Accordingly, fitness bands dynamically modify the exercise goals using user performance and tiredness levels. The integration of wearables into broader healthcare networks is made possible by these customized services, enabling guarantees of ongoing adoption by consumers and real-world artificial seamless integration in given circumstances of the environment.

Wearable data can be converted into electronic health records, also known as EHRs, using FHIR technology standards, which makes it easier for doctors to monitor patients and make decisions based on information in real time. Wearables are rapidly paired with telemedicine programs, automated assistants, and AI-driven triage tools to provide remote medical treatment, illness management, and medication compliance. Additionally, wearables have been making their way throughout the long-neglected field of mental health tracking. To measure psychological well-being, wearables use information collected by sensors from sleep, heart rate, skin conductance, and even voice tone. Bright headbands that track brainwave activity (EEG) can identify stress or cognitive exhaustion, and AI provides real-time psychological wellness alerts, individualized mindfulness operations, and methods for calming down.

Wearability expands beyond the traditional form factors of watches and bands because of novel materials and implantable technology. For postoperative care or sports performance monitoring, glow-in-the-dark sportswear with integrated conductive fibres is ideal since it can non-invasively monitor posture, respiration, and muscle activity. On the other hand, implantable biosensors provide patients with previously unheard-of medical monitoring without compromising their quality of life, allowing for prolonged, continual surveillance of patients who are seriously ill. In totality, the development of AI-enabled wearables is not incremental stages but a qualitative leap in health delivery, experience, and optimization. These wearables enable early diagnosis, enhance treatment, and enable patients to engage in their health experiences through pervasive, innovative, and personalized monitoring. Health monitoring will be easier, effective, and innovative than ever in the future because of the rapid rate of technology development, especially in biomedical engineering, artificial intelligence, and human-centred design.

6. Limitations and Challenges of AI Wearables

While the potential for AI-based wearables to revolutionise healthcare is enormous, several technical, ethical, clinical, and operational limitations restrict their application and penetration. These would have to be overcome to enable safe, equitable, and effective deployment of the devices in clinical and consumer environments.

6.1 Data Accuracy and Reliability

The inconsistent and variable sensor data is a significant drawback of wearable technology. Elements, including poor device location, skin tone, motion artefacts, perspiration, temperature fluctuations, or limited battery life, may harm the accuracy of data gathering. A major development that incorporates wearables into larger health systems is clinical interoperability within the environment. Wearable data may be converted into electronic health records (EHRs) using FHIR standards, making it easier for doctors to monitor patients and make real-time data-driven decisions. Wearables are rapidly paired with telemedicine services, virtual assistants, and AI-driven triage tools to provide remote medical treatment, illness management, and medication compliance.

6.2 Lack of Clinical Validation and Regulatory Approval

Few devices have been subjected to rigorous clinical trials or approved by regulatory bodies like the FA or CE. Their data are not clinical-grade data. There is, therefore, a gap between clinically grade and consumer-grade devices. It is also hard to compare devices or their performance in different populations and conditions without standardized testing and verification procedures.

6.3 Data Privacy and Security

The continuous collection of personal behavioral and psychological data by wearable devices presents serious user privacy, consent, and data security issues. Unless adequately secured, the data is susceptible to hacking, unauthorized access, or abuse by advertisers, insurers, or third-party vendors. Data breaches are further exacerbated when cloud services are used for AI processing and storing data. Global adherence to regulations like GDPR and HIPAA is still tricky, particularly for manufacturers and startups that function across many countries.

6.4 Algorithmic Bias and Health Inequity

Wearable AI systems will most likely be built on data that does not necessarily reflect various populations on age, gender, race, socioeconomic status, or health. Algorithmic bias will result, wherein some populations will see a far better-performing wearable than others. Women during their menstruation or people of darker skin tones can see less accurate heart rate monitoring. These differences can create health inequalities, particularly among the poor or marginalized.

6.5 Hardware Limitations and Energy Consumption

High-power AI computation, wireless communication, and real-time sensing are all power-intensive consumers, but wearable technology does not have a long battery life. Long-term monitoring is then not so convenient and beneficial due to this trade-off. Hardware considerations such as processor power, device lifespan, and storage space also limit the on-device deployability of AI models.

6.6 Interoperability with Health Care Systems

The second major challenge is non-interoperability with other health infrastructure, like telemedicine, hospital information systems, and electronic health records (EHRs). Without information interoperability, the clinical usefulness of wearables would be lost. Further, errors, overload, and liability issues would discourage healthcare providers from depending on or using information acquired from wearable devices.

6.7 Cost and Accessibility

High-end wearables with advanced AI functions are too costly and out of reach for poor communities. This digital divide hampers the democratization of health technology and worsens healthcare inequality, especially in resource-poor or rural areas. Affordability, trends in reimbursement, and insurance coverage are crucial to their uptake. While AI-based wearables introduce new solutions for continuous, real-time health monitoring, their widespread use is constrained by data quality, clinical validity, privacy, bias, user behavior, and system integration. These imitations are addressed through multidisciplinary collaboration between technologists, healthcare professionals, regulators, and ethicists. For the advancement of technology to successfully and safely assist all facets of society, future developments must prioritize transparent AI, standardized evaluation applications, inclusive design, and safe data environments.

7. Conclusion

A revolutionary change regarding healthcare is occurring at the nexus of wearable technology and AI. With the promise of timely illness identification, ongoing disease surveillance, and providing individuals with tailored information on their health and well-being, the intelligent systems provide real-time, uninterrupted health monitoring. AI-powered wearables are rapidly changing precautionary and participative health care paradigms, from managing cardiovascular disease and diabetes to alerting caregivers in an emergency. Although these developments are notable, there are still a lot of issues, such as sensor accuracy, algorithmic bias, clinical confirmation, confidentiality of information, integrating systems, and the cost of healthcare. Confidence, connectivity, humanitarian construction, healthcare integration, and technology innovation are critical to success. By overcoming each of these obstacles, their potential in various healthcare settings can be realized. Wearable AI technology is both a force for advancement and a technology disruptor, as the conversation thus far has shown. They must be created as empowerment tools rather than as causes of injustice or suffering if they want to achieve their full potential.

7.1 Prospects for the Future

The following recommendations are made for future development and research to go beyond existing limitations and to develop more effective, universal, and therapeutically helpful approaches:

- **Development of Clinically Validated AI Models:** Future wearables must utilize AI algorithms trained on high-quality, diverse clinical data sets. The models must be clinically validated and stringently tested based on medical device regulations. Standard benchmarks and test protocols will be the way to gain credibility and acceptance of wearables in the clinic.

- **Prioritize Explainable and Transparent AI:** AI algorithms in wearables must be configured to deliver explainable outcomes to establish trust among clinicians and patients. Data processing and decision-making transparency will boost user understanding and facilitate better clinician oversight.
- **Improved Power Efficiency and Edge AI Integration:** Advances in low-power processors and on-device (edge) AI processing will improve energy efficiency, enabling longer battery life and real-time response without relying on cloud resources. This is necessary to ensure continuous and unbroken monitoring.
- **Enhancing Information Privacy and Federated Learning:** Using privacy-protecting machine learning techniques, such as federated learning, AI models can be trained on decentralized data provided by numerous users without revealing personal data. This will facilitate data protection, law enforcement, and model accuracy.
- **Inclusive and Accessible Design:** To bridge the digital health gap, next-generation wearables must be affordable, socially acceptable, and accessible to everyone, regardless of age, skin color, gender, or socioeconomic status. Inclusive design principles will make the benefits of those technologies accessible to all equally.
- **Smooth Integration with Healthcare Infrastructure:** Information gathered through wearable technology must work with current clinical decision support systems (CDSS) and electronic health records (EHRs). Interoperability will enable doctors to readily utilize wearable data for diagnosis, monitoring, and treatment planning.
- **Behavioral Health and Mental Wellbeing Monitoring:** Next-generation AI-based wearables must possess the ability to extend their functionality in monitoring mental health metrics, such as mood, stress, or sleep, using affective computing and passive sensing. This would allow for early intervention against cognitive and mental illnesses.
- **Cross-Disciplinary Collaboration and Policy Frameworks:** Multi-stakeholder collaboration between policymakers, ethicists, clinicians, and technologists will be needed to govern the safe and practical application of AI wearables. International policy guidelines, ethical norms, and policy frameworks will promote responsible innovation.

AI-driven wearable technologies constitute a powerful combination of computing power, sensor technology, and person-centred healthcare. At maturity, they have the potential to revolutionize health systems by changing the paradigm from treatment to prediction, prevention, and personalization. With sustained investment in research, ethical innovation, and systems integration, AI wearables can emerge as keystone technologies for future healthcare, providing life-saving insights, improving quality of life, and making healthcare proactive, personalized, and participatory for all.

References

1. Banaee, H., Ahmed, M. U., and Loutfi, A. (2022). Data mining for wearable sensors in health monitoring systems: A review of recent trends and challenges. *Journal of Biomedical Informatics*, 127, 104024.
2. Gao, Y., Li, M., Wang, X., and Zhou, B. (2023). Clinical validation of wearable-based AI systems: Challenges and future perspectives. *IEEE Transactions on Medical Technology*, 72(3), 123–132.
3. Jovanov, E., and Milenkovic, A. (2021). Body area networks for ubiquitous healthcare applications: Opportunities and challenges. *Journal of Medical Systems*, 45(2), 1–14.
4. Kumar, S., Jain, A., and Srivastava, R. (2022). Enhancing user adherence in AI-powered health wearables through adaptive personalization. *Digital Health*, 8, 20552076221093974.
5. Lee, J., and Lim, S. (2020). Factors influencing user acceptance of smart wearables in healthcare. *Telemedicine and e-Health*, 26(9), 1106–1112.
6. Li, H., Zhang, Y., and Zhou, Y. (2022). Smart wearables in chronic disease management: A review of current capabilities and future prospects. *Healthcare Technology Letters*, 9(5), 137–145.
7. Liu, F., Wang, Y., and Chen, H. (2020). Real-time arrhythmia detection using wearable ECG and deep learning. *IEEE Access*, 8, 145388–145398.
8. Mittelstadt, B. D., Allo, P., Taddeo, M., Wachter, S., and Floridi, L. (2016). The ethics of algorithms: Mapping the debate. *Big Data & Society*, 3(2), 2053951716679679.
9. Pantelopoulos, A., and Bourbakis, N. (2008, August). A survey on wearable biosensor systems for health monitoring. In: *2008 30th Annual International Conference of the IEEE Engineering in Medicine and Biology Society* (pp. 4887–4890). IEEE.
10. Rajpurkar, P., Hannun, A. Y., Haghpanahi, M., Bourn, C., and Ng, A. Y. (2017). Cardiologist-level arrhythmia detection with convolutional neural networks. arXiv preprint, arXiv:1707.01836.
11. Shi, W., Cao, J., Zhang, Q., Li, Y., and Xu, L. (2020). Edge computing: Vision and challenges. *IEEE Internet of Things Journal*, 3(5), 637–646.
12. Sun, C., Guo, H., and Yang, J. (2023). Federated learning for privacy-preserving health monitoring in wearables. *IEEE Transactions on Artificial Intelligence*, 2(1), 88–98.
13. Yue, X., Wang, H., Jin, D., Li, M., and Jiang, W. (2021). Healthcare data gateways: Found healthcare intelligence on blockchain with novel privacy risk control. *Journal of Medical Systems*, 45(4), 105.
14. Bhamidipaty, V., Bhamidipaty, D. L., Guntoory, I., Bhamidipaty, K. D. P., Iyengar, K. P., Botchu, B., and Botchu, R. (2025). Revolutionizing healthcare: The impact of AI-powered sensors. *Generative Artificial Intelligence for Biomedical and Smart Health Informatics*, 355–373. Wiley Online Library.
15. Etli, D., Djurovic, A., and Lark, J. (2024). The future of personalized healthcare: AI-driven wearables for real-time health monitoring and predictive analytics. *Current Research in Health Sciences*, 2(2), 10–14.
16. Mirica, K. A. (2024). Unlocking the potential of wearable sensors in healthcare and beyond. *ACS Sensors*, 9(2), 533–534.
17. Kumar, M. (2022). AI-powered wearables for continuous patient monitoring: Improving chronic disease management and preventive care. *International Scientific Journal of Engineering and Management (ISJEM)*, 2583–6129.

18. Sarker, M. T. H. (2025). Case study analysis of AI-powered sensor fabrics for continuous health monitoring in chronic disease management. *Strategic Data Management and Innovation*, 2(1), 160–180.
19. Wah, K., and Ng, J. (2024). Wear the future of healthcare: Revolutionizing healthcare with AI-driven wearables for enhanced health and wellness. Available at SSRN. https://ssrn.com/abstract=5194254
20. Oluwagbade, E. (2024). Wearable AI technologies for continuous health monitoring: The future of preventive healthcare. [Manuscript in preparation]
21. Secara, I.-A., and Hordiiuk, D. (2024). Personalized health monitoring systems: Integrating wearable and AI. *Journal of Intelligent Learning Systems and Applications*, 16(2), 44–52. Scientific Research Publishing.
22. Paul, J. (2025). Real-time predictive health monitoring using AI-driven wearable sensors: Enhancing early detection and personalized interventions in chronic disease management. [Manuscript in preparation]
23. Komalasari, R. (2024). AI-powered wearables revolutionizing health tracking and personalized wellness management. *Timor Leste Journal of Business and Management*, 6, 42–50.
24. Durairaj, S. (2025). Hybrid key management WSN protocol to enhance network performance using ML techniques for IoT application in cloud environment. *Peer-to-Peer Networking and Applications*, 18(4), 1-17.
25. Durairaj, S., and Sridhar, R. (2024). MOM-VMP: Multi-objective mayfly optimization algorithm for VM placement supported by principal component analysis (PCA) in cloud data center. *Cluster Computing*, 27(2), 1733–1751.
26. Krishnan, R., and Durairaj, S. (2024). Reliability and performance of resource efficiency in dynamic optimization scheduling using multi-agent microservice cloud-fog on IoT applications. *Computing*, 106(12), 3837–3878.
27. Durairaj, S., and Sridhar, R. (2024). Coherent virtual machine provisioning based on balanced optimization using entropy-based conjectured scheduling in cloud environment. *Engineering Applications of Artificial Intelligence*, 132, 108423.

CHAPTER

10

Training the Healthcare Workforce: Virtual Simulations and AI

V. Kavitha[1], S. Poonkodi[1*], S. Hemavathi[1], K. Suresh[2], K. Jayasakthi Velmurugan[3] and Raja Rajakani[4]

[1] Department of Computing Technologies, School of Computing, SRM Institute of Science and Technology, Kattankulathur, Tamil Nadu, India
[2] Department of Computational Intelligence, School of Computing, SRM Institute of Science and Technology, Kattankulathur, Tamil Nadu, India
[3] Department of Computer Science and Engineering, Saveetha School of Engineering, Saveetha Institute of Medical and Technical Sciences, Tamil Nadu, Chennai, India
[4] Plant Plastic Research Centre, Seoul National University, Seoul, South Korea

Virtual simulations and AI are emerging technologies that are transforming the training and education of the healthcare workforce within the metaverse. With an increasing shortage of skilled healthcare workers, these intelligent and immersive digital ecosystems offer training that can be scaled and is realistic and adjustable. These systems allow learners to rehearse procedures, make decisions, and receive specialized feedback within a controlled environment based on actual clinical scenarios. AI provides real-time analytics, dynamic learning pathways, and interactions with simulated patients through natural language processing and machine learning, elevating these virtual simulations. The metaverse facilitates innovation even further by enabling collaborative remote training in virtual ecosystems that are not bound by geography. Professionals in medicine can train, teach, and learn from each other in real time. This abstract analyzes how these technologies are transforming the landscape of medical education, highlighting their main uses in training and skill development, while also discussing the opportunities and challenges they present for AI-driven healthcare education in the virtual metaverse environments.

*Corresponding author: poonkods3@srmist.edu.in

DOI: 10.1201/9781003679370-10

1. Introduction

The adoption of new technologies, such as Artificial Intelligence (AI), Virtual Reality (VR), and the Metaverse is transforming the healthcare industry profoundly, fostering more rapid changes than ever before. Conventional training approaches rely heavily on content, minimal practical exposure, and the presence of a mentor. Nowadays, traditional training approaches are being supplemented or, in some cases, completely replaced by on-demand intelligent environments that are accessible anytime and anywhere, as well as immersive and interactive.

Diagnostics and education are now conducted using AI, which helps reduce the burden of providing personalized and flexible learning by analyzing individual performance and identifying gaps in knowledge and content for learners [2]. Similarly, medical professionals and students can participate in realistic clinical cases, practice procedures, and enhance their critical decision-making skills in near-real healthcare environments using VR simulations and the metaverse [3]. These technologies are vital in helping to address the gaps in providing experiential learning and knowledge retention, minimizing the chances of medical errors in real clinical practice [4].

Worldwide health systems face challenges, such as a limited number of workers, a rapidly growing elderly population, increasingly complex cases, and the need to learn new skills. Therefore, there is a pressing need for a new approach to professional education and career development. It is becoming more and more necessary every day [5]. The implementation of AI and virtual reality in the metaverse is one of the most effective solutions for ensuring equity in training a large number of healthcare workers. They are also excellent for collaborative learning, where professionals from various fields and different places work in virtual environments to improve teamwork and communication skills [6].

This chapter focuses on introducing the effects of AI, virtual simulations, and metaverse applications in training healthcare professionals, highlighting their essential role in transforming healthcare education. The chapter emphasizes improving clinical skills and reducing errors to create a workforce that is more adaptable, advanced, and agile, capable of handling the rapidly changing field of medicine [7, 8].

1.1 Overview of the Metaverse in Healthcare

The metaverse is a collective virtual shared space created by the convergence of virtually enhanced physical reality and physically persistent virtual reality. It is driven by the convergence of exciting new technologies—virtual and Augmented Reality (AR), mixed reality, and blockchain—Artificial Intelligence. In the healthcare domain, the metaverse is referred to as a disruptive force that changes the way care is provided, physicians cooperate, and medical education is performed [1].

By utilizing avatars, motion trackers, haptic feedback, and virtual twins, the metaverse operates to give users the ability to communicate with one another in real time in a 3D space. With this technology, our doctors can train, consult, diagnose, and operate in an augmented or digitally simulated world. The concept of the metaverse has opened the door to immersive technologies beyond place-based and remote isomorphism and has the potential to realize natural and effective human-computer interaction [5].

The healthcare industry stands to benefit the most from the metaverse in terms of improving medical training and clinical skills education. Advanced medical training often suffers from a paucity of space and excruciatingly costly infrastructure, ethical issues surrounding the employment of cadavers, the necessity of patient-facing interactions, and the need for diverse clinical exposures. The metaverse provides risk-free, repeatable, and thorough training environments that overcome these issues. Advanced virtual reality-equipped simulated operating theaters, emergency rooms, anatomy dissection labs, and ICUs provide students and trainees with advanced simulation of complex procedures for practice.

The metaverse is unique in its potential to enhance equitable opportunities in medical education and professional training. Through the use of the cloud and decentralization, medical students, nurses, surgeons, and other specialists can attend virtual learning sessions to engage in case seminars and participate in team training exercises. This is beneficial for countries with a scarcity of qualified medical professionals or those with restricted access to postgraduate training. There are plans to build virtual medical teaching hospitals, research centers, and other educational medical institutions, which would enable virtual ward rounds, interdisciplinary simulations, and collaborative diagnostics.

Simultaneously, as metaverse technologies advance, they will increasingly integrate with biometric sensors and real-time patient data, as well as the digital twin models we are developing to enhance their realism and clinical relevance for the patient experience. In the future, the healthcare metaverse could offer personalized training as per the student's skill level and enable AI-based feedback and assessment. Paired with blockchain, they might also ensure secure credentialing, certification, and tracking of professional competencies. Thus, the metaverse isn't just a newfangled tool; it's a shift in the paradigm of how medical personnel are trained, how healthcare is provided, and how patients interact with their care experiences.

2. Role of Artificial Intelligence in the Healthcare Metaverse

AI forms the intelligent infrastructure of the healthcare metaverse, creating personalized, adaptive, and highly interactive educational, diagnostic, and patient care environments. In immersive 3D virtual worlds, AI features pervasively in the ecosystem, from simulations to avatars, data analytics, and communication tools that enable realistic and interactive virtual healthcare. We depict in Figure 1 the intermediary layer, AI, that connects Extended Reality (XR) interfaces to various intelligent parts of the Healthcare metaverse. AI drives simulators, virtual avatars, and decision-making aids used in personalized training, diagnosis, and clinical skills development.

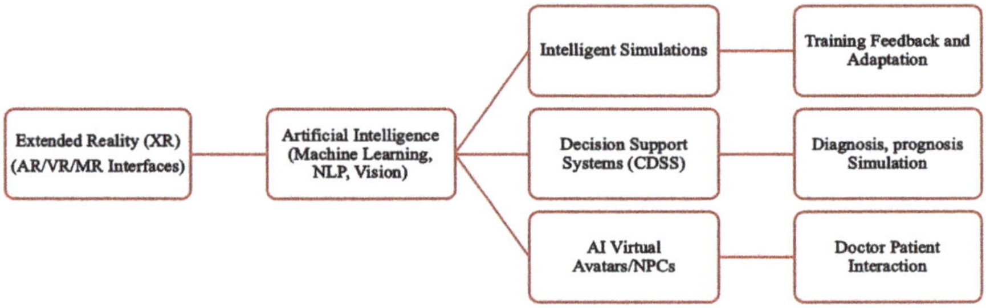

Figure 1: Integration of AI in the healthcare metaverse ecosystem.

2.1 AI in Personalized Virtual Simulations

AI algorithms personalize medical observations in the metaverse. These intelligent systems can evaluate user performance, track real-time decisions, and provide instantaneous feedback to learners, hence making the training more personalized and effective. Machine learning models record behavior tendencies and modulate the complexity/content of scenarios by evaluating the learner's level of performance and past mistakes, creating an ongoing learning cycle [9].

1. NAI-Driven Virtual Patients and Instructors

AI enables the creation of realistic and interactive virtual patients capable of simulating various medical conditions, psychological responses, and even emotions. Using DL models and NLP capabilities, these avatars can emulate dialogues from patients, descriptions of symptoms, and emotional expressions to grant learners occasions to develop technical skills as well as soft skills, such as empathy, active listening, and communication with the patient [10].

Clinical cases can also be supported by AI-based virtual mentors or teachers, who help users learn or practice these ideal cases, correct them on the fly, and ask them questions that stimulate critical thinking. These teachers function as an intelligent tutoring system in virtual learning, enhancing engagement and reducing cognitive load [11].

2. Automation and Clinical Decision Support

In addition to education, AI significantly contributes to automating many tasks within healthcare metaverses. Such prerequisites may include things like virtual triage, diagnostic support, and clinical decision-making support. AI systems process symptom information, images, and a patient's history. To aid in the differentiation of diagnoses, suggest treatment plans, and model patient outcomes. These peripheral characteristics are also being integrated into training packages to allow trainees to practice not just skill-based skills but also operationalization of uncertainty [12].

AI-powered Clinical Decision Support Systems (CDSS) also help users understand the rationale behind treatment decisions, which results in increased diagnostic accuracy and patient safety during virtual consultations or simulations [13].

3. AI and Data Analytics in Simulation Environments

During training, the healthcare metaverse interacts with the users as it records substantial biometric data. AI, along with big data analytics, analyzes this data to identify learning curves, performance trends, and training gaps. Institutions can use these findings to evaluate course effectiveness, reform curricula, or modify training based on evidence [14].

For instance, heat maps with in-brain tracking data can be processed to determine attentiveness to key areas during the procedure. This step informs systems of the provision of personalized feedback within a VR-based simulation.

4. AI with XR

The smart metaverse relies on AI as its healthcare backbone. XR technologies, combined with AI, consist of AR, VR, and MR. XR offers an engaging user interface, while AI provides cognitive functions such as perception, reasoning, learning, and more adaptation. After this, they created a digital health ecosystem that is responsive, patient-centered, and continuously evolving, and this lifts clinical efficiency, patient safety, and medical education to unprecedented heights.

2.2 Introduction to Digital Twins in Healthcare

The notion of digital twins in healthcare designates the development of realistic, virtual models of patients, organs, healthcare facilities, or clinical processes. These versions are then regularly integrated with data from various sources, such as electronic health records (EHRs), wearables, imaging, genomics, and other environmental sources, generating even more up-to-date models. With such synchronized digital twins, the healthcare providers can simulate, analyze, and predict a wide range of medical circumstances accurately [15, 16].

In terms of clinical learning and staff training, digital twins have the potential to be disruptive. With these patient-specific models, students and practitioners can develop, virtually, a disease, observe how effective the treatments are, and even tweak their clinical decision-making. For instance, a digital twin of a heart can be used to teach and understand how arrhythmias, myocardial infarctions, or drug effects influence it over time, as reflected by the physiological parameters of a particular patient [17]. This mode of learning goes beyond passive, book-based learning with a focus on engaging, interactive, and personalized case studies.

In addition to individual patients, digital twins are under development for entire healthcare systems—such as hospital departments, Intensive Care Units (ICUs), and emergency departments. These macro-level twins mimic operations like bed utilization, workflows for staff, and equipment usage, allowing administrators and policymakers to maximize resource allocation, model public health crises, and experiment with new models for delivering healthcare without affecting real-world operations [18].

When they become part of the healthcare metaverse, digital twins are even more significant. Through the conjunction of AI with XR, such as VR and AR, digital twins become smart, immersive, and interactive training tools. AI, for example, can help identify the digital twin of a model's behavior and predict preventive measures before mistakes occur. Besides, XR tools enable the learners to have direct contact with these models in 3D environments [19]. This combination not only facilitates hyper-personalized care planning, diagnostic prediction, and precision education but also makes digital twins a basic unit in the future of intelligent healthcare systems [20].

2.3 Key Applications of the Metaverse, AI, and Digital Twins in Healthcare

The healthcare metaverse brings together VR, AR, AI, and blockchain for a highly interactive, intelligent, and immersive healthcare experience. Such

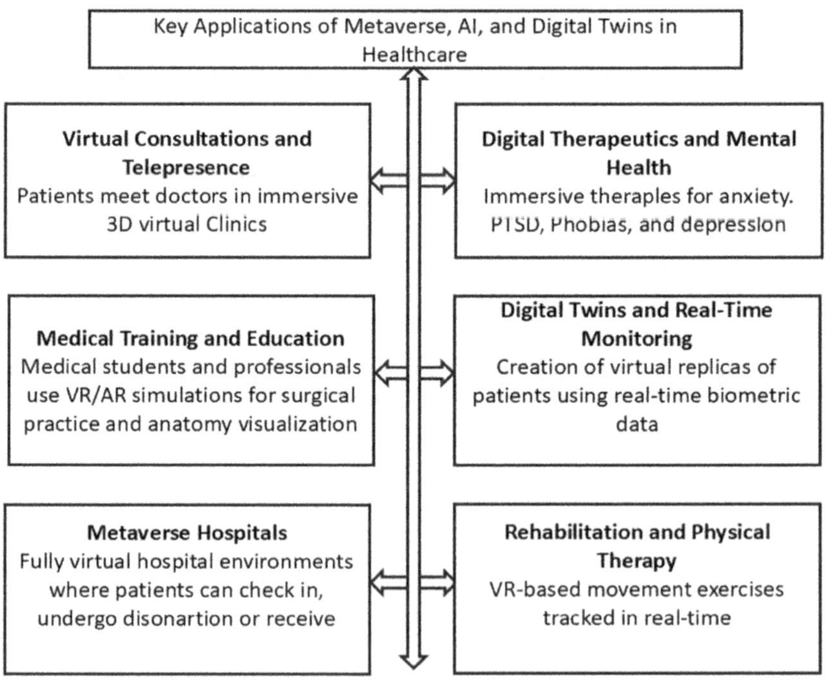

Figure 2: Key applications of metaverse, AI, and digital twins in healthcare.

innovative technology improves patient care, medical education, operational efficiency, and therapeutic results. Figure 2 shows the key applications of the metaverse in the healthcare sector and descriptions are as follows:

1. Virtual Consultations and Telepresence

Metaverse platforms are propelling telemedicine into the future by transforming virtual consultations into incredibly real and immersive 3D worlds. A more vivid and natural interactive experience is provided instead of video conferencing. Here, patients can engage with doctors in actual virtual clinics utilizing the avatars that they have made for themselves and thus bringing the experience closer to a face-to-face one. For example, XRHealth and the Second Life Medical Community are among the organizations experimenting with the metaverse in the healthcare sector.

2. Medical Training and Education

VR/AR simulations present opportunities to interact and safely practice without risk, like:

- **Surgical simulations:** Surgeons can perform a virtual operation on a patient repeatedly in a virtual operating theatre until they get it right without the risk of harming a real patient.
- **Anatomy visualization:** 3D models of organs and systems can be explored from all angles, helping students understand spatial relationships more effectively.
- **Certification and assessment:** AI algorithms track learner performance, offer real-time feedback, and assess readiness for real-world application.

For example, tools such as Touch Surgery and Osso VR provide surgical training in a virtual reality environment.

3. Digital Therapeutics and Mental Health

The metaverse has become a playground of virtual worlds with unlimited potential to create digital therapeutics, and this goes beyond mental health treatment. Immersive virtual environments give highly controlled, safe spaces for therapy.

- **Exposure therapy:** Combatants of PTSD, anxiety disorders, or phobias are generally very cautious in their exposure to the various things that might trigger a condition. Such things might include a VR space that is safe and where they can be assisted by a therapist in the process of this gradual exposure.
- **Behavioral tracking:** Robots can observe the way we express ourselves, our tone of voice, and how interested we are during each session so that treatment can be more personalized.
- **Group therapy:** Patients can opt to be part of a virtual reality-based anonymous support group as a solution to combating loneliness. The only drawback, according to VR, is the lack of nonverbal communication between the participants.

One of the examples is VR platforms such as Limbix and MindMaze, which provide virtual reality sessions of psychological treatment for young adults and veterans.

4. Digital Twins and Real-Time Monitoring

In this context, digital twins are virtual representations of physical patients. They are constructed using data captured in real-time from devices like wearable sensors, medical devices, and EHRs.

- **Personalized medicine:** A patient's digital twin can help decide the most suitable drug or therapy plan without actually trying the patient; thus, trials are kept to a minimum.
- **Predictive analytics:** By utilizing AI, a digital twin can predict the future location of a disease, potentially enabling early intervention.
- **Remote monitoring:** The digital twin is a virtual model of a patient that can be used for long-term health monitoring.

For example, Siemens Healthineers and Philips are conducting research on patient-specific digital.

5. Metaverse Hospitals

The metaverse hospital concept embodies a fully virtual medical care provision environment where conducting medical consultations, diagnostics, and minor treatments is done only through virtual means.

- **Virtual check-ins:** Patients can complete the registration, carry out symptom analysis, and also fill out forms without leaving their homes.
- **Hybrid staffing:** These spaces are the life of both AI-based avatars and real people who furnish the service, thus providing efficient and scalable service.
- **Emergency triage:** The algorithms of AI distribute priority for the different cases of urgency based on the data obtained from the sensors that the human being wears.

As an illustration, in the year 2022, the Ministry of Health of the UAE inaugurated the very first virtual hospital in the metaverse for the world, which was a source of consultations as well as healthcare information.

6. Physical Therapy and Rehabilitation

VR-based physical therapy modules are revolutionizing rehabilitation processes by monitoring patient movement, posture, and progress in real time.

- **Gamification environments:** Patients are positioned within game-like environments that promote movement and adherence.
- **Remote monitoring:** Therapists can observe patient progress remotely and modify exercise regimens accordingly.
- **Improved motivation:** Real-time feedback and interactive visuals keep patients engaged with their recovery.

For instance, Neuro Rehab VR and Karuna Labs provide interactive rehab solutions that enhance the recovery of stroke and trauma patients.

3. Virtual Simulations in Healthcare Training

Virtual simulations mimic actual medical situations in completely immersive virtual environments, providing students with a secure and risk-free setting to discover, err, and hone their clinical and decision-making abilities through repeated practice. Such sophisticated learning instruments use technologies like VR, AR, AI, and 3D modeling to simulate hospital environments, patient encounters, and intricate medical procedures with high fidelity and interactivity.

It becomes especially valuable in preparing health practitioners to undertake high-risk, time-critical, or technically demanding procedures, such as surgery, trauma management, resuscitation algorithms, and critical care therapies. In this context, small errors during practice can be fatal, making it difficult to provide early practical exposure, which is valuable but potentially hazardous.

Virtual simulations allow students—who are aspiring doctors, surgery students, nurses, or EMTs—to:

- Systematically practice with complex processes, including laparoscopic surgery, intubation, or central line placement.
- Experience virtual emergencies such as polytrauma or cardiac arrests in real time.
- Select voluntarily and view consequence-free experiments to assist with reflecting and learning from mistakes.

For example, a surgery student operating a VR platform can simulate the complete process of appendectomy step-by-step and review the feedback from every task, from cutting to stitching. The virtual world reduces mistakes involving choosing the wrong instrument or damaging tissue near where surgery occurs, so students can learn from the best techniques without any involvement with live patients.

Aside from promoting interdisciplinary education, these simulators also train students by giving them collaborative environments made up of doctors, nurses, anesthetists, and paramedics. In doing so, students are allowed to practice these skills, such as communication, situational awareness, leadership, and teamwork, which are crucial in high-pressure clinical situations but hard to learn from lectures or even from observation.

Additionally, virtual simulations' scalability and flexibility can enable their related training programs to be facilitated from any geographic location. Even where resources are limited, a kind of training such as this guarantees students receive a like, standardized education without any influence from their place or institutional resources. Such training becomes even more important within pandemic planning or global health programs, where a significant number of health practitioners should be trained expeditiously or upskilled.

Virtual simulations, more than any other, provide room for data-driven evaluation. These aspects of learning—interaction, decision, timing, and outcome—can be registered and then analyzed to offer detailed feedback, personalized instruction, and a more objective evaluation of competency than traditional observation-based methods.

3.1 Advantages of Virtual Simulations

Virtual simulations have been proven to be a very useful tool in healthcare education, as they grant many advantages to the training quality and accessibility.

1. Safe and Controlled Environment

Virtual simulations provide a new approach to the healthcare profession, as they make the training of the candidates more accessible and of higher quality. Virtual simulations allow learners to practice a procedure many times without risking harm or making mistakes in the patients. Such an approach not only boosts experimentation but also allows the students and the professionals to admit mistakes, learn from them, and perfect their techniques with less stress. Such an approach is especially important when it comes to performing high-risk procedures, such as conducting a surgery or an emergency; if there are real-world errors, then it will not be beneficial. Elaborate surgical tasks, crucial decision points, and strenuous situations can be performed multiple times, if need be, helping confidence and competence during real-world application (BioMed Central).

2. Standardization

Clinical education typically varies significantly based on the patient's condition, the instructor's teaching style, and the hospital's protocol. Using virtual simulations, one can eliminate rid of such variability by offering learners the same consistent and structured experiences. Additional virtual platforms can also be accessed anywhere, making the training available even in places that are difficult to access; thus, the training becomes more decentralized. These changes will allow students to have the same experiences and to put them into practice accordingly. The differences in patient work or instructor styles are eliminated.

3. Feedback and Performance Monitoring

Performance tracking and feedback are also important virtues of virtual simulations. Unlike conventional training, which often relies on subjective observation, simulations offer objective feedback based on comprehensive analytics. All actions, ranging from choosing instruments to timing and accuracy, are tracked and analyzed. The students receive immediate feedback, and they can recognize their strengths and weaknesses. This data-driven process enables individualized learning, adjusting the learning process as per each learner's requirements and development.

3.2 Key Applications of Virtual Simulations

1. Surgical Simulations

Among others, Osso VR is one of the VR platforms that digitally transformed surgical education by creating captivating and interactive worlds for doctors and medical students, where they can repeat difficult operations—like tibial intramedullary nailing and knee arthroplasty—in a virtual operating room. These platforms simulate everything that exists in the clinical setting; thus, the trainees can improve their technical skills without any danger to the patients.

On numerous occasions, researchers have largely emphasized the advantages of VR-based surgical training:

- **Faster procedure completion:** VR-trained participants were able to complete surgical procedures 20–25% faster than those trained through traditional methods. This indicates not only improved familiarity with the steps involved but also greater confidence and efficiency in execution.
- **Enhanced surgical accuracy:** One of the most striking outcomes was a 230% improvement in performance scores, showing that VR users performed significantly more surgical steps correctly. This result reflects a deeper understanding of procedural protocols and precise execution of techniques.
- **Fewer errors and higher ratings:** VR-trained individuals required fewer corrections from supervising surgeons during evaluations and received higher scores on global performance assessments, indicating superior preparedness and lower likelihood of mistakes in real-life surgical settings.

These results indicate that virtual reality emulations lend a strong hand to procedural accuracy, safety confirmation, and technical skills retention among the surgery candidates. On the one hand, speeding the learning curve, and on the other, repeated exercises allowed by the controlled situation; the likes of Osso VR are making it possible for the future surgical labor force to be more skilled and efficient (ossovr.com).

2. Nursing and Paramedic Training

Nursing and paramedicine students benefit greatly from high-fidelity virtual reality simulation, which provides realistic, hands-on learning in a safe environment. The simulations allow students to rehearse critical clinical skills and soft skills multiple times to build their confidence and enhance performance without jeopardizing real patients. VR-based training has significantly improved several areas.

- **Insertion of intravenous catheters:** VR enables students to continually practice IV insertion procedures, allowing them to develop hand-eye coordination, depth perception, and procedural accuracy.
- **Wound care procedures:** Simulation scenarios ensure that students are familiar with the correct process in cleaning wounds, dressing wounds, and

preventing infections, which reinforces best patient hygiene and recuperation practices.

- **Therapeutic communication and patient handover:** VR modules mimic actual real-time conversations with patients and peers, such that students can build competent communication approaches and enhance their self-confidence in clinical dialogue.

Regarding outcomes, one included review exploring the effect of VR on nursing education reported improvement in many skill sets:

- Students were able to think critically and make decisions during clinical VR situations, which was captured through problem-solving ability improvement with effect sizes of 0.2 to 0.9.
- Empathetic and clear communication with patients, as well as overall communication skills improvement, were captured through effect sizes between 0.4 and 0.7.
- Major professional competencies, clinical reasoning, collaboration, and ethics in professional conduct are also enhanced with engaging VR technology, with effect sizes of 0.3 to 0.9 pointing to substantial gains across multiple aspects of professional practice (sources: PubMed, TIME, BioMed Central).

Furthermore, another study comparing immersive virtual reality (VR) simulation training with traditional teaching methods reported a significant boost in confidence when performing basic life support (BLS) among paramedics and midwifery students. They reported the mean confidence score to have improved by 6.71 ($p < 0.001$), highlighting vocational preparedness concerning practical skills through VR-designed training.

In summary, these discoveries underscore the cumulative, intensive value of modern healthcare education, integrating staples of critical thinking, confidence, and enhanced communication, all made possible with the use of modern VR simulations, proving them to be an important educational asset.

3. Emergency Medicine and Crisis Response

Virtual simulations are essential for educating healthcare workers in emergency medicine and crisis response, offering controlled and immersive environments for the most demanding, time-sensitive situations. During training, learners completely remove the risk to actual patients, enabling them to manage real-life emergencies with precision and confidence. Situations such as cardiac arrest, trauma resuscitation, and mass casualties expose trainees to fostering essential problem-solving skills, collaboration, and swift action in critical thinking. Key benefits of VR-based emergency training include:

- **Simulation of high-stress situations:** Simulations replicate actual emergencies such as cardiac arrests and multi-victim traumas, which enable students to learn how to remain calm, quickly evaluate situations, and make correct decisions under stress.

- **Risk-free skill acquisition:** Students can repeat emergency procedures without risking injury to actual patients, which is particularly valuable for unusual but life-threatening conditions.
- **Enhanced triage and crisis management:** Colleges such as Ohio State University employ VR platforms to mimic patients presenting at the emergency department with severe conditions, enabling students to improve the accuracy of their triages, set interventions in the right order, and manage scarce resources efficiently (TIME, BioMed Central).
- **Collaboration and communication amongst the team:** Virtual situations typically present several roles, which assist learners in building interprofessional working and concise communication—aptitudes that are critical during emergency response.

VR simulations provide a realistic and safe environment for skill-building, confidence-building, and mental preparation needed in emergency medicine. Through repeated exposure to critical events, these platforms prepare healthcare professionals to provide timely and effective care in actual crisis scenarios.

4. AI-Powered Learning in Healthcare

An AI-powered learning module in healthcare describes the integration of Artificial Intelligence (AI) technologies to enhance learning and decision-making in the healthcare environment. It integrates beginner-level and professional technologies, including machine learning, natural language processing, deep learning, and computer vision, to assist with clinical training, healthcare services, patient management, and healthcare delivery. Artificial intelligence (AI) has revolutionized healthcare by easing the identification, treatment, and tracking of patients. Elevating more individualized treatments and generating more accurate diagnoses, this technology is significantly enhancing healthcare research and its outputs. Medical practitioners can find disease signs and patterns that would otherwise go unnoticed because of AI's rapid analysis of large volumes of clinical data.

AI has a wide range of uses in healthcare, from estimating results from electronic medical records to analyzing radiological images for early detection. Healthcare systems may become smarter, faster, and more efficient in treating millions of people globally by utilizing artificial intelligence in clinics and hospitals. In healthcare, artificial intelligence marks a significant step forward, revolutionizing patient care while lowering provider costs and enhancing patient outcomes.

4.1 AI in Healthcare Education

- Improve medical education
- Boost the accuracy of diagnosis
- Forecast patient results

- Make treatment plans better
- Encourage the use of patient-specific medication
- Encourage continuous education for medical professionals

4.2 AI in Healthcare Obstacles

Investing in AI for the above-mentioned purposes, the technology's problems must be resolved, but due to a lot of ethical and legal concerns that might not be relevant in other contexts, such as:

- Ensuring data privacy and cybersecurity for sensitive information
- Training with a large volume of relevant clinical datasets
- Integration with the existing IT system
- Securing trust from current physicians and clinics
- Following current international regulations
- Implementation of data governance and ethical oversight frameworks

Job-related safety and the precision of patients are also significant factors when employing AI in healthcare. To start observing patterns in medical data, understand the relationship between different diagnoses and treatments, and provide accurate recommendations tailored to each patient, AI systems need to be trained. Moreover, since it requires a full understanding of how modern technology operates to function smoothly, the incorporation of AI into existing IT systems may make the task more complicated for medical professionals. Finally, the effective use of AI in the field of healthcare is relevant only when receiving the support and trust that medical workers give. Physicians have to trust that the AI tool provides them with relevant advice, and it will not deceive them. They should especially have transparency, as the doctors need to understand how the AI system is making its judgment to ensure it is based on its reliability and current medical standards research. To ensure that the use of AI systems is ethical and does not pose any problems for the safety of patients, it is necessary to comply with the government standards.

1. AI in Optimizing and Scheduling

A primary operations is the efficient scheduling and admission of patients, which affects the effectiveness of healthcare delivery. AI integration in this domain improves certain procedures:

2. Admission of Patients

AI modules are especially good at spotting trends in patient transfers, admissions, and discharges, which makes it possible for patients to access the required facilities more easily. AI can help with the strategic allocation of resources, including beds, staff, and equipment, to suit patient demands by anticipating times of high demand. AI systems, for example, can predict daily or seasonal variations in patient admissions, enabling hospitals to modify bed availability and personnel levels based on the obtained data. The general patient experience is improved with this proactive approach.

3. Dynamic Scheduling Systems

AI-powered scheduling platforms are transforming the way procedures and appointments are set up. To generate the best schedules, these systems can examine a variety of factors, including patient preferences, healthcare provider availability, and the urgency of care. Doing so, they maximize the use of healthcare professionals and resources by lowering last-minute cancellations and missed appointments. Additionally, by rescheduling non-urgent appointments without causing major delays, these AI systems can adjust in real time to changes such as emergency instances.

To improve patient satisfaction and efficiency in the outpatient department, researchers developed a unique appointment scheduling model based on the Markov decision process framework, taking into account patient preferences to increase their satisfaction. Several experiments have been conducted to assess the system's performance, and the results indicate excellent convergence behavior accuracy.

4. Cutting Waiting Times

Cutting waiting times in ERs and outpatient clinics is one of the main advantages of AI in patient flow. Hospital employees can effectively manage patient wait times by taking proactive measures with the help of AI's ability to forecast patient influx and identify potential issues and delays. Better triage procedures and speedier patient assignment to the right care are what this entails for emergency rooms.

Improving the precision and effectiveness of diagnostic procedures can be done by:

- Increasing the accuracy of diagnosis
- Reducing diagnostic mistakes
- Increasing the pace of diagnostic procedures
- Automated documentation and reporting
- Integrating diagnostic information

5. Illustrations of AI Systems in Imaging

With many AI systems being developed and utilized to analyze images from MRIs, CT scans, and other modalities, artificial intelligence has made significant progress in the field of medical imaging.

6. AI in Monitoring and Patient Care

An era of more effective and efficient patient monitoring is promised by the initiation of AI in healthcare, which represents a paradigm change. This section examines the use of AI to improve patient care. Three main topics are covered here: wearable technology driven by AI for ongoing monitoring, the effects of virtual nursing assistants, and AI's application in telemedicine and remote patient interaction. These AI applications are enhancing healthcare delivery and empowering individuals to have more control over their own health and well-being.

7. Wearable Technology Driven by AI for Constant Monitoring

Wearables with AI allow patient monitoring by combining real-time vital sign analysis, such as heart rate, blood pressure, blood glucose, and oxygen saturation, with ease. To provide a holistic monitoring of a patient's health, they can record additional physiological data such as electroencephalography (EEG) and peripheral physiological signals like photo plethysmography (PPG).

8. AI in Remote Patient Engagement and Telemedicine

The effectiveness and accessibility of healthcare are being transformed by the incorporation AI into telemedicine and remote patient contact. Healthcare professionals can assess patients remotely and tailor virtual consultations based on patient data improving telehealth platforms with sophisticated diagnostic and consultation services. While AI's use in predictive analytics and remote patient monitoring enables proactive care for chronic illnesses and foresees possible health difficulties, chatbots and virtual assistants driven by AI enable patient engagement, providing support and services.

9. AI in Potential Healthcare

AI's quick development indicates a revolutionary future for the medical field. This chapter's last portion examines how the next developments and possible uses of AI in healthcare will affect the provision of healthcare system as a whole. We will also examine how AI affects public health and how it can be used to address global health emergencies like pandemics. AI introduces adaptive intelligence into healthcare training by personalizing content, providing real-time feedback, and simulating intelligent patient behaviors.

5. The Metaverse: A Virtual Healthcare Ecosystem

The Metaverse, using technologies like virtual reality (VR), augmented reality (AR), artificial intelligence (AI), and blockchain, is an immersive, interactive digital environment that combines the real and virtual worlds. By establishing a virtual healthcare environment, the metaverse transforms the way patients, physicians, and educators communicate, educate, and provide treatment.

In the upcoming stage of our global digital growth, the metaverse is expected to play a significant role. Together with continuous social and behavioral change, emerging technologies and the conceptual and technological innovation of digital platforms—including the blurring of "virtual" and "physical" environments—will continue to develop, allowing us to interact with each other in more ways and places.

Both consumers and businesses around the world are committed to this change. According to a recent metaverse poll, 82% of US corporate leaders anticipate that metaverse integration will become "business as usual" in three years or less, while 66% of them claim that their organizations are actively interacting with the metaverse.

Metaverse service applications are becoming a more important and promising sector of the healthcare sector. The healthcare sector understands the principles and dedication to metaverse services as a crucial component of strategic planning for the sector's long-term goals. Although there is potential for metaverse services in the healthcare sector, these opportunities are complex and sometimes conflicting because they depend on the sub-sector. Without a methodical way to assess the development of possible business opportunities, it is extremely challenging to appropriately match the present metaverse service requirements of a business model with its related technology.

The strategic choice can be costly in terms of technology and operations planning issues if a particular metaverse service aim is selected with little regard for other goals.

5.1 Applications of the Metaverse in Healthcare

The metaverse in healthcare refers to the combination of an immersive virtual universe, augmented reality (AR), virtual reality (VR), artificial intelligence (AI), and blockchain technologies in the healthcare system. Below are the important use cases of the metaverse in healthcare described in Figure 3.

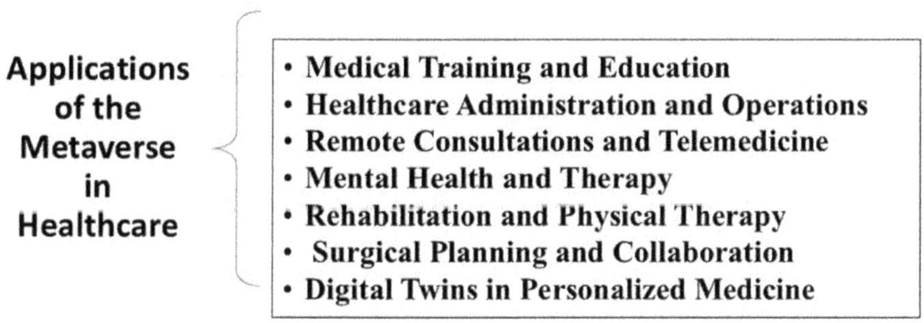

Figure 3: Applications of the metaverse in healthcare.

1. **Medical Training and Education**

- **Virtual simulations:** Students and practitioners can learn to conduct surgical procedures or diagnose patients through interactive lesions with virtual patients in completely safe VR settings.
- **Enhanced understanding of body parts:** 3D images of the human body aid in learning and understanding complex anatomical structures.
- **Remote skill development:** Self-directed training offered through interactive modules enables skills training in the field of medicine away from medical schools or training hospitals.

2. **Remote Consultations and Telemedicine**

- **Avatar-based virtual clinics:** Patients view doctors in an avatar-based virtual clinic in the Metaverse.

- **Improved patient interaction:** Telemedicine consultations that are more immersive and personal in comparison to traditional video conferences.

3. **Mental Health and Therapy**

- **Interaction with others:** Virtual support groups and therapy sessions are beneficial to those who are isolated or unable to travel outside of their homes.
- **VR therapy environments:** VR experiences are used for treating PTSD, anxiety, and phobias.

4. **Rehabilitation and Physical Therapy**

- **Remote monitoring:** It is possible for therapists to supervise sessions remotely and provide feedback.
- **Exercises with gamification:** VR environments make physiotherapy fun and track progress in real-time.

5. **Surgical Planning and Collaboration**

- **Virtual collaboration:** Surgeons around the world can plan surgeries and exchange expertise via a virtual space.
- **3D visualization:** The use of 3D digital twins of patients enables surgeons to rehearse complex surgery.

6. **Digital Twins in Personalized Medicine**

- **Patient avatars:** Develop virtual models of patients integrated with real-time data for health tracking and predictive analytics.
- **Treatment simulations:** Assess treatment response in the virtual version before applying it in the real-world treatment.

7. **Healthcare Administration and Operations**

- **Non-clinical staff training:** Get virtual training in emergency drills, equipment handling, and hospital logistics.
- **Virtual hospitals:** Hospitals that operate within a virtual environment can manage administrative operations, communication with patients, and staff training.

5.2 Elements of a Healthcare Metaverse

Healthcare Metaverse is an immersive virtual ecosystem that combines healthcare services with advanced digital technologies. The following are the key elements that make up a healthcare metaverse:

1. **Ecosystem Digital Twins**

Using real-time data and simulations, digital twins are virtual representations of real-world objects, such as hospitals, medical devices, or even human organs.

Role in the Medical Field

- Model the anatomy and organ systems of humans.
- Estimate how surgical treatments will turn out.

- To increase efficiency, model hospital workflows.
- Prior to deployment, test medical equipment in a virtual setting.

Benefits

- Makes individualized care possible.
- Lowers the dangers of testing in the real world.
- Improves diagnostic prediction.
- Aids in the planning of intricate surgeries without the need for physical intervention.

Example

Siemens Healthcare, for instance, simulates blood flow and forecasts how procedures or drugs would affect specific patients using digital twins of their hearts.

2. Smart Avatars

AI-driven digital characters who serve as assistants, teachers, patients, or healthcare professionals in the metaverse are known as smart avatars.

Role in the Medical Field

- Avatars are used by physicians and nurses to provide remote consultations.
- AI-powered patient avatars are used to train by simulating symptoms.
- When it comes to administrative duties like scheduling or patient inquiries, avatars can help.
- Wellness coaching and medication reminders are offered by personalized health assistants.

Benefits

- Makes telepresence and remote care easier.
- Provides pupils with realistic training simulations.
- Improves accessibility and engagement around the clock.
- Enhances the comfort of patients in virtual environments.

Example

XRHealth guides patients through VR-based therapy for pain and anxiety management using AI-driven therapist avatars.

3. Virtual Classrooms

In the metaverse, virtual classrooms are immersive, three-dimensional learning environments that replicate actual medical settings for instruction and training.

Role in the Medical Field

- Use 3D visuals to deliver interactive, live lectures.
- Use simulation labs to rehearse procedures or conduct virtual dissections.
- Collaborate with mentors and peers across the world.
- Replay situations to improve comprehension and fix mistakes.

Benefits

- A secure environment for honing important techniques.
- Provides experiential and visual learning without the dangers of the real world.
- Improves retention of information through immersion.
- Encourages access to knowledgeable educators and international cooperation.

Example

Case Western Reserve University offers 3D anatomy lessons using the Microsoft HoloLens, allowing students to examine and walk about human organs in augmented reality.

6. Applications in Workforce Training

As healthcare systems evolve, there is a greater demand to train medical workers in a more efficient, safe, and effective manner. Technological advancements, such as virtual simulations, AI, and metaverse-based ecosystems, are taking the lead in providing workforce training for the healthcare sector. This collaboration is revolutionizing conventional medical education by turning it into engaging, hands-on, information-rich learning experiences.

6.1 Virtual Simulations in Healthcare Training

Virtual simulations are computer-created environments designed to replicate real clinical scenarios that might happen. These include:

- **VR surgery simulation of a VR surgery training:** Doctors can perform operations with a realistic sensation provided by VR headsets.
- **Emergency response simulation:** A healthcare team can practice managing unexpected situations like cardiac arrest or traumatic incidents in a virtual setting environment.
- **The anatomical exploration:** The students are able to navigate through the human anatomy in 3D interactively.

Advantages

- Without any danger to real patients
- Scenarios that can be repeated to achieve mastery
- Immediate feedback on performance

6.2 AI-Powered Training

Artificial Intelligence energizes healthcare education by providing brains and flexibility:

- **Virtual patients:** AI-operated characters simulate one's symptoms, emotions, and interactions for the training in communication and diagnosis.
- **Personalized learning paths:** AI can evaluate a trainee's strong and weak areas and, therefore, create tailored modules for the improvement of their performance.

- **Performance analytics:** AI registers the performance of the user, recognizes skill gaps, and offers ways to improve.

6.3 Metaverse Virtual Ecosystems

The metaverse blends VR, AR, and digital twins to fabricate persistent, collaborative virtual worlds. In healthcare:

- **Collaborative learning:** Students as well as instructors who are from different parts of the world can interact in common virtual hospitals or classrooms.
- **Remote mentorship:** Professionals can support the trainees by guiding them through the shared 3D spaces of the procedure.
- **Role-based simulations:** Groups can do role-specific simulations (e.g., doctor, nurse, paramedic) simultaneously, so they can not only practice but also enhance interprofessional communication.

6.4 Key Applications in Workforce Training

- **Medical student education**: Initial hands-on experience in clinical environments precludes engaging with actual patients.
- **Nursing training:** Practicing bedside care along with medication delivery and patient supervision.
- **Surgical skill acquisition:** Advanced virtual surgery simulation with tactile response for precise hand movements.
- **Advanced specialized education:** Remote sessions for certification updates and skills maintenance.
- **AI simulations:** Fostering empathy and cross-cultural understanding through virtual interactions.

AI, the metaverse, and virtual simulation are transforming the way healthcare professionals are trained. As these technologies offer a personalized and engaging learning experience, traditional training is overcome, and the workforce is prepared to handle complex problems in the real world. This integration of tools promotes universal, scalable, and intelligent learning, which is an indication of the evolution of medical education. By enhancing surgical skills in VR platforms with haptic feedback, simulating real-time multiuser emergency response scenarios, allowing nursing professionals to interact with AI-driven patient avatars for better communication, and presenting simulated epidemics and vaccination strategies to prepare for effective public health responses, metaverse and AI-based training solutions are revolutionizing healthcare education.

7. Benefits of AI and Virtual Ecosystems

- Scalability
- Accessibility
- Cost Efficiency

- Customization
- Data-Driven Insights

Technological advancements have reshaped workforce training in healthcare education through virtual ecosystems and artificial intelligence (AI). The use of these technologies is not limited to traditional classrooms or hospitals; they are redefining medical training with more effective, engaging, and high-impact innovations.

7.1 Risk-Free Learning Environments

Healthcare professionals can now leverage AI for virtual simulations to:

- Effectively practice procedures to obtain useful experience that they can use in real clinical work.
- Improve their abilities without endangering patients in the real world.
- Students can experience virtual immersion by viewing real-world patients and seeing how they respond and show complications.
- Learners gain confidence and competence during practice before real clinical exposure.

7.2 AI-Powered Learning Adaptation

AI is adept at modifying guide content and tracks based on individual performance:

- The system's design enables the creation of individualized learning journeys and tailored prompts, dynamically adjusting to each user's demonstrated comprehension and performance during assessment periods.
- Provides real-time evaluations and performance analyses against a range of established metrics.
- Highlights critical aspects of evaluation, giving targeted revision strategies and pointers.
- Every learner can engage and unlearn in tandem for efficient revisions and optimally streamlined learning and practice.

7.3 Better Teamwork in the Metaverse

The metaverse provides a shared, persistent 3D virtual space where health staff can: join group training sessions, communicate with peers and guides from anywhere globally, and participate in multi-user simulations like emergency response drills or surgical procedures.

7.4 Ongoing and Distant Teaching

AI and online platforms give access at any time, from anywhere, to learning tools and practice. Professionals get to upskill without having to leave their workplaces.

It supports lifelong learning and continuous professional development. Training can be conducted in low-resource or remote areas without teaching hospitals.

7.5 Data-Driven Competency Evaluation and Certification

AI systems can measure and compare:

- Performance metrics for skills
- Response time
- Accuracy in simulated decision-making

These metrics can be applied to:

- Credentialing and certification
- Regulatory compliance
- Monitoring readiness for actual clinical tasks

7.6 Cost and Resource Efficiency

Relative to conventional training, virtual spaces minimize:

- The necessary physical equipment, mannequins, or actual patients
- Off-site training, travel, and accommodation costs
- Instructor time, through effective content delivery and assessment
- Makes healthcare training scalable and cost-effective.

Artificial intelligence and virtual worlds within the metaverse are revolutionizing healthcare workforce training to be more interactive, responsive, and accessible. Such technologies facilitate more intelligent learning among healthcare workers, international collaboration, and enhanced patient care. As such technologies continue to advance, they will facilitate closing training gaps and a more capable, future-proof healthcare workforce.

8. Challenges and Considerations

- **Technological Constraints:** Implementing virtual and AI-powered training tools requires substantial investments and technical expertise.
- **Access Disparities:** Not everyone has equal access to the internet and necessary digital tools.
- **Privacy and Ethical Concerns:** Managing learners' data and potential over-surveillance raise critical ethical questions.
- **Lack of Standards:** There is currently no unified framework to regulate virtual training systems.

8.1 Key Challenges in AI and Virtual Training Ecosystems

Although AI, virtual simulations, and the metaverse are transforming healthcare education, their implementation presents several challenges. Figure 4 describes key challenges in AI and virtual training ecosystems.

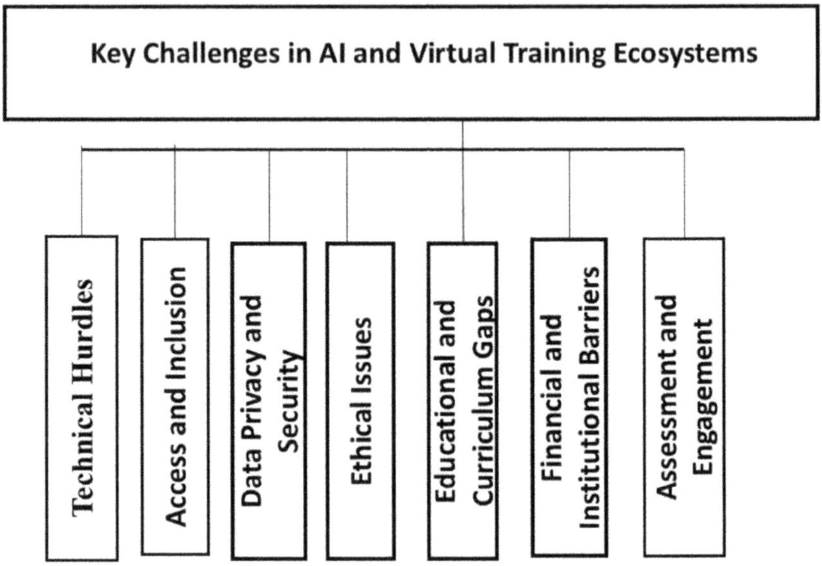

Figure 4: Key challenges in AI and virtual training ecosystems.

1. **Technical Hurdles**

- **Infrastructure demands:** Deploying metaverse training requires high-end technology, such as VR/AR gear, fast internet, and powerful computing system resources, often limited in underfunded areas.
- **Complex integration:** Integrating AI, VR technologies, and educational systems necessitates smooth and precise technological interoperability.
- **Network performance:** For live, interactive, real-time training, dependable and low-latency networks are critical.

2. **Access and Inclusion**

- **Digital inequity:** The disparity in accessing advanced systems and technological tools might impede some learners from fully engaging.
- **Cultural and language accommodation:** Virtual systems should be designed to consider users of different cultures and languages.
- **Learning curve with users:** The use of more advanced immersive technologies may be challenging for elderly and less technologically proficient users.

3. **Data Privacy and Security**

- **Dealing with private information:** To improve performance, AI technologies gather performance data, which poses privacy concerns and approval issues.
- **Privacy violations:** Unauthorized access and exploitation of private information are common in online classrooms.
- **Legal compliance:** Online tools must follow regulatory frameworks such as HIPAA and GDPR to ensure user and patient privacy.

4. **Ethical Issues**

- **Algorithmic bias:** If Artificial Intelligence is trained on biased data, it may provide inaccurate and discriminatory results
- **Simulation limitations:** The use of simulation is not a complete substitute for actual clinical exposure, although it is valuable.
- **Balance of control:** In training decisions made by Al, human oversight must be maintained.

5. **Educational and Curriculum Gaps**

- **No standard curriculum:** There's a lack of uniform guidelines for creating and evaluating metaverse-based learning.
- **Need for content updates:** Medical simulations must be regularly revised to reflect the latest practices.
- **Instructor preparedness:** Educators need training to effectively support AI-integrated learning environments.

6. **Financial and Institutional Barriers**

- **Upfront investment:** A virtual training environment requires a significant amount of infrastructure and development funding.
- **Institutional resistance:** In some organizations, it may be difficult to move from conventional methods to more innovative ones.
- **Long-term viability:** These systems require ongoing technical, financial, and educational support to remain viable.

7. **Assessment and Engagement**

- **Effectiveness measurement:** In real-world situations, it is still hard to assess the impact of virtual training.
- **Learner fatigue:** A heavy use of simulations may reduce the engagement of learners and reduce learning efficiency.

The use of artificial intelligence and virtual simulations has the potential to revolutionize healthcare education. For their adoption to be successful, however, equity, privacy, ethics, and measurable outcomes must all be addressed. To develop inclusive and effective training systems, educators, institutions, developers, and policymakers must collaborate.

9. Future Directions

Technological innovations in training:

- AR/VR in medical curricula
- AI-powered continuous learning programs
- Global virtual universities for health training
- Neuroadaptive interfaces tracking focus and emotions

Healthcare professionals are being trained in intelligent, immersive, and globally accessible ways through the use of emerging technologies.

1. Next-Level Personalization with AI

The AI will take the following steps to support ultra-personalized training

- A real-time adaptive approach to content and difficulty based on learner performance.
- Based on the job role and skill level of learners, designing customized learning paths is necessary.
- By incorporating emotional realism into simulations, communication skills can be enhanced.

2. Advanced Metaverse Training Hubs

Platforms will evolve into:

- Enable international collaboration within shared virtual clinical settings.
- Provide digital twins of real hospitals for realistic training on actual protocols.
- Offer virtual internships simulating real hospital experiences.

3. AI Mentors and Virtual Tutors

Among the features of future systems will be intelligent assistants that:

- Use natural language to answer learners' queries.
- Monitor progress and guide human mentors.
- Simulate dynamic cases that evolve with learner decisions.

4. Integration with Real-World Health Data

As part of future systems, intelligent assistants will be able to

- Practice on real (anonymized) patient scenarios.
- Simulations using actual medical device data.
- Seamless transition between theoretical learning and real-time healthcare settings.

5. Regulation and Ethical AI Development

The following will be prioritized for upcoming advancements:

- Designing unbiased algorithms.
- Establishing international standards for certification and quality.
- Strengthening privacy and cybersecurity measures.

6. Ongoing Learning and Skill Refreshers

Through artificial intelligence, lifelong learning can be promoted in the following ways:

- Knowledge and procedures that are up-to-date are easily accessible.
- A game-based approach to learning can increase motivation.
- An individual's learning pattern should be taken into consideration when preparing skill refreshers.

7. Collaborative and Culturally Aware Training

The benefits of virtual platforms are as follows:

- Training in multidisciplinary teams, reflecting real clinical collaboration.
- Culturally competent care by simulating diverse patient populations.

Integrating AI, simulations, and metaverse platforms can transform healthcare education. Additionally, these tools can enhance technical competence, teamwork, and decision-making skills. To achieve their full potential, these advancements must be implemented with a focus on inclusivity, ethics, and long-term sustainability.

References

1. Barsom, E. Z., Graafland, M., and Schijven, M. P. (2016). Systematic review on the effectiveness of augmented reality applications in medical training. *Surgical Endoscopy*, 30(10), 4174–4183, doi: 10.1007/s00464-016-4800-6.
2. Oh, S., Kim, J. H., Choi, S. W., Lee, H. J., and Hong, J. S. (2021). Application of artificial intelligence in healthcare: Review and future directions. *J. Korean Med. Sci.*, 36(3), e6, doi: 10.3346/jkms.2021.36.e6.
3. Yang, Y., Zhang, H., and Sun, M. (2022). Metaverse in medicine: Applications, challenges, and future directions, *JMIR Med. Inform.*, 10(12), e39569, doi: 10.2196/39569.
4. Mesko, B., and Győrffy, Z. (2022). The role of artificial intelligence in precision medicine and the future of personalized healthcare. *npj Digit. Med.*, 5(1), 1–6, doi: 10.1038/s41746-021-00534-6.
5. World Health Organization. (2021). Digital Health Education: Addressing the Health Workforce Digital Skills Gap. Geneva, Switzerland: WHO [Online]. Available: https://www.who.int/publications/i/item/9789240020504
6. Accenture. (2022). The Future of Healthcare in the Metaverse [Online]. Available: https://www.accenture.com/us-en/insights/health/metaverse-healthcare
7. American Medical Association. (2020). The Future of Medical Education: Artificial Intelligence and the Learning Health System [Online]. Available: https://www.ama-assn.org
8. IBM Institute for Business Value. (2022). Digital Twins in Healthcare: Bridging the Physical and Digital Worlds [Online]. Available: https://www.ibm.com/thought-leadership/institute-business-value/report/digital-twin-healthcare
9. Topol, J. (2019). High-performance medicine: The convergence of human and artificial intelligence. *Nat. Med.*, 25, 44–56, doi: 10.1038/s41591-018-0300-7.
10. Georgiou, M., Papadopoulos, E., and Tzovaras, D. T. (2022). Virtual reality training tools for the metaverse in medicine: A review. *Comput. Biol. Med.*, 149, 106066, doi: 10.1016/j.compbiomed.2022.106066.
11. Woolf. (2009). *Building Intelligent Interactive Tutors: Student-centered Strategies for Revolutionizing e-learning.* Morgan Kaufmann.
12. Esteva, M., Robicquet, A., and Ramsundar, B. (2019). A guide to deep learning in healthcare. *Nat. Med.*, 25, 24–29, doi: 10.1038/s41591-018-0316-z.
13. Berner, D. M., and La Lande, T. J. (2007). Overview of clinical decision support systems. In: *Medical Informatics*, pp. 330–366. Springer.

14. Romero, M. E. S., Gutierrez, C. E., and Sanchez, M. A. (2021). Big data analytics and AI in medical simulation environments. In: *Proc. IEEE Int. Conf. Healthcare Informatics*, pp. 1–8.
15. Bruynseels, D., de Sio, S., and de Vries, P. B. E. (2018). Digital twins in health care: Ethical implications of an emerging engineering paradigm. *Frontiers in Genetics*, 9, 31, https://doi.org/10.3389/fgene.2018.00031
16. Björnsson, E., Borrebaeck, C., Elander, N., Gasslander, T., Gawel, D. R., Gustafsson, M. et al. (2020). Digital twins to personalize medicine. *Genome Med.*, 2(1), 4. doi: 10.1186/s13073-019-0701-3
17. Topol, K. (2019). The Topol review: Preparing the healthcare workforce to deliver the digital future. *NHS Health Education England*, Available: https://topol.hee.nhs.uk/
18. Barricelli, E., Casiraghi, and Fogli, D. (2019). A survey on digital twin: Definitions, characteristics, applications, and design implications. *IEEE Access*, 7, 167653–167671, https://doi.org/10.1109/ACCESS.2019.2953499
19. Tao, G., Zhang, W., and Zhang, S. (2020). Digital twin-driven smart healthcare system design framework. *IEEE Access*, 8, 211902–211913, https://doi.org/10.1109/ACCESS.2020.3039803
20. Rasheed, M., Qayyum, A., and Hassan, M. I. (2022). Digital twin for Healthcare 4.0: A survey and future research directions. *IEEE Access*, 10, 36626–36650. https://doi.org/10.1109/ACCESS.2022.3162961

CHAPTER

11

AI for Global Healthcare Equity: Bridging Healthcare Gaps in the Metaverse

Anitha K. L.[1], Jitha Janardhanan[2], Rahul D.[3*] and Dhanya V. Kurup[4]

[1] Department of Computer Science, Mar Ivanios College, Thiruvananthapuram, Kerala, India

[2] Department of Computer Applications, Presidency College, Bangalore, Karnataka, India

[3] Department of Futures Studies, University of Kerala, Thiruvananthapuram, Kerala, India

[4] Department of Computer Science and Engineering, College of Engineering Aranmula, Kerala, India

A revolutionary approach to solving worldwide medical inequities has emerged with the convergence of digital twin technology, artificial intelligence (AI), and the metaverse. For offering assertive, accurate, and customized care, electronic replicas of patients, pharmaceuticals, or medical facilities can be integrated into metaverse contexts. This chapter explores how these technologies boost the scheduling of therapy, enable distant diagnosis and measures, and address unique medical issues. These technologies allow healthcare providers to assess uncertainty, visualize disease progression, and measure medication effectiveness by instantly recreating patients' physiological and behavioral traits, without requiring human intervention. These characteristics can be used to improve healthcare facilities, simulated medical centers, and interactive medical educational spaces that operate under virtual environments worlds.

1. Introduction

The Metaverse represents a new concept in the world of computing, with tremendous promise for medicine, offering authentic hits across consumers and

*Corresponding author: drahul198@gmail.com

DOI: 10.1201/9781003679370-11

healthcare providers. It depicts the integration of several underlying methods, notably AI, VR, AR, the internet of health care products, robots, and quantum technology. Healthcare professionals may offer online discussions, resemble immediate form patient models (digital twins), and offer predicted therapy via insights based on data through the use of artificial intelligence in simulated settings. These collaborations make it cost-effective. Digital health systems can totally alter traditional approaches to healthcare as they become more robust, ensuring all people have a reasonable opportunity for outstanding medical care, despite geographical location or economic status.

1.1 Contextualizing Global Healthcare Inequities

Most healthcare and rehab services emphasize equitable healthcare. Similar to various countries, Canada's demographic is deteriorating, while 22% of its citizens live with some form of impairment. Integration, equality, diversity, and cultural resonance remain vital as the metaverse expands to reach everyone. Computer literacy education and adaptations for individuals with bodily, visually appealing, and hearing impairments should be part of the Metaverse's deployment. In this case, an online webcam that captures fingers as well as head motion is essential for anyone who's blind or has poor eyesight.

Haptic technology, which enables interaction through the sensation of contact remotely, helps users interact with devices along with other clients. Using complete bodysuits equipped with haptic feedback gauges and detectors that transmit pressure, motion, and various types of movement accurately in real-time helps track communication between people and physicians through immersive virtual reality experiences [1].

Biofeedback, an autonomy learning strategy, is used to regulate the psychophysiological state actively. Someone might change their physiological situation by manipulating data sources while paying attention to their response. With execution, this biofeedback process may assist anyone by regulating their psychophysiological emotions along with their moods. Patients focusing on biological signs that are usually unconscious, such as heart rate, respiration rate, or temperature, may develop strategies to overcome undesirable responses to various types of strains.

Galvanic Skin Response is a physiological indicator that keeps track of fluctuations in the electric conductivity of the epidermis and depends on the degree of moisture. Sweating, although not apparent, rises with a person's degree of mental excitement, regardless of anxiety, enthusiasm, or fright. Electricity conductance, which GSR sensors monitor as an index for mental exertion, is affected by the variation in body moisture. It is a tool to detect anxiety in patients, which can be implemented in environments with dim lights, soothing music ambience that reduces stress. Technologies that utilize AR and VR offer improved therapies by offering patients effortless, enjoyable treatments customized for their preferences.

In the long run, the Metaverse integrates interconnected equipment, live data analysis, and dynamic design to change health care to a global, comprehensive environment. It's especially crucial for regions with persistently low health funding.

1.2 The Promise of Emerging Technologies in Bridging Gaps

Additionally, there is an increasing acceptance of the promise of breakthroughs like blockchain, telemedicine, DT, AI, and the metaverse to decrease healthcare inequalities in remote regions, especially in low and middle-income countries. Artificial Intelligence plays a vital role in improving health by aiding with health care choices, predicting treatment, and optimizing medical processes. Artificial intelligence platforms could support physicians in remote or resource-limited areas by managing medical records, predicting epidemics, and providing quick medical assistance guidance. AI chatbots successfully overcome shortages of workers and reduce the need for personal sittings, deliver health guidance and assessments in native languages in remote regions of India and sub-Saharan Africa. DT builds replicas of people, physical parts, or hospitals to improve holistic treatment. Furthermore, such simulations enable personalized therapeutic planning, clinical modeling, and prediction in areas where medical care is not typically utilized. The beneficial tools for bypassing geographic and structural constraints include those associated with virtual healthcare and mobile health care (mHealth), SMS notifications, mobile-based medical notifications, along with online counselling, which improve accessibility to medical services and therapeutic regimen compliance. One instance that shows how flexible online tools could boost health care operations in crisis-prone regions is the WHO's mHero program in Liberia, which employs mobile devices for assisting health professionals on the ground during pandemics.

Blockchain technique offers data privacy and availability constitute additional critical aspects of equitable healthcare. It ensures continuous healthcare via distributed and secure healthcare records for relocated individuals or those lacking legal identification.

2. Foundations of AI in Healthcare

AI can significantly reduce inconsistencies in medical services, improve patient care, and boost expertise, caregiver satisfaction, and patient safety during the treatment pathway. Examples include remotely tracking patients, using smart gadgets/sensors to detect various factors. Innovations in the medical sector provide a solution for medical expenses. The various AI applications include sleep pattern detecting wireless devices such as the Emerald and Google Nest. A recent paper exploring the potential of non-invasive heartbeat tracking with wireless speakers is another major contribution of AI. Wearable gadgets, such as wristwatches, may be linked to artificial intelligence chatbots that provide patients with information on how to enhance their conduct, sleep, and holistic wellness. With the help of various Artificial Intelligence, retinal diabetes management has shown significant improvement results.

2.1 Overview of AI Techniques: ML, DL, NLP

AI can be subdivided into machine learning and deep learning, adding intelligence to applications. ML generally can be broadly classified into three distinct groups: reinforcement learning (RL), unsupervised learning, and supervised learning [2]. The labeled data in supervised learning can be used for classifying various diseases in health care, such as detecting cancerous cells. Unsupervised learning does not provide annotation for data, like clustering patients with identical symptoms of disease. In Reinforcement Learning, agents acquire knowledge from instruction or by error and trial. The model learns by building an approach for maximizing rewards. Deep Learning algorithms give outstanding predictions in image, video, and speech analysis [3]. Intelligent medical cognition: AI with NLP can enhance medical workflows by automating administrative tasks such as tracking patient interactions in e-health records. This allows doctors to focus more on client service [4].

2.2 Role of AI in Diagnostics, Decision Support, and Predictive Analytics

Artificial intelligence (AI), which involves gaining knowledge, solving problems, and reasoning, is used for analyzing large amounts of data, including genetic information, images, and electronic health records (EHRs), with the goal of predicting disease progression, improving therapies, and increasing the chances of recovery. The extracted information from electronic health records with various algorithms can be used for technology that helps estimate the appropriate amount of medicines, forecast whether an individual would react to therapy, and assess the patient's outlook [5].

The predictions in immunotherapy have been done by various researchers using omics database created by analyzing cancer, stromal, and immune cells are utilized to find the outcome of the machine learning algorithm are used to solve breast implantation surgeries, predicting the problems after colorectal, hepatic, and pancreatic surgeries for the patients utilizing the dataset generated by National Surgical Quality Improvement Program (NSQIP). These ML and DL models provide the merits and demerits of these scenarios, thereby making patients aware of the consequences [6].

3. Understanding the Metaverse in a Healthcare Context

The idea of the Metaverse has fascinated people worldwide, combining immersive technologies with digital innovation. Although it started primarily in the realms of gaming and entertainment, its uses are quickly broadening into essential fields like healthcare. In this context, the Metaverse signifies the merging of technologies like Virtual Reality, Augmented Reality, and Extended Reality into a cohesive virtual environment. The system has enabled admins, patients, and medical personnel to collaborate, evaluate, manage, and teach in online environments, which leads to impacts. The medical metaverse is a growing, appealing, and collaborative simulation where sophisticated techniques could be utilized to categorize, deliver, or improve medical care. Wearable sensors, intelligent devices, and avatars enable people to explore this simulated environment. Such advancements made it feasible to track vital signs, mimic clinical procedures, monitor biological structure, and provide online consulting. It offers holistic and collaborative provisions, as opposed to conventional telemedicine, which requires video conferences and static platforms. Users and healthcare providers may employ virtual reality and augmented reality to explore the healthcare space, undertake live replicas, and study 3D illustrations of healthcare problems.

3.1 Metaverse Transformation

The Metaverse has evolved from a concept in science fiction into a quickly emerging digital reality. The word "metaverse" was created by Neal Stephenson in 1992 [7]. In this literary work, he blended real and virtual characters with a three-dimensional virtual realm called the metaverse. This thriving cyberspace allows individuals to partake in various tasks, including purchasing and education. Essentially, the metaverse refers to a world that exists beyond our physical reality. It is imagined as a parallel virtual reality universe where users can engage as digital avatars, offering connected, immersive, and real-time experiences. This environment aims to support a designer's budget by offering virtual spaces that are compassionate and fostering a dispersed economy [8].

3.2 Architecture of the Metaverse for Medical Applications

The architecture of the Metaverse in the Medical field is shown in Figure 1. Metaverse is the future internet, which offers an online space to humans in which they can live another lifespan. With any kind of intelligent devices smartphones to head-mounted displays, humans can freely enter in online world to interact and communicate with avatars or digital objects. Metaverse is an integration of personal and online spaces. It offers an independent, entirely immersive spatiotemporal virtual environment where humans can work, purchase property, socialize, learn, go to concerts, visit libraries, parks, and engage in many more real-world activities. The metaverse is a broad realm that supports socialization, immersive interactions, real-world construction, and expansibility, where users can freely transform. The predictions show that humans will spend a minimum of an hour a day on the Metaverse [9]. Today, the metaverse has gained significant popularity. Essentially, it is often described as a futuristic iteration of the Internet. Utilizing AR, VR, and XR, users will navigate the metaverse's

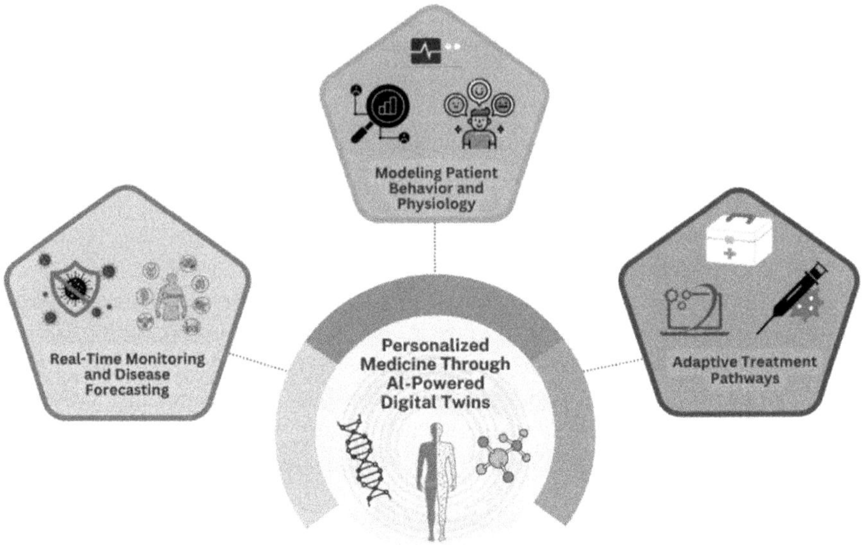

Figure 1: Architecture of the metaverse in healthcare.

virtual realms much like we browse websites with a mouse cursor today. So far, major companies like Google, Microsoft, and Meta have invested heavily in evolving the metaverse as the next development of cyberspace. In the future, the metaverse is expected to become an immersive digital ecosystem that integrates social interaction, work, entertainment and commerce. In the coming years, it is expected to flourish that cyberspace will flourish by revolutionizing service environments across various sectors, including healthcare, education, and smart industries [10–12].

The Metaverse architecture in healthcare brings together various cutting-edge technologies to develop immersive, interactive, and intelligent healthcare environments. It fundamentally combines VR, AR, and MR to facilitate 3D simulations of medical situations, including surgical planning, remote consultations, and virtual tours of hospitals.

3.2.1 Medical Training

The Metaverse healthcare system offers a healthcare experience of service that is immersive, recreational, and interactive, tailored to individual patients' needs. The Metaverse consists of advanced technology revolutions such as Artificial Intelligence (AI), AR, VR, telepresence, digital twinning, and blockchain, which have a significant effect on healthcare [13]. The Metaverse facilitates medical professionals and students to study in a hands-on, risk-free setting. Platforms based on a VR model, actual medical procedures where students can conduct surgeries, emergency interventions, and diagnosis in a risk-free context without actual patients. 3D anatomical models improve learning beyond textbooks.

International collaboration is facilitated, with trainees from various countries interacting in the same virtual operating room.

3.2.2 Virtual Hospitals

The metaverse refers to a world made by human beings with digital technology that can interact with the physical world. In particular, humans can experience the virtual space in person with the help of VR glasses, which is a type of metaverse [14]. In the Metaverse, medical practitioners can establish virtual clinics or hospitals. Patients visit these clinics through an avatar, connect with physicians, undergo examinations, and then get medications in an approach that's identical to those in conventional clinics. It provides greater exposure to health services and is rarely available by location, particularly to underprivileged and faraway persons. Using a variety of clinical imaging applications built into the system, clinicians can engage with patients more intimately and engagingly than possible using typical online conversations, and medical records may be considered three-dimensional models.

3.2.3 Mental Health Therapy

The metaverse provides dynamic, distant, and often avatar-based emotional treatments through the use of complex VR settings. It permits clients to acquire treatment remotely from anywhere in the world, providing advantages such as ease, privacy, and tailored settings for procedures like sunlight exposure treatment, meditation, and mental health treatment. It may enhance performance and participation by replicating actual events or pleasant locations, especially with conditions such as social anxieties, stress, and post-traumatic stress disorder (PTSD). However, it additionally brings up questions regarding availability, privacy of data, and the quality of therapist-client exchanges in cyberspace. During the guidance of a clinician, individuals may participate in scenarios within a virtual environment. As a human who feels hesitant to meet in person, the Metaverse provides privacy, ease, and pleasure via interpersonal counselling meetings, relaxing regions, and mindfulness initiatives.

3.2.4 Physical Therapy

Physical therapy with VR enables patients who have suffered strokes, injuries, or surgery to undergo gamified rehabilitation through immersive games. Patients receive real-time feedback to improve their posture and compliance with treatment. With AI and motion tracking, therapy can be customized and modified as the recovery continues. Encouragement and rewards can be given to patients in the virtual environment, which enhances rehabilitation.

3.2.5 Surgical Planning

The Metaverse in medicine assists in diagnostic imaging, surgical simulation, rehabilitation, and management of patient health [15]. In addition, the Metaverse can encourage patients to perform the necessary physical exercises continuously based on the treatment protocols. AR and MR are utilized by surgeons to plan intricate operations by seeing patient-specific anatomy in 3D. Digital twins of organs or tumors are analyzed before cuts are made, enabling more accurate interventions. During procedures, AR can overlay real-time data—such as vitals, blood flow, or tumour site—onto the operating field to improve surgeon precision and decision-making. The interactive metaverse offers solutions for these issues by offering human-computer interaction in the form of customized services [16]. Researchers explored the applicability and feasibility of the metaverse in the field of medicine and found that the development of the metaverse adopts the digitization of real experience from real to virtual and from virtual to real. AI physicians, medical operations, training in medicine, healthcare robots, and pharmaceutical research and development are a few healthcare paradigms of the metaverse [17].

3.3 Immersive Technologies: VR, AR, XR

3.3.1 Virtual Reality (VR)

It is an immersive experience entirely composed without any world knowledge. The virtual world will be represented exquisitely, but this system does not consider the real environment [18]. Users can view the virtual world, walk and navigate, and touch virtual features or objects using virtual reality technology. It can also be created by specially constructed rooms with several big screens, though it is most often created by VR headsets with a head-mounted screen and tiny display in the vicinity of the eyes.

3.3.2 Augmented Reality (AR)

An Augmented Reality system adds virtual (computer-generated) objects to the real world, making the virtual objects appear to be in the same space as the real world [19]. An AR system should juxtapose virtual and real objects in an actual environment, operate in real-time and interactively, and synchronize real and virtual objects with one another. Augmented Reality (AR) enriches the real world by superimposing digital information—like images, text, and 3D models—upon the physical environment in real time. While VR eliminates reality, AR augments reality, enabling consumers to stay conscious of their surroundings even as they receive context-dependent digital augmentations. This is most often accessed through smartphones, tablets, or AR headsets.

3.3.3 Extended Reality (XR)

Extended Reality (XR) encompasses all immersion technologies, such as Virtual Reality (VR), Augmented Reality (AR), and Mixed Reality (MR). XR is the entire range of digital-physical interaction, fusing real and virtual worlds in different proportions. This enables users to toggle between completely immersive and real-world augmentation, depending on the scenario and device. XR is being used more and more across sectors such as healthcare, education, manufacturing, retail, and remote collaboration. For example, a healthcare provider may practice in VR, access real-time data in AR during an operation, and engage with digital twins in MR. For education, XR enables students to conduct interactive science experiments, listen to virtual lectures, or visit virtual museums. Companies use XR for virtual product development, immersive advertising, and hybrid offices where people get together as avatars.

4. Digital Twin Technology in Medicine

4.1 Definition and Key Concepts

An online replica or model of an individual's physique or specific body parts is created in the medical field, incorporating historical and current data from smartwatches, devices, medical records, images, and other medical sources data. The modeling of one's physical and pathological procedures, the simulated version, allows for predicting and preparing customized therapy for everyone simulations. The simulations were generated precisely for all patients employing their unique hereditary, emotional, and medical records. It presents continuous tracking by revealing variations in the patient's present medical condition.

4.2 Types of Digital Twins: Patient, Equipment, and Facility Models

In the field of medicine, it can be categorized into the following:

4.2.1 Patient Digital Twin

It is an online real-time replica of an individual patient that incorporates input from multiple resources, like smartwatches, genes, diagnostic images, electronic health records (EHRs), and real-time detectors. Through replicating a patient's physiologic and pathologic procedures, this customized simulation enables healthcare practitioners to forecast the advancement of an illness, assess treatment plans accurately, and customize treatment options for every patient. It enables faster treatment, improved long-term disease management, personalized medical care, and a secure method to assess complicated treatment prospects, representing the patient's state.

4.2.2 Equipment Digital Twin

The simulation of a healthcare device employs data collected via integrated sensors, IoT technology, and user logs to recreate the operational efficiency and functionality of the device. It eliminates malfunctions through spotting initial signs of damage or collapse, anticipates service requirements, and offers constant insight into the condition of devices. It guarantees that vital devices like infusion pumps, ventilation systems, surgical robots, and magnetic resonance imaging (MRI) machines remain accessible to be used securely. It provides security for patients and the quality treatments in clinics with low maintenance and repairs.

4.2.3 Facility Digital Twin

It simulates the design, operations, and settings of healthcare facilities like clinics or hospitals. It provides an extensive overview of the facility's performance by incorporating information on location, material utilization, employee and patient movement, and IoT-supported infrastructure. It enhances energy efficiency, resource administration, crisis preparation, and hygiene practices. It assists in organizational management and improves the overall efficiency, adaptability, and security of medical centers by simulating numerous operational settings.

4.3 Benefits of Digital Twins in Clinical Practice

These techniques provide precise, anticipatory, and customized medical care, giving noteworthy advances in healthcare. Doctors may forecast the progress of a condition, evaluate various therapies, and customize treatment strategies without risking patients by generating digital data simulations of actual patients in context. Improved choices and outcomes become feasible through it, particularly for complicated or hazardous circumstances as chemotherapy care, cardiac conditions, and surgeries. Through continually recording health information from gadgets or devices and observing anomalies before indications develop, these also enable rapid detection and proactive treatment. They also enhance treatment planning and resource allocation, enabling hospitals to decrease trial-and-error practices, reduce complications, and lower the cost of healthcare. In a multidisciplinary team, digital twins also strengthen communication through a common, visual representation of the patient's state. Consequently, clinical processes are streamlined, patient safety is enhanced, and delivery of health care becomes more responsive and evidence-based.

5. Personalized Medicine Through AI-Powered Digital Twins

It is transforming personalized medicine through the development of virtual copies of individual patients that incorporate their distinct biological, physiological, and lifestyle profiles. Personalized Medicine Through AI-Powered Digital Twins is shown in Figure 2. These virtual models are updated in real time through information from electronic health records, genomics, medical imaging, wearable technologies, and real-time biosensors. Artificial intelligence is used to analyze the rich data, detect patterns, and forecast how a patient will react to certain treatments or disease developments. Physicians can employ digital twins to model different therapeutic situations—e.g., different drug regimens or the outcome of surgery—specifically for the patient's profile. This enables more precise diagnoses, better-planned treatments, and fewer side effects. Consequently, AI-driven digital twins shift medicine from the one-size-fits-all model and toward personalized, predictive, and preventive care.

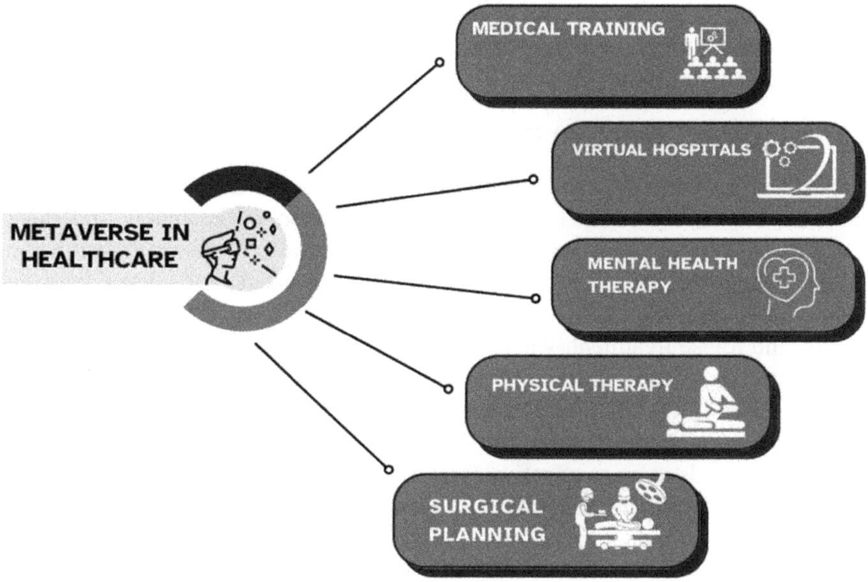

Figure 2: Personalized medicine through AI-powered digital twins.

5.1 Real-Time Monitoring and Disease Forecasting

The seamless incorporation of sensors, portable, and health information into an ongoing simulated approach facilitates immediate patient tracking. Physicians can analyze health indicators, detect minor physical shifts, and respond swiftly whenever abnormal patterns appear with the assistance of instant syncing. Digital twins may predict the emergence or evolution of conditions, including septicemia, cardiac arrest, or pulmonary drop, prior to medical signs emerging through the use of machine learning and computational intelligence. Preventative services, including initiatives happening earlier to avoid issues, reduce hospitalizations, and enhance patient outcomes, are rendered feasible by such anticipatory ability.

5.2 Modeling Patient Behavior and Physiology

Digital twins for medicine may recreate a patient's routines, which impact their medical condition, as well as their biological processes. They provide an extensive and continuous visualization of a patient by combining information from devices, mobile medical applications, medical records, and lifestyle habits, such as dietary habits, fitness, sleeping habits, and medication compliance. These simulations can replicate physiologic procedures, like digestion, respiration, and arterial factors, in addition to the way such activities respond to therapies or external stimuli. Furthermore, psychological simulation assists doctors in understanding how much external variables or practices enhance the likelihood of illness or the quality of medication. Integrated analysis of the human body and mind may help prevent disease over time, anticipate how changes in routine or environment might influence the progression of disease, or lead to more tailored, effective treatments procedures.

5.3 Adaptive Treatment Pathways

By replicating, tracking, and adapting healthcare procedures according to a patient's fluctuating state, DT allows the formation of adaptable treatment approaches. Digital twins enable a flexible, personalized approach compared to traditional therapies, which tend to be consistent and dependent on demographic information. Doctors may evaluate various approaches, foresee effects, and revise treatment, when necessary, via immediate health information, like laboratory results, images, or sensor assessments, to modify the simulated model frequently. As the patient's emotional or disease condition develops, this versatility ensures that therapies are optimal. Adapting treatment paths through digital twins leads to more effective care, better outcomes, and a lower chance of over- or under-treatment, regardless of whether they address persistent illnesses like diabetes or complex conditions like cancer.

6. Collaborative Medical Training in the Metaverse

6.1 Simulation-Based Learning with Digital Twins

Medical simulators tailored to each patient enhance judgment in emergency rooms and critical care units by utilizing datasets from real patients and AI-driven DT. They offer secure, viable, and inclusive educational spaces that enhance clinical cognitive.

Heart-simulations with DT: Simulate heart rhythm, circulatory systems, and therapeutic responses utilizing actual data sets with AI guided by fundamental sciences. It offers in-silico medication testing and tailored planning for procedures, like stents or bypass surgeries.

AI-based population-based modelling trains for broad emergencies, optimizes medical supplies, and predicts medical hazards.

Distress responder simulators offer appealing, collaborative contexts in trauma treatment protocols, boosting partnership and enhancing resilience for crises.

Digital twins for pharmacology: Real-time medical components, gene data, and simulated organs are integrated to model how an individual metabolizes and responds to medications. These models provide tailored observations about medication intake, dispersion, metabolic processes, and expulsion by replicating

Table 1: Use Cases of Digital Twin (DT), AR/VR, and Blockchain (BC)

DT + Augmented/ Virtual Reality	Augmented Reality glasses are used to experience the DT of machines by experts.
DT + BC	DT data are secured with BC.
BC + Augment/ Virtual Reality	Blockchain verifies ownership of virtual assets (like NFTs) used in VR spaces or AR applications.
All above	BC ensures secure recording of sensor information and history, and augmented reality visualizes a DT of traffic.

body processes, such as liver and kidney activity, integrating pharmacogenomic accounts, and constantly upgrading with patient information through sensors or electronic healthcare records. Medical choices and pharmacological training have been enhanced, negative therapeutic effects reduced, and more secure, better drug selection has become feasible. Table 1 shows the use cases of digital twin, AR/VR and blockchain.

6.2 Cross-Border Professional Training and Collaboration

Collaborative educational techniques improve the educational procedure, enhance insight into information, and promote current growth in abilities. Collaborative learning and the metaverse share similar features that make both a great fit [20].

Professionals may meet, interact, and investigate jointly in online learning spaces that exist in the metaverse. Such sets enable imaginative play, models, and brainstorming sessions. In simulated educational environments, avatar-based networking connects learners closely and promotes collaboration and expertise sharing. The immersion method simulators enhance the growth of concrete abilities through regulated, practical sessions [21]. Table 2 highlights the role of metaverse in multiple fields.

Table 2: Metaverse in Various Fields

Areas	**Use Cases**
Teaching/ Learning	Virtual experience gives immense pleasure and knowledge while learning civics, science, like the study of planets, archaeology, etc.
Health Care	Enhances healthcare efficiency with distant monitoring of patients, virtual nursing attention, and emergency assistance.
Industrial Sector	Optimizing, planning, and designing in various product stages with the help of virtualization makes effective testing and development of the product.
Art	Creating a virtual exhibition of various monuments that cannot be touched across dispersed regions.
Communal/ Cultural Area	Widen the communal areas through various social platforms, thereby reducing real-world constraints.

With My Virtual Lab, a virtual world platform, the National University of Singapore trains students to transition smoothly to practical laboratories by allowing them to simulate lab processes risk-free and develop confidence and hands-on skills. Reliance utilizes a digital twin for training staff members, easing complex manufacturing constraints.

Heineken organized Tiger Beer's initial food fair in the metaverse after COVID. While purchasing food from street vendors and having it served directly to the doorstep through a partnered delivery company, consumers might have explored three-dimensional markets in their own customized avatar, linking with everybody else, enjoying activities, and meeting vendors. Pop-rock musician Bastian Baker illustrated the metaverse's potential to foster close bonds and execute an exclusive concert via a simulated event [22].

6.3 Role of AI in Adaptive Learning Environments

A particular type of tailored instruction referred to as "adaptable learning" makes use of sophisticated technological tools—often based on analytical techniques and ML thinking—to alter the learning procedure using current data regarding how a student is doing [23]. Through the use of educational data mining (EDM) methods that collect external, demographic, intellectual, emotional, and interpersonal features, the student model creates an outline of every learner. Population statistics (such as their ages, region), evaluations, job completion initiatives, previous experience, intellectual capacities, educational choices, behavioral characteristics, confidence, inspiration, online access, impact, and hardware requirements are all examples of those characteristics. Surveys, user activity tracking, or machine learning techniques may be employed to collect information on such features. For evaluating moods and attention, gadgets that

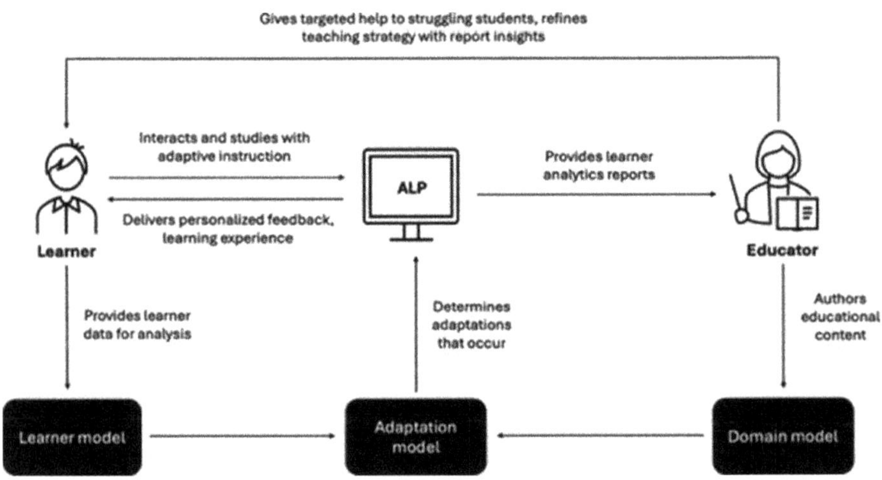

Figure 3: Pictorial representation of AL structure.

collect our heartbeats, eye movement, or looks can be integrated. Through the use of speech recognition devices to gather learners' oral remarks in context whenever they perform the study module, their emotional status may be determined. By employing these methods, the student paradigm stays active and continually alters the student's traits as he or she advances through their academic journey. Figure 3 presents a visual overview of AL structure.

Item Response Theory (IRT) is a mathematical paradigm commonly observed in platforms for adaptable assessment. It facilitates assessing a pupil's degree of expertise through assessing the way they execute specific tasks or queries. By adapting the degree of complexity for the inquiries to the learners' ability, IRT systems can assist in personalized instruction. Topics within the adaptable educational method evolve in the moment based on the learner's response. The following issue may become tougher when a learner responds to the query effectively; when they respond to a topic incorrectly, the method offers an easier topic or offers further assistance. Tools such as Socratic from Google implement adaptable questions that aid learners in progressively understanding concepts.

7. Challenges and Limitations

7.1 Technological Barriers: Connectivity, Hardware, Infrastructure

Fast connectivity a low-latency broadband are vital to the metaverse's capability for realistic experiences, excellent quality visuals, and real-time interactions. Consumers commonly encounter delays or complete shutdowns due to the lack of reliable links, which degrades engagement and makes the web page ineffective. As an example, low connection costs could lead to delays or breakdowns for a learner engaging in a virtual surgical procedure via virtual reality headgear over distant health care learning, especially in poor or remote regions.

Hardware Constraints: Earbuds, protective gear, gadgets, and other augmented and virtual reality equipment needed to access the metaverse are costly and often demand significant processing units. Such hardware is unavailable to numerous people. If a university implements metaverse-based chemical labs, numerous learners will not be allowed to take part as they have no choice of virtual reality (VR) headphones or the necessary graphics-capable systems.

Infrastructure Limitations: Supporting metaverse systems requires a reliable energy source, an efficient system, cloud services, and edge computing tools. The technological framework required to cope with such enormous and constant computing workloads has been inadequate in numerous fields. An apparel company creates a 3D simulated shop wherein clients may use simulations to test out clothes. The software becomes slow, inactive, or fails when the cloud service can't support many users around the world at the same time because of server limits or inappropriate geographical coverage.

7.2 Interdisciplinary Gaps and Scalability

The metaverse cuts across several disciplines—computer science, AI, networking, psychology, ethics, education, design, and others. These areas usually exist in silos, with varying terminologies, approaches, and priorities. This makes collaboration challenging, with the consequence being slowed innovation and fragmented or incompatible systems. Scalability is an indicator of the extent to which the metaverse could handle large online spaces, trillions of customers simultaneously, and current data with no slowdowns [24]. Nowadays, systems often complain about evaluating load, network constraints, and the need for cloud services, especially when sessions incorporate depth visuals, artificial intelligence, and sensor feeds.

7.3 Cultural and Socioeconomic Factors

The societal and intellectual variables that affect participation, involvement, and accessibility have an immense effect in the metaverse, which holds promise for an exciting future filled with global connection. Avatars, simulated environments, and language norms are primarily intended to resemble European figures, which restricts other cultures' participants in portraying what they are in the app. Efficient global collaboration is made harder by copyright rules, linguistic barriers, and differences in cultural norms.

Financial alternatives like online freelance jobs, new financial technology trades, and land possession thus help prosperous consumers, despite limiting poor people. Such digital spaces reflect inequalities in academic achievement and job opportunities. Moreover, companies in advanced nations prefer to reside at the heart of metaverse network regulation, resulting in beneficial policy formulation and social integrity. Autonomous governing frameworks, sponsored accessibility, equitable architecture methods, and historically relevant writing are all required for tackling this problem.

Socially and economically, the metaverse demands costly gadgets, rapid connectivity, and an advanced range of online literacy, all of which tend to be unattainable in remote or impoverished locations. When trying to tackle these challenges, autonomous governing approaches subsidize access, equitable designing methods, and socially acceptable writing must be used.

8. Future Outlook and Research Directions

Hyper-realistic simulations that offer flawless collaboration, tailored interactions, and autonomous rules are anticipated to depict the metaverse's potential future. Nevertheless, it must be achieved by addressing major barriers to safety, diversity, moral oversight, and compatibility. Developing extensible infrastructure, enhancing realistic experiences, ensuring user privacy and safety, and exploring the societal impacts of extended online participation are among the primary fields of subsequent study. The growing integration of virtual and bodily dimensions demands cross-domain cooperation to influence the metaverse's ethical and sustainable growth.

8.1 Toward a Global Health Metaverse

The healthcare Metaverse concept sees advanced modern innovations like BC, AI, AR/VR, and IoT merging to build a solitary, integrated, holistic digital realm that fosters global collaboration in investigations, training, and health services. World campuses and immersive augmented and virtual reality simulators will improve healthcare learning and instruction by simplifying the exchange of skills and enhancing talent building. Internet of Things gadgets and artificial intelligence-driven avatars could offer personalized and proactive treatment, while blockchain would guarantee the secure and open exchange of medical data internationally. Blockchain, which, in the context of the other conjunction, guarantees a secure and open global transfer of medical data. Public health awareness campaigns can utilize immersive platforms to create awareness and foster wellness worldwide. While promising, some issues need to be addressed, such as the digital divide, data privacy issues, costs of implementation, and ethical issues. With a strategic investment and global collaboration, the Global Health Metaverse has the potential to transform equitable and efficient healthcare globally.

8.2 Integration with Blockchain, IoT, and 6G

6G networks are imagined to be the breakthrough in the next era of communication systems that would solve the issues of speed-up of details, including millions of uses of information faced by present fifth generation (5G) networks. A few major radical technologies in 6G, along with current 5G candidate designs, will ensure the desired quality of experience (QoE) to achieve ubiquitous wireless connectivity for the Internet of Everything (IoE) from the telecommunication sector to digital smart industries. Blockchain technology (BCT) has attracted immense attention to handle the openness, decentralized management, frequency shortage, and intrinsic integrity, connectivity, protection, and safety, and is being developed for smart applications areas such as Industrial IoT (IIoT) and Industry 5.0 applications. The incompatibility between the demands of most disruptive, highly data-driven IoT applications and the capabilities of 5G networks guided the need for a decentralized BCT-based 6G architecture. A few blockchain research initiatives have appeared in recent years on industrial IoT and 6G communications; therefore, industry-focused research is still at its nascent stage [25].

8.3 Roadmap for Equitable Implementation

The roadmap should start with closing the digital divide by expanding internet access, making devices affordable, and teaching digital literacy to marginalized communities groups. The government and the private sector must collaborate to develop inclusive regulations and norms that focus on accessibility, linguistic diversity, and cultural sensitivity. Ethical and legal foundations must be established to deal with data privacy, user rights, content moderation, and AI bias to protect vulnerable users. Furthermore, public-private partnerships and international agencies can assume a central role in providing funding for infrastructure, facilitating local innovation ecosystems, and developing capacity in education and training.

9. Conclusion

Artificial Intelligence, Digital Twin, and the Metaverse are collaborating to offer treatment worldwide that provides fresh, extendable solutions to past atrocities. AI-enabled DT empowers physicians to provide customized and proactive treatment by replicating clients' physiological and behavioral data in real time. Through overcoming geographical constraints, this kind of preventive service facilitates rapid disease learning, continuous and persistent sickness tracking, along treatment regimen alterations. By integrating the Metaverse and Digital Twins, clinicians enhance their skills in ways that were previously inaccessible to people in remote locations, ultimately increasing access to treatment and improving the quality of healthcare education and practice. In particular, such tools may enhance opportunities for large-scale healthcare models that could improve resource allocation, train policymakers, and create simulations that can dynamically monitor the impact of treatments. Despite the tremendous possibilities for favorable outcomes, accomplishing such opportunities requires a thorough understanding of the confidentiality and moral issues that must be addressed. Obtaining societal acceptance entails preserving information, ensuring virtual fairness, and fostering trust among patients and medical practitioners. Toward responsible handling of such issues, collaboration among technicians, doctors, administrators, and even scientists becomes crucial. In summary, emerging innovations possess tremendous potential for enhancing medical assistance, yet their deployment needs to be strategically planned to ensure that all individuals benefit.

References

1. Victor, N., Chengoden, R., Huynh-The, T., Yenduri, G., Madhusanka, L., and Gadekallu, T. R. (2022). *Metaverse for Healthcare: A Survey on Potential Applications, Challenges, and Future Directions*. arXiv. https://doi.org/10.48550/arXiv.2209.04160.
2. Akkaya, N., and Aras, B. (2023). A framework for equitable virtual rehabilitation in the metaverse era. *Frontiers in Rehabilitation Sciences*, 4, 1241020. https://doi.org/10.3389/fresc.2023.1241020

3. Ford, T. J., Buchanan, D. M., Azeez, A., Benrimoh, D. A., Kaloiani, I., Bandeira, I. D. et al. (2023). Taking modern psychiatry into the metaverse: Integrating augmented, virtual, and mixed reality technologies into psychiatric care. *Frontiers in Digital Health*, 5, 1146806. https://doi.org/10.3389/fdgth.2023.1146806
4. Kourtesis, P. (2024). A comprehensive review of multimodal XR applications, risks, and ethical challenges in the Metaverse. *Multimodal Technologies and Interaction*, 8(11), 98. https://doi.org/10.3390/mti8110098
5. Rahul, D., George, S., and Amritha, P. S. (2025). Metaverse-powered human-computer interaction and application. In: *Applying Metaverse Technologies to Human-Computer Interaction for Healthcare* (pp. 38). CRC Press.
6. Bajwa, J., Munir, U., Nori, A., and Williams, B. (2021). Artificial intelligence in healthcare: Transforming the practice of medicine. *Future Healthcare Journal*, 8(2), e188–e194. https://doi.org/10.7861/fhj.2021-0095
7. Dixon, D., Sattar, H., Moros, N., Kesireddy, S. R., Ahsan, H., Lakkimsetti, M. et al. (2024). Unveiling the influence of AI predictive analytics on patient outcomes: A comprehensive narrative review. *Cureus*, 16(5), e59954. https://doi.org/10.7759/cureus.59954
8. Kim, S. (2020). *Metaverse: Digital World, World of Emerging Items*. 1st ed. Hwaseong: PlanB Design.
9. Zhang, T., Gao, L., He, C., Zhang, M., Krishnamachari, B., and Avestimehr, A. S. (2022). Federated learning for the Internet of Things: Applications, challenges, and opportunities. *IEEE Internet of Things Magazine*, 5, 24–29.
10. Wang, Y., Su, Z., Zhang, N., Xing, R., Liu, D., Luan, T. H. et al. (2023). A survey on metaverse: Fundamentals, security, and privacy. *IEEE Commun. Surveys Tuts.*, 25(1), 319–352, 1st Quart.
11. Dionisio, J. D. N., Iii, W. G. B., and Gilbert, R. (2013). 3D virtual worlds and the metaverse: Current status and future possibilities. *ACM Comput. Surveys*, 45(3), 1–38.
12. Mozumder, M. A. I., Sheeraz, M. M., Athar, A., Aich, S., and Kim, H.-C. (2022). Overview: Technology roadmap of the future trend of metaverse based on IoT, blockchain, AI technique, and medical domain metaverse activity. In: *Proc. 24th Int. Conf. Adv. Commun. Technol.* (*ICACT*), pp. 256–261.
13. Lee, L.-H. , Braud, T., Zhou, P., Wang, L., Xu, D., Lin, Z. et al. (2021). All one needs to know about metaverse: A complete survey on technological singularity, virtual ecosystem, and research agenda. *Foundations and Trends in Human–Computer Interaction*, 18(2–3), 100–337.
14. Park, S.-M. and Kim, Y.-G. (2022). A metaverse: Taxonomy, components, applications, and open challenges. *IEEE Access*, 10, 4209–4251.
15. Lippert, K., Khan, M. N. R., Rabbi, M. M., Dutta, A., and Cloutier, R. (2021). A framework of metaverse for systems engineering. In: *Proc. 2021 IEEE Int. Conf. Signal Processing, Information, Communication & Systems* (*SPICSCON*), Dhaka, Bangladesh, pp. 50–54.
16. Bansal, G., Rajgopal, K., Chamola, V., Xiong, Z., and Niyato, D. (2022). Healthcare in metaverse: A survey on current metaverse applications in healthcare. *IEEE Access*, 10, 119914–119946.
17. Deebak, B. D., Memon, F. H., Khowaja, S. A., Dev, K., Wang, W., and Qureshi, N. M. F. (2022). In the digital age of 5G networks: Seamless privacy-preserving authentication for cognitive-inspired Internet of Medical Things. *IEEE Trans. Ind. Informat.*, 18(12), 8916–8923.

18. Xu, J., Jiang, C., Wei, W., and Li, Y. (2022). The research of medical metaverse application under the background of the normalization of the new crown epidemic. In: L. J. Zhang (ed.), *Metaverse–Metaverse*. Cham, Switzerland: Springer pp. 68–80.
19. Kim, S. K., Kang, S.-J., Choi, Y.-J., Choi, M.-H., and Hong, M. (2017). Augmented-reality survey: From concept to application. *KSII Transactions on Internet and Information Systems*, 11(2), 982–1004.
20. Skarbez, R., Smith, M., and Whitton, M. C. (2021). Revisiting milgram and Kishino's reality-virtuality continuum. *Frontiers Virtual Reality*, 2, Art. 647997.
21. Azuma, R., Baillot, Y., Behringer, R., Feiner, Julier, S., and MacIntyre, B. (2001). Recent advances in augmented reality. *IEEE Comput. Graph. Appl.*, 21(6), 34–47.
22. Zaidi S. S. B., Adnan, U., Lewis, K. O., and Fatima, S. S. (2024). Metaverse-powered basic sciences medical education: Bridging the gaps for lower middle-income countries. *Ann Med.*, 56(1), 2356637. doi: 10.1080/07853890.2024.2356637. Epub 2024 May 24. PMID: 38794846; PMCID: PMC11132556.
23. Zarei, T., Emery, M., Saredakis, D., Lee, G. A., Stubbs, B., Szpak, A., and Loetscher, T. (2024). Being there together for health: A systematic review on the feasibility, effectiveness and design considerations of immersive collaborative virtual environments in health applications. arXivpreprint arXiv:2412.04760. https://arxiv.org/abs/2412.04760https://www.weforum.org/stories/2023/07/global-collaboration-village-metaverse-real-world-impact/
24. Tan, L. Y., Hu, S., Yeo, D. J., and Cheong, K. H. (2025). Artificial intelligence-enabled adaptive learning platforms: A review. *Computers and Education: Artificial Intelligence*, 9, 100429. https://doi.org/10.1016/j.caeai.2024.100429
25. Jahid, A., Alsharif, M. H., and Hall, T. J. (2023). The convergence of blockchain, IoT and 6G: Potential, opportunities, challenges and research roadmap. *Journal of Network and Computer Applications*, 217, Article 103677. https://doi.org/10.1016/j.jnca.2023.103677

CHAPTER 12

The Role of Blockchain and AI in Securing Health Transactions in the Metaverse

Subhayan Nag[1], Dawn Sivan[2], Veena Raj[3] and K. Satheesh Kumar[1*]

[1] School of Digital Sciences, Kerala University of Digital Sciences, Innovation, and Technology, Thiruvananthapuram, Kerala – 695317, India

[2] Centre for Advanced Intelligent Materials, Faculty of Industrial Sciences and Technology, Universiti Malaysia Pahang Al-Sultan Abdullah, 26300 Kuantan, Pahang, Malaysia

[3] Faculty of Integrated Technologies, Universiti Brunei Darussalam Gadong, Bandar Seri Begawan BE1410, Brunei

This chapter examines the role of blockchain and artificial intelligence in the healthcare metaverse. Virtual and augmented reality provide spaces for remote consultation, training, and clinical work. Artificial intelligence is added for different tasks: threat detection, identity checks, and decision support. The reason is simple—patient data is sensitive, and without secure systems, there can be no trust. Blockchain offers a decentralized and tamper-resistant way to move records, while keeping transfers transparent. Examples already exist. Virtual doctor visits are one. Beyond virtual consultations, experiments now extend to digital health marketplaces and the automation of claims. Extended-reality platforms are also being tested for clinical research. Each shows the value of combining these tools. Still, serious challenges remain. HIPAA and GDPR compliance, scaling costs, energy use, system interoperability, and fairness in AI decisions cannot be ignored. Future work will likely involve 6G networks, the Internet of Everything, and cryptography resistant to quantum attacks. The claim is straightforward: technology alone will not make healthcare in the metaverse safe. Clear standards, careful design, and strong protection of patient rights are required.

*Corresponding author: satheesh.kumar@duk.ac.in

DOI: 10.1201/9781003679370-12

1. Overview of the Metaverse in Healthcare

The emergence of the metaverse presents a range of transformative applications for the healthcare sector [1, 2]. It's also a great way to train for complex operations, since you can practice in a really realistic 3D environment. It's built on things like virtual reality (VR), augmented reality (AR), the Internet of Medical Things (IoMT), and all sorts of wearable tech and sensors [3]. The COVID-19 pandemic really sped things up, pushing us toward more remote monitoring and patient care. At first, it was mostly about virtual clinics where patients could chat with doctor avatars and get educational materials. But it's expanded to include things like digital twins, AI simulations, and interactive media, offering a lot more support for training, rehab, and managing long-term illnesses [4].

In healthcare, the metaverse is built on layered technologies that integrate immersive interfaces, data services, and secure infrastructures. The VR/AR systems and user interface enable teleconsultations, remote surgeries, and rehabilitation. [5]. The service layer links IoMT with cloud and edge computing devices to process biomedical data across physical and virtual spaces [6]. The data integrity and confidentiality among distributed participants are protected by a secure infrastructure layer [7]. Unlike conventional telemedicine, the metaverse embeds clinical workflows within immersive replicas of hospitals and laboratories [8]. These layers support diagnostics, simulations, and personalized care planning by accessing real-time data. This virtual environment also provides collaboration spaces for medical teams to jointly design treatment strategies [9].

As these technologies deal with highly sensitive health data, their implementation posses major security and interoperability challenges. Platforms within the metaverse must ensure the management of secure and verifiable transactions, including updates to electronic health records and processing insurance claims. In this scenario, blockchain is a relevant technology by providing decentralization, traceability, and tamper resistance [10, 11]. When combined with AI for threat detection and identity management, the integration of blockchain technology enables efficient, secure, and patient-centred digital health ecosystems [12].

2. Need for Secure Health Transactions

Various healthcare transactions within the metaverse include updating electronic health records (EHRs), transferring diagnostics, exchanging lab results, authorizing prescriptions, processing insurance claims, and managing patient consent [13]. These transactions within the metaverse occur between patients, clinicians, insurers, and regulators via avatars and intelligent agents [1]. The real-time and cross-border character of the interactions amplifies the complexity of ensuring security measures.

Given the sensitivity of health data, breaches can result in identity theft, fraud, and erosion of trust [14]. In metaverse contexts, risks intensify as IoMT devices and wearables generate high-frequency, granular physiological data [15], expanding the vulnerability surface. Gaps in identity verification, data transmission, or storage become potential attack points. Regulatory frameworks like HIPAA (US) and GDPR (EU) impose strict controls on health data handling [16, 17]. Ensuring compliance in decentralized virtual environments is difficult due to jurisdictional conflicts, ambiguous consent mechanisms, and a lack of standards for lawful cross-border data exchange [18, 19].

Traditional healthcare systems rely on centralized authorities for data security. This model falters when multiple autonomous entities must manage and verify records without a central intermediary [20]. In such cases, systems must ensure tamper-evidence, confidentiality, authenticity, and non-repudiation. Blockchain offers immutability and distributed consensus, allowing secure and auditable transactions even in hostile conditions [21]. Artificial intelligence enhances this with threat detection, adaptive access control, and predictive analytics [22]. Combined, these technologies provide a robust foundation for secure and compliant healthcare transactions in the metaverse.

3. Convergence of Blockchain and AI in Digital Health

Individually, blockchain technology and artificial intelligence have demonstrated significant benefits in healthcare, and used together, they offer complementary strengths for securing digital health ecosystems [23]. Blockchain provides a decentralized, tamper-resistant ledger to record transactions, whereas AI can intelligently analyze data patterns, detect anomalies, and automate decision-making. Experts anticipate that blockchain, in conjunction with peer technologies like AI and IoT, will play a critical role in transforming healthcare operations in the near future [24]. It can offer innovative solutions within the healthcare sector. Blockchain-based electronic health records offer mechanisms for preserving data integrity and managing access. Building on this foundation, AI algorithms can utilize the secured records to support clinical decision-making and to detect fraudulent behavior. Blockchain's immutable logs can anchor AI outputs to verified data sources, and AI can enhance blockchain by strengthening security and optimizing performance. This interplay is visible in the new tele-health models as they merge immersive platforms, blockchain-based data exchange, and AI-powered analytics. The verifiability of blockchain and the adaptability of AI can create a system that improves care quality, efficiency, and patient focus.

4. Foundations of the Metaverse in Healthcare

4.1 Key Components: VR, AR, XR, and IoT in Health Services

The concept of a healthcare metaverse draws on multiple technologies already familiar in clinical research. Virtual reality has been used to construct simulated clinics and operating rooms, while augmented reality allows medical data to be superimposed on physical settings. One common example is the projection of imaging scans onto the patient's body during a remote consultation, although limitations in alignment and resolution remain a concern. Mixed reality environments extend these approaches further. Collectively, these systems are described as extended reality (XR) and are being explored for training, remote interventions, and patient education [25].

Alongside XR, connected devices play an equally important role. Wearables and domestic health sensors supply continuous streams of information—heart rate, glucose levels, or blood pressure—that can be accessed in virtual consultations. This linkage allows clinicians to observe vital signs during an appointment rather than relying only on retrospective reports. In this arrangement, XR provides the interaction layer, and the Internet of Things (IoT) contributes the clinical data that makes those encounters meaningful. The scope is not limited to visualization alone; these tools already enable avatar-based consultations and simulated surgeries for training. Running in parallel is the Internet of Things (IoT), which provides connectivity between physical devices and virtual platforms, allowing continuous data exchange across both domains.

Wearable medical devices and home health sensors continuously collect patient data (heart rate, blood pressure, glucose levels, etc.), which are then fed into the metaverse environment in real time. This fusion of IoT with XR allows healthcare providers in a virtual clinic to monitor live vital signs or view streaming data from smart medical devices during an appointment. The confluence of these components—immersive XR interfaces for user interaction, and IoT networks for data acquisition—forms the backbone of metaverse health services. Underlying cloud and edge computing infrastructure is also crucial to render graphics, maintain low-latency communication, and perform AI computations that augment the experience (such as real-time language translation or symptom analysis). Collectively, VR/AR/XR and IoT technologies establish a highly interactive, data-driven platform on which advanced health applications can be built [25].

4.2 Data Flows and Transaction Types in Virtual Health Environments

In a healthcare metaverse, data flows continuously among patients, providers, and devices within immersive virtual environments. A typical VR-based telemedicine session involves multimodal exchanges: live audio/video, text messages, medical images (e.g., scans, lab reports), and real-time IoT sensor data from devices like ECG monitors or glucose sensors [26]. These interactions constitute health transactions requiring secure capture and management.

During a virtual consultation, a patient's avatar may automatically share vital signs with the physician. Clinical actions—such as prescriptions or referrals—are transactions to be logged and executed. Other examples include virtual consent signing, retrieval of EHR data into the XR space, and financial operations like co-payments or billing. For instance, a patient may use a metaverse-based pharmacy to purchase medication or IoT health devices as digital assets, initiating secure payments and updating medication records.

These processes depend on tight integration between XR platforms and health information systems. Virtual session data must be written back to hospital databases or personal health records. Without standardized coordination, maintaining consistency and security is difficult.

Figure 1 depicts this flow in a blockchain-supported health metaverse: XR applications connect patients and clinicians to IoT devices and external records, while a blockchain logs each key transaction—such as data access, device output, and orders—into an immutable ledger [27]. This approach ensures a verifiable audit trail and a unified record of activity, supporting clinical use, billing, and regulatory compliance.

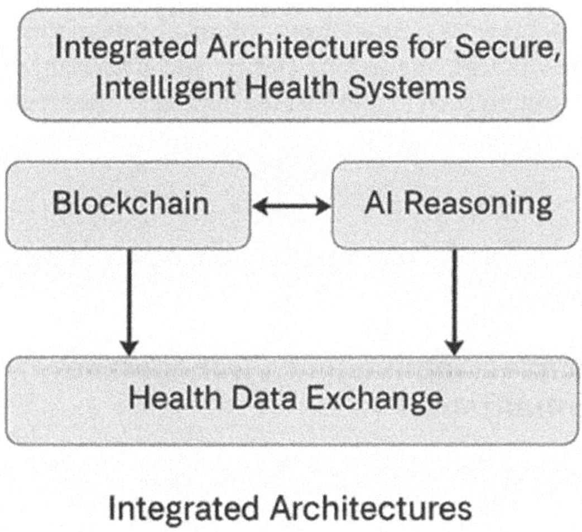

Figure 1: The block diagram of the architecture of the blockchain and AI-assisted health metaverse.

4.3 Risks and Challenges in Health Data Exchange in the Metaverse

The metaverse presents new opportunities for healthcare delivery, but it simultaneously increases the risks associated with data management. Privacy and confidentiality remain central issues, particularly since virtual environments can expose far more information than traditional telehealth encounters [28]. Weak platform security may expose sensitive data, including audio, spatial inputs, and facial cues, posing serious privacy risks. Verifying clinician identity is also challenging in avatar-based settings since unauthorized users could fabricate records or spread misinformation in the absence of strong authentication.

The cybersecurity threats also increase with prescriptions, diagnostics, and sensor data being vulnerable to interception or manipulation. A tampered vital-sign stream could mislead clinical decisions, raising the risk of error. Linking XR systems with IoT devices and health records creates more points of failure, and poor synchronization can result in inconsistent data across platforms. Interoperability remains difficult, especially when systems follow different standards.

Cross-border data flows introduce further complications. Legal uncertainty arises over which jurisdiction's privacy laws apply, and enforcing compliance is difficult when patients and physicians are in different countries. Ethical concerns also emerge, including reduced empathy in virtual interactions and the risk of AI-driven bias in clinical decisions.

Questions may also arise regarding consent related to whether a patient fully understands what it means to agree in immersive avatar-based environments. These are some of the non-technical challenges associated with providing secure metaverse frameworks. Apart from technical safeguards, we must ensure proper policy development, regulatory clarity, and user training for successful implementation. Through such a multifaceted approach, healthcare data exchange in the metaverse can remain secure, legally compliant, and resilient to ethical scrutiny [29].

5. Blockchain Technology for Secure Health Transactions

5.1 Core Principles: Immutability, Transparency, and Decentralization

Blockchain is a distributed ledger designed to meet the security concerns of data management. Its immutability means that once records such as consent logs are entered, any later change leaves evidence and is traceable. In a blockchain, transactions are interconnected through cryptographic chains, which render data tampering visible and maintain an audit trail for medical actions, including prescriptions and diagnostic entries.

Transparency plays a key role in applying blockchain to healthcare. It builds trust by making transactions and data exchanges verifiable, which can improve outcomes and streamline resource use. In a consortium setup, hospitals can access transaction logs without exposing patient identities, thanks to encryption. This lets insurers confirm procedures before issuing payments and supports shared accountability.

Blockchain's decentralized design spreads ledger nodes across hospitals, clinics, and insurers, reducing reliance on any single party. Entries are confirmed through consensus, lowering the risk of tampering or failure. Even if some nodes go offline, others maintain system integrity. Together, transparency, immutability, and decentralization provide a robust infrastructure for healthcare [30, 31], enabling secure data exchange even among institutions with limited mutual trust.

5.2 Blockchain Architectures: Public, Private, Consortium in Healthcare

Blockchain architectures differ in privacy, scalability, and security—each influencing their applicability in healthcare. Public blockchains, such as Bitcoin and Ethereum, offer full transparency and immutability [32], but broadcasting encrypted health transactions can violate privacy laws. Their limited throughput and latency also hinder real-time medical use. However, public chains can anchor hashed references to health data or support verifiable credentials, like digital physician licenses, without revealing sensitive information.

Private blockchains restrict access to a single organization. A hospital may use one to manage prescriptions or internal record access. These chains are fast, customizable, and maintain data within the institution. Yet, trust remains centralized—participants must rely on the hosting organization. While suitable for internal audit trails, private blockchains do not solve interoperability or distributed trust.

Consortium (permissioned) blockchains offer a compromise. Operated by vetted stakeholders—such as hospitals and insurers—they enable shared control while preserving confidentiality. Platforms like Hyperledger Fabric or Quorum support role-based access and consensus validation. In regional health exchanges, such systems allow secure sharing of patient summaries or medication lists. Transactions are endorsed by multiple nodes, ensuring tamper resistance without public exposure. This model combines privacy with a shared, verifiable log.

Interoperability across blockchain types is under active exploration [33]. Techniques like hashed time-lock contracts and IPFS-based storage enable secure data exchange between, for example, Ethereum and Hyperledger Fabric. These cross-chain bridges suggest a future where public, private, and consortium networks coexist—linked by standards that allow trusted health data and credentials to follow patients across platforms.

5.3 Smart Contracts for Health Data Management

Smart contracts are programs deployed on a blockchain that execute automatically once predefined conditions are satisfied. In healthcare, they can enforce rules for data access and management without manual intervention, which simplifies workflows and helps maintain compliance [34]. One application is the handling of patient consent: access to genetic data may be permitted only when a valid digital consent token is present. When consent is signed, for example, through a metaverse interface, the contract can update permissions and enable queries, easing administrative work and reducing the chance of error. The same principle can be applied in insurance. Claims may be checked automatically against recorded medical services. If procedure codes align with policy status, payment is released without delay; if inconsistencies arise, the contract can halt the process and flag the claim for review. Such mechanisms allow near real-time adjudication, contrasting with slower manual processing.

In metaverse-based healthcare, smart contracts can respond to sensor data. Consider a heart monitor that detects arrhythmia during a virtual rehabilitation session: the event could trigger a contract that alerts the cardiologist and temporarily opens access to emergency records. Hospitals can also use contracts to structure data-sharing agreements, specifying the scope of access and enforcing conditions directly through the ledger [35]. Every permitted query is logged, creating a record that combines transparency with immutability. Prototype systems already show how patients can manage access to encrypted health records through contracts. In these cases, the program validates both the requester's credentials and the patient's explicit consent before releasing information. This shift places greater control in the patient's hands while ensuring compliance is technically enforced.

Taken together, smart contracts operate as digital administrators. They are capable of automating diverse tasks—scheduling, referrals, prescription management, and even research data sharing. Because the logic is embedded in code, transactions become verifiable and consistent, which reduces opportunities for error or manipulation and supports fairer processes.

5.4 Interoperability Standards and Cross-Chain Solutions

For blockchain to be effective in healthcare, it must interoperate with existing health IT systems and other blockchain networks. A key enabler is adherence to health data standards. HL7 FHIR (Fast Healthcare Interoperability Resources) provides a structured format for clinical data. When integrated with smart contracts, FHIR ensures that transactions—such as medication orders or lab results—are semantically consistent and interpretable across systems. Several implementations use blockchain to store hashes or pointers to FHIR-compliant records off-chain, combining blockchain's trust and traceability with FHIR's semantic interoperability. Cross-chain interoperability is equally critical [36]. Different healthcare consortia may operate separate blockchains—for EHRs, insurance, or patient-owned data. Technologies like atomic swaps and hash time-locked contracts enable secure, conditional data exchange across chains. For example, patient consent issued on a national health blockchain could be validated by a pharmaceutical blockchain to authorize access to de-identified data, without revealing private details.

Relay or oracle networks provide another method, allowing one chain to monitor another. An oracle could detect a hospital discharge event on a private chain and trigger a claim process on an insurer's blockchain. Many standards bodies are developing protocols for authenticated cross-chain communication. Governance initiatives by HIMSS and the EU's European Health Data Space aim to harmonize blockchain use across jurisdictions.

A working prototype by Sonkamble et al. [48] demonstrated EHR exchange between Ethereum and Hyperledger Fabric using hashed time-lock contracts and

IPFS-based storage. A secure session key allowed synchronized updates across chains, ensuring continuity of care as patients move between networks. While still emerging, such models point toward a future where the health metaverse is powered by multiple interoperable blockchains. Achieving this vision will require coordination across standards, governance, identity, and technical protocols [24].

6. Artificial Intelligence in Health Data Security

6.1 AI for Threat Detection and Anomaly Monitoring

Machine learning (ML) is increasingly applied to detect threats and anomalies in complex data systems. In healthcare, AI-based monitoring helps protect patient records and maintain transaction integrity by spotting patterns that suggest cyberattacks or technical failures [37]. For instance, an ML intrusion detection system can learn typical hospital activity and highlight anomalies, such as odd record access or unusual sensor readings. This is particularly relevant in the metaverse, where diverse inputs—voice, video, biomedical streams—exceed human monitoring capacity. Models such as neural networks and clustering algorithms can even pick up subtler signals, from deepfake avatars to spoofed device outputs.

Researchers have also examined hybrid frameworks that link AI with blockchain to improve the security of IoT-based healthcare [38]. One reported demonstration combined an Isolation Forest algorithm with a private blockchain to analyze real-time IoT health data [39]. The AI module detected tampering and replay attacks with complete accuracy, while the blockchain maintained immutable records of the anomalies for later auditing. Beyond detection, these frameworks can initiate automated responses. If suspicious activity is detected, for instance, a smart contract may revoke access or shift the network into a safer operating mode.

Researchers are now exploring AI for securing medical devices, with malware detection as a major focus. Algorithms can scan firmware or analyze telemetry to identify patterns linked to malicious signatures, protecting IoT endpoints that connect to healthcare systems in the metaverse. Here, AI functions as a continuous surveillance layer, operating at a pace far beyond human monitoring. When its outputs are coupled with blockchain's verifiable audit log, the result is faster identification of threats and a stronger basis for forensic review.

6.2 AI-Driven Identity Verification and Fraud Prevention

Identity checks are critical for secure virtual healthcare. AI assists through biometrics such as facial or voice recognition. In metaverse clinics, avatars can be matched to stored profiles, with liveness tests added to prevent spoofing. These safeguards apply to both patients and clinicians; for example, only licensed physicians' avatars may enter restricted consultation areas. Blockchain credentials can add another layer, where smart contracts release health records only after valid biometric confirmation.

AI is increasingly used to detect fraud in insurance and billing. Rule-based systems rarely keep pace with new schemes, but ML and LLMs can learn from past data to spot anomalies such as unusual billing patterns or procedures that do not fit patient demographics. In virtual settings, these tools may also expose avatar impersonation or staged consultations.

A recent study linked blockchain with an LLM to detect fraudulent claims [40]. Records were stored on-chain, while the model—supported by Retrieval-Augmented Generation—reviewed claims for inconsistencies such as repeated notes or mismatched treatments. Accuracy was reported at 98%. An integrated chatbot explained flagged cases in plain language, giving investigators quicker insight.

Integrating AI into identity verification and claims handling offers a way to limit fraud, identity theft, and other forms of data abuse. Such systems run in the background, confirming that avatars are linked to real individuals and that transactions rest on valid records. When something looks irregular, the platform can send alerts or trigger pre-defined contract actions. Taken together, these measures strengthen confidence in digital healthcare systems.

6.3 Privacy-Preserving AI Models (Federated Learning, Split Learning)

Researchers increasingly use AI to improve healthcare analytics and security. However, many models still require centralized access to sensitive patient data, which creates privacy concerns. To address this, new training methods have been introduced that let algorithms learn from decentralized datasets. One such method is Federated Learning (FL) [41, 42]. In this approach, each participating site—such as a hospital or clinic—keeps its data locally while contributing updates to a shared model. These updates are combined to improve performance without ever sharing the raw data. Coordination is usually handled by a central server, though blockchain-based alternatives have also been explored.

Federated learning allows multiple institutions to train shared models, such as for disease prediction, without exchanging raw data. Privacy regulations restrict the direct exchange of data from virtual reality platforms and Internet of Things (IoT) devices in healthcare applications. Federated and related distributed learning techniques have been investigated as a way to train models without centralizing sensitive information. Studies indicate that, when implemented with secure aggregation, such models can approach the accuracy of those developed on pooled datasets, while remaining consistent with legal requirements such as GDPR and HIPAA. Applications reported so far include diagnostic image classification and forecasting of hospital outcomes.

Split learning represents a complementary strategy. In this approach, initial layers of a model are executed within the hospital environment, and only the intermediate representations are transmitted to an external server for further processing. This structure limits direct data exposure and can be adapted to resource-constrained devices, for example, wearables that transmit extracted features rather than raw signals.

Multi-institutional training introduces privacy risks that are not present in single-site studies. Researchers have therefore examined cryptographic techniques —most notably homomorphic encryption and secure multiparty computation— to limit what can be inferred from exchanged model parameters. Blockchain has likewise been evaluated in pilot studies as a means of recording contributions, enforcing agreed protocols through smart contracts, and preserving transparent audit records. Together, these methods illustrate how privacy-preserving AI development can be made compatible with existing legal and ethical frameworks.

6.4 AI-Enabled Decision Support in Health Transaction Validation

Artificial intelligence has been applied to strengthen compliance monitoring and the protection of health data. In prescribing, experimental systems link electronic health records with blockchain frameworks to check safety parameters [43]. These systems review information such as medication history, allergy records, and laboratory values before validating a prescription. When discrepancies arise— for example, a potentially harmful dose or a contraindicated combination—they generate alerts for clinical review. Unlike rule-based software, learning models can also capture evolving patterns of risk, offering an additional safeguard.

Insurance workflows present a different focus. Here, AI is being tested to evaluate whether submitted claims correspond to covered procedures and whether the supporting documentation is sufficient. Integrating these checks with secure audit mechanisms can assist insurers in maintaining regulatory compliance while reducing manual workload [44].

It can compare claims against patient history or clinical guidelines. If everything looks fine, a smart contract could approve payment. If not, it could hold the claim, log the reason (like missing records), and send it for review.

AI can also act as a trusted source of external info, feeding smart contracts with verified facts. Say a health program needs to check whether someone's fitness data shows improvement. AI can process the off-chain data and return a result with a confidence score. The contract then uses this, without heavy processing on the blockchain. Accuracy can be improved by checking results from different AI tools or confirming them cryptographically.

AI is also useful in operations. If an ICU is likely to run out of beds, a system could trigger actions—redirecting patients, warning ambulances, updating databases, and arranging secure data transfers [45]. Each step can be logged on the blockchain, making later checks easier.

Even with all this automation, AI is not the final decision-maker. Doctors still need to have the last word. The system can explain its suggestions by pointing to evidence or guidelines [46]. If a doctor disagrees, that choice should be recorded too. In this role, AI helps keep things consistent, lowers the load of routine work, and creates traceable logs. When connected to smart contracts, it adds both structure and flexibility to how care is managed.

7. Synergy of Blockchain and AI in the Metaverse

The integration of blockchain and AI in healthcare metaverse systems enables secure, intelligent operations. Blockchain manages transactions and ensures data integrity, while AI processes data to support diagnostics, risk forecasting, and workflow decisions. A typical system includes an interaction layer (XR/IoT interface), a blockchain layer to log consent and activities, and an AI layer that analyses data for clinical insights. These layers synchronize their operations. Blockchain events may trigger AI actions, and AI results can be logged on-chain for transparency.

Telemedicine systems already reflect this integration. Consultations generate multimodal data—text, voice, sensor readings—secured via blockchain. AI tools, including explainable models like Grad-CAM or LIME, interpret the data and assist in diagnosis. Blockchain verifies that AI works on authentic inputs. Smart contracts govern access, store outputs, and release anonymized data as needed. Large files or continuous streams typically remain off-chain, with their hashes stored on-chain to prove origin. Federated training allows models to learn across distributed datasets, while blockchain coordinates updates and logs parameters.

Smart contracts gain flexibility when linked to AI. Rather than relying solely on fixed rules, they can query AI systems to guide actions. A telehealth scheduler might balance urgency and clinician schedules using AI before confirming an appointment. Wellness incentives can depend on personalized targets derived from wearable data. Tokens are released only if conditions are met. In insurance, AI can evaluate claims and provide justifications in real time, while smart contracts preserve the audit trail.

In current healthcare applications, most artificial intelligence modules operate outside the blockchain, which raises questions about the trustworthiness of exchanged information. Several approaches have been proposed to strengthen reliability, including hashed timestamps, oracle-based validation, and multi-agent consensus layers. In clinical research settings, such as ongoing trials, additional controls—human approval steps or quorum-style validation—are often considered necessary to reduce the risk of unintended updates.

Efforts have also turned to system performance. Predictive models have been tested to anticipate transaction surges, while optimization routines adjust validator scheduling, block timing, and reputation scores. Within more complex architectures, including sharded ledgers and directed acyclic graphs, adaptive controllers informed by machine learning are being explored to manage routing and task distribution.

Energy demand remains a further obstacle. Some experimental designs prioritize low-consumption nodes or scale activity to off-peak periods.

Reinforcement learning has been applied in simulation studies to model network behavior and propose protocol changes, although implementation usually depends on governance filters.

Taken together, these developments point to a division of labour. Blockchain provides verifiable ledgers and decentralized governance; learning systems contribute analysis and generate proposals. Pilot studies describe cases where institutional agents monitor service use or anomalies [47] and where smart contracts allocate resources. Concepts such as Distributed Autonomous Health Organizations (DAHOs) extend this vision, yet the evidence consistently shows that clinical judgment and ethical safeguards must remain decisive.

8. Case for Hybrid Decentralized-Intelligent Health Networks

Recent studies discuss how blockchain and artificial intelligence might be combined to support health services in metaverse environments. The blockchain layer is intended to provide tamper-resistant records and decentralized coordination, while machine-learning modules are applied to the analysis of those records and to decision support tasks.

Proposals in the literature suggest that shared ledgers could be used to record consents, requests for services, and treatment events. Some studies move beyond simple record keeping, proposing that analytic agents examine ledger entries to flag potential deterioration or missed follow-up appointments. Exploratory initiatives have shown smart contracts configured to raise alerts and manage follow-up scheduling, although these remain limited in scope. These initiatives remain experimental, and implementation is limited by institutional rules and oversight requirements. These experiments remain preliminary, and any automated intervention is still subject to governance checks and institutional approval.

Some recent works have examined governance structures within blockchain-enabled health systems. Instead of relying on unilateral control, contract rules can be written so that major changes require the approval of multiple stakeholders. This principle underpins proposals for Distributed Autonomous Health Organizations (DAHOs), where case records, analytic modules, and resource flows are coordinated through encoded logic. Authors who advance these designs emphasise that automated triggers are insufficient on their own. Clinical judgment and ethical oversight remain central, and governance layers must be designed to preserve that authority. Technical resilience is an additional motivation. Without dependence on a central server, the risk of single-point failure is reduced, while adaptive algorithms can redistribute tasks or forecast potential disruptions. Preliminary trials suggest that such hybrid arrangements—linking decentralized infrastructure with institutional oversight—may enhance coordination across providers. Some reports also note improved transparency and greater institutional trust, though evidence is still limited and further evaluation is required.

9. Use Cases and Applications

A blockchain- and AI-supported metaverse could transform telemedicine by enabling patient–clinician interaction through avatars in virtual clinics. Patients report symptoms via voice or gestures, while clinicians review 3D scans and health records. Blockchain logs all actions, and smart contracts enforce consent in line with HIPAA's minimum-necessary rule [49, 50]. AI systems, limited to verified blockchain-linked data, can cross-reference symptoms with history to suggest diagnoses. Patients see what's accessed, improving trust. Prescriptions and referrals may be issued as single-use tokens, with personal data stored off-chain. Smart contracts automate billing, insurance checks, and payments. If issues arise, provider and insurer avatars can resolve them directly. AI assistants support patients through coverage steps, reducing administrative burden and allowing more focus on care.

Clinical trials also benefit. Virtual visits let participants join remotely, stream sensor data, and consult with trial staff. Blockchain ensures audit trails, manages consent, and tracks protocol adherence. AI monitors safety and flags anomalies, while smart contracts help enforce jurisdiction-specific rules in global trials. Federated learning and transparent model logs reduce bias. Researchers can collaborate in shared virtual labs, review dashboards, and record findings directly to the chain, improving speed, cost-efficiency, and regulatory alignment.

10. Security, Privacy, and Compliance Considerations

Healthcare systems must comply with regulations like HIPAA and GDPR, which govern how patient data is handled [50]. Blockchain and AI introduce new tools for compliance, but also bring technical and legal complexity. HIPAA's requirements—privacy, access, and breach notification—can be met with permissioned blockchains using encryption, access control, and immutable logs. GDPR's data rights, including portability and erasure, can be addressed by off-chain storage and encryption key deletion. Pseudonymization and decentralized identifiers further strengthen privacy. The European Union's AI Act places particular emphasis on explainability and traceability. One technical response has been to record model inputs and outputs on blockchain ledgers so that decisions can later be reconstructed and audited. This approach is still experimental, but it offers a way to align machine-learning systems with emerging regulatory expectations.

Questions about cross-border data exchange remain unresolved. Several proposals describe using blockchain to keep original health data within national systems while transmitting only anonymized or de-identified results. Smart contracts have been explored as enforcement tools, ensuring that local laws continue to apply even when data is processed elsewhere. Deletion proofs provide a further safeguard: the chain records evidence of removal without retaining the underlying file. Some authors also suggest that regulators could run read-only nodes to monitor compliance in real time. Comparable requirements appear in existing rules such as 21 CFR Part 11 in the United States and Canada's PIPEDA, which together encourage the design of privacy-first architectures.

Zero-knowledge proofs (ZKPs) are being tested as a means of validating information without exposing underlying data. For example, a patient might demonstrate eligibility for a trial, or an insurer might verify compliance, without direct access to sensitive files. ZKPs have also been applied to fine-grained access control, such as confirming patient consent without revealing identity. When combined with decentralized identity systems, cryptographic protocols including zk-SNARKs and STARKs make privacy-preserving verification technically feasible, though practical deployment is still at an early stage.

In distributed health infrastructures, identity management is therefore not a peripheral issue but a central design problem. Ongoing work considers how secure identifiers can support both regulatory compliance and patient trust [ref]. Self-sovereign identity (SSI) allows patients to carry verified credentials issued by trusted entities. A virtual clinic visit might require only a credential, not a full form. Clinicians' digital profiles can link to professional licenses to prevent fraud. These systems require robust key management, including recovery protocols and multi-device wallets. SSI also enables real-time, role-based access—say, limiting permissions to an on-shift nurse—and makes consent traceable and enforceable.

11. Technical Challenges and Research Gaps

The healthcare metaverse will generate continuous data streams from wearables, VR diagnostics, AI tools, and smart contracts. Managing this requires scalable, low-latency blockchain-AI infrastructure. Public chains like Ethereum lack throughput for real-time care, and even private chains can choke on high-frequency IoT inputs. Off-chain storage and Layer-2 solutions help by aggregating and anchoring data. Sharding can split workloads by data type or patient group, though keeping consistency across shards is non-trivial.

Real-time decisions should run on edge AI, while blockchains handle logging. Edge nodes reduce geographic latency, and peer-to-peer encrypted messaging supports regional processing. Imaging and other heavy content should remain off-chain, with hashes stored for verification. A layered setup—local chains feeding into a broader consortium chain—can balance speed and auditability. Lightweight devices can push updates through IoT gateways that batch and sign data. Streaming ML with blockchain-verified alerts enables high-throughput monitoring. While costly, gains from automation and fraud reduction may justify the investment.

Interoperability remains a key challenge. Integration with EHRs, devices, and metaverse platforms demands consistent standards. HL7 FHIR helps bridge to EHRs, but newer data types—like motion capture or AI-based health scores—don't fit easily. APIs and middleware can help convert formats, with blockchain ensuring verifiable logs. Device standards like IEEE 11073 and FHIR Device resources enable consistent wearable data capture. Blockchain supports data provenance, while decentralized IDs and consent frameworks give patients control over access.

Clinician-facing tools need to reduce friction: single sign-on, integrated messaging, and billing support are essential. Coding systems must evolve to describe virtual services and trigger smart-contract-based claims. If virtual platforms become primary record sources, reconciliation and migration protocols will be vital. Blockchain overlays can help unify distributed data and support longitudinal care. Frameworks like IHE may require updates to support decentralized records and on-chain registries.

Metaverse-scale systems also raise sustainability concerns. Early blockchains were energy-intensive, but shifts to proof-of-stake and PBFT have cut consumption [52]. AI brings its own demands. Strategies include efficient algorithms, model compression, edge computing, and renewable energy use. Blockchain-based carbon auditing and device lifecycle tracking can support green compliance [51]. Data centers might use passive cooling or capture waste heat. Hospitals can scale systems based on demand and embed sustainability into procurement policies.

Bias, transparency, and trust in healthcare AI require active governance. Unbalanced training data can produce inequitable outcomes, such as skin tone bias in dermatology models [53]. Blockchain can log demographics and model behavior for auditing. Developers should apply debiasing techniques and validate on diverse datasets. Explainability tools like SHAP or LIME, when stored on-chain, allow decision review and appeals. Periodic oversight, override mechanisms, and traceable outputs help sustain trust.

Federated learning and personalization can expand training data and improve fairness. Patients should be able to inspect AI decisions, inputs, and rationales through secure portals. Blockchain can store model certifications and regulatory status. Involving users in system design helps ensure AI outputs support safe, informed decisions. Combined with blockchain's traceability, this approach strengthens accountability in AI-enabled care.

12. Future Directions

Healthcare is moving toward semi-autonomous systems where blockchain and AI take over many administrative tasks [54]. Scheduling, billing, and logistics may soon operate with limited human input [55]. In smart hospitals, AI agents could use wearable data to manage appointments and prescriptions, while smart contracts handle insurance and protocol enforcement. Staff and resources might be allocated dynamically using AI-driven forecasts. Blockchain-backed data commons could support secure, privacy-preserving research and early outbreak detection. As routine roles shrink, new positions like system architects and algorithm ethicists may emerge. Personal AI tools could assist with monitoring and coordination. Security challenges remain, driving the adoption of AI threat detection and blockchain for information integrity.

Full automation is still far off, but partial deployments are in the near future. Blockchain-AI systems promise more responsive and patient-centered care.

Technologies like 6G, IoE, and quantum computing will accelerate this shift. 6G's low latency may enable remote surgery and real-time diagnostics [56, 57]. Edge computing can reduce lag by placing AI and blockchain nodes closer to the patient. IoE will generate health data from everyday environments, processed by AI and secured through blockchain. This allows earlier intervention and improved continuity of care.

Quantum computing threatens current cryptography, making the adoption of quantum-safe algorithms necessary. At the same time, it could transform genomics, drug development, and AI. Verifying quantum outputs on classical systems, however, remains unresolved. With dense 6G deployments, every medical device becomes traceable. Blockchain can log device activity and simplify compliance, but the expanded attack surface demands unified security standards across sectors.

Sustainable deployment requires global policy alignment and updated standards. Protocols must support interoperability, identity management, and secure data sharing. Extensions to HL7 FHIR, SNOMED, and IEEE standards will be needed to support decentralized infrastructure and prevent system fragmentation.

Governance may fall to consortia of providers, regulators, technologists, and patients, with smart contracts enforcing agreed rules and ensuring data rights. Regulatory frameworks such as HIPAA, GDPR, and the EU AI Act will shape how systems handle privacy, transparency, and contract auditability. Decentralized identifiers and verifiable credentials will support secure, platform-independent access. Legal structures must also define accountability for AI errors and contract failures. Incentives, like those used for EHR adoption, may speed uptake of compliant systems. A phased rollout might begin with global guidelines (1–3 years), followed by pilots (3–5 years), and eventual regulatory embedding within a decade.

Integration will move gradually, depending on infrastructure, policy, and public acceptance. In the short term, AI and smart contracts will assist with claims, triage, and prescription checks. Within five to ten years, routine tasks such as billing, diagnostics, and scheduling could operate semi-autonomously. Oversight will still be needed for higher-risk clinical work. Long term, AI could handle preliminary analysis in fields like radiology and pathology, with uncertain cases escalated. Blockchain ensures integrity and auditability. Virtual care for common conditions may become routine, while automated systems balance resources across services.

Trust will determine adoption speed. As systems prove reliable, especially among younger, tech-literate populations, confidence will grow. Major platforms may emerge, but consortia and open standards will be needed to prevent monopolies and ensure equity. Technically, improvements in explainable AI, integration of multimodal data, and personalized preventive models are expected. Blockchain could enable patient-controlled data access or monetization, supporting broader research efforts.

Ethical risks remain. Algorithmic bias, loss of personalization, and data misuse require professional safeguards and ongoing audits. Still, with proper governance, blockchain and AI together offer a viable path to more transparent, efficient, and equitable healthcare systems.

13. Conclusions and Key Messages

This chapter reviewed proposals for combining blockchain with artificial intelligence in health systems built for metaverse applications. Blockchain is discussed mainly for its capacity to store records in a tamper-resistant and decentralized form, while AI is considered in connection with automation and decision support. Examples appear in fraud monitoring, data exchange, and claims processing, although most accounts describe trials or pilot systems rather than operational deployments. A consistent concern in this literature is patient privacy. Suggested approaches include privacy-by-design frameworks, layered consent processes, and compliance with regulations such as GDPR. Cryptographic tools—encryption, permissioned ledgers, and zero-knowledge proofs—have been investigated to limit disclosure while retaining usability. Other studies point to audit trails and anomaly-detection methods as additional safeguards.

Interoperability with existing infrastructures is a further obstacle. International standards such as HL7 FHIR and ICD have been identified as necessary foundations, yet practical adoption has been uneven. Researchers also note that AI models should be explainable, validated across multiple datasets, and deployed with user training if they are to be accepted in clinical practice. Governance receives particular attention: several proposals stress the need for multi-party participation, with smart contracts sometimes suggested as a way of encoding procedural rules. Work on scalability has considered edge computing, sharding, and side-chain designs, while the arrival of 6G networks and advances in quantum computing are expected to place new demands on performance and security.

References

1. Ali, S. Abdullah, Armand, T. P. T., Athar, A., Hussain, A., and Ali, M. et al. (2023). Metaverse in healthcare integrated with explainable AI and blockchain: Enabling immersiveness, ensuring trust, and providing patient data security. *Sensors*, 23(2), 565.
2. Wang, G., Badal, A., Jia, X., Maltz, J. S., Mueller, K., Myers, K. J. et al. (2022). Development of metaverse for intelligent healthcare. *Nature Machine Intelligence*, 4(11), 922–929.
3. Hulsen, T. (2023). Applications of the metaverse in medicine and healthcare. *Advances in Laboratory Medicine*, 5(2), 159–165.

4. Ghaempanah, F., Moasses Ghafari, B., Hesami, D., Hossein Zadeh, R., Noroozpoor, R., Moodi Ghalibaf, A. et al. (2024). Metaverse and its impact on medical education and health care system: A narrative review. *Health Science Reports*, 7(9), e70100.
5. Chengoden, R., Victor, N., Huynh-The, T., Yenduri, G., Jhaveri, R. H., Alazab, M. et al. (2023). Metaverse for healthcare: A survey on potential applications, challenges and future directions. *IEEE Access*, 11, 12765–12795.
6. Greco, L., Percannella, G., Ritrovato, P., Tortorella, F., and Vento, M. (2020). Trends in IoT based solutions for health care: Moving AI to the edge. *Pattern Recognition Letters*, 135, 346–353.
7. Chinnasamy, P., Albakri, A., Khan, M., Raja, A. A., Kiran, A., and Babu, J. C. (2023). Smart contractenabled secure sharing of health data for a mobile cloud-based e-health system. *Applied Sciences*, 13(6), 3970.
8. Bansal, G., Rajgopal, K., Chamola, V., Xiong, Z., and Niyato, D. (2022). Healthcare in metaverse: A survey on current metaverse applications in healthcare. *IEEE Access*, 10, 119914–119946.
9. Taylor, M. J., Shikaislami, C., McNicholas, C., Taylor, D., Reed, J., and Vlaev, I. (2020). Using virtual worlds as a platform for collaborative meetings in healthcare: A feasibility study. *BMC Health Services Research*, 20(1), 442.
10. Kim, E. J., and Kim, J. Y. (2023). The metaverse for healthcare: Trends, applications, and future directions of digital therapeutics for urology. *International Neurourology Journal*, 27(Suppl 1): S3.
11. Carlos Ferreira, J., Elvas, L. B., Correia, R., and Mascarenhas, M. (2024). Enhancing EHR interoperability and security through distributed ledger technology: A review. In: *Healthcare*, 12, 1967. MDPI.
12. Bathula, A., Gupta, S. K., Merugu, S., Saba, L., Khanna, N. N., Laird, J. R. et al. (2024). Blockchain, artificial intelligence, and healthcare: The tripod of future—A narrative review. *Artificial Intelligence Review*, 57(9), 238.
13. Kumar, A., Singh, A. K., Ahmad, I., Singh, P., Anushree, Verma, P. K. et al. (2022). A novel decentralized blockchain architecture for the preservation of privacy and data security against cyberattacks in healthcare. *Sensors*, 22(15), 5921.
14. Ayo-Farai, O. (2023). Cybersecurity in healthcare: A review of strategies and challenges in the USA. *Acta Electronica Malaysia*, 25–33.
15. Gupta, A., Khan, H. U., Nazir, S., Shafiq, M., and Shabaz, M. (2023). Metaverse security: Issues, challenges and a viable ZTA model. *Electronics*, 12(2), 391.
16. Regulation P. (2016). Regulation (EU) 2016/679 of the European Parliament and of the Council. Regulation (EU). 10–3.
17. Accountability Act. (1996). Health insurance portability and accountability act of 1996. *Pub. Law*, 104(1996), 191.
18. Razmetaeva, Y., Ponomarova, H., and Bylya-Sabadash, I. (2021). Jurisdictional issues in the digital age. *Ius Humani, Revista de Derecho*, 10, 167.
19. Vayena, E., Blasimme, A., and Sugarman, J. (2023). Decentralised clinical trials: Ethical opportunities and challenges. *The Lancet Digital Health*, 5(6), e390-4.
20. Abughazalah, M., Alsaggaf, W., Saifuddin, S., and Sarhan, S. (2024). Centralized vs. decentralized cloud computing in healthcare. *Applied Sciences*, 14(17), 7765.
21. Ahmed Teli, T., and Masoodi, F. (2021). Blockchain in healthcare: Challenges and opportunities. In: *Proceedings of the International Conference on IoT-based Control Networks & Intelligent Systems (ICICNIS)*.

22. Adekunle, J. J., Sodipe, A. O., Ayanfe, D., Abdulwahab, C. C. U., Ibeneme, S. O., and Bin-Uyo, M. O. (2024). AI shield: Leveraging artificial intelligence to combat cyber threats in healthcare. *Iconic Research and Engineering Journals*, 8(3), 184–195.
23. Ghosh, P. K., Chakraborty, A., Hasan, M., Rashid, K., and Siddique, A. H. (2023). Blockchain application in healthcare systems: A review. *Systems*, 11(1), 38.
24. Ferreira, J. C., Elvas, L. B., Correia, R., and Mascarenhas, M. (2024). Enhancing EHR interoperability and security through distributed ledger technology: A review. *Healthcare*, 12(19), 1967.
25. Kaur, N., and Gupta, L. (2025). Explainable AI assisted IoMT security in future 6G networks. *Future Internet*, 17(5), 226.
26. Ghadi, Y. Y., Mazhar, T., Shahzad, T., Amir Khan, M., Abd-Alrazaq, A., Ahmed, A. et al. (2024). The role of blockchain to secure Internet of Medical Things. *Scientific Reports*, 14(1), 18422.
27. Dubovitskaya, A., Baig, F., Xu, Z., Shukla, R., Zambani, P. S., Swaminathan, A. et al. (2020). ACTIONEHR: Patient-centric blockchain-based electronic health record data management for cancer care. *Journal of Medical Internet Research*, 22(8), e13598.
28. Saberi Kamarposhti, M., Ng, K. W., Chua, F. F., Abdullah, J., Yadollahi, M., Moradi, M. et al. (2024). Post-quantum healthcare: A roadmap for cybersecurity resilience in medical data. *Heliyon*, 10(10), e31406.
29. Horgan, D., Hajduch, M., Vrana, M., Soderberg, J., Hughes, N., Omar, M. I. et al. (2022). European health data space—An opportunity now to grasp the future of data-driven healthcare. *Healthcare*, 10(9), 1629.
30. AbdelSalam, F. M. (2023). Blockchain revolutionizing healthcare industry: A systematic review of blockchain technology benefits and threats. *Perspectives in Health Information Management*, 20(3), 1.
31. Fang, H. S. A., and Tan, T. H. (2021). Blockchain technology in the healthcare industry: Trends and opportunities. *Journal of Industrial Information Integration*, 22, 100217.
32. Azaria, A., Ekblaw, A., Vieira, T., and Lippman, A. (2016). Medrec: Using blockchain for medical data access and permission management. In: *2016 2nd International Conference on Open and Big Data (OBD)*. IEEE, pp. 25–30.
33. Ben Othman, S., and Getahun, M. (2025). Leveraging blockchain and IoMT for secure and interoperable electronic health records. *Scientific Reports*, 15(1), 12358.
34. Pham, A., Edelson, M., Nouri, A., and Kuo, T. T. (2024). Distributed management of patient datasharing informed consents for clinical research. *Computers in Biology and Medicine*, 180, 108956.
35. Zhang, P., White, J., Schmidt, D. C., Lenz, G., and Rosenbloom, S. T. (2018). FHIRChain: Applying blockchain to securely and scalably share clinical data. *Computational and Structural Biotechnology Journal*, 16, 267–278.
36. Darshan, M., Amet, M., Srivastava, G., and Crichigno, J. (2023). An architecture that enables crosschain interoperability for next-gen blockchain systems. *IEEE Internet of Things Journal*, 10(20), 18282–18291.
37. Anjum, M., Kraiem, N., Min, H., Dutta, A. K., Daradkeh, Y. I., and Shahab, S. (2025). Opportunistic access control scheme for enhancing IoT-enabled healthcare security using blockchain and machine learning. *Scientific Reports*, 15(1), 7589.
38. Xie, Q., and Ding, Z. (2025). Provably secure and lightweight blockchain based cross hospital authentication scheme for IoMT-based healthcare. *Scientific Reports*, 15(1), 6461.

39. Wang, X., Yue, X., Tariq, N., and Sajid, A. (2025). A hybrid AI and blockchain-powered IoT framework for anomaly detection and data security in smart city healthcare systems. *Processes*, 13(5), 1466.
40. Singh, G., Singh, P., and Singh, M. (2025). Advanced Real-Time Fraud Detection Using RAG-Based LLMs. arXiv. abs/2501.15290.
41. Munusamy, S., and Jothi, K. R. (2025). Blockchain-enabled federated learning with edge analytics for secure and efficient electronic health records management. *Scientific Reports*, 15(1), 27524.
42. Bhasker, B., Rao, P. M., Saraswathi, P., Patro, S. G. K., Bhutto, J. K., Islam, S. et al. (2025). Blockchain framework with IoT device using federated learning for sustainable healthcare systems. *Scientific Reports*, 15(1), 26736.
43. Islayem, R., Musamih, A., Salah, K., Jayaraman, R., and Yaqoob, I. (2025). Enhancing medical digital twins within metaverse using blockchain, NFTs and LLMs. *Internet of Things* (Netherlands), 32, 101648.
44. Zhang, G., Zhang, X., Bilal, M., Dou, W., Xu, X., and Rodrigues, J. J. P. C. (2022). Identifying fraud in medical insurance based on blockchain and deep learning. *Future Generation Computer Systems*, 130, 140–154. Available from: https://www.sciencedirect.com/ science/article/pii/S0167739X21004878.
45. Fan, Y., Zhang, W., Wu, G., Zhang, L., Long, C., Tan, G. et al. (2025). Shard-DAG: A scalable and secure block-DAG sharding scheme for AI-driven 6G networks. *Digital Communications and Networks*, 11(6), 1738–1750.
46. Rivera, S. C., Liu, X., Chan, A., Denniston, A., Calvert, M., Darzi, A. et al. (2020). Guidelines for clinical trial protocols for interventions involving artificial intelligence: The SPIRIT-AI extension. *Nature Medicine*, 26, 1351–1363.
47. Calain, P. (2006). From the field side of the binoculars: A different view on global public health surveillance. *Health Policy and Planning*, 22(1), 13–20.
48. Sonkamble, R. G., Shirke-Deshmukh, S., Katkar, V., Lunagaria, M., Tejani, G .G., and Mousavirad, S. J. (2025). A blockchain secured metaverse framework for scalable and immersive telemedicine. *Scientific Reports*, 15, 26655.
49. Said, A., Yahyaoui, A., and Abdellatif, T. (2024). HIPAA and GDPR compliance in IoT Healthcare Systems. In: Mosbah, M. et al. (eds). *Advances in Model and Data Engineering in the Digitalization Era*. MEDI 2023. Communications in Computer and Information Science, vol. 2071. Springer, Cham. https://doi.org/10.1007/978-3-031-55729-3_16
50. Ettaloui, N., Arezki, S., and Gadi, T. (2024). An overview of blockchain-based electronic health records and compliance with GDPR and HIPAA. In: Farhaoui, Y., Hussain, A., Saba, T., Taherdoost, H., Verma, A. (eds). *Artificial Intelligence, Data Science and Applications*. ICAISE 2023. Lecture Notes in Networks and Systems, vol. 838. Springer, Cham. https://doi.org/10.1007/978-3-031-48573-2_58
51. World Bank. (2017). Climate-Smart Healthcare: Low-Carbon and Resilience Strategies for the Health Sector. © World Bank. http://hdl.handle.net/10986/27809 License: CC BY 3.0 IGO.
52. Li, L., Chen, Y., and Lin, B. (2021). Intrusion detection analysis of Internet of Things considering Practical Byzantine Fault Tolerance (PBFT) algorithm. *Wireless Communications and Mobile Computing*, 2021(1), 6856284.
53. Brancaccio, G., Balato, A., Malvehy, J., Puig, S., Argenziano, G., and Kittler, H. (2024). Artificial intelligence in skin cancer diagnosis: A reality check. *Journal*

of Investigative Dermatology, 144(3), 492–499. Available from: https://www.sciencedirect.com/science/ article/pii/S0022202X23029640.
54. Kumar, A., Masud, M., Alsharif, M. H., Gaur, N., and Nanthaamornphong, A. (2025). Integrating 6G technology in smart hospitals: Challenges and opportunities for enhanced healthcare services. *Frontiers in Medicine*, 12.
55. Kalør, A., Durisi, G., Coleri, S., Parkvall, S., Yu, W., Mueller, A. et al. (2024). Wireless 6G connectivity for massive number of devices and critical services. arXiv, abs/2401.01127.
56. Fernández-Caramés, T. (2020). From pre-quantum to post-quantum IoT security: A survey on quantum-resistant cryptosystems for the Internet of Things. *IEEE Internet of Things Journal*, 7, 6457–6480.
57. Rajak, S., Summaq, A., Kumar, M. P., Ghosh, A., Elumalai, K., and Chinnadurai, S. (2024). Revolutionizing healthcare with 6G: A deep dive into smart, connected systems. *IEEE Access*, 12, 194150–194170.

CHAPTER

13

Artificial Intelligence, Metaverse, Blockchain Mediated Diagnosis, Prevention and Treatment of Alzheimer's Disease

S. Sheik Asraf[1*], P. Nagaraj[2], V. Muneeswaran[3] and Muhammad Fazal Ijaz[4]

[1] Department of Biotechnology, School of Bio, Chemical and Processing Engineering, Kalasalingam Academy of Research and Education, Virudhunagar, India

[2] Department of Computer Science and Engineering, School of Computing, SRM Institute of Science and Technology, Tiruchirappalli, SRM Nagar, Trichy, India

[3] Department of Electronics and Communication Engineering, School of Electronics, Electrical and Biomedical Technology, Kalasalingam Academy of Research and Education, Virudhunagar, India

[4] Centre for Artificial Intelligence Research and Optimization (AIRO), Design and Creative Technology, Torrens University Australia, 196 Flinders Street, Melbourne, Victoria, 3000, Australia

Alzheimer's disease (AD) is one of the neurological health issues that can be detected, prevented, and for which personalized treatment can be provided. Blockchain (BC) technology, metaverse technology (MV), and artificial intelligence (AI) have the potential to tackle AD. AI provides the precise diagnosis of AD with the help of machine learning (ML), deep learning (DL), natural language processing (NLP), support vector machines (SVM), and random forest (RF). MV provides neurological tests, treatment, awareness, and assistance options for AD patients with the help of virtual reality (VR), augmented reality (AR), digital twins, 3D Avatars, and social spaces. BC provides personalized medicine options for AD through unchangeable documents, intelligent contracts, decentralization, tokenization, rewards, and trails of audits. This chapter provides insights into AD, MV, and BC technologies' contribution to diagnosing, preventing, and treating Alzheimer's Disease.

*Corresponding author: s.sheikasraf@klu.ac.in

DOI: 10.1201/9781003679370-13

1. Introduction and Overview

Alzheimer's disease (AD) is one of the neurological problems that can be detected, prevented, and for which treatment can be provided, as shown in Figure 1. Blockchain (BC) technology, Metaverse technology (MV), and Artificial Intelligence (AI) have the potential to challenge AD. AI delivers an accurate analysis of AD. MV provides nerves examinations, treatment, responsiveness, and support options for AD patients. BC offers tailored medication options for AD. This chapter offers an understanding of the involvement of AD, MV, and BC skills for analyzing, inhibiting, and handling Alzheimer's Disease.

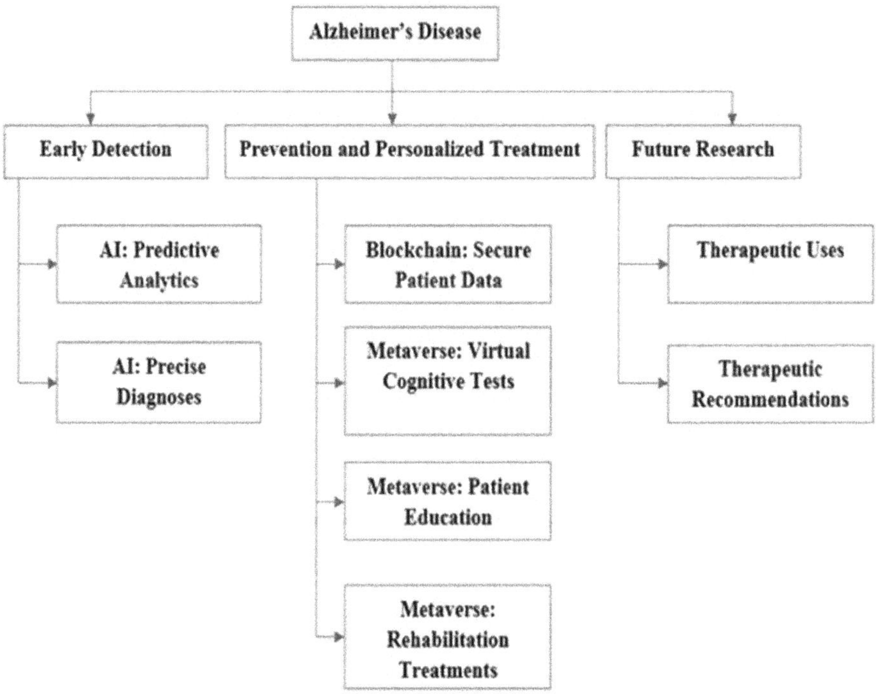

Figure 1: Overview of artificial intelligence, metaverse, blockchain mediated diagnosis, prevention, and treatment of Alzheimer's disease.

2. Artificial Intelligence's Contribution to Diagnosis, Prevention, and Treatment of Alzheimer's Disease

Various aspects of modern-day life, including transportation, medicine, and business, have been supported by developments in AI. Modern-day mechanical devices evaluate information efficiently because of deep learning (DL) techniques such as CNN and RNN. Figure 2 shows that these techniques have made driverless cars and smart homes possible due to improvements in audio and video recognition systems [1]. Optimized decision-making is made possible because of reinforced learning [2]. Image-based diagnosis, the discovery of drugs, and personalized medicine have been made possible because of AI. Classifying cancer types based on imaging techniques is made possible due to AI algorithms, thereby increasing the accuracy of diagnosis and reducing costs, as reported by Hunter et al. (2022) [3]. Protein structures can be predicted using AI [4]. AI has made the treatment of AD more efficient due to the classification of patients, risk assessment, and accurate diagnosis [5].

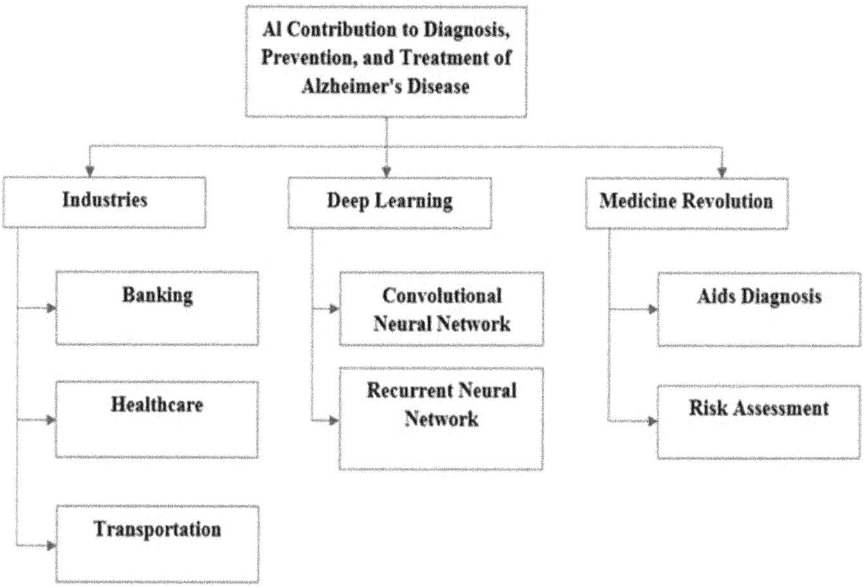

Figure 2: Artificial intelligence's contribution to diagnosis, prevention, and treatment of Alzheimer's disease.

Artificial Intelligence's contribution to the diagnosis, prevention, and treatment of Alzheimer's disease is immense [6]. Diagnosis and assignment of AD, as shown in Table 1, are made possible due to AI-based ensembles such as machine learning (ML) and DL [7]. ML and neuropsychological measurements have made the diagnosis of progression of AD more accurate [8]. According to a recent study conducted between 2009 and 2020, 90% accuracy was achieved in DL-based CNN algorithms in AI research on brain MRI analysis. Intellectual weakness and structural variations during the progression of AD were known due to advancements in AI [9].

DL techniques are being explored for early diagnosis of AD, with potential applications in genetic research, picture classification, and natural language processing [10]. Using brain MRI scans, DL techniques for early AD diagnosis

Table 1: Comparison of AI Techniques for Alzheimer's Diagnosis

AI Method	**Application in the Diagnosis of Alzheimer's**	**Benefits**	**Restrictions**
Machine Learning (ML)	Cognitive scores, MRI, and PET scan picture classification	High precision and early detection	Large labeled datasets are necessary
Deep Learning (DL)	Automatically extracting features from neuroimaging images	Excellent efficiency; little manual preprocessing	Computationally demanding; inherently opaque
Natural Language Processing (NLP)	Examination of patient histories, clinical records, and cognitive tests	Extracts patterns that are not based on images	Bias in language and models, sensitive to the quality of the data
Support Vector Machines (SVM)	Uses biomarker information and neuroimaging to categorize cognitive deterioration	Dependable results with tiny datasets	Scalability issues with big datasets
Random Forest (RF)	Prediction based on a variety of biological and clinical factors	Excellent interpretability; effectively manages missing data	Able to overfit complicated data without adjusting

are discussed, along with their drawbacks, difficulties, and potential future study areas [11]. The use of AI in the research of AD is hindered by shortcomings in theoretical frameworks, systematic biological analysis, and database management [12]. The application of AI, ML, feature extraction, and image processing methods in computer-aided diagnostic systems to identify AD in elderly patients has been studied recently [13]. Explainable AI (XAI) is being explored for AD detection, encompassing various frameworks and methodologies, and its potential for accurate diagnosis [14].

AI technologies like CNN, RNN, and Graph CNN are being utilized for primary recognition of AD, a severe brain condition causing cognitive impairment [15]. A new technique uses EEG signals to detect early stages of dementia, including AD, using noise addition, hybrid approaches, and variational autoencoders. The method improves classification accuracy by 2–7% and 3% when more data is included [16]. Xception with Adam, a low-cost, non-invasive AI-based dementia screening approach, demonstrated strong relationships with MMSE scores [17]. Recent studies have addressed missing data handling and equipment issues by analyzing multimodality picture data using ML and AI for AD diagnosis and prognosis [18]. A model using SHapley Additive exPlanations and a random forest classifier accurately diagnoses and identifies AD course from 1048 participants, offering 87.08% and 93.95% cross-validation accuracy [19]. Neuroimaging is essential for the initial detection of AD, and although AI can improve diagnostic accuracy, it has limitations, such as issues with generalization, limited data, absence of a gold standard, skepticism, and patient privacy concerns [20]. A proposed model for early AD detection outperforms PCA, reduces false-negative rates, and outperforms the Kaggle dataset for MRI neuroimaging diagnosis using a composite hybrid feature selection and stacked hybrid classification system [21].

By utilizing big data and interdisciplinary cooperation, AI can reduce the failure rates of clinical trials for AD and AD-related dementia [22]. Research indicates that using longitude data from electronic health records, decision support systems based on reinforcement learning (RL) can improve therapy for patients with AD, exceeding therapies recommended by professionals [23]. AI can aid in initial discovery, treatment, and caregiver support for AD, but ethical concerns, such as algorithmic accuracy, data privacy, and depersonalization, require collaborative efforts [24]. Using a pre-trained data2vec model, a new AI-powered system can identify and predict the severity of AD through language recordings, showing potential for early diagnosis and severity assessment in community settings [25]. The incorporation of DL and AI in non-invasive data for early AD diagnosis is revolutionizing the field of non-invasive medicine [26]. To determine different regions for AD and MCI, explainable AI was used to examine how AD affected the connections in the brains of 432 individuals [27].

A network-based AI technique recognized 103 AD risk genes and druggable targets, revealing three medications, pioglitazone, febuxostat, and atenolol, as effective in reducing AD incidence [28]. DL and MRI scans are precision-enhanced in detecting AD, achieving 98.88% testing accuracy and 99.7% binary data accuracy, thus enhancing medical treatment and solutions [29]. An AI-based AD diagnosis model achieved high sensitivity, specificity, and c-statistic values using data from 7932 patients, reducing missed diagnoses and ensuring proper use of medical resources [30]. Early AD analysis using AI and technological tools is being investigated; however, this requires a large body of information, a data pool, and thorough research [31]. To prevent serious loss of brain function, people are being diagnosed with AD using Explainable Artificial Intelligence (XAI) and algorithms such as CNN and VGG-16 [32]. Recent work utilized leucocyte epigenomic biomarkers to accurately predict AD, using AI techniques and genome-wide DNA methylation analysis for minimal invasiveness [33]. The documentation of initial biomarkers and molecular fingerprints in AD is being transformed by developments in neuroimaging, blood-based biomarkers, neurochemical profiling, AI, and ML algorithms [34]. AI-driven approaches for AD-agnostic drug discovery, such as computer-generated showing, de novo strategy, and drug-target interface calculation, find novel indications, pinpoint AD targets, and discuss upcoming difficulties [35]. Using algorithms and databases like ROSE, researchers are employing AI to detect, diagnose, and prognosticate

AD based on retinal scans, showing excellent sensitivity and accuracy [36]. DL computer system identified new Alzheimer's treatment targets using ML and latent features, inferring candidate chemicals and key genes, potentially improving medication repositioning tactics [37]. Fifteen studies utilizing radiomics and AI for AD diagnosis and monitoring show potential for improved clinical outcomes and quality of life [38]. A recent study explored the challenges of clinical trials for AD, such as high screen dropout rates and unequal participant distribution, along with potential applications of AI in these studies [39].

AAD, the seventh greatest cause of mortality worldwide, may be detected using AI algorithms, such as DL and ML, which will enhance clinical assessments and early diagnosis [40]. Homeostasis of NKT and GMP may be related to AD, according to a new study that used ML to examine blood transcriptome alterations in AD and find possible blood biomarkers [41]. For early AD diagnosis, a new study used a multi-level stacking model that beats single-modality methods that include explainable AI, stacking training, and stacking testing [42]. An accessible and scalable speech-based AI system reduced false positives and PET scans while enhancing early detection of cognitive impairment and amyloid beta positivity in AD [43]. A recent study explored the use of AI and ML algorithms for precise diagnosis of AD, highlighting future research directions and clinical implications [44]. A recent study suggested that combining AI and eye biomarkers using multimodal imaging could enhance the accuracy of early AD diagnosis [45]. Ethical concerns over AI-assisted AD prediction have led to early diagnosis training for doctors to ensure autonomy, beneficence, non-maleficence, and justice [46]. Because structural MRI is inexpensive and radiation-efficient, AI approaches are being used for AD early detection and diagnosis [47]. XAI has significantly improved the reliability of medical choice provision systems and AI-based AD forecasts [48]. An ML predictor for AD diagnoses achieved 93% accuracy using transcriptome data from both AD patients and non-AD individuals, highlighting β-amyloid oxidative stress and mitochondrial translation as key factors [49]. AD, a worldwide wellbeing concern, is influenced by factors such as AI and ML, as well as dietary choices, particularly Mediterranean-DASH diets [50]. Using MRI cortical features from 162 patients, the study created AI-based technology for early AD prediction, producing precise multi-predictor nomograms [51]. A study using cfDNA and DL successfully diagnosed AD in 3684 individuals with differentially methylated CpGs, achieving 94.5% sensitivity and specificity [52]. The stigma surrounding AD hinders research, handling, and primary detection, but advancements in NLP and AI, along with secure, decentralized data transport techniques, can mitigate this issue [53]. The 3D ResNet-18-RF AI-ensembled network excels in classifying cognitive impairment development using ADNI dataset variables, primarily focusing on the gray matter to white matter ratio [54]. InceptionResNetv2 outperformed other networks in a study utilizing AI and evidence-based medication to evaluate the prediction ability of MRI-based hippocampus volume measures for AD risk [55]. AI is changing how AD is understood and diagnosed, helping medical professionals with patient strategizing, conversion estimate, and the creation of individualized treatment plans [56]. Potential AD pathogenesis was shown by a study that used AI and ML to recognize plasma metabolites as an investigative tool for AD and moderate cognitive impairment [57]. Researchers have developed support vector machines and deep CNNs for early detection of AD, with the deep convolutional network design achieving 100% accuracy during training and 98.8% accuracy in test results [58]. A study using AI algorithms and reasoning scores predicted AD and mild cognitive impairment diagnosis, highlighting gender impacts, education's protective effect, and functional decline [59]. According to the study, future research should employ standardized methods and clinical integration, which shows that AI-assisted hippocampus segmentation is most accurate in AD but less accurate in mild reasoning impairment [60]. AI methods like fuzzy logic, ML, and NLP can improve AD diagnosis and treatment, but challenges like inconsistent data and moral dilemmas need to be addressed [61]. AI developments in therapeutic image examination and AD detection, with particular attention to CNN's 95.70% accuracy for DL models and brain MRI scans [62]. The use of AI and ML is being utilized to improve early analysis and tailored handling of AD, while addressing data diversity and ethical concerns [63]. A study utilized AI, ML, and neural networks to comprehend the aggregation of AD protein using graphics processing units [64]. By overcoming obstacles such as high dimensionality, lost information, and dataset inequity, AI approaches such as state-space models, DL techniques, and digital twins are being utilized to forecast the course of AD in a tailored manner [65]. The Alzheimer's Therapeutic Research Institute study found AI-based adverse happening encoding outperformed traditional clinician coding in a trial of 1000 contrary proceedings, highlighting the potential of AI and human expertise [66]. AI is being utilized in the diagnosis, management, and treatment of brain disorders like AD, enhancing precision, forecasting, and personalized treatment regimens [67]. AI's potential in managing AD is highlighted for its proactive care, personalized therapies, and improved patient outcomes, while also addressing data privacy concerns [68]. AI develops an end-to-end system, analyzes existing approaches, proposes new tactics, assesses the risk of AD, and conducts a population-level online video-based hand movement test [69]. DL models and other therapy techniques are being researched for using AI in AD diagnosis and treatment [70].

AI algorithms were used in a network pharmacology-based method to predict the bioactivities of herbs like *Ardisia japonica, Ligusticum chuanxiong, Lippia nodiflora,* and *Mirabilis jalapa* for potential Traditional Chinese Medicine treatments [71]. AI research that evaluated the relationship between blood-based indicators of AD and naturalistic driving behavior found that the model's predicted accuracy increased to 0.80 [72].

Successive 98%, 95%, and 91% accuracy was achieved in early diagnosis and identification of AD using DL algorithms and MRI scans [73]. AI DL models have been used for diagnosis, prevention, and treatment of AD [74]. The ORAI2 gene has been identified as the best biomarker for the diagnosis of AD using ML algorithms [75]. A recent study looked into how AI DL models have been used for diagnosis, prevention, and treatment of AD [76]. β-amyloid and early cognitive deterioration were identified by AI models and were used to diagnose the course of AD using PET scans [77]. Early diagnosis and identification of AD using DL algorithms and MRI scans showed good performance versus known biomarkers [78]. In a recent study, speech-based ML was used to study significant variations in the duration of speech, gaps, prosodic essentials, and phrases of sentences, with the help of speech-based ML to detect AD [79].

Through developments in AI-enabled platforms, early detection, genomic analysis, and autonomous research systems, a recent study demonstrated the important role that AI plays in speeding up biomedical research, especially in the area of AD [80]. AI is being used to automate processes and enhance decision-making in AD diagnosis, improving care quality and cutting expenses [81]. According to a new study, molecular docking techniques improve drug-target interaction modeling, speeding up drug development and enhancing AD treatment approaches, while AI algorithms provide more accurate predictions in AD medication repurposing [82]. According to a recent study, CNN is the best AI model for early AD identification using neuroimaging data, surpassing SVM and RF models [83]. According to a recent study, natural language processing may be used to detect linguistic characteristics linked to AD, slight damage, and cognitively undamaged people, as well as for continuous cognitive impairment screening [84]. With a high accuracy of 95.65%, a DL dragonfly algorithm has effectively predicted the early stages of AD using multi-modality imaging methods [85]. AI and ML techniques for AD prediction face challenges, such as information confidentiality, algorithmic prejudice, computational resources, and ethical issues [86].

3. Using Metaverse in Diagnosis, Prevention, and Treatment of Alzheimer's Disease

Using cognitive tests and MRI data from the ADNeuroimaging Initiative 2 dataset, a recent study created a virtual reality environment for senior citizens with remarkable accuracy and precision [87], as shown in Figure 3. The MV, a combination of data science, VR, AI, and digital twins, offers potential solutions for cognitive decline and mental health issues [88] as shown in Table 2. MV therapy, which might retain human memories and be used as a future treatment in the Internet business, was one of the non-pharmacological therapies for AD studied in recent research [89]. Recent research highlighted the potential of generative AI in the MV by examining how it may help older adults with everyday problems, including reasoning weakening, dementia, AD, hearing damage, and loneliness [90].

With its potential to hyperalert the brain, prevent AD, and help comprehend neurodegenerative illnesses through visual arts, the MV presents a serious

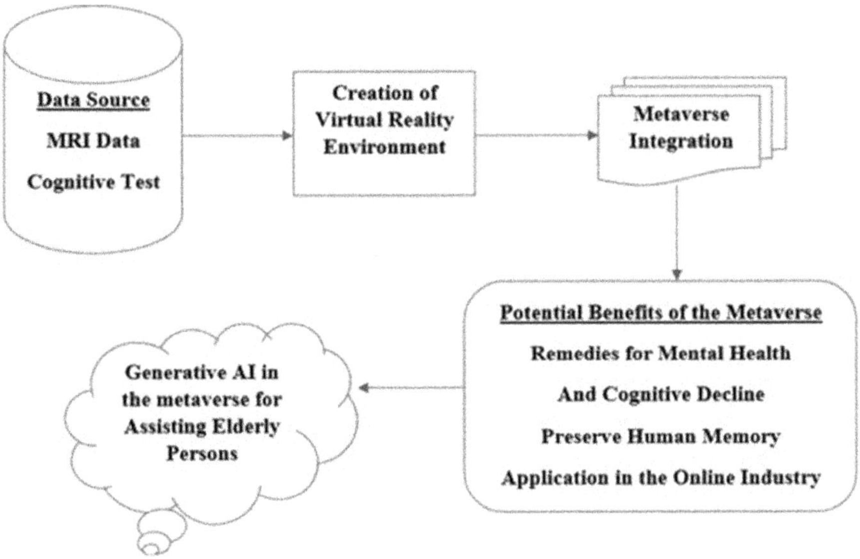

Figure 3: Using metaverse in diagnosis, prevention, and treatment of Alzheimer's disease.

Table 2: Role of Metaverse Components in Alzheimer's Care

Component of the Metaverse	Role in the Treatment of Alzheimer's	Advantages	Difficulties
Virtual Reality (VR)	Memory drills, cognitive stimulation, and immersive treatment	Increases recollection, fosters engagement, and creates safe spaces	Accessibility: Some users experience motion sickness
Augmented Reality (AR)	Environmental signals, task reminders, and navigation assistance	Interaction in the real world helps and lessens confusion	Hardware is needed; field applications are limited
Digital Twins	Individualized patient health and behavior simulation	Allows for predictive analysis and precision care	High data needs and privacy issues
3D Avatars & Social Spaces	Encourages emotional support and social connection	Lessens loneliness and promotes dialogue	Need the assistance of caregivers and computer literacy
Platforms for the Metaverse	An integrated ecosystem for patient monitoring and care management	Access to care in one place; multisensory experience	Cost and infrastructure obstacles

challenge to human physiology and psychology [91]. In the medical field, virtual and augmented reality are increasingly used for post-stroke therapy, pre-operative preparation, image-guided surgery, teaching medical anatomy, pain management, and training Alzheimer's patients' cognitive skills [92]. By distinguishing common and modality-specific characteristics, the M-AVAE DL system improves MV brain age predictions and overcomes the difficulties of integrating complicated MRI data and noisy measurements for the detection of age-related neuropathologies like AD [93]. Digital Therapeutics (DTx) improves patient engagement and improves patient outcomes by using AI and XR technology to deliver real-time, individualized treatments for a diversity of diseases, including AD [94].

4. Blockchain for Safe and Moral Diagnosis, Prevention, and Treatment of Alzheimer's Disease

To recover data quality and speed, a recent study used BC-based DNN in healthcare control systems, as shown in Figure 4. This resulted in 98% accuracy

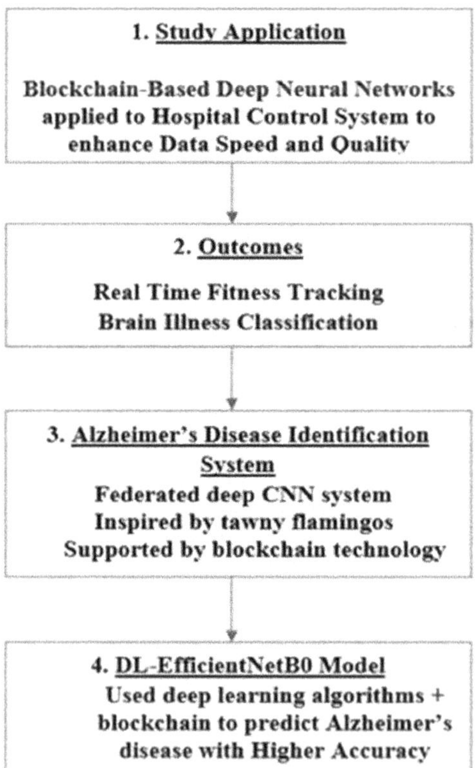

Figure 4: Blockchain for safe and moral diagnosis, prevention, and treatment of Alzheimer's disease.

in instantaneous suitability pursuit and the categorization of brain diseases, including AD [95]. With a tawny flamingo-based federated deep CNN and BC support, researchers have developed a disease detection system for Alzheimer's that boasts excellent sensitivity, specificity, and accuracy at training percentages of 80 [96].

Table 3 shows how BC technology and DL algorithms are being used to predict AD, with the DL-EfficientNetB0 model achieving a 99.14% accuracy rate in classifying 3182 images [97].

Table 3: Blockchain Benefits in Alzheimer's Diagnosis and Research

A feature of blockchain	Use in the Field of Alzheimer's	Advantage	Things to Think About
Unchangeable Documents	Protecting diagnostic data and medical histories	Keeps data from being altered and guarantees its integrity	Adherence to regulations (e.g., GDPR, HIPAA)
Intelligent Contracts	Automating research participation agreements and patient consent	Builds trust and makes consent management easier	Implementation complexity
Decentralization	Data exchange between entities that is secure	Reduces single-point failure and fosters more collaboration	Format standardization is required
Tokenization and Rewards	Using tokens or incentives to entice patients to provide data	Increases involvement in clinical research	Concerns about health data monetization and ethics
Trails of Audits	Monitoring the use and access of data in research	Complete openness makes responsibility easier	Strong access controls are necessary

5. Integrated Framework: Blockchain, Metaverse, and AI Working Together

With a 9% increase in discrimination accuracy over structural MRI techniques, the AI system that uses magnetic resonance imaging greatly improves early AD diagnosis [98]. AD and clinical scores are strongly correlated, according to the RADAR-AD project, an IMI program that uses a virtual reality game to assess cognitive impairment [99]. Using open data-sharing programs and multi-omics research, a recent study examined AI technologies for AD detection and prediction, highlighting the effectiveness of ML and DL [100]. ML algorithms are frequently utilized to identify AD, an intelligence illness causing dementia in older individuals, emphasizing the importance of early detection for effective treatments [101]. Despite moral and information excellence concerns, AI is enhancing early AD detection using imagery, biomarkers, and medical records, perhaps leading to increased precision and early treatments [102]. A recent study used CNN to diagnose AD early, achieving 97% accuracy, precision, recall, and F1-score, which are crucial for early treatment [103]. Despite issues with data consistency, interpretability, and ethical considerations, AI improves AD research and clinical treatment through neuroimaging analysis, biomarker identification, cognitive evaluation, and predictive modelling [104]. Although difficulties show that more work is needed, AI-enhanced MRI technology increases the effectiveness, accuracy, treatment options, and patient outcomes of AD diagnosis [105]. Using a 3D CNN architecture, a recent study compared ML with DL models for early AD diagnosis, with 98.92% and 98.3% identification rates, respectively [106]. As AI techniques are applied in research, they can help identify AD by evaluating medical images, answering both known and unanswered issues [107]. A recent study explored how AI can be utilized to develop new diagnostic methods for AD, highlighting its potential for early detection, classification, and progression prediction [108]. AI can use DL to develop innovative treatments for delirium, a major consequence of AD that leads to hospitalization in the elderly [109]. AI is likely to improve healthcare by predicting the risk of AD, evaluating accuracy, reliability, and cost-effectiveness, and addressing ethical and legal issues [110]. Advancements in medical image processing and analysis, focusing on ML and deep feature extraction techniques, are paving the way for AI-based AD diagnosis [111]. Using high-quality spectra and ML approaches, MRS is being investigated for the discovery of biomarkers in AD, with potential applications in neurodegenerative illnesses [112].

Using a dataset of 6400 preprocessed pictures, a recent study used AI to categorize MRI scans into AD stages, improving accuracy and efficiency with a 99.6% classification rate [113]. Using α-mangostin as a hit chemical, researchers found a new PDE4 inhibitor, 13d, which had neuroprotective and anti-inflammatory properties, highlighting the promise of AI-driven drug development for AD [114]. Using RN-SSAS for small sample sizes and multiple categories, the World Health Organization promotes higher AD screening rates with a focus on early detection and intervention [115].

Drug development and molecular taxonomic classification of neurodegenerative illnesses like AD are made possible by data-driven technology like AI [116]. Diagnostic imaging methods, biomarkers, and processed neuroimaging data required for early AD diagnosis are made possible because of AI [117]. Routine brain imaging and computer-aided diagnosis supplements AI's potential in early AD diagnosis [118]. Ethical, philosophical possibilities and hazards in the diagnosis and treatment of AD are a concern [119]. The benefits and limitations of AI and MRI data in analyzing AD have produced many success stories [120]. A non-linear neural network utilizing Explainable AI (XAI) to establish diagnostic techniques for AD has been implemented in a recent study [121].

Researchers have developed prediction models for AD using supervised ML on the OASIS dataset, with the Naïve Bayes classifier showing the highest accuracy at 97.5% [122]. A study that combined AI with cutting-edge imaging methods discovered a connection between elevated angiogenesis and Aβ accumulation, indicating that AI may help with AD early identification and therapy [123]. Early AD diagnosis has improved thanks to AI advancements, especially in natural language processing (GPT-3 from OpenAI has an accuracy rate of 0.8028), but public usage issues still exist [124]. To improve diagnosis accuracy in the categorization of EEG signals for AD, frontotemporal dementia, and healthy age-matched controls, a recent study employed ML algorithms and ensemble learning approaches [125].

The use of AI-based digital phenotyping to diagnose neurological conditions like Alzheimer's is increasing, but ethical issues are raised by the technology's limited decision-making ability and potential hazards, which require risk mitigation techniques [126]. A recent study introduced an early detection method for AD using GWAS, DL models, and XAI to identify genetic markers and enhance transparency in DL model decisions [127]. AI software based on brain MRI helps doctors diagnose and treat AD by giving precise information for early diagnosis and tracking the progression of the disease in patients with memory impairment [128]. The Random Forest model achieved the highest accuracy and precision, while the Naive Bayes model demonstrated the greatest sensitivity, according to a recent evaluation of categorization models using EEG data from both healthy individuals and Alzheimer's patients [129]. AI-driven analysis significantly outperformed traditional techniques in a study involving 145 Alzheimer's patients, achieving 92% accuracy, 90% sensitivity, and 94% specificity while reducing diagnostic variability and improving inter-pathologist agreement. [130]. A recent study presented a computer system that uses conditional random fields and inception deep neural networks to diagnose AD early using AI approaches [131]. The importance of preprocessing methods in improving MRI images for AI-based AD detection was recently highlighted in a study, which also emphasized the necessity for uniform pipelines and more research to increase accuracy [132]. AI is improving diagnostic techniques, providing individualized risk assessments, enabling prompt therapies, and improving early diagnosis of AD using ML and data analysis [133]. Data "tiling" is being used by the AI for AD cooperation to examine more than 15,000 genomes to find novel genetic markers in the development and risk of AD [134]. The DL model ResNet-50 demonstrates AI's potential for early diagnosis by accurately classifying Alzheimer's patients using MRI images, even when facing class imbalance and subtle brain changes [135]. A recent study achieved over 94% accuracy in ML approaches for AD identification by using ensemble boosting algorithms such as XGBoost, LightGBM, Gradient Boosting, and SHAP for feature selection [136]. With a 66% F-1 score, 76% sensitivity, and 93.5% specificity, a 3D ResNet-18-RF AI-ensembled network outperformed traditional techniques in the correct classification of cognitive impairment progression using the ADNI dataset [137]. Although early AD diagnosis is being improved by AI and ML, moral issues, including patient permission, data security, and privacy, are still unresolved [138].

Using neuroimaging data, ML and domain adaptation approaches are being employed for early AD diagnosis; nevertheless, difficulties still exist because of variations in data distribution [139]. To diagnose AD early, recent research investigated AI technologies such as ML, CNN, GCNN, and CNN [140]. A recent study suggested early diagnosis of AD using MRI images and cerebrospinal fluid biomarkers classified using ML and DL models [141]. Recent research improved the interpretability of ML models for AD early detection by utilizing Explainable AI (XAI) methodologies [142]. Algorithms for AD early diagnosis are being developed using DL and ML to improve patient outcomes and quality of life [143]. Using AI models and virtual screening technologies, researchers have found that co-activation of GHSR1α and DRD1 can restore hippocampal synaptic and cognitive function in AD [144]. AI, particularly ML and DL, is greatly enhancing the early identification of AD [145]. With an accuracy of 95.7%, sensitivity of 94.1%, and specificity of 96.2%, DNCP, a DL-based technique for early AD diagnosis, outperformed state-of-the-art models in recent research [146]. Although more study is required to fully grasp AI's potential for susceptibility analysis and management, it holds promise for early AD discovery and treatment, especially in China's aging population [147]. A recent study investigated the use of DL and ML classifiers, namely Extra Tree and Gradient Boosting, as an affordable diagnostic method for early preclinical AD [148]. To improve patient care and management, a recent study presented a revolutionary AI-based technique for forecasting the progression of AD using LSTM, Random Forest, and Gradient Boosting Machines [149]. While the AD+P network found ADPN linked to delusions and cognitive loss, DL predicted psychosis in AD by finding neural connections [150]. A study on blood-based biomarkers (BBBMs) and ML algorithms for early detection of AD has identified four key indicators for effective early detection [151]. A study using AI revealed that 92.3% of Alzheimer's patients struggle with smiles, with smile/neutral-NC scores strongly correlated with subcortical volume [152]. Although more research is needed to fully understand its usefulness, AI's potential in early AD detection could improve treatment outcomes and therapeutic planning [153]. A recent study evaluated the effectiveness of medical AI in diagnosing and treating AD, highlighting its limitations and suggesting innovative solutions for China's clinical decision support system [154].

By examining the patterns of illness progression, the MV may be able to forecast the course of conditions like Alzheimer's [155]. With encouraging outcomes in depression treatment and cognitive rehabilitation for Alzheimer's illnesses, studies demonstrate VR's ability to address mental health issues and cognitive impairments [156]. To overcome obstacles like concealed data and limited control, BC technology can organize and distribute large amounts of healthcare data, enabling the development of an Alzheimer's risk calculator using AI techniques [157]. By addressing computational complexity and privacy issues, the decentralized expert system, which combines BC technology with AI, seeks to improve early AD detection [158].

6. Conclusion

Alzheimer's disease, a severe nervous illness, requires early detection, prevention, and personalized treatment. BC, MV, and AI technologies can help with predictive analytics, precise diagnoses, virtual cognitive tests, rehabilitation treatments, patient education, and caregiver assistance. BC ensures patient-centric healthcare by protecting sensitive data. Future research aims to explore future therapeutic uses, ethical considerations, and technical frameworks, examining how BC, AI, and the MV could alter AD diagnosis.

Acknowledgement

The authors thank Kalasalingam Academy of Research and Education and SRM Institute of Science and Technology, Tiruchirappalli Campus, for providing the computational resources to complete this research work efficiently.

References

1. Alam, Mahbubul, Manar D. Samad, Lasitha Vidyaratne, Alexander Glandon, and Khan M. Iftekharuddin. (2020). Survey on deep neural networks in speech and vision systems. *Neurocomputing*, 417, 302–321.
2. Lee, Daeyeol, Hyojung Seo, and Min Whan Jung. (2012). Neural basis of reinforcement learning and decision making. *Annual Review of Neuroscience*, 35(1), 287–308.
3. Hunter, Benjamin, Sumeet Hindocha, and Richard W. Lee. (2022). The role of artificial intelligence in early cancer diagnosis. *Cancers*, 14(6), 1524.
4. Jiménez-Luna, José, Francesca Grisoni, Nils Weskamp, and Gisbert Schneider. (2021). Artificial intelligence in drug discovery: Recent advances and future perspectives. *Expert Opinion on Drug Discovery*, 16(9), 949–959.
5. Fabrizio, C., Termine, A., Caltagirone, C., and Sancesario, G. (2021). Artificial intelligence for Alzheimer's disease: Promise or challenge? *Diagnostics*, 11(8), 1473.
6. Zhang, W., Li, Y., Ren, W., and Liu, B. (2023). Artificial intelligence technology in Alzheimer's disease research. *Intractable & Rare Diseases Research*, 12(4), 208–212.
7. El-Sappagh, S., Alonso-Moral, J. M., Abuhmed, T., Ali, F., & Bugarín-Diz, A. (2023). Trustworthy artificial intelligence in Alzheimer's disease: State of the art, opportunities, and challenges. *Artificial Intelligence Review*, 56(10), 11149–11296.
8. Battista, P., Salvatore, C., Berlingeri, M., Cerasa, A., and Castiglioni, I. (2020). Artificial intelligence and neuropsychological measures: The case of Alzheimer's disease. *Neuroscience & Biobehavioral Reviews*, 114, 211–228.

9. Frizzell, T. O., Glashutter, M., Liu, C. C., Zeng, A., Pan, D., Hajra, S. G., ... and Song, X. (2022). Artificial intelligence in brain MRI analysis of Alzheimer's disease over the past 12 years: A systematic review. *Ageing Research Reviews*, 77, 101614.
10. Aditya Shastry, K., and Sanjay, H. A. (2024). Artificial Intelligence techniques for the effective diagnosis of Alzheimer's Disease: A review. *Multimedia Tools and Applications*, 83(13), 40057–40092.
11. Yao, Z., Wang, H., Yan, W., Wang, Z., Zhang, W., Wang, Z., and Zhang, G. (2023). Artificial intelligence-based diagnosis of Alzheimer's disease with brain MRI images. *European Journal of Radiology*, 165, 110934.
12. Mishra, R., and Li, B. (2020). The application of artificial intelligence in the genetic study of Alzheimer's disease. *Aging and Disease*, 11(6), 1567.
13. Subasi, A. (2020). Use of artificial intelligence in Alzheimer's disease detection. *Artificial Intelligence in Precision Health*, 257–278.
14. Viswan, V., Shaffi, N., Mahmud, M., Subramanian, K., and Hajamohideen, F. (2024). Explainable artificial intelligence in Alzheimer's disease classification: A systematic review. *Cognitive Computation*, 16(1), 1–44.
15. Yang, K., and Mohammed, E. A. (2020). A review of artificial intelligence technologies for early prediction of Alzheimer;s disease. arXiv preprint arXiv:2101.01781.
16. Sadegh-Zadeh, S. A., Fakhri, E., Bahrami, M., Bagheri, E., Khamsehashari, R., Noroozian, M., and Hajiyavand, A. M. (2023). An approach toward artificial intelligence Alzheimer's disease diagnosis using brain signals. *Diagnostics*, 13(3), 477.
17. Umeda-Kameyama, Y., Kameyama, M., Tanaka, T., Son, B. K., Kojima, T., Fukasawa, M., ... and Akishita, M. (2021). Screening of Alzheimer's disease by facial complexion using artificial intelligence. *Aging (Albany NY)*, 13(2), 1765.
18. Liu, X., Chen, K., Wu, T., Weidman, D., Lure, F., and Li, J. (2018). Use of multimodality imaging and artificial intelligence for diagnosis and prognosis of early stages of Alzheimer's disease. *Translational Research*, 194, 56–67.
19. El-Sappagh, S., Alonso, J. M., Islam, S. R., Sultan, A. M., and Kwak, K. S. (2021). A multilayer multimodal detection and prediction model based on explainable artificial intelligence for Alzheimer's disease. *Scientific Reports*, 11(1), 2660.
20. Mirkin, S., and Albensi, B. C. (2023). Should artificial intelligence be used in conjunction with Neuroimaging in the diagnosis of Alzheimer's disease? *Frontiers in Aging Neuroscience*, 15, 1094233.
21. Farid, A. A., Selim, G. I., and Khater, H. A. A. (2020). Applying artificial intelligence techniques to improve clinical diagnosis of Alzheimer's disease. *European Journal of Engineering Science and Technology*, 3(2), 58–79.
22. Cheng, F., Wang, F., Tang, J., Zhou, Y., Fu, Z., Zhang, P., ... and Cummings, J. (2024). Artificial intelligence and open science in discovery of disease-modifying medicines for Alzheimer's disease. *Cell Reports Medicine*, 5(2).
23. Bhattarai, K., Rajaganapathy, S., Das, T., Kim, Y., Chen, Y., ... and Zong, N. (2023). Using artificial intelligence to learn optimal regimen plan for Alzheimer's disease. *Journal of the American Medical Informatics Association*, 30(10), 1645–1656.
24. Habibi, F., Ghaderkhani, S., Shokoohi, M., Banari, T., Morsali, M., Abadi, R. N. S., and Kiamehr, H. (2025). Harnessing artificial intelligence in Alzheimer's disease management: Navigating ethical challenges in AI. *AI and Ethics*, 1–17.
25. Agbavor, F., and Liang, H. (2022). Artificial intelligence-enabled end-to-end detection and assessment of Alzheimer's disease using voice. *Brain Sciences*, 13(1), 28.

26. Vrahatis, A. G., Skolariki, K., Krokidis, M. G., Lazaros, K., Exarchos, T. P., and Vlamos, P. (2023). Revolutionizing the early detection of Alzheimer's disease through non-invasive biomarkers: The role of artificial intelligence and deep learning. *Sensors*, 23(9), 4184.
27. Amoroso, N., Quarto, S., La Rocca, M., Tangaro, S., Monaco, A., and Bellotti, R. (2023). An eXplainability Artificial Intelligence approach to brain connectivity in Alzheimer's disease. *Frontiers in Aging Neuroscience*, 15, 1238065.
28. Fang, J., Zhang, P., Wang, Q., Chiang, C. W., Zhou, Y., Hou, Y., ... and Cheng, F. (2022). Artificial intelligence framework identifies candidate targets for drug repurposing in Alzheimer's disease. *Alzheimer's Research & Therapy*, 14, 1–23.
29. Farooq, A., Anwar, S., Awais, M., and Alnowami, M. (2017, September). Artificial intelligence based smart diagnosis of Alzheimer's disease and mild cognitive impairment. In: *2017 International Smart Cities Conference* (*ISC2*) (pp. 1–4). IEEE.
30. Fujita, K., Katsuki, M., Takasu, A., Kitajima, A., Shimazu, T., and Maruki, Y. (2022). Development of an artificial intelligence-based diagnostic model for Alzheimer's disease. *Aging Medicine*, 5(3), 167–173.
31. Verma, R. K., Pandey, M., Chawla, P., Choudhury, H., Mayuren, J., Bhattamisra, S. K., ... and Obaidur Rahman, S. (2022). An insight into the role of Artificial Intelligence in the early diagnosis of Alzheimer's disease. *CNS & Neurological Disorders – Drug Targets*, 21(10), 901–912.
32. Sudar, K. M., Nagaraj, P., Nithisaa, S., Aishwarya, R., Aakash, M., and Lakshmi, S. I. (2022, April). Alzheimer's disease analysis using Explainable Artificial Intelligence (XAI). In: *2022 International Conference on Sustainable Computing and Data Communication Systems* (*ICSCDS*) (pp. 419–423). IEEE.
33. Bahado-Singh, R. O., Vishweswaraiah, S., Aydas, B., Yilmaz, A., Metpally, R. P., Carey, D. J., ... and Radhakrishna, U. (2021). Artificial intelligence and leukocyte epigenomics: Evaluation and prediction of late-onset Alzheimer's disease. *PLOS One*, 16(3), e0248375.
34. Etekochay, M. O., Amaravadhi, A. R., González, G. V., Atanasov, A. G., Matin, M., Mofatteh, M., ... and Praticò, D. (2024). Unveiling new strategies facilitating the implementation of artificial intelligence in neuroimaging for the early detection of Alzheimer's disease. *Journal of Alzheimer's Disease*, 99(1), 1–20.
35. Qiu, Y., and Cheng, F. (2024). Artificial intelligence for drug discovery and development in Alzheimer's disease. *Current Opinion in Structural Biology*, 85, 102776–102776.
36. Ashayeri, H., Jafarizadeh, A., Yousefi, M., Farhadi, F., and Javadzadeh, A. (2024). Retinal imaging and Alzheimer's disease: A future powered by Artificial Intelligence. *Graefe's Archive for Clinical and Experimental Ophthalmology*, 262(8), 2389–2401.
37. Tsuji, S., Hase, T., Yachie-Kinoshita, A., Nishino, T., Ghosh, S., Kikuchi, M., ... and Tanaka, H. (2021). Artificial intelligence-based computational framework for drug-target prioritization and inference of novel repositionable drugs for Alzheimer's disease. *Alzheimer's Research & Therapy*, 13(1), 92.
38. Bevilacqua, R., Barbarossa, F., Fantechi, L., Fornarelli, D., Paci, E., Bolognini, S., ... and Maranesi, E. (2023). Radiomics and artificial intelligence for the diagnosis and monitoring of Alzheimer's disease: A systematic review of studies in the field. *Journal of Clinical Medicine*, 12(16), 5432.
39. Seo, Y., Jang, H., and Lee, H. (2022). Potential applications of artificial intelligence in clinical trials for Alzheimer's disease. *Life*, 12(2), 275.

40. Maleki, S. F., Yousefi, M., Sobhi, N., Jafarizadeh, A., Alizadehsani, R., and Gorriz-Saez, J. M. (2024). Artificial intelligence in eye movements analysis for Alzheimer's disease early diagnosis. *Current Alzheimer Research*, 21(3), 155–165.
41. Sh, Y., Liu, B., Zhang, J., Zhou, Y., Hu, Z., and Zhang, X. (2021). Application of artificial intelligence modeling technology based on fluid biopsy to diagnose alzheimer's disease. *Frontiers in Aging Neuroscience*, 13, 768229.
42. Al Mohimeed, A., Saad, R. M., Mostafa, S., El-Rashidy, N. M., Farrag, S., Gaballah, A., ... and Saleh, H. (2023). Explainable artificial intelligence of multi-level stacking ensemble for detection of Alzheimer's disease based on particle swarm optimization and the sub-scores of cognitive biomarkers. *IEEE Access*, 11, 123173–123193.
43. Fristed, E., Skirrow, C., Meszaros, M., Lenain, R., Meepegama, U., Papp, K. V., ... and Weston, J. (2022). Leveraging speech and artificial intelligence to screen for early Alzheimer's disease and amyloid beta positivity. *Brain Communications*, 4(5), fcac231.
44. Bazarbekov, I., Razaque, A., Ipalakova, M., Yoo, J., Assipova, Z., and Almisreb, A. (2024). A review of artificial intelligence methods for Alzheimer's disease diagnosis: Insights from neuroimaging to sensor data analysis. *Biomedical Signal Processing and Control*, 92, 106023.
45. Chaitanuwong, P., Singhanetr, P., Chainakul, M., Arjkongharn, N., Ruamviboonsuk, P., and Grzybowski, A. (2023). Potential ocular biomarkers for early detection of Alzheimer's disease and their roles in artificial intelligence studies. *Neurology and Therapy*, 12(5), 1517–1532.
46. Ursin, F., Timmermann, C., and Steger, F. (2021). Ethical implications of Alzheimer's disease prediction in asymptomatic individuals through artificial intelligence. *Diagnostics*, 11(3), 440.
47. Zhao, X., Ang, C. K. E., Acharya, U. R., and Cheong, K. H. (2021). Application of Artificial Intelligence techniques for the detection of Alzheimer's disease using structural MRI images. *Biocybernetics and Biomedical Engineering*, 41(2), 456–473.
48. Vimbi, V., Shaffi, N., and Mahmud, M. (2024). Interpreting artificial intelligence models: A systematic review on the application of LIME and SHAP in Alzheimer's disease detection. *Brain Informatics*, 11(1), 10.
49. Chiricosta, L., D'Angiolini, S., Gugliandolo, A., and Mazzon, E. (2022). Artificial intelligence predictor for Alzheimer's disease trained on blood transcriptome: The role of oxidative stress. *International Journal of Molecular Sciences*, 23(9), 5237.
50. Soares Dias Portela, A., Saxena, V., Rosenn, E., Wang, S. H., Masieri, S., Palmieri, J., and Pasinetti, G. M. (2024). Role of artificial intelligence in multinomial decisions and preventative nutrition in Alzheimer's disease. *Molecular Nutrition & Food Research*, 68(13), 2300605.
51. Zeng, R., Yang, B., Wu, F., Liu, H., Wu, X., Tang, L., ... and Guo, D. (2025). Early prediction of Alzheimer's disease using artificial intelligence and cortical features on T1WI sequences. *Frontiers in Neurology*, 16, 1552940.
52. Bahado-Singh, R. O., Radhakrishna, U., Gordevičius, J., Aydas, B., Yilmaz, A., Jafar, F., ... and Vishweswaraiah, S. (2022). Artificial intelligence and circulating cell-free DNA methylation profiling: Mechanism and detection of Alzheimer's disease. *Cells*, 11(11), 1744.
53. Pilozzi, A., and Huang, X. (2020). Overcoming Alzheimer's disease stigma by leveraging artificial intelligence and blockchain technologies. *Brain Sciences*, 10(3), 183.

54. Hasan, M. M., Rahman, S., Parmar, H., and Chowdhury, S. K. (2024). A novel Artificial Intelligence (AI) method to classify and predict the progression of Alzheimer's disease. *bioRxiv*, 2024–06.
55. Zhou, J., Zhao, M., Yang, Z., Chen, L., Liu, X., and Alzheimer's Disease Neuroimaging Initiative. (2024). Exploring the value of MRI measurement of hippocampal volume for predicting the occurrence and progression of Alzheimer's disease based on artificial intelligence deep learning technology and evidence-based medicine meta-analysis. *Journal of Alzheimer's Disease*, 97(3), 1275–1288.
56. Tripathi, S., Sharma, Y., and Kumar, D. (2025). Unraveling the mysteries of Alzheimer's disease using Artificial Intelligence. *Reviews on Recent Clinical Trials*, 20(2), 124–141.
57. Yilmaz, A., Ustun, I., Ugur, Z., Akyol, S., Hu, W. T., Fiandaca, M. S., ... and Graham, S. F. (2020). A community-based study identifying metabolic biomarkers of mild cognitive impairment and Alzheimer's disease using artificial intelligence and machine learning. *Journal of Alzheimer's Disease*, 78(4), 1381–1392.
58. Davodabadi, A., Daneshian, B., Saati, S., and Razavyan, S. (2023). Mathematical model and artificial intelligence for diagnosis of Alzheimer's disease. *The European Physical Journal Plus*, 138(5), 474.
59. Sadegh-Zadeh, S. A., Nazari, M. J., Aljamaeen, M., Yazdani, F. S., Mousavi, S. Y., and Vahabi, Z. (2024). Predictive models for Alzheimer's disease diagnosis and MCI identification: The use of cognitive scores and artificial intelligence algorithms. *NPG Neurologie-Psychiatrie-Gériatrie*, 24(142), 194–211.
60. Wu, Q., Huang, C., Zhang, J., Zhang, Z., and Zhu, X. (2025). Artificial Intelligence-assisted hippocampal segmentation and its diagnostic value for Alzheimer's disease: A meta-analysis. *Academic Radiology*, 32(8), 4785–4796.
61. Pimprale, V. S., and Gadade, H. D. (2025, March). The role of Artificial Intelligence in the diagnosis of Alzheimer's Disease – A comprehensive review. In: *2025 International Conference on Machine Learning and Autonomous Systems (ICMLAS)* (pp. 720–725). IEEE.
62. Subasi, A., Kapadnis, M. N., and Bulbul, A. K. (2022). Alzheimer's disease detection using artificial intelligence. In: *Augmenting Neurological Disorder Prediction and Rehabilitation Using Artificial Intelligence* (pp. 53–74). Academic Press.
63. Mohammed, S., and Malhotra, N. (2024, December). Machine learning and artificial intelligence for enhanced Alzheimer's disease detection: A state-of-the-art review. In: *2024 4th International Conference on Ubiquitous Computing and Intelligent Information Systems (ICUIS)* (pp. 19–26). IEEE.
64. Martin, W., Sheynkman, G., Lightstone, F. C., Nussinov, R., and Cheng, F. (2022). Interpretable artificial intelligence and exascale molecular dynamics simulations to reveal kinetics: Applications to Alzheimer's disease. *Current Opinion in Structural Biology*, 72, 103–113.
65. Koksalmis, G. H., Soykan, B., Brattain, L. J., and Huang, H. H. (2025). Artificial intelligence for personalized prediction of Alzheimer's disease progression: A survey of methods, data challenges, and future directions. arXiv preprint arXiv:2504.21189.
66. Jimenez-Maggiora, G. A., Donohue, M. C., Rafii, M. S., Raman, R., and Aisen, P. S. (2025). Artificial intelligence-enabled safety monitoring in Alzheimer's disease clinical trials. *The Journal of Prevention of Alzheimer's Disease*, 12(1), 100002.
67. Abbasi, H., Afrazeh, F., Ghasemi, Y., and Ghasemi, F. (2024). A shallow review of artificial intelligence applications in brain disease: Stroke, Alzheimer's, and

Aneurysm. *International Journal of Applied Data Science in Engineering and Health*, 1(2), 32–43.

68. Al Haji, S., and Mross, E. (2024). Artificial Intelligence Application in Alzheimer's Disease. Penn State University. https://doi.org/10.26207/s1tk-w524
69. Li, R. (2024). Using artificial intelligence (AI)-based computer vision methods to investigate associations between hand movement and Alzheimer's Disease (AD) risk. Doctoral dissertation, University of Tasmania.
70. Saray, U., and Çavdar, U. (2023, December). Investigating the role of artificial intelligence in the diagnosis and treatment of Alzheimer's disease. In: *VIII International Scientific and Vocational Studies Congress* (BILMES 2023), (pp. 132–137). Turkey.
71. He, X., Zhao, L., Zhong, W., Chen, H. Y., Shan, X., Tang, N., and Chen, C. Y. C. (2020). Insight into potent leads for Alzheimer's disease by using several artificial intelligence algorithms. *Biomedicine & Pharmacotherapy*, 129, 110360.
72. Bayat, S., Roe, C. M., Schindler, S., Murphy, S. A., Doherty, J. M., Johnson, A. M., ... and Babulal, G. M. (2023). Everyday driving and plasma biomarkers in Alzheimer's disease: Leveraging artificial intelligence to expand our diagnostic toolkit. *Journal of Alzheimer's Disease*, 92(4), 1487–1497.
73. Benba, A., and Kerchaoui, A. (2023). Automatic detection of Alzheimer's disease based on artificial intelligence. *Informatyka, Automatyka, Pomiary w Gospodarce i Ochronie Środowiska*, 13(1), 18–21.
74. Ali, I., and Manda, V. K. (2025). Artificial intelligence for predicting progression and personalizing healthcare to Alzheimer's disease patients. In: *AI-Driven Personalized Healthcare Solutions* (pp. 155–190). IGI Global Scientific Publishing.
75. Sekaran, K., Alsamman, A. M., George Priya Doss, C., and Zayed, H. (2023). Bioinformatics investigation on blood-based gene expressions of Alzheimer's disease revealed ORAI2 gene biomarker susceptibility: An explainable artificial intelligence-based approach. *Metabolic Brain Disease*, 38(4), 1297–1310.
76. Dabbaghi, K. G., Khosravirad, Z., Jamalnia, S., GhorbaniNia, R., Mahmoudikohani, F., Zakeri, H., and Khastehband, S. (2023). The use of artificial intelligence in the management of neurodegenerative disorders: Focus on Alzheimer's disease. *Galen Medical Journal*, 12, 1.
77. Doering, E. (2025). *Artificial Intelligence and Positron Emission Tomography for the Timely Diagnosis and Prognosis of Alzheimer's Disease*. Doctoral dissertation, Universität zu Köln.
78. Coluzzi, D., Bordin, V., Rivolta, M. W., Fortel, I., Zhan, L., Leow, A., and Baselli, G. (2025). Biomarker investigation using multiple brain measures from MRI through explainable artificial intelligence in Alzheimer's disease classification. *Bioengineering*, 12(1), 82.
79. Favaro, A., Motley, S., Samus, Q. M., Butala, A., Dehak, N., Oh, E. S., and Moro-Velazquez, L. (2022). Artificial intelligence tools to evaluate language and speech patterns in Alzheimer's disease. *Alzheimer's & Dementia*, 18, e064913.
80. Subramanian, P. S. (2025). The transformative role of artificial intelligence in accelerating biomedical research: A focus on Alzheimer's disease. *Journal of Computer Science and Technology Studies*, 7(4), 375–379.
81. Galety, M. G., and Gupta, S. (2022). Artificial intelligence in the detection of Alzheimer's disease. In: *Bio-Inspired Algorithms and Devices for Treatment of Cognitive Diseases Using Future Technologies* (pp. 136–155). IGI Global Scientific Publishing.

82. Zulhafiz, N. A., Teoh, T. C., Chin, A. V., and Chang, S. W. (2025). Drug repurposing using artificial intelligence, molecular docking, and hybrid approaches: A comprehensive review in general diseases vs Alzheimer's disease. *Computer Methods and Programs in Biomedicine*, 108604.
83. Abdelfattah, A., Sajjad, W., Soomro, I. A., Tariq, M., Maqbool, L., and Rafique, A. A. (2025). Harnessing artificial intelligence in early detection and diagnosis of Alzheimer's disease: Current and future applications. *Indus Journal of Bioscience Research*, 3(2), 199–212.
84. Nyongesa, C. A., Hogarth, M., and Pa, J. (2025). Artificial intelligence-driven natural language processing for identifying linguistic patterns in Alzheimer's disease and mild cognitive impairment: A study of lexical, syntactic, and cohesive features of speech through picture description tasks. *Journal of Alzheimer's Disease*, 13872877251339756.
85. Annapurna, K., Marlin, S., Krishnan, V. G., and Kumar, N. P. S. (2023, May). A novel prediction of Alzheimer's disease by using artificial intelligence. In: *2023 7th International Conference on Intelligent Computing and Control Systems* (ICICCS) (pp. 530–535). IEEE.
86. Sekhar, M. G. (2024). Predicting Alzheimer's Disease Using Artificial Intelligence and Machine Learning: A Comprehensive Analysis [Preprint]. OSF Preprints.
87. Bazargani, J. S., Rahim, N., Sadeghi-Niaraki, A., Abuhmed, T., Song, H., and Choi, S. M. (2024). Alzheimer's disease diagnosis in the metaverse. *Computer Methods and Programs in Biomedicine*, 255, 108348.
88. Zhou, H., Gao, J. Y., and Chen, Y. (2022). The paradigm and future value of the metaverse for the intervention of cognitive decline. *Frontiers in Public Health*, 10, 1016680.
89. Qian, P., Yang, D., and Bai, C. (2023). Metaverse: freezing the time. *Clinical eHealth*, 6, 29–35.
90. Mitra, D. S. (2023). Generative AI and metaverse: Companionship and assisted living for elderly people. Available at SSRN 4843464.
91. Chen, M. (2023, August). Brain study to understand destructive Alzheimer disease and artificial intelligence (AI) technology in art creation. In: *2023 IEEE 6th International Conference on Knowledge Innovation and Invention* (*ICKII*) (pp. 270–272). IEEE.
92. Ford, T. J., Buchanan, D. M., Azeez, A., Benrimoh, D. A., Kaloiani, I., Bandeira, I. D., ... and Williams, N. R. (2023). Taking modern psychiatry into the metaverse: Integrating augmented, virtual, and mixed reality technologies into psychiatric care. *Frontiers in Digital Health*, 5, 1146806.
93. Usman, M., Rehman, A., Shahid, A., Rehman, A. U., Gho, S. M., and Lee, A. (2024). Advancing metaverse-based healthcare with multimodal neuroimaging fusion via multi-task adversarial variational autoencoder for brain age estimation. *IEEE Journal of Biomedical and Health Informatics*. Advance online publication.
94. Lee, A. G. (2024). AI-and XR-powered digital therapeutics (DTx) innovations. In: *Digital Frontiers-Healthcare, Education, and Society in the Metaverse Era.* IntechOpen.
95. Singh, B., Tatiya, M., Shrivastava, A., Verma, D., Srivastava, A. P., and Rana, A. (2022, October). Detection of Alzheimer's disease using deep learning, blockchain, and IoT cognitive data. In: *2022 2nd International Conference on Technological Advancements in Computational Sciences* (*ICTACS*) (pp. 863–869). IEEE.

96. Mandawkar, U., and Diwan, T. (2024). Ensemble activation enabled deep classifier for Alzheimer's disease detection in the blockchain-enabled distributed edge environment. *International Journal of Information Technology*, 1–18.
97. Sanjay, V., and Swarnalatha, P. (2023). Blockchain-based deep learning approach for Alzheimer's disease classification. In: *Handbook of Research on Deep Learning Techniques for Cloud-Based Industrial IoT* (pp. 92–105). IGI Global.
98. Silva, J. R. (2021). Artificial intelligence system for the automatic detection of Alzheimer's Disease using Magnetic Resonance Imaging (MRI). Master's thesis, Universidade Catolica Portuguesa (Portugal).
99. Sood, M., Harms, R., Bügler, M., Tarnanas, I., Coello, N., and Fröhlich, H. (2021). Evaluating digital device technology in Alzheimer's disease via artificial intelligence. *Alzheimer's & Dementia*, 17, e053574.
100. Comito, C., Pizzuti, C., and Sammarra, M. (2023, November). Overview of artificial intelligence methods for Alzheimer's disease prediction and progression. In: *2023 17th International Conference on Signal-Image Technology & Internet-Based Systems* (*SITIS*) (pp. 22–29). IEEE.
101. Gambhir, A., Bansal, A., Rawat, S., and Sah, A. (2024). Artificial intelligence and machine learning models for Alzheimer's disease. In: *Using Traditional Design Methods to Enhance AI-Driven Decision Making* (pp. 102–117). IGI Global Scientific Publishing.
102. Panwar, D., Sharma, P., Sharma, S., Goyal, M., and Goyal, K. (2024). Role of artificial intelligence in cognitive assessment and early detection of Alzheimer's disease. In: *AI-driven Alzheimer's Disease Detection and Prediction* (pp. 190–210). IGI Global.
103. Ziyad, S. R., Alharbi, M., and Altulyan, M. (2023). Artificial intelligence model for Alzheimer's disease detection with convolution neural network for magnetic resonance images. *Journal of Alzheimer's Disease*, 93(1), 235–245.
104. Ismail, Y., and Voleti, V. K. (2024). A review on usage of artificial intelligence for early detection and management of Alzheimer's disease. *Journal of Pharma Insights and Research*, 2(5), 007–013.
105. Das, T., Nayak, C. K., and Pattnayak, P. (2024, March). Alzheimer's disease diagnosis using artificial intelligence and MRI images of the brain. In: *2024 3rd International Conference for Innovation in Technology* (*INOCON*) (pp. 1–6). IEEE.
106. Alarjani, M. (2023, September). Detect Alzheimer's disease from neuroimaging using artificial intelligence techniques. In: *2023 3rd International Conference on Computing and Information Technology* (*ICCIT*) (pp. 192–200). IEEE.
107. Arulprakash, A., Ponmaniraj, S., and Divya, A. (2023, December). Application of artificial intelligence technique to detect Alzheimer's disease. In: *2023 Intelligent Computing and Control for Engineering and Business Systems* (*ICCEBS*) (pp. 1–5). IEEE.
108. Rathod, P. (2024). A study on artificial intelligence and its role in redefining Alzheimer's disease diagnostics. *Vidhyayana – An International Multidisciplinary Peer-Reviewed E-Journal*, ISSN 2454-8596, 10(si1), 627–636.
109. Ai, R., Xiao, X., Deng, S., Yang, N., Xing, X., Watne, L. O., ... and Fang, E. F. (2025). Artificial intelligence in drug development for delirium and Alzheimer's disease. *Acta Pharmaceutica Sinica B*. 15(9), 4386–4410.
110. Ganasegeran, K., Ch'ng, A. S. H., and Looi, I. (2021). Artificial intelligence for risk prediction of Alzheimer's disease: A new promise for community health screening

in the older aged. In: *Handbook of Decision Support Systems for Neurological Disorders* (pp. 71–88). Academic Press.

111. Kapadnis, M. N., Bhattacharyya, A., and Subasi, A. (2023). Artificial intelligence based Alzheimer's disease detection using deep feature extraction. In: *Applications of Artificial Intelligence in Medical Imaging* (pp. 333–355). Academic Press.
112. Seriramulu, V. P., Suppiah, S., Lee, H. H., Jang, J. H., Omar, N. F., Mohan, S. N., ... and Ahmad, U. (2024). Review of MR spectroscopy analysis and artificial intelligence applications for the detection of cerebral inflammation and neurotoxicity in Alzheimer's disease. *The Medical Journal of Malaysia*, 79(1), 102–110.
113. Jassar, N. A., and Fraiwan, L. (2024, November). Automated identification of Alzheimer's disease stages based on magnetic resonance imaging scans using artificial intelligence techniques. In: *2024 Second Jordanian International Biomedical Engineering Conference* (*JIBEC*) (pp. 113–118). IEEE.
114. Sang, Z. P., Xue, T., Xing, Q. R., Zhang, Q. Y., Chen, H. S., Wang, X., ... and Luo, H. B. (2025). Discovery of α-mangostin derivatives as novel PDE4 inhibitors for the treatment of Alzheimer's disease: An artificial intelligence-driven synergized strategy. *Chinese Chemical Letters*, 111318.
115. Xu, X., and Yan, X. (2022, August). A convenient and reliable multi-class classification model based on explainable artificial intelligence for Alzheimer's disease. In: *2022 IEEE International Conference on Advances in Electrical Engineering and Computer Applications* (*AEECA*) (pp. 671–675). IEEE.
116. Emon, M. A. E. K. (2021). Mechanism-based Stratification of Alzheimer's and Parkinson's Disease using Artificial Intelligence. Doctoral dissertation, Bonn, Rheinische Friedrich-Wilhelms-Universität, 2021.
117. Gupta, R., and Iftekhar, Z. (2024). Artificial intelligence for Alzheimer's disease detection: Enhancing biomarker analysis and diagnostic precision. *Chemistry Proceedings*, 16(1), 25.
118. Logan, R., Zerbey, S. S., and Miller, S. J. (2021). The future of artificial intelligence for Alzheimer's disease diagnostics. *Advances in Alzheimer's Disease*, 10(4), 53–59.
119. Wiltfang, J., Esselmann, H., and Barnikol, U. B. (2021). The use of artificial intelligence in Alzheimer's disease-personalized diagnostics and therapy. *Psychiatrische Praxis*, 48(S 01), S31–S36.
120. Nisha, A. V., Rajasekaran, M. P., Rajeev, S. K., Wilson, A., Sunil, S., and Soorya, M. (2024, October). Advancements in artificial intelligence-based Alzheimer's disease classification using magnetic resonance imaging: A comprehensive review. In: *2024 4th International Conference on Sustainable Expert Systems* (*ICSES*) (pp. 742–749). IEEE.
121. Varghese, A., George, B., Sherimon, V., and Al Shuaily, H. S. (2023). Enhancing trust in Alzheimer's disease classification using explainable artificial intelligence: Incorporating local post hoc explanations for a glass-box model. *Bahrain Medical Bulletin*, 45(2).
122. Ali, H., Imtiaz, H., Rehman, A. U., Javaid, S., Ali, T. M., Alshammeri, M., ... & Kumar, H. (2024, July). An applied artificial intelligence technique for early-stage Alzheimer's disease prediction. In: *2024 International Conference on Emerging Trends in Networks and Computer Communications* (*ETNCC*) (pp. 1–8). IEEE.
123. Alagumuthukrishnan, S., Sanuvala, G., Ebinezer, M. J. D., and Vidhya, B. V. (2024). Exploring angiogenesis and artificial intelligence in Alzheimer's disease: Implications for early detection and therapeutic strategies. *Journal of Angiotherapy*, 8(8), 1–10.

124. Abid, M., Asif, M., Khemane, Z., Jawaid, A., Khan, A. W., Naveed, H., ... and Siddiq, M. A. (2024). Advances in artificial intelligence for diagnosing Alzheimer's disease through speech. *Annals of Medicine and Surgery*, 86(7), 3822–3823.
125. Hachamnia, A. H., Mehri, A., and Jamaati, M. (2025). Integrating neuroscience and artificial intelligence: EEG analysis using ensemble learning for diagnosis Alzheimer's disease and frontotemporal dementia. *Journal of Neuroscience Methods*, 110377.
126. Dino, F. R., Pressman, P. S., Cohen, K. B., Dubljevic, V., Jarrold, W., Foltz, P. W., ... and Hunter, L. E. (2025). Ethics in digital phenotyping: Considerations regarding Alzheimer's disease, speech and artificial intelligence. *Journal of Medical Ethics*. Advance online publication. https://doi.org/10.1136/jme-2024-110252
127. Alzoubi, R., Turky, A., Hussain, A., and Foufou, S. (2024, December). Interpretable deep learning for Alzheimer's disease through genetic data and explainable artificial intelligence. In: *2024 IEEE/ACM International Conference on Big Data Computing, Applications and Technologies* (*BDCAT*) (pp. 50–59). IEEE.
128. Kim, H. W., Rieu, Z., Kim, D., and Lim, H. K. (2023). Clinical utilization of brain magnetic resonance imaging-based artificial intelligence software in the spectrum of Alzheimer's disease: Case series. *Journal of Korean Neuropsychiatric Association*, 62(2), 86–94.
129. Arabaci, B., Öcal, H., and Polat, K. (2024, May). Detection of Alzheimer's disease from EEG signals using explainable artificial intelligence analysis. In: *2024 32nd Signal Processing and Communications Applications Conference* (*SIU*) (pp. 1–4). IEEE.
130. Mehdar, K. M., Elshafie, S. E. M., Shediwah, A. M., Sayed, H. K. A., Omar, I., Suliman, M., ... and Alshammari, K. (2024). Unveiling the synergy between artificial intelligence and histopathology for advancing Alzheimer's disease diagnosis. *Azerbaijan Pharmaceutical and Pharmacotherapy Journal*, 23, 1–5.
131. Shayegan, M. A., and Moloudi, Z. (2021). Diagnosis of Alzheimer's disease by MRI images using artificial intelligence. *Journal of Gorgan University of Medical Sciences*, 23(1), 135–147.
132. Viswan, V., Hajamohideen, F., Subramanian, K., Shaffi, N., and Mahmud, M. (2025). Enhancing insights: Unravelling the potential of preprocessing MRI for artificial intelligence based Alzheimer's disease classification. *Machine Learning Models and Architectures for Biomedical Signal Processing*, 125–151.
133. Mangi, P. J., and Rajyaguru, J. D. (2023). Artificial intelligence applications in early diagnosis of Alzheimer's disease. *International Journal of Scientific Research in Engineering and Management*, 7(12), 1–5.
134. Zaranek, S. W., Zaranek, A. W., Amstutz, P., Bao, J., Chen, J., ... and Alzheimer's Disease Neuroimaging Initiative (as a consortium author) for the AI4AD Initiative. (2024). Discovering genetic signatures associated with Alzheimer's disease in tiled whole genome sequence data: Results from the Artificial Intelligence for Alzheimer's Disease (AI4AD) Consortium. *medRxiv*, 2024–08.
135. Noviandy, T. R., Idroes, G. M., Purnawarman, A., Imran, I., Lestari, N. D., Hastuti, S., and Idroes, R. (2024). Enhancing early detection of Alzheimer's disease through MRI using explainable artificial intelligence. *Indonesian Journal of Case Reports*, 2(2), 43–51.
136. Raghupathy, B. K., Reddy, M. R., Theeda, P., Balasubramanian, E., Namachivayam, R. K., and Ganesan, M. (2025). Harnessing Explainable Artificial Intelligence

(XAI) based SHAPLEY values and ensemble techniques for accurate Alzheimer's disease diagnosis. *Engineering, Technology & Applied Science Research*, 15(2), 20743–20747.

137. Hasan, M. M., Rahman, S., Parmar, H., and Chowdhury, S. K. (n.d.). A novel Artificial Intelligence (AI) ensembled method to identify Alzheimer's disease progression [Unpublished manuscript]. Texas Tech University.
138. Sanjaykumar, G. S., Malviya, R., and Uniyal, P. (2025). Digital twins (Artificial Intelligence and Machine Learning) for diagnosis of Alzheimer's disease: Ethical and regulatory aspects. *Recent Advances in Computer Science and Communications*, 18(4), E180624231083.
139. Naveen, N., and Cholli, N. G. (2024). Artificial intelligence for automatic detection of Alzheimer's disease: Resolving domain shift problems to create reliable models. Authorea Preprints.
140. Wei, M., Li, Y., Liang, M., Xi, M., and Tian, H. Artificial intelligence approaches for early detection and diagnosis of Alzheimer's disease: A review. *Acad J Sci Technol.*, 5(3), 21–215.
141. Chahal, A., Almir, K., Diab, A., Zakaria, F., and Hamawy, L. (2024, November). Early detection of Alzheimer's disease using artificial intelligence based on CSF biomarkers & MRI images. In: *2024 International Conference on Smart Systems and Power Management* (*IC2SPM*) (pp. 6–11). IEEE.
142. Nawaz, A., and Ahmad, A. (2023, September). Explainable artificial intelligence in medical diagnostics: Insights into Alzheimer's disease. In: *Joint European Conference on Machine Learning and Knowledge Discovery in Databases* (pp. 312–319). Cham: Springer Nature Switzerland.
143. Das, S., Monani, U. J., and Jena, B. Leveraging artificial intelligence-based deep learning for early diagnosis of Alzheimer's disease: A comparative analysis of neural network approaches. In: *Machine Learning for Neurodegenerative Disorders* (pp. 138–150). CRC Press.
144. Tang, Z. Q., Zhao, L., Chen, G. X., and Chen, C. Y. C. (2021). Novel and versatile artificial intelligence algorithms for investigating possible GHSR1α and DRD1 agonists for Alzheimer's disease. *RSC Advances*, 11(12), 6423–6446.
145. Kumaran, G., Narayanan, S., Murugan, S., and Krishnamurthy, M. (2025). A brief review on Alzheimer's disease and utilization of artificial intelligence techniques as an aid to early diagnosis. *World Journal of Pharmaceutical Research*, 14(2), 316–329.
146. Malar, R. J., Devanandam, K., Kumar, C. H., and Afaneh, S. (2024, December). DNCP: A robust artificial intelligence based Alzheimer's disease detection methodology by using deep neural classification principle. In: *2024 International Conference on Innovative Computing, Intelligent Communication and Smart Electrical Systems* (*ICSES*) (pp. 1–6). IEEE.
147. Wang, H., and Wang, G. (2021). Application of artificial intelligence in the prevention, diagnosis and treatment of Alzheimer's disease: New hope for dealing with aging in China. In: *Computer Methods in Medicine and Health Care* (pp. 103–108). IOS Press.
148. Bóbeda, J., Etxebarria-Elezgarai, J., Perez-Herrera, L. V., García-González, M. J., Alonso, E., García-Sebastián, M., ... and López-Linares, K. (2024, June). Alzheimer's disease classification by artificial intelligence using microscopy images of dried human body fluids. In: *International KES Conference on Innovation in Medicine and Healthcare* (pp. 57–66). Singapore: Springer Nature Singapore.

149. Kaliappan, S., Ali, H. M., Maranan, R., and Sunil, G. (2024, January). Mining healthcare data for predictive modeling and prognosis of Alzheimer's disease progression with artificial intelligence. In: *2024 International Conference on Advancements in Smart, Secure and Intelligent Computing* (*ASSIC*) (pp. 1–7). IEEE.
150. Nguyen, N., Gomar, J. J., Truong, J. N., Barbero, J., Do, P. P., Rommal, A., ... & Vo, A. (2025). An artificial intelligence-derived metabolic network predicts psychosis in Alzheimer's disease. *Brain Communications*, 7(3), fcaf159.
151. Al-Nuaimi, A. H., Nsaif, M. K., and Al-Juboori, S. (2025). Developing an artificial intelligence framework for identifying fusion blood-based biomarkers in Alzheimer's disease. *Journal of Information Systems Engineering and Management*, 10(36), 443–458.
152. Iizuka, T., Kameyama, Y. U., Fukasawa, M., Akishita, M., and Kameyama, M. (2023). Impaired ability to smile in Alzheimer's disease is associated with reduced brain volume of nucleus accumbens and pallidum, revealed by artificial intelligence. *Alzheimer's & Dementia*, 19, e082571.
153. Iman, R., and Mobinizadeh, M. (2023). Investigation of Artificial intelligence in Alzheimer's disease. *Health Technology Assessment in Action*, 7(4). https://doi.org/10.18502/htaa.v7i4.14555
154. LI, S., and Zhang, X. (2022). The application of clinical decision support system based on medical artificial intelligence in Alzheimer's disease. *Chinese Journal of Geriatrics*, 115–119.
155. Jamshidi, M., Dehghaniyan Serej, A., Jamshidi, A., and Moztarzadeh, O. (2023). The meta-metaverse: Ideation and future directions. *Future Internet*, 15(8), 252.
156. Hemmings-Jarrett, K., Plowright, K., and Jarrett, J. (2025). Metaverse leisure experiences: Implications for seniors in developing countries – A case study. *World Leisure Journal*, 1–23.
157. Sorino, P. (2022, July). Blockchain and AI to build an Alzheimer's risk calculator. In: *International Conference on Web Engineering* (pp. 432–436). Cham: Springer International Publishing.
158. Behfar, S. K., Behfar, Q., and Hosseinpour, M. (2023). Architecture of data anomaly detection-enhanced decentralized expert system for early-stage Alzheimer's disease prediction. arXiv preprint arXiv:2311.00373.

CHAPTER
14

Limitations and Challenges of AI and Metaverse in Healthcare Applications

Shaik Khaja Mohiddin[1*], Shaik Sharmila[2], Venkatagurunatham Naidu Kollu[3], Royyuru Srikanth[4] and Mohammad Khamruddin[5]

[1] Department of CSE, Siddhartha Academy of Higher Education, Deemed to be University, Vijayawada, Andhra Pradesh – 520007, India

[2] Department of IT, Vignan's Nirula Institute of Technology and Science for Women, Peda Palakalur, Guntur, Andhra Pradesh – 522009, India

[3] Department CSE, Koneru Lakshmaiah Education Foundation, Vaddeswaram, Andhra Pradesh – 522302, India

[4] Department of Computer Science & Engineering, Vardhaman College of Engineering, Hyderabad, Telangana – 501218, India

[5] Department of Computer Science, College of Computer Science and Information Technology, Jazan University, Jazan, Saudi Arabia

Intelligent health, combined with the Metaverse, created a new avenue of personalized medicine, virtual care, real-life rehabilitation, and smart diagnostics. Although the technologies present unprecedented potential to revolutionize the way healthcare is delivered, there exist weaknesses and challenges in relation to deploying these technologies. At the chapter level, we can analytically address the technological, ethical, legal, infrastructural, and socio-cultural risks and challenges that obstruct the successful implementation of AI and Metaverse use in medical environments. The basic problems include data privacy, security, interoperability, biased data caused by algorithms, the need for substantial capital, decreased digital literacy in a regulated world, and concerns about the legal and regulatory framework. This chapter also considers patient-centric and provider-centric concerns, including a lack of trust and disruption of the working process and equity in accessibility. Keeping case studies in mind and considering

*Corresponding author: mail2mohiddin@gmail.com

DOI: 10.1201/9781003679370-14

a real-world example of where this technology is working or failing in public works proposals, it is a great way to move forward in the future. The chapter ends by suggesting such strategic responses to these challenges, a redesign of governance, development of skills training, ethically oriented cross-disciplinary cooperation, and the use of AI. The purpose of this chapter is therefore the recommendation of a model to be adhered to by researchers, technologists, and policymakers in pursuit of the creation of health systems that promote lives and communities.

1. Introduction

1.1 Overview of AI in Healthcare

The mechanism that empowers machines to acquire, reason, and self-correct, reproducing human cognition, is AI and ML. AI incorporated systems that dictate the roost nowadays on domains such as medical imaging, disease prediction, and drug discovery, and personalized treatment recommendations are just a few common applications of AI in the contemporary world. One example of this is that deep learning algorithms have been capable of identifying radiographs and MRIs more accurately than humans, leading to fewer diagnostic errors and providing background to medical practitioners when making clinical judgments. Another application that AI is well known for is improving operational efficiency by automating repetitive clerical work and optimizing resources in hospitals [1]. Nevertheless, the quality of data to bin the models, the fight for models' transparency, and regulatory approval prevent the growth of AI in clinical applications.

1.2 Role of Metaverse in Healthcare

The Metaverse offers an alternative to traditional closed rooms, allowing its use in healthcare experiences, diagnosis, and treatment within virtual environments like never before, as well as in rehabilitation and medical education. Applications ranging from surgery simulations, mental health therapy, to training budding medical professionals in real and near-zero risk environments are examples where Virtual Reality (VR) and Augmented Reality (AR) technologies are being leveraged. Digital health innovations are enhancing accessibility and patient involvement, particularly in remote or underserved areas [2]. Nevertheless, the application of Metaverse systems within the healthcare sector remains in its early stages, hindered by challenges such as high costs, the need for clinical approval, and user adoption.

AI Metaverse Deployment Timeline in Healthcare: Data collection in healthcare, model development, and subsequent integration into healthcare systems and deployment in virtual environments, ending with patient-provider interaction. All points of critical risk, namely privacy, bias, interoperability

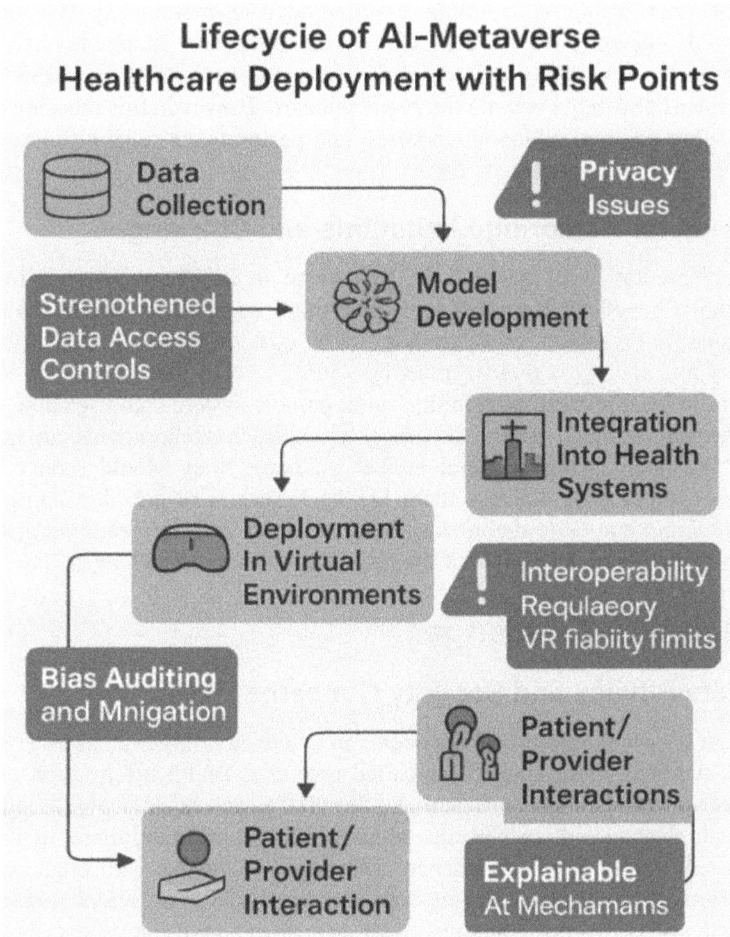

Figure 1: Lifecycle of AI-metaverse healthcare deployment with risk points.

challenges, regulatory uncertainty, and VR fidelity limits, are highlighted by red alerts. Data access controls, fairness auditing, standardized protocols, and explainable AI mechanisms are also on the list of corresponding mitigation strategies (in green). It emphasizes the importance of risk management in all phases of deployment to ensure the safe, ethical, and effective adoption of AI Metaverse healthcare technologies daily.

1.3 Convergence of AI and Metaverse Technologies

Metaverses driven by AI are the first step to intelligent, interactive, and personalized digital healthcare experiences. This can be achieved by predicting behavior insights and forecasting a person's natural language interactions and

VR experiences using AI, enabling real-time decision-making [3]. The solutions are virtual hospitals, AI-powered diagnostic tools, and adaptable therapeutic areas provided by these technologies. They can support overworked health professionals and help expand remote patient care. However, this crossing causes data synchronization, ethical boundaries, and performance reliability issues that should be properly addressed.

1.4 Need for Exploring Limitations and Challenges

The implementation of AI and the Metaverse in healthcare is sure to bring forth many beneficial consequences, but there are also a lot of limitations and concerns presented by technology. The cost of building an AI-powered economy and society is that we must be willing to set aside issues like privacy, algorithmic bias, legal responsibility, interoperable systems, and scalable digital infrastructure, among others. In cases where such technologies are applied without adequate protection and ethical guidance, they would reduce health disparities rather than increase them [4]. Therefore, a responsible approach to innovation and equitable digitalization in healthcare reform should be promoted through widespread debate about the technical risks and challenges.

2. Technical Challenges

2.1 Data Privacy and Security Concerns

To design legally competitive AI systems in healthcare, larger datasets of patient records, medical, and personal (so-called protected health information or PHI) will be required. In most jurisdictions, the GDPR and HIPAA regulations may differ; data sharing and cross-border operations might make it difficult to maintain a consistent approach to compliance. The origin of attacks with other patients, in the form of adversarial threats, can sometimes lead to patient records and clinical decision-making outcomes being lost or distorted due to data breaches, especially when trust and safety are compromised. Differential privacy, federated learning, and encryption techniques offer certain mitigation measures; however, these do not realistically cover the range of risks in the practice because of the complexity of implementation, infrastructure disparities, and constraints [5]. Good risk management requires good governance and standard procedures along with ongoing audit facilitation.

2.2 Interoperability and Integration Issues

Based on data from various healthcare systems, successfully implementing AI tools can be complex due to differing standards for data collection, isolated EHR systems, and varying protocols even within the same region. Integration of technical standards, organizational policy, and workflow frameworks is the concept of health data interoperability [6]. AI modules are not connected with all points of the patient records, which demonstrates a lack of full and accurate information and a disjointed vision of the clinical uses. That is why, nowadays, research is focused on the creation of integrated but interoperable digital ecosystems by harmonizing the metadata schema and clinical terminologies. Legacy systems, governance fragmentation, and non-standardization, however, are pulling growth at a snail's pace.

2.3 Computational Complexity and Infrastructure Demands

Neural network scaling can then be added in the form of frameworks, which can keep a server bogged down, or it can spend hours running on a desktop. Models often developed by the developer are executed in GPUs or edge server cloud clusters and use interconnected servers to perform this type of networking to work with high-resolution images that require real-time analysis, and on which model retries are plentiful. Hospitals are not usually in a position to carry redundancy as their IT is highly susceptible, and they have low-latency networks and hybrid edge-cloud solutions installed. Ineffective resource allocation can lead to system failure or performance decline, along with a lack of good observability and strong governance.

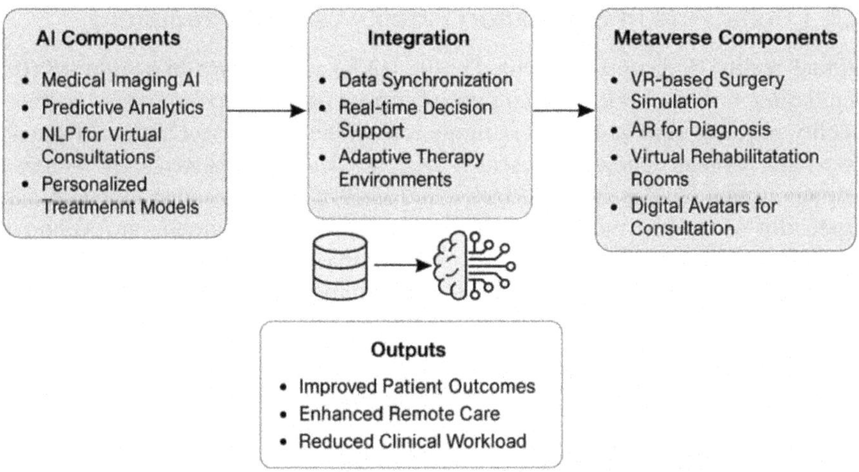

Figure 2: Integration of AI and the metaverse in healthcare.

The example of AI-specific workflows also complicates infrastructure planning because such processes are typically dynamically scaled and have inconsistent inference requirements, both of which are not optimized by standard IT.

The above illustration depicts the integration of Artificial Intelligence and the Metaverse technologies to introduce a contemporary solution to healthcare. AI-powered medical image analysis, predictive analytics, NLP-driven virtual consultations, AR-assisted diagnosis, virtual rehabilitation rooms, digital avatars for engaging with VR-based surgery simulations, and VR digital avatars for surgery engagement. Data integration layer enables real-time decision support and data synchronization, leading to better patient outcomes and reduced clinical workload. The presented solutions prove that a convergence between AI and immersive technologies has the potential to be used and help improve efficiency, accessibility, and personal care delivery in healthcare.

2.4 Model Interpretability and Explainability in Clinical Settings

In high-stakes clinical domains like emergency or critical care, AI often produces outputs that are opaque ("black-box"), creating trust and accountability gaps among clinicians. Sabotage or unexplained predictive errors can lead to diagnostic mistakes. Explainable AI (XAI) methods such as visual attribution maps, feature relevance ranking, and post-hoc model simplification help clinicians understand model behaviour [7]. Yet, many XAI techniques lack standardization, and balancing interpretability with model performance remains challenging. Regulatory bodies increasingly demand transparency, but existing explainability frameworks are still evolving.

2.5 Limitations in Simulation Fidelity (VR/AR Precision)

Virtual reality (VR) and augmented reality (AR) applications in healthcare (for simulation, training, or therapy) often suffer from fidelity gaps compared to high-fidelity physical simulators. These limitations include imperfect haptic feedback, graphical realism deficiencies, sensor inaccuracies, or restricted user interface responsiveness [8]. Users might lack some realism with procedural simulations, especially where fine motor skills or tactile sensitivity are important. Although VR allows creating a training environment that is scalable and safe, lower visuomotor performance gains and worsened muscle memory retention in real-world circumstances are observed as challenges.

3. Ethical and Legal Limitations

3.1 Consent and Transparency Issues

It is difficult to imagine healthcare with meaningful informed consent being provided in the case of AI-enabled and Metaverse-accessed healthcare that functions. The concept of a one-time consent form in its traditional form is hardly adequate when it comes to data that can be repurposed, exchanged, or even processed in the domain of AI models, the latest generation trained in the virtual domain. In the case of long-playing virtual worlds, one may be inclined to argue that a patient can know only so much when it comes to letting the research community know that he or she is using data or digital behavior [9]. Making it more organized and informing the user about how long certain data will be stored enables Smart Lock to infer a division in consent in this case as well. To some extent, we can also observe that dynamic consent models, which allow the two-way flow to persist, are becoming more common. The medical facilities and technologies that lack obvious, easily approved by patients consent processes run the danger of slowly undermining consumer confidence and can violate long-standing ethical or legal standards.

3.2 Bias and Fairness in AI Algorithms

Algorithmic bias threatens fair healthcare delivery when AI systems trained on skewed or unrepresentative datasets yield discriminatory outputs, especially along racial, gender, and socioeconomic lines. The literature demonstrates that AI models frequently perpetuate biases present in historical data, resulting in differential diagnosis, resource distribution, or care recommendations [10]. This gap can only be closed by proactively auditing training data, enforcing fairness-aware algorithmic approaches, or embedding ethical frameworks such as consensus guidelines on fairness, accountability, and traceability (Fair), from the FUTURE-AI. These guidelines highlight the importance of continual fairness assessment throughout the AI lifecycle.

3.3 Regulatory Uncertainty in Metaverse-Based Treatments

The use of Metaverse virtual and immersive healthcare solutions would put a portion of practitioners into a legal gray zone. There are several inquiries about the extent to which traditional medical device laws, privacy frameworks, such as HIPAA or GDPR, and reimbursement policies for telehealth will be applied in lasting virtual environments [11]. E.g., can a VR therapy session with standard digital health codes be billed? For harm caused by a digital avatar, where does the fault lie? Numerous regulatory bodies worldwide (EU, South Korea, Japan) are looking at potential frameworks to regulate some use cases of the metaverse; however, little is clear at this point. This uncertainty is heightened by gapped expectations for providers and technologists seeking to deliver care in virtual spaces.

3.4 Accountability and Legal Liability in Virtual Care

When AI systems or Metaverse platforms contribute to clinical decisions or care delivery, assigning accountability becomes complex. Traditional legal frameworks largely assume a singular human clinician is responsible. In contrast, today's AI-supported workflows may involve algorithmic recommendations, automated avatars, and virtual agents [12]. In cases of error or harm, it's unclear whether legal liability lies with the clinician, healthcare institution, AI vendor, or the platform operator. Several reviews confirm that current regulation remains fragmented, as no unified legal framework currently governs AI-infused diagnostics or virtual care supply chains.

Figure 3 presents a layered view of how technology components such as AI Models, VR/AR Platforms, and Interoperability Frameworks interact with diverse challenge categories, including technical, ethical/legal, data-related, patient-centric, provider-centric, financial/infrastructure issues, and R&D gaps. These challenges collectively impact healthcare through accessibility gaps, trust issues, scalability limitations, and equity concerns. The visual emphasizes the interconnected nature of these barriers and the need for multi-faceted solutions to ensure responsible AI–Metaverse adoption in healthcare.

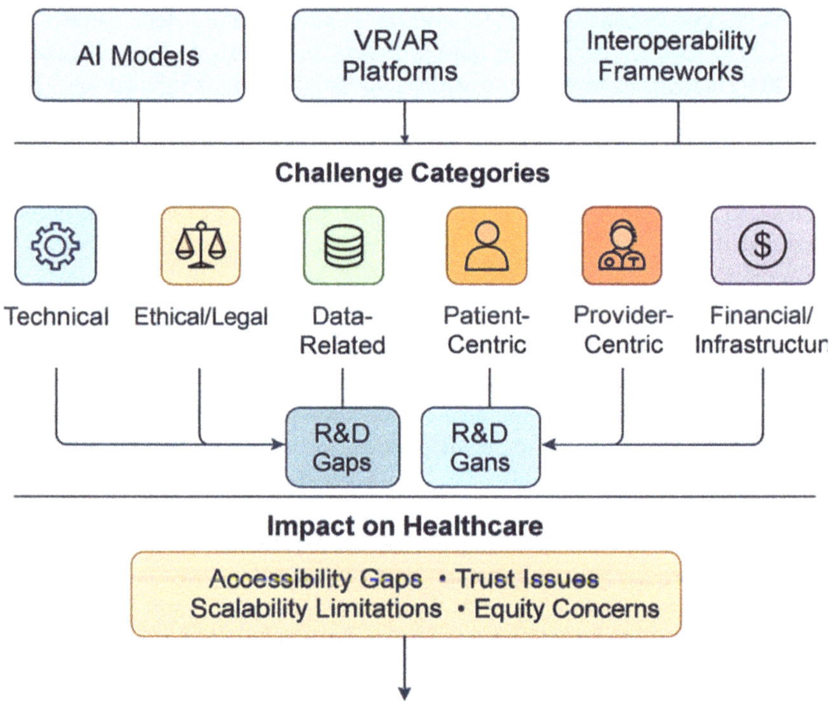

Figure 3: Holistic view of AI-Metaverse integration challenges in healthcare.

4. Data-Related Limitations

4.1 Incomplete or Poor-Quality Medical Data

Information from the unstructured electronic health records (EHRs), which are incomplete, lack values, and have varying formats and unstructured data, is fed to healthcare AI systems and stored in databases to influence model performance quite significantly. Predictive models trained on incomplete EHR data (which are not evidence-based but coded based on evidence) tend to generalize better to underserved groups and can, in fact, widen health disparities; however, they are less effective [13]. Another way this can cause issues is that if the information is incorrect or distorted, then once again, intelligent AI won't be able to help because of the all too familiar garbage-in, garbage-out problem. This is why the weakening process of gathering data, its cleaning, and the systematic validation is expected to be provided before AI is integrated into the everyday clinical procedure.

4.2 Real-Time Data Handling in Virtual Environments

This is a vital skill for documenting, manipulating, and responding to real-time physiological and behavioral data that are important in metaverse and virtual care settings. Latency, sensor noise, and communication bandwidth constraints tend to upset or delay the information streams. Any faults in real-time tracking, such as the head movements, heart rate, or eye-gaze position, will diminish therapeutic fidelity and patient engagement. High-quality network reliability and real-time error correction are necessary to ensure precise system-level synchronization of AI models for proper functionality in an immersive environment.

4.3 Annotation, Labelling, and Standardization Challenges

One of the major challenges for medical AI is the quality of labeled datasets. Annotation requires experts in the field, and as a result, ground truth labels can be noisy due to disagreements among raters or poor labeling practices. No uniform labelling protocols and schema harmonization to build on results in a non-uniform training of AI models, particularly among institutions [14]. Such a problem is more serious in a subject like medical imaging, where annotations are expensive and subjective. Compared to previous paradigms like the METRIC paradigm, which has 15 data quality dimensions covering completeness, consistency, timeliness, and appropriate labeling, it follows a common standard that guides the preparation and validation of datasets.

4.4 Ownership and Control of Health Data in the Metaverse

This is especially true in healthcare, where we are adopting immersive technologies like the Metaverse, with data ownership quickly becoming a complex issue. Who owns the patient and provider data created as a result of transactions and interactions in this virtual world: The Patient, Provider, or Platform/Developer? The EHR models of the past presuppose ownership that is transferred to the institution; however, in a continued virtual environment, the power to take a control may be divided and disseminated among numerous actors. The Collaborative Healthcare Data Ownership (CHDO) approaches imply common governance, role-based access to data, and a blockchain that allows transparency. Such models attempt to reconcile patient agency, provider responsibilities, and ethical maturation of AI in immersive and decentralized eco-systems of healthcare provision [15].

5. Patient-Centric Challenges

5.1 Accessibility and Digital Literacy Barriers

The applicability of AI-driven or Metaverse-enabled healthcare would otherwise be lost in the absence of quality internet, easy-to-use interfaces, and desired digital skills. The chief obstacles to virtual care and teleconsultations are: access hurdles in rural, senior, or low-income homes and among the digitally excluded. Provision of services: If available, limited literacy or experience with the devices also curtails their use effectively [16]. To overcome these barriers, there is a need for an inclusive design approach, user-friendly interfaces, provision of devices or support to manage connectivity challenges, and a digital literacy curriculum. Policymakers and designers of digital health innovations must mitigate these risks to avoid further exacerbating existing health inequities.

5.2 Trust in AI-Driven and Virtual Consultations

Patients' trust in AI-mediated or virtual health interactions hinges on transparency, reliability, and perceived human oversight. Lack of confidence in system accuracy, fears about data misuse, and unfamiliarity with avatar-led consultations can undermine acceptance. According to research on trust and medical AI, users are more likely to embrace these systems when developers ensure explainability, certifications, and clinician-verified decisions [17]. Establishing standardized communication about AI limitations, efficacy, and oversight is essential to building and maintaining trust in virtual care settings.

5.3 Discomfort and Side Effects from VR/AR Experiences

Immersive interventions using VR/AR can cause adverse effects for some users, such as motion sickness (cybersickness), eye strain, dizziness, or disorientation. These physical and cognitive side effects may be more intense in older individuals or those with vestibular or visual sensitivity. Extended VR sessions may also trigger nausea or fatigue, limiting usability [18]. Ensuring patient safety requires careful environment calibration, session time limits, accessibility options, and personalized comfort settings to minimize discomfort and optimize therapeutic outcomes.

5.4 Socioeconomic Disparities in Access to Metaverse Healthcare

In many ways, socioeconomic status (SES) is a key determinant of patients' access to state-of-the-art healthcare technologies. Limited access to essential devices like smartphones, smart wearables, broadband internet, and health tech literacy among lower-income, minority, or marginalized groups has created a digital divide. This gap restricts their participation in wearable-based monitoring or immersive Metaverse care. In the absence of intentional policies for access and community support, Metaverse healthcare innovations could actually serve to exacerbate rather than ameliorate extant inequities, thereby potentially undermining their intended inclusive impact [19].

6. Healthcare Provider Challenges

6.1 Resistance to Technology Adoption

The field of AI and XR offers improved detection performance, sensitivity, specificity, or predictive power compared to current standard methods, but healthcare professionals often hesitate to adopt these new tools, fearing they will disrupt their established workflows, increase perceived workload, or diminish their professional autonomy. Sociometrical resistance was frequently rooted in the lack of compatibility with the current processes, and a concern about the degradation of the clinician-patient relations in the case of AI support. The latter will require handling the issue of context, as well as the inclusion of clinical-studies implementation in the initial stages of the design and deployment process [20].

6.2 Training and Skill Gaps for AI and XR Tools

Most clinicians lack the necessary digital and domain-specific training to be proficient in AI-enhanced decision tools or immersive XR environments. A scoping review of key healthcare professional competencies revealed significant gaps in AI-related fundamentals and ethical reasoning, practice, and the importance of formal professional development courses [22]. Without specific training—especially in ethics, data interpretation, and real-time interface use—health systems are likely to underutilize and misuse these technologies.

6.3 Workflow Disruptions and Time Constraints

The use of AI and XR technology threatens to interrupt current clinical processes due to additional steps and increased cognitive load, especially when it has not been properly integrated into electronic health records or standard practices. Clinical decision support system studies indicate that the adoption failures are often attributable to duplication of manual data entry and fatigue in context-switching. Such disruptions may result in clinician rejection of the tool in busy environments such as the outpatient clinic or emergency department. Integration and usability tests should be seamlessly integrated to reduce friction [23].

6.4 Overreliance on Automated Systems

Clinicians may over-rely on AI recommendations, accepting them without critical evaluation, a phenomenon known as automation bias. Literature on AI dialogue systems shows users often accept AI-generated outputs even in the face of errors or hallucinations. In clinical environments, this can degrade decision

Table 1: Healthcare Provider Challenges

Challenge	Description	Impact on Providers	Example Case	Recommended Action
Resistance to Adoption	Hesitation due to workflow disruption fears	Low adoption rate	Clinicians rejecting AI diagnostic tools	Early clinician involvement in design
Skill Gaps	Lack of AI/XR literacy and training	Misuse or underutilization	Improper VR rehab operation	Structured training programs
Workflow Disruptions	Poor EHR integration is causing extra steps	Reduced productivity	AI alerts requiring duplicate data entry	Seamless system integration
Overreliance on Automation	Blindly trusting AI outputs	Diagnostic errors	Missed tumor due to AI misclassification	Human-in-the-loop safeguards
Time Constraints	Limited time to learn new tools	Poor onboarding experience	Avoidance of AI-enabled consultation systems	Phased implementation and microlearning

quality and clinical vigilance. Institutions must implement human-in-the-loop safeguards, alert mechanisms for out-of-distribution outputs, and clinician training on system limitations [24].

7. Financial and Infrastructural Constraints

7.1 High Cost of Implementation

Implementing AI and Metaverse-based healthcare solutions requires significant upfront investment. Basic AI integration can cost between $40,000–50,000, while comprehensive custom solutions can exceed $100,000–1 million, depending on system complexity, infrastructure, and compliance needs [25]. These costs include secure data pipelines, high-performance computing, integration with EHR systems, and regulatory certifications. Smaller clinics and startups often cannot justify such expenses without clear evidence of value, making early-stage innovation financially risky.

7.2 ROI Uncertainty for Hospitals and Startups

Despite its promise, AI healthcare projects often have unclear or delayed returns on investment. Many pilot programs do not scale due to variable outcomes, integration challenges, and compliance burdens. Clinics implementing AI systems may incur costs without realizing sufficient reductions in operating expenses, and hospitals may struggle to recoup investments without clear reimbursement pathways or institutional support [26]. This uncertainty can deter decision-makers, especially when budgets are tight.

7.3 Scalability and Sustainability Issues

Scaling AI and XR technologies across healthcare systems introduces complexity: infrastructure must support model retraining, software updates, edge-cloud deployments, and embedded governance. Many institutions lack in-house expertise or technical capacity to sustain long-term operations [27]. Without robust maintenance, oversight, and funding models, deployed tools risk becoming outdated or unmanageable, ultimately hindering scalability.

Table 2: Financial and Infrastructural Constraints

Constraint	Description	Cost Impact	Example Case	Mitigation Strategy
High Cost of Implementation	Large upfront investment for AI/XR systems	\$40,000–\$1M+ depending on scope	AI-integrated EHR upgrade	Public-private partnerships
ROI Uncertainty	Delayed or unclear returns on investment	Budget reluctance in hospitals	Small clinics avoiding AI pilot projects	Define measurable KPIs before deployment
Scalability Issues	Challenges in expanding the system to multiple sites	Increased maintenance costs	VR rehab is limited to urban hospitals	Cloud-based scaling with edge integration
Sustainability Gaps	Lack of long-term operational funding	Obsolescence risk	AI tools discontinued after funding ends	Establish recurring revenue/ funding models
Infrastructure Limitations	Lack of GPU/ cloud resources and reliable internet	Downtime, reduced efficiency	Low-resource rural healthcare centers	Hybrid cloud-edge deployment
Global Inequity	Uneven technology distribution across countries	Widening health disparities	Metaverse tools are only available in high-income regions	Subsidized tech programs for LMICs

7.4 Inequity in Technological Distribution Globally

Innovative healthcare technologies are frequently rolled out first in high-income countries, raising concerns about global equity. Limited infrastructure, financing, and digital literacy in low- and middle-income countries (LMICs) mean that populations who might benefit most from AI and virtual health tools are often excluded. Absent targeted investment and inclusive policy frameworks, these innovations risk creating a wider digital divide in health outcomes.

8. Research and Development Gaps

8.1 Lack of Long-Term Clinical Validation

Most AI models in healthcare are validated through short-term, controlled clinical studies, with far fewer undergoing long-term or real-world effectiveness evaluation. This leaves a gap in understanding how models evolve in dynamic clinical environments, potentially leading to performance drift or failure over time. To address this, frameworks like "AI for IMPACTS" advocate for continuous monitoring, governance, and socio-technical integration, making longitudinal assessment part of standard validation protocols [28]. Without long-term oversight and iterative validation, deploying AI tools in real-world care settings remains risky and unsustainable.

8.2 Limited Standardized Datasets for Training AI

Clinical AI development is often hindered by disjointed datasets, inconsistent coding systems, and variable preprocessing pipelines that complicate reproducibility and model generalizability. Surveys at ML4H conferences have highlighted the need for standardized datasets and benchmark tasks to ensure transparent comparison and reliable performance evaluation [29]. Efforts to curate and share standardized datasets such as EHRSHOT, INSPECT, and MedAlign are emerging, but broader adoption remains limited. This fragmentation impedes scalable, cross-institutional AI adoption.

8.3 Inadequate Cross-Disciplinary Collaboration

Many AI tools are developed in technology silos without input from clinicians, ethicists, or healthcare administrators, leading to narrow solutions that don't address real-world workflows. Cross-disciplinary frameworks are needed to unify technical robustness with clinical relevance, user acceptance, and governance. Reviews reveal a systemic lack of integrated design, evaluation, and deployment processes, which slows adoption and limits clinical impact [30]. Bridging this divide is essential for developing AI tools that are both technically sound and contextually appropriate.

8.4 Overhyped Expectations Versus Real Outcomes

Public enthusiasm often amplifies AI's promise in healthcare well beyond current capabilities, fueling unrealistic expectations. Media coverage of breakthroughs ranging from diagnostic tools to virtual consultation avatars overshadows the

Table 3: Research and Development Gaps

Gap Area	Description	Impact on Healthcare AI/Metaverse	Example Case	Potential Solution
Lack of Long-Term Clinical Validation	Limited longitudinal studies and monitoring	Risk of performance drift, reduced trust	AI tool accuracy declining over time	Continuous monitoring frameworks like AI for IMPACTS
Limited Standardized Datasets	Variations in data formats and coding systems	Hinders reproducibility and generalization	Different EHR systems in hospitals	Development of unified datasets (EHRSHOT, INSPECT)
Inadequate Cross-Disciplinary Collaboration	Lack of joint work between clinicians, developers, and ethicists	Narrow solutions not fitting clinical workflows	AI tools failing integration tests	Interdisciplinary design teams
Overhyped Expectations	Public/media exaggeration of capabilities	Disillusionment and poor adoption	IBM Watson Oncology case	Transparent reporting and realistic projections
Weak Benchmarking Practices	Absence of standardized evaluation metrics	Hard to compare models fairly	Conflicting study outcomes	Creation of benchmark tasks for each use case

limited real-world impact and adoption hurdles. Industry analyses show that fewer than 20% of digital health innovations achieve robust clinical validation or sustained deployment, highlighting the mismatch between hype and reality [31]. Responsible framing, tempered by rigorous evidence and transparent reporting, is critical to avoid disillusionment and ensure meaningful progress.

9. Case Studies and Real-World Examples

9.1 AI Diagnostic Tools: Successes and Shortcomings

AI-powered diagnostic tools have shown remarkable performance in controlled environments. For instance, Microsoft's AI Diagnostic Orchestrator reached 85.5% accuracy on complex medical cases, far surpassing the 20% accuracy achieved by experienced physicians under time constraints. In India, a multi-site AI chest X-ray model achieved precision and recall exceeding 99%, improving diagnostic speed and reducing radiologist workload at scale. These successes illustrate AI's potential when trained on massive, diverse datasets [32]. However, limitations persist; tools often perform poorly when integrated into routine care, with variable accuracy across populations, reliance on clinical context, and risk of automation bias when clinicians blindly follow AI recommendations.

9.2 Metaverse Platforms in Telemedicine: Trial Outcomes

Early trials of immersive teleclinics suggest promise in mental health and cognitive assessments. A recent study of social VR platforms explored neuropsychological testing within the Metaverse and found immersive approaches improved patient engagement and assessment fidelity. Another systematic review of digital therapies like NightWare and EndeavorRx reported clinically validated improvements in PTSD, anxiety, and ADHD, though concerns over privacy, accessibility, and therapeutic sustainability were noted [33].

9.3 Virtual Rehabilitation: Promise and Pitfalls

Metaverse-based rehabilitation has shown significant functional benefits. Studies report that stroke survivors using VR-based therapies regained upper limb function faster than conventional therapy cohorts, with increased motivation and engagement. A design framework published in 2023 emphasized equity, interoperability, and patient-centered design as essential to avoid exacerbating disparities in access to immersive rehabilitation services [34]. However, challenges include device affordability, digital literacy barriers, and therapy adherence over time.

9.4 Lessons from Failed Implementations

A high-profile cautionary tale is the collapse of Babylon Health, an AI-fueled virtual clinic that served millions globally but ultimately went bankrupt. Regulatory concerns, unverifiable diagnostic claims, and failure to meet clinical standards led to widespread controversy and closure. Similarly, IBM Watson's oncology initiative, initially valued at billions, was discontinued after failing to deliver clear clinical or financial benefits, shedding light on the risk of hype without rigorous real-world validation [35].

10. Recommendations and Mitigation Strategies

10.1 Policy and Governance Improvements

Effective policy and governance are foundational to ensuring the responsible deployment of AI and Metaverse technologies in healthcare. Organizations and policymakers should adopt sector-specific governance frameworks that include accountability, auditability, and clear decision rights, even suggesting independent AI oversight functions and certification systems. Initiatives like the OECD AI Principles, UN advisory recommendations, and healthcare-specific governance studies emphasize the need for comprehensive policies that balance innovation with ethical safeguards while promoting transparency, equity, and global collaboration [36].

10.2 Promoting Transparency and Explainability

Promoting explainability ensures clinicians and patients can understand how AI systems arrive at decisions. Policymakers and institutions should encourage Explainable AI (XAI) approaches that are accessible and tailored to users with differing expertise. Standards and regulations currently evolving in the EU, US, and UK must define minimum acceptable transparency levels and accountability structures, helping close the gap between technical model explanations and user comprehension [37].

10.3 Enhancing User-Centric Design

Health AI and Metaverse systems must be designed with end users, patients, clinicians, and support staff in mind. User-centered design frameworks advocate iterative prototyping, usability testing, and feedback loops to ensure interfaces are intuitive, bias-aware, and contextually appropriate. Emerging studies highlight the importance of clinical stakeholder engagement from the earliest stages of design, a structured design checklist tailored to healthcare workflows and settings [38].

10.4 Capacity Building and Interdisciplinary Training

Bridging clinician and technical communities is essential: healthcare workers should receive training in AI literacy, data interpretation, and ethical implications, while AI designers benefit from domain insights. Multi-sector collaborations, such as India's AI Centers of Excellence and Indo AI initiatives, demonstrate how interdisciplinary capacity building can create sustainable ecosystems for healthcare innovation [39]. This enables shared understanding, better adoption, and long-term resilience.

11. Future Directions

11.1 Towards Responsible AI in the Metaverse

Responsible AI in the Metaverse involves governance, design, and ongoing ethical oversight. This would require it to be equipped with privacy-preserving technologies such as federated learning, blockchain-based access control, transparent audit logs, human-in-the-loop checkpoints, and more. Systems in the metaverse should be designed to protect user rights and mitigate risks by creating more mechanisms through frameworks like Trustworthy AI fairness, robustness, explainability, and accountability. To illustrate, institutional protocols should mandate audits, risk assessment, and incident reporting, which ensure the integrity of virtual healthcare provision.

11.2 Emerging Standards and Frameworks

New standards are being developed to bridge gaps and support Metaverse healthcare systems that provide interoperable and secure connections between AI, blockchain, and healthcare interoperability. It also includes support such as blockchain-based federated learning models and smart contract-based models for secure EHR access, as integrity, provenance, privacy, and other aspects are governed by bodies and industry groups that develop reference architectures. These architectures help create secure, interoperable systems that can operate across different institutions. These templates make open, fair, and equal service provision in digital healthcare immersive.

11.3 Opportunities for Equitable Global Adoption

Federated learning may be a turning point in offering more comprehensive global healthcare, on the condition that the patient privacy of those with chronic illnesses is not violated. And, preserving patient privacy, low-resource areas can access common wisdom. It can be developed and deployed not only by health systems in low- and middle-income countries but also worldwide when paired with edge computing and the affordability of XR devices in the coming years. Such strategies make innovations in healthcare using the Metaverse democratic on a worldwide basis.

11.4 Role of Quantum Computing and Federated Learning

Such healthcare AI transformative trajectories in the virtual environment are Quantum Computing and Federated Learning (QFL). Quantum machine learning has the potential to accelerate the diagnosis, enhance the precision of simulations, and introduce real-time customization to the Metaverse [40]. Conversely, quantum extension and non-quantum federated learning can be used to create a privacy-compliant model trained across a network of nodes. Both NeXus EAI and X-RnD will combine their technologies to deliver more efficient, powerful, and secure AI applications in healthcare through the Virtual Reality platform.

12. Conclusion

That is what the implementation of Artificial Intelligence (AI) and Metaverse technologies in healthcare aims to do: improve patient outcomes by making services faster, more accessible, operationally efficient, and affordable. Impractical as it may sound, this technology also has its pitfalls and issues, which need to be addressed to make sure the implementation of the technique is done safely, ethically, and sustainably. The authors have discussed a wide range of challenges in this chapter, including not only technical issues like data privacy, interoperability, and model explainability, but also ethical concerns such as bias, consent, and liability. Several issues related to infrastructure, funding, and patient orientation with supporting policy and provider preparedness, and long-term research validation are also presented. The trick is balancing caution with the integration of these technologies. Over-trusting automation, sending information prematurely without proper validation, and inaccessibility can all potentially increase care disparities or create new risk points. A better approach is to focus more precisely on responsible AI development, equitable design, multi-disciplinary collaboration, and deploying in real-world scenarios to minimize the gap between impact and innovation. The new frontier of feed-forward vision must necessarily include the future AI, which is ethical, explainable, inclusive, and interoperable with self-in-epistemic-reflection AI, woven entirely into the Metaverse. The synergy among technology, clinicians, and patients, and sustainable success will be realized through continuous expansion of its own governance, stakeholder alignment, continuous learning cycles, and feedback loops. In so doing, the health community will lead to accountable yet transformational digital health ecosystems.

References

1. Kandeel, M. (2024). Revolutionizing healthcare: Harnessing the power of artificial intelligence for enhanced diagnostics, treatment and drug discovery. *International Journal of Pharmacology*, 20(1), 1–10.
2. Chengoden, R., Victor, N., Huynh-The, T., Yenduri, G., Jhaveri, R. H., Alazab, M. et al. (2022). Metaverse for healthcare: A survey on potential applications, challenges and future directions, arXiv preprint.
3. Lin, J., Gao, H., Li, C., Ning, Z., Wu, Y., and Gu, L. (2023). Artificial intelligence–Empowered metaverse in healthcare: Framework, challenges, and future directions, *IEEE Transactions on Industrial Informatics*, 19(4), 5622–5632.
4. Morley, M., et al. (2020). Ethical and legal challenges of artificial intelligence-driven healthcare. *Nature Machine Intelligence*, 2, 361–364.
5. Khalid, N., Qayyum, A., Bilal, M., Al-Fuqaha, A., and Qadir, J. (2023). Privacy-preserving artificial intelligence in healthcare: Techniques and applications. *Computers in Biology and Medicine*, 158, 106848.
6. Torab-Miandoab, A., Samad-Soltani, T., Jodati, A., and Rezaei-Hachesu, P. (2023). Interoperability of heterogeneous health information systems: A systematic literature review. *BMC Medical Informatics and Decision Making*, 23, Article 18.
7. Okada, Y., Ning, Y., and Ong, M. E. H. (2023). Explainable artificial intelligence in emergency medicine: An overview. *Clinical and Experimental Emergency Medicine*, 10(4), 354–362.
8. Halbig, A., Babu, S. K., Gatter, S., Latoschik, M. E., Brukamp, K., and von Mammen, S. (2022). Opportunities and challenges of virtual reality in healthcare: A domain experts inquiry. *Frontiers in Virtual Reality*, 3, Article 837616
9. Kaye, J., Whitley, E. A., Lund, D., Morrison, M., Teare, H., and Melham, K. (2015). Dynamic consent: A patient interface for twenty-first century research networks. *European Journal of Human Genetics*, 23(2), 141–146.

10. Jiménez-Luna, J., Skuta, C., and Gilmer, A. (2022). FUTURE-AI: Guiding principles and consensus strategy for trustworthy AI in medical imaging. *Nature Machine Intelligence*, 4(7), 536–540.
11. Song, D. Y., Lee, Y., and Im, M. (2023). Healthcare in the metaverse: Perspectives, challenges, and future directions. *Healthcare Informatics Research*, 29(2), 87–96.
12. Cestonaro, G., Avesani, M., and Graziano, F. (2023). Medical liability and artificial intelligence: A systematic literature review. *Healthcare*, 11(2), 195.
13. Getzen, J., and Long, Q. (2023). Incomplete electronic health records may drive bias in predictive models. Penn LDI Research Update, Feb. 15, 2023.
14. Schwabe, D., Becker, K., Seyferth, M., Klaß, A., and Schaeffter, T. (2024). The METRIC-framework for assessing data quality for trustworthy AI in medicine: A systematic review. *npj Digital Medicine*, 7, Art. 203.
15. Liu, S. and Guo, L. R. (2024). Data ownership in the AI-powered integrative health care landscape. *JMIR Medical Informatics*, 12, Art. e57754.
16. Latif, A., Qamar, F. A., Haider, M. A., Saeed, M. A., and Rehman, W. U. (2021). Digital literacy and accessibility: Barriers to AI-based healthcare adoption. *Frontiers in Digital Health*, 3, 1–10.
17. Murphy, Kathleen, Erica Di Ruggiero, Ross Upshur, Donald J. Willison, Neha Malhotra, Jia Ce Cai et al. (2021). Artificial intelligence for good health: A scoping review of the ethics literature. *BMC Medical Ethics*, 22.1, 14.0.
18. Rebenitsch, A., and Owen, C. (2013). Review on cybersickness in applications and visual displays. *Virtual Reality*, 17(2), 101–125.
19. Chatterjee, T. R. and Nath, S. (2023). Equity challenges in metaverse healthcare: A socioeconomic lens. *Journal of Global Health Reports*, 7, 1–5.
20. Hassan, M., Kushniruk, A., and Borycki, E. (2024). Barriers to and facilitators of artificial intelligence adoption in healthcare: A scoping review. *Journal of Medical Internet Research Human Factors*, 11(1), Article e48633.
21. Gazquez-Garcia, J., Sánchez-Bocanegra, C. L., and Sevillano, J. L. (2025). Systematic review of key skills required for future health professionals. *Journal of Medical Internet Research Medical Education*, 11, Article e58161.
22. Khan, Z., Adil, T., Oduoye, M. O., Khan, B. S., and Ayyazuddin, M. (2024). Assessing the knowledge, attitude and perception of extended reality (XR) technology in Pakistan's healthcare community in an era of artificial intelligence. *Front. Med.*, 11, 1456017.
23. Greenhalgh, T., Wherton, J., Papoutsi, C., Lynch, J., Hughes, G., Hinder, S. et al. (2017). Beyond adoption: A new framework for theorizing technology-supported change in healthcare. *Journal of Medical Internet Research*, 19(11), Article e367.
24. Zhai, C., and Wibowo, A. (2024). The effects of over-reliance on AI dialogue systems on critical thinking and decision-making. *Smart Learning Environments*, 11, Article 16.
25. The Cost of Implementing AI in Healthcare in 2025. *Aalpha*, Jul. 31 2025.
26. Aalpha. (2025). The Cost of Implementing AI in Healthcare in 2025, *Aalpha Blog*, 2025.
27. Medical Centres Compete to Achieve 'Smart Hospital' Status. *Financial Times*, Mar. 5 2025.
28. Jacob, C., Brasier, N., Laurenzi, E., Heuss, S., Mougiakakou, S.-G., Cöltekin, A. et al. (2025). AI for IMPACTS: A comprehensive framework for evaluating the long-term real-world impacts of artificial intelligence–powered clinician tools. *Journal of Medical Internet Research*, 27, e67485.

29. Reflections from Research Roundtables at ML4H 2024. arXiv, Feb. 2025.
30. El Arab, R. A., Abu-Mahfouz, M. S., Abuadas, F. H., Alzghoul, H., Almari, M., Ghannam, A., & Seweid, M. M. (2025). Bridging the gap: From AI success in clinical trials to real-world healthcare implementation—A narrative review. *Healthcare*, 13(7), Article 701.
31. Saria, S., and Butte, A. (2018). Better medicine through machine learning: What's real, and what's artificial? *PLoS Medicine*, 15(12), Art. e1002721. doi: 10.1371/journal.pmed.1002721
32. Esteva, T., Kuprel, B., Novoa, R. A., Ko, J., Swetter, S. M., Blau, H. M., & Thrun, S. (2017). Dermatologist-level classification of skin cancer with deep neural networks. *Nature*, 542(7639), 115–118. doi: 10.1038/nature21056.
33. Cho, Y. S., Kim, J., and Kim, J. Y. (2023). A telemedicine platform using virtual reality and AI for remote diagnosis and consultation. *IEEE Access*, 11, 20334–20345. doi: 10.1109/ACCESS.2023.3247534.
34. Duffell, L. C., Wiles, A. D., and Jackson, A. J. (2022). Effectiveness of virtual reality in rehabilitation of neurological conditions: A review. *Journal of NeuroEngineering and Rehabilitation*, 19(1), 1–13. doi: 10.1186/s12984-022-01013-9.
35. Ghassemi, A., Naumann, J., and Perez, E. F. (2022). Practical limitations in deploying AI systems in healthcare settings: Lessons learned from case studies. *npj Digital Medicine*, 5(1), 33.
36. Taeihagh, M. A. (2021). Organizational governance of emerging technologies: AI adoption in healthcare. *Policy & Society*, 40(2), 137–154.
37. Nannini, L., Balayn, A., and Smith, A. L. (2023). Explainability in AI policies: A critical review of communications, reports, regulations, and standards in the EU, US, and UK. arXiv, Apr. 2023.
38. Jung, I. C., Schuler, K., Zerlik, M., Grummt, S., Sedlmayr, M., & Sedlmayr, B. (2025). Overview of basic design recommendations for user-centered explanation interfaces for AI-based clinical decision support systems: A scoping review. *Digital Health*, 11, 1–16.
39. Crawford, M., Simmons, M., and Lee, N. T. (2025). Health and AI: Advancing responsible and ethical AI for all communities. *Brookings*, Mar. 3 2025.
40. Sahu, A., Ma, H., and Kumar, S. R. (2025). Quantum computing and machine learning in medical decision making: Current progress and future prospects. *Algorithms*, 18(3), Art. 156. doi: 10.3390/a18030156.

Index

About the Editors

Dr. Balasubramaniam S is an assistant professor at the School of Computer Science and Engineering, Kerala University of Digital Sciences, Innovation and Technology, Digital University Kerala (DUK), Thiruvananthapuram, Kerala, India. Prior to joining DUK, he was with the School of Computer Science and Engineering, Vellore Institute of Technology (VIT), Chennai, where he worked as a senior associate professor. He has around 15+ years of experience in teaching, applied research, and industry. He completed his postdoctoral research in the Department of Applied Data Science at Noroff University College, Kristiansand, Norway. He holds a Ph.D degree in Computer Science and Engineering from Anna University, Chennai, India, in 2015. He has published more than 30 research papers in reputed SCI/WoS/Scopus indexed Journals. He has been granted one Australian patent and two Indian Patents and has also published two additional Indian patents. He has presented papers at conferences, received a best paper award, contributed 40 chapters in edited books, and served as an Editor for 15 books published by international publishers. His research and publication interests include machine learning, deep learning, federated learning-based healthcare and security applications, cloud computing security, Generative AI, and Agentic AI.

Google Scholar: https://scholar.google.co.in/citations?user=1KGLST0AAAAJ &hl=en
Academic url: https://duk.ac.in/personnel/balasubramaniam-s/
Orcid Id: https://orcid.org/my-orcid?orcid=0000-0003-1371-3088
LinkedIn: https://www.linkedin.com/in/dr-balasubramaniam-s-6873533b/

Prof. Seifedine Kadry has a bachelor's degree in 1999 from Lebanese University, an MS degree in 2002 from Reims University (France) and EPFL (Lausanne), a Ph.D in 2007 from Blaise Pascal University (France), HDR degree in 2017 from Rouen University (France). At present, his research focuses on Data Science, education using technology, system prognostics, stochastic systems, and applied mathematics. He is an IET and AAIA fellow, and he is a full professor of data science at the Department of Computer Science and Mathematics, Lebanese American University, Beirut, Lebanon.

Google Scholar: https://scholar.google.com/citations?hl=en&user=EAVEmg0AAAAJ
Academic url: https://www.noroff.no/en/contact/staff/53-academic/423-seifedine-kadry
LinkedIn: https://www.linkedin.com/in/seifedine-kadry/

For Product Safety Concerns and Information please contact our EU representative GPSR@taylorandfrancis.com
Taylor & Francis Verlag GmbH, Kaufingerstraße 24, 80331 München, Germany

www.ingramcontent.com/pod-product-compliance
Ingram Content Group UK Ltd.
Pitfield, Milton Keynes, MK11 3LW, UK
UKHW021513250926
475702UK00043B/282
* 9 7 8 1 0 4 1 1 0 5 8 5 5 *